REFERENCE LIBRARY OF BLACK AMERICA

REFERENCE LIBRARY OF BLACK AMERICA

Volume III

Edited by

Kenneth Estell

Distributed by Afro-American Press

Reference Library of Black America is based upon the sixth edition of *The African American Almanac*, published by Gale Research Inc. It has been published in this 5-volume set to facilitate wider usage among students.

Linda Metzger, *Senior Editor*
Kenneth Estell, *Editor*
Monica Hubbard, *Contributing Editor*
David G. Oblender, *Associate Editor*
Victoria Coughlin, Paula Cutcher-Jackson, *Contributing Asociate Editors*
Janie Wilcox, *Contributing Assistant Editor*

Simon Glickman, Joyce Harrison, Carmen Johnson, Michael Knes, *Writers*
Beth Baker, Kimberly Burton Faulkner, William J. Moses, David Sprinkle, *Copyeditors*

George Hobart, *Photo Researcher*

Jeanne Gough, *Permissions Manager*
Margaret A. Chamberlain, *Permissions Supervisor (Pictures)*
Barbara Wallace, *Permissions Assistant*
Sandra C. Davis, *Permissions Supervisor (Text)*
Michele M. Lonoconus, *Permissions Assistant*

Victoria B. Cariappa, *Research Manager*
Maureen Richards, *Research Supervisor*
Donna Melnychenko, *Editorial Associate*

Mary Beth Trimper, *Production Director*
Evi Seoud, *Assistant Production Manager*
Mary Kelley, *Production Assistant*

Cynthia Baldwin, *Art Director*
Barbara J. Yarrow, *Graphic Services Supervisor*
Mark C. Howell, *Cover Designer*
Mary Krzewinski, *Page Designer*
Willie F. Mathis, *Camera Operator*
Nicholas Jakubiak, *Desktop Publisher*
Sherrell L. Hobbs, *Desktop Publisher*

Benita L. Spight, *Data Entry Supervisor*
Gwendolyn S. Tucker, *Data Entry Group Leader*
Nancy K. Sheridan, *Data Entry Associate*

The paper used in this publication meets the minimum requirements of American National Standard for Information Sciences—Permanence Paper for Printed Library Materials, ANSI Z 39.48-1984. ™

Printed in the United States of America
Printed in 1995

Advisory Board

Contributors

Stephen W. Angell
Associate Professor of Religion, Florida A&M University

Robin Armstrong
Adjunct Lecturer, University of Michigan, Dearborn

Claudette Bennett
Bureau of the Census, United States Department of Commerce

John Cohassey

Allen G. Harris
President, Air Force Association,
General Dainiel James Chapter

Hayward Derrick Horton
Assistant Professor of Sociology, Iowa State University

George Johnson
Professor of Law, Howard University School of Law

Faustine C. Jones-Wilson
Professor of Education, Howard University; Editor, *The Journal of Negro Education*

Donald Franklin Joyce
Director, Felix G. Woodward Library, Austin Peay State University

Kwame Kenyatta
Detroit Board of Education; New African People's Organization

Mark Kram
Sportswriter, *Philadelphia Daily News*

Marilyn Hortense Mackel
Associate Professor, Western State University College of Law, Judge Pro Tempore,
Los Angeles County Superior Court, Juvenile Department

Ionis Bracy Martin
Lecturer, Central Connecticut State University

Dan Morgenstern
Director, Institute for Jazz Studies, Rutgers University

Wilson J. Moses
Professor of History, Pennsylvania State University

Richard Prince
National Association of Black Journalists

Nancy Rampson

Michael D. Woodard
Director, Los Angeles Institute for Multicultural Training;
Visiting Scholar, UCLA Center for Afro-American Studies

Contents

Volume III

Volume IV

Volume V

Introduction

The Reference Library of Black America is based upon the sixth edition of *The African-American Almanac*, first published in 1967 as *The Negro Almanac* and since cited by *Library Journal* as an outstanding reference work.

New Features in This Edition

All material was extensively reviewed by the editor and a board of prominent advisors and, where appropriate, updated and/or expanded. For example, the expanded chapter on national organizations now includes a history of black organizations in the United States and provides biographical information on leaders of major associations, past and present. The chapter on fine art now includes coverage of the applied arts—architecture, industrial design, fashion design, and graphic art—and a directory of museums in the United States.

Some chapters which appeared in the fifth edition were totally rewritten to focus on issues facing contemporary African-Americans. In particular the chapters on law, employment and income, the family, and education, were rewritten to reflect new and changing concerns within the black community regarding such issues as racism in the criminal justice system, factors in employment and unemployment, family structure and stability, and African-centered education.

Several completely new topics were added to this edition, including: a chapter on Africans in America since the first arrival of Africans in the Western Hemisphere through the Civil War and Reconstruction; a chapter on black nationalism covering the history of cultural nationalism and Pan-Africanism in the United States; a chapter on popular music covering contemporary music forms, including rhythm and blues, soul, gospel, rap, and country music. In addition, an appendix listing African-American recipients of selected major awards is new to this edition.

While many chapters have been expanded, others which appeared in the fifth edition have been incorporated into new or existing sections of the book. For example, biographical profiles included in the chapters on women and on prominent African Americans have been absorbed into existing chapters.

Content and Arrangement

Information in this edition of *The Reference Library of Black America* appears in twenty-seven subject chapters. Many chapters open with an essay focusing on historical developments or the contributions of African Americans to the subject area, followed by concise biographical profiles of selected individuals.

Although the individuals featured in this edition represent only a small portion of the African-American community, they embody excellence and diversity in their respective fields of endeavor. Where an individual has made a significant contribution in more than one area, his or her biographical profile appears in the subject area for which he or she is best known, and cross references in other chapters lead the user to the profile.

In order to facilitate further research, a bibliography and list of publishers is provided. The bibliography has been divided into two major divisions: "Africana" and "African Americana." Within these two divisions titles are arranged alphabetically by author under categories indicative of their subject matter.

More than eight hundred maps and illustrations aid the reader in understanding the topics and people covered in the work. A name and keyword index provides access to the contents.

11

Politics

11

Politics

African Americans in National Politics: 1990–1993 ■ African-American Government Officials

Essay by David G. Oblender

■ AFRICAN AMERICANS IN NATIONAL POLITICS: 1990–1993

Throughout the past several decades, African Americans have been selected for political offices in ever-increasing numbers. The year 1992 was no exception. One of the most significant political developments of 1992 was the election of the first black

Representatives Maxine Waters (center), Eleanor Holmes Norton (far left), and Charles Hayes (right), 1991.

United States Senate		
Illinois	Carol Moseley Braun*	Democrat
United States House of Representatives		
Alabama	Earl Hilliard*	Democrat
California	Ron Dellums	Democrat
California	Julian Dixon	Democrat
California	Maxine Waters	Democrat
California	Walter Tucker*	Democrat
Connecticut	Gary Franks	Republican
Florida	Corrine Brown*	Democrat
Florida	Carrie Meek*	Democrat
Florida	Alcee Hastings*	Democrat
Georgia	Sanford Bishop*	Democrat
Georgia	John Lewis	Democrat
Georgia	Cynthia McKinney*	Democrat
District of Columbia	Eleanor Holmes Norton	Democrat
Illinois	Bobby Rush*	Democrat
Illinois	Mel Reynolds*	Democrat
Illinois	Cardiss Collins	Democrat
Louisiana	William Jefferson	Democrat
Louisiana	Cleo Fields*	Democrat
Maryland	Kweisi Mfume	Democrat
Maryland	Albert Wynn*	Democrat
Michigan	John Conyers	Democrat
Michigan	Barbara Rose Collins	Democrat
Mississippi	Bennie Thompson*	Democrat
Missouri	William Clay	Democrat
Missouri	Alan Wheat	Democrat
New Jersey	Donald Payne	Democrat
New York	Floyd Flake	Democrat
New York	Ed Towns	Democrat
New York	Major Owens	Democrat
New York	Charles Rangel	Democrat
North Carolina	Eva Clayton*	Democrat
North Carolina	Melvin Watt*	Democrat
Ohio	Louis Stokes	Democrat
Pennsylvania	Lucien Blackwell	Democrat
South Carolina	Jim Clyburn*	Democrat
Tennessee	Harold Ford	Democrat
Texas	Eddie B. Johnson*	Democrat
Texas	Craig Washington	Democrat
Virginia	Bobby Scott*	Democrat

*Elected to first term November 1992.

African-American representatives in the U.S. Congress, 1993

United States Senate			
Hiram R. Revel	Republican	Mississippi	1870-1871
Blanche K. Bruce	Republican	Mississippi	1875-1881
Edward W. Brooke	Republican	Massachussetts	1967-1979
United States House of Representatives			
Joseph H. Rainey	Republican	South Carolina	1870-1879
Jefferson F. Long	Republican	Georgia	1870-1871
Robert B. Elliott	Republican	South Carolina	1871-1874
Robert C. DeLarge	Republican	South Carolina	1871-1873
Benjamin S. Tumer	Republican	Alabama	1871-1873
Josiah T. Walls	Republican	Florida	1871-1873
Richard H. Cane	Republican	South Carolina	1873-1875; 1877-1879
John R. Lynch	Republican	Mississippi	1873-1877; 1882-1883
James T. Rapier	Republican	Alabama	1873-1875
Alonzo J. Ransier	Republican	South Carolina	1873-1875
Jeremiah Haralson	Republican	Alabama	1875-1877
John A. Hyman	Republican	North Carolina	1875-1877
Charles E. Nash	Republican	Louisiana	1875-1877
Robert Smalls	Republican	South Carolina	1875-1879
James E. O' Hara	Republican	North Carolina	1883-1887
Henry P. Cheatharn	Republican	North Carolina	1889-1893
John M. Langston	Republican	Virginia	1890-1891
Thomas E. Miller	Republican	South Carolina	1890-1891
George W. Murray	Republican	South Carolina	1893-1895; 1896-1897
George W. White	Republican	North Carolina	1897-1901
Oscar DePriest	Republican	Illinois	1929-1935
Arthur W. Mitchell	Democrat	Illinois	1935-1943
William L. Dawson	Democrat	Illinois	1943-1970
Adam C. Powell Jr.	Democrat	New York	1945-1967; 1969-1971
Charles C. Diggs Jr.	Democrat	Michigan	1955-1980
Robert N. C. Nix	Democrat	Pennsylvania	1958-1978
Augustus F. Hawkins	Democrat	California	1963-1990
John Conyers Jr.	Democrat	Michigan	1965-
William L. Clay	Democrat	Missouri	1969-
Louis Stokes	Democrat	Ohio	1969-
Shirley Chisholm	Democrat	New York	1969-1982
George W. Collins	Democrat	Illinois	1970-1972
Ronald V. Dellums	Democrat	California	1971-
Ralph H. Metcalfe	Democrat	Illinois	1971-1978
Parren H. Mitchell	Democrat	Maryland	1971-1987
Charles B. Rangel	Democrat	New York	1971-
Walter E. Fauntroy	Democrat	District of Columbia	1971-1990
Yvorme B. Burke	Democrat	California	1973-1979
Cardiss Collins	Democrat	Illinois	1973-
Barbara C. Jordan	Democrat	Texas	1973-1978
Andrew Young	Democrat	Georgia	1973-1977
Harold E. Ford	Democrat	Tennessee	1975-
Julian C. Dixon	Democrat	California	1979-
William H. Gray	Democrat	Pennsylvania	1979-1991
Mickey Leland	Democrat	Texas	1979-1989
Melvin Evans	Republican	Virgin Islands	1978-1980
Bennett McVey Steward	Democrat	Illinois	1979-1980
George W. Crockete	Democrat	Michigan	1980-1990
Mervyn M. Dymally	Democrat	California	1981-1992
Gus Savage	Democrat	Illinois	1981-1992
Harold Washington	Democrat	Illinois	1981-1983
Katie Hall	Democrat	Indiana	1982-1984
Major Owens	Democrat	New York	1983-
Edolphus Towns	Democrat	New York	1983-
Alan Wheat	Democrat	Missouri	1983-
Charles Hayes	Democrat	Illinois	1983-1992
Alton R. Waldon Jr.	Democrat	New York	1986-1987
Mike Espy	Democrat	Mississippi	1987-1992
Floyd Flake	Democrat	New York	1987-
John Lewis	Democrat	Georgia	1987-
Kweisi Mfume	Democrat	Maryland	1987-
Donald M. Payne	Democrat	New Jersey	1988-
Barbara Rose Collins	Democrat	Michigan	1990-
Gary Franks	Republican	Connecticut	1990-
William Jefferson	Democrat	Louisiana	1990-
Eleanor Holmes Norton	Democrat	District of Columbia	1990-
Craig Washington	Democrat	Texas	1990-
Lucien Blackwell	Decocrat	Pennsylvania	1991-

African Americans in the Forty-first to One Hundred Second Congresses

woman, Carol Moseley Braun, to the United States Senate. Braun, a native of Chicago, Illinois, shocked political observers by scoring a stunning upset over incumbent Senator Alan Dixon in the Democratic primary on March 17, 1992. In the November 1992 election, she easily defeated her Republican challenger, Richard Williamson, by a wide margin. Among Braun's many assets is her eclectic base of political supporters, which includes African Americans, feminists, Jews, trade unionists, and working people. She is considered a strong, independent woman who holds firmly to her beliefs, yet is able to compromise when necessary. Braun is a strong supporter of abortion rights, environmental protection, educational and health care reform, and job creation. Braun, whose term in the Senate expires in 1998, is only the fifth African American to serve in the Senate and only the second since Reconstruction. Her election to the United States Senate is an important victory for African Americans and women alike.

The 1992 national elections increased the number of African American representatives in Congress. Thirty-nine African Americans occupy seats in the current 103rd Congress, compared with only 25 African-American representatives in the 102nd Congress. African Americans elected to their first Congressional term in November 1992 include: Earl Hilliard (Alabama); Walter Tucker (California); Alcee Hastings (Florida); Sanford Bishop (Georgia); Bobby Rush (Illinois); Mel Reynolds (Illinois); Cleo Fields (Louisiana); Albert Wynn (Maryland); Jim Clyburn (South Carolina); Eddie B. Johnson (Texas); and Bobby Scott (Virginia). Four of the new Congressional representatives are women. They are: Corrine Brown (Florida); Carrie Meek (Florida); Cynthia McKinney (Georgia); and Eva Clayton (North Carolina). Many of the gains in representation can be attributed to an increasing acceptance of African Americans as viable political candidates. Also, the process of redistricting has benefitted minority political candidates. Redistricting occurs every ten years and involves the reapportionment of all 435 seats in the United States House of Representatives according to population shifts among the 50 states.

On November 3, 1992, Americans elected a new president, Bill Clinton. President Clinton's cabinet includes seven African Americans. Ron Brown, former Democratic National Committee chairman, was chosen as Secretary of Commerce. He is the first African American to hold this post. Also, Clinton chose Jesse Brown to serve as head of the Veterans Affairs Department. Brown, a former director of the Disabled Veterans of America, is the first African-American veteran affairs secretary. On December 24, 1992, the position of Secretary of Agriculture was awarded to Michael Espy. Espy, a Congressman from Mississippi, was elected in 1986 and was the first African American from Mississippi to serve in Congress since Reconstruction. Another African American, Lee P. Brown, was selected as head of the Office of National Drug Control Policy. Brown is a former police commissioner from New York City. He is faced with the difficult challenge of balancing the desire for tough penalties for drug offenders with the urgent need for drug rehabilitation and anti-drug education. Hazel R. O'Leary, one of two African-American women selected for cabinet positions, was chosen as Secretary of Energy. O'Leary, who served as an energy regulator during the Ford and Carter administrations, brings a wealth of experience to her new position. The position of surgeon general was awarded to Dr. Joycelyn Elders. Elders is a talented physician known for her innovative research on diabetes. She is also a controversial figure who has clashed with conservatives regarding her views concerning abortion rights and her support of contraception in school health clinics. Also, Clifton R. Wharton, Jr. was chosen as deputy secretary of state. Wharton is an economist and a business executive.

■ AFRICAN-AMERICAN GOVERNMENT OFFICIALS

Thomas Bradley (1917–)
Former Mayor

Bradley was born December 29, 1917 in Calvert, Texas. In 1924 he moved with his family to Los Angeles. Bradley graduated from Polytechnic High School in 1937 and attended the University of California, Los Angeles on an athletic scholarship. He excelled at track before quitting college in 1940 and joining the Los Angeles Police Department.

While a member of the police force Bradley worked as a detective, community relations officer and in the departments juvenile division. In the early 1950s Bradley began studying law at two Los Angeles colleges, Loyola University and later at Southwestern University. He was awarded an LL.B. from Southwestern University in 1956. Bradley stayed with the LAPD until 1961 when he entered private law practice.

Tom Bradley

In 1963 Bradley became the first African American elected to the Los Angeles City Council. He was re-elected in 1967 and 1971. In a hotly contested 1973 election Bradley became mayor of Los Angeles winning 56% of the vote.

Bradley has served as president of the National League of Cities and the Southern California Association of Governments. He belongs to the Urban League of Los Angeles and is a founding member of the NAACP's Black Achievers Committee. On the National level he has served on President Gerald Ford's National Committee on Productivity & Work Quality and on the National Energy Advisory Council. Bradley has won numerous awards and honors including the University of California's Alumnus of the Year (1974), the Thurgood Marshall Award (1974), Award of Merit given by the National Council of Negro Women (1978) and the NAACP's Springarn Medal (1985).

Bradley retired as mayor of Los Angeles in 1993.

Carol Moseley Braun (1947–)
United States Senator

Carol Moseley was born in Chicago on August 16, 1947. She received her B.A. from the University of Illinois in 1969 and her J.D. from the University of Chicago Law School in 1972. While attending law school Braun worked as a legal intern and an associate attorney for a number of private law firms.

After graduating from law school Braun was an assistant U.S. attorney for the northern district of Illinois from 1973 until 1977.

Carol Moseley Braun, the first black woman elected to the United States Senate.

In 1979 she was elected an Illinois state representative from the 25th district, where she became known as an ardent supporter of civil rights legislation. After a bid for the lieutenant governorship was thwarted, Braun was elected Cook County recorder of deeds in 1986. In 1992 Braun became the nation's first African-American woman elected to the United States Senate.

In 1980 and 1982 Braun won the Best Legislation Award presented by the Independent Voters of Illinois. She has also won the National Association of Negro Business & Professional Womens Clubs' Community Recognition Award (1981), the Chicago Alliance of Black School Educators' Recognition of Excellence in Education Award (1981) and the Afro-American Voters Alliance Community Recognition Award in 1982.

Braun belongs to the League of Black Women, Operation PUSH, Federal, Illinois and Chicago Bar Association and the Women's Political Caucus.

Sidney John Barthelemy (1942–)
Mayor

Barthelemy was born in New Orleans on March 17, 1942. He attended Epiphany Apostolic Junior College from 1960 to 1963 and received a B.A. from the St. Joseph Seminary in 1967. Two years later he earned a Masters in Social Work from Tulane University.

After graduation Barthelemy worked in administrative and professional positions at a wide variety of organizations including Total Community Action (1967–1969), Adult Basic Education Program (1968–1969), Parent-Child Center, Family Health Inc. (1969–1971), Urban League of New Orleans (1969–1972), and the Parent-Child Development Center (1971–1972).

From 1972 to 1974 Barthelemy was the director of the Welfare Department of the City of New Orleans. In 1974 he was elected to the Louisiana State Senate. In 1978 Barthelemy left the state legislature after winning a seat on the New Orleans City Council where he stayed until his election as mayor in 1986.

Barthelemy has taught at Xavier University as an associate professor of sociology (1974–1986), and at Tulane University and the University of New Orleans. He has been the vice-chairman for voter registration for the Democratic National Party (1988–1989), second vice-president for the National League of Cities (1988) and president of the Louisiana Conference of Mayors (1989).

Barthelemy belongs to the NAACP, National Association of Black Mayors, Democratic National Committee, National Institute of Education, National League of Cities and the New Orleans Association of Black Social Workers.

He has won numerous awards including Outstanding Alumnus of Tulane University, and the Louisiana Chapter of the National Association of Social Workers' Social Worker of the Year Award (1987). He has

Sidney Barthelemy campaigning for reelection in 1990

also won the American Freedom Award presented by the Third Baptist Church of Chicago (1987), the American Spirit Award given by the United States Air Force Recruiting Service (1989) and the NAACP's New Orleans Chapter Daniel E. Byrd Award (1990).

Mary Frances Berry (1938–)
Former Assistant Cabinet Member, Civil Rights Commissioner

Mary Frances Berry was born in 1938 and received her B.A. degree from Howard University in 1961 and her masters degree in 1962. In 1966, she received a Ph.D. from the University of Michigan and her J.D. from its law school in 1970. Berry worked several years as a professor of history and law at several universities throughout the United States. She was appointed Assistant Secretary of Education, United States Department of Health, Education and Welfare by President Jimmy Carter in 1977, and became commissioner and vice chairman of the United States Commission on Civil Rights in 1980. She was "fired" from the Civil Rights Commission by President Ronald Reagan in 1983. In a compromise with Congress, Berry was reinstated.

She currently is a Geraldine R. Segal professor of American Social Thought at the University of Pennsylvania.

Julian Bond (1940–)
Former State Representative

Throughout his successful career and personal and political adversity, Julian Bond has been labeled everything from a national

Mary Frances Berry (middle) speaks at a news conference in 1984.

Julian Bond

hero to a national traitor. He has faced violent segregationists and his own political failures and scandals. In spite of everything, he has kept his head above water and has remained an influential voice in politics, education and the media.

Julian Bond was born on January 14, 1940 to well-educated parents. His father, an eminent scholar and president of Lincoln University in Pennsylvania, wanted Julian to follow his footsteps into the world of academics. Although Julian attended fine private schools, he showed little desire for educational pursuits. In 1960, Bond attended Morehouse College in Atlanta where he was a mediocre student. While at Morehouse, however, Bond developed an interest in civil rights activism. He and several other students formed the Atlanta Committee on Appeal for Human Rights (COHAR). Along with other members, Bond participated in several sit-ins at segregated lunch counters in downtown Atlanta. The activities of Bond and his cohorts attracted the attention of Dr. Martin Luther King and the Southern Christian Leadership Conference (SCLC). King invited Bond and other COHAR members to Shaw University in North Carolina to help devise new civil rights strategies. At this conference, the Student Nonviolent Coordinating Committee (SNCC) was created. The SNCC eventually absorbed COHAR and Bond accepted a position as the SNCC director of communications. By 1966, Bond had grown tired of the SNCC and decided to embark on a new career in politics.

In 1966, Bond campaigned for a seat in the Georgia House of Representatives. He won the election and prepared to take his seat in the Georgia legislature. However, Bond was soon embroiled in a bitter controversy when he publicly announced that he opposed U.S. involvement in Vietnam and supported students who burned their draft cards to protest against the Vietnam War. These statements outraged many conservative members of the Georgia House of Representatives and, on January 10, 1966, they voted to prevent Bond's admission to the legislature. Bond sought legal recourse to overturn this vote and the case eventually went to the U.S. Supreme Court. On December 5, 1966, the Court ruled that the Georgia vote was a violation of Bond's First Amendment right of free speech and ordered that he be admitted to the legislature. The members of the Georgia House of Representatives reluctantly allowed Bond to take his seat, but treated him as an outcast.

Bond's battle with the Georgia House of Representatives would not be his last experience as the center of controversy. In 1968, Bond and several other members of the Georgia Democratic Party Forum protested Governor Lester Maddox's decision to send only six African-American delegates out of 107 to the Democratic National Convention. Bond and his supporters arrived at the convention and set up a rival delegation. After several bitter arguments with Georgia's official delegation, Bond's delegation had captured nearly half of Georgia's delegate votes. Bond's actions made him a national hero to many African Americans. He became the Democratic Party's first black candidate for the U.S. vice-presidency, a position he declined.

Throughout the 1970s, Bond was no longer in the national spotlight. In 1974, he became president of the Atlanta branch of the NAACP and served until 1989. Also, Bond was elected to the Georgia Senate in 1975 and remained a member until 1987. In 1976, he refused a cabinet position in the Carter administration. Although Bond continued to express his political views as a writer and lecturer, his popularity plummeted dramatically.

The 1980s proved to be a difficult for Julian Bond on both a professional and personal level. Bond ran for a seat in the U.S. Congress in 1986, but lost the election. In 1989, he divorced his wife after twenty-eight years of marriage. Shortly thereafter, he became embroiled in a paternity suit. He initially denied the allegations, but admitted in May 1990 to fathering the child and was ordered to pay child support. Bond remarried in March 1990.

Today, Julian Bond is retired from political life. He remains extremely active, however. He has served as a visiting professor at Drexel University, Harvard University, the University of Virginia, and American University. He is a popular lecturer and writer and is often called upon to comment on political and social issues. Bond has hosted a popular television program *America's Black Forum* and narrated the highly acclaimed public television series *Eyes on the Prize.*

Edward W. Brooke (1919–   )

Former United States Senator

During his two terms in the United States Senate, Edward W. Brooke, the first black to be elected to that body since 1881, defied conventional political wisdom. In a state that was overwhelmingly Democratic and in which blacks constituted only 3% of the population, he was one of its most popular political figures and a Republican.

He first achieved statewide office in 1962 when he defeated Elliot Richardson to become Attorney General. He established an outstanding record in that post and in 1966 was elected to the Senate over former Massachusetts governor Endicott Peabody.

Born into a middle-class Washington, DC environment, Brooke attended public schools locally and went on to graduate from Howard. Inducted into an all-black infantry unit during World War II, Brooke rose to the rank of captain and was ultimately given a Bronze Star for his work in intelligence.

Returning to Massachusetts after the war, Brooke attended the Boston University Law School, compiling an outstanding academic record and editing the *Law Review* in the process. After law school, he established himself as an attorney and also served as chairman of the Boston Finance Commission.

Brooke was later nominated for the attorney general's office, encountering stiff opposition within his own party. He eventually won both the Republican primary and the general election against his Democratic opponent.

Upon entering the national political scene, Brooke espoused the notion that the Great Society could not become a reality until it was preceded by the "Responsible Society." He called this a society in which "it's more profitable to work than not to work. You don't help a man by constantly giving him more handouts."

Edward Brooke, 1966.

When first elected, Brooke strongly supported United States participation in the Vietnam War, though most black leaders were increasingly opposing it. However, in 1971, Brooke supported the McGovern-Hatfield Amendment which called for withdrawal of the United States from Vietnam.

As might be expected, matters of race rather than foreign affairs were to become Brooke's area of expertise. Reluctant and subdued, Brooke proceeded carefully at first, waiting to be consulted by President Nixon and loyally accepting the latter's apparent indifference to his views. However, as pressure mounted from the established civil rights groups and impatient black militants he decided to attack the Nixon policies. Brooke was roused into a more active role by the administration's vacillating school desegregation guidelines, its "firing" of HEW official Leon Panetta, and the nominations to the Supreme Court of judicial conservatives Clement Haynsworth and G. Harrold Carswell.

In 1972 Brooke was reelected to the Senate overwhelmingly, even though Massachusetts was the only state not carried by his party in the presidential election. While Brooke seconded the nomination of President Nixon at the 1972 Republican Convention, he became increasingly critical of the Nixon administration. He also began to appear publicly at meetings of the Congressional Black Caucus, a group he had tended to avoid in the past. Brooke was considered a member of the moderate-to-liberal wing of the Republican Party.

In 1978, Brooke's bid for a third term in the Senate was defeated by Democrat Paul

Tsongas and he returned to his private law practice.

Ronald H. Brown (1941–)
Cabinet Member

Born in Washington, DC on August 1, 1941 Brown was raised in Harlem and attended White Plains High School and Rhodes and Walden Preparatory Schools in New York. He graduated from Middlebury College in Middlebury, Vermont with a B.A. in political science in 1962. Upon graduating he enlisted in the army and achieved the rank of captain while serving in West Germany and Korea. Brown then graduated from New York City's St. Johns University Law School in 1970.

While attending law school Brown began working for the National Urban League's job training center in the Bronx, New York in 1968. He continued with them until 1979, working as general counsel, Washington spokesperson, deputy executive director and vice-president of Washington operations. In 1980 he resigned to become chief counsel of the United States Senate judiciary committee and in 1981 general counsel and staff coordinator for Senator Edward Kennedy. In that year he also became a partner in the Washington law firm of Patton, Boggs & Blow. In 1989 Brown was appointed Chairman of the Democratic National Committee and thus the first African American to head a major American political party. In 1993 Brown was appointed Commerce Secretary by President Bill Clinton.

Ron Brown opening the 1992 Democratic National Convention.

Ron Brown

Brown belongs to the American Bar Association and is a trustee of the University of the District of Columbia, Middlebury College and Harvard University's JFK School of Government.

Blanche K. Bruce (1841–1898)
Former United States Senator

Blanche Kelso Bruce was born a slave in Farmville, Prince Edward County, Virginia on March 1, 1841. He received his early formal education in Missouri, where his parents had moved while he was still quite young, and later studied at Oberlin College in Ohio.

In 1868, Bruce settled in Floreyville, Mississippi. He worked as a planter and eventually built up a considerable fortune in property.

In 1870, Bruce entered politics and was elected sergeant-at-arms of the Mississippi Senate. A year later he was named assessor of taxes in Bolivar County. In 1872 he served as sheriff of that county and as a member of the Board of Levee Commissioners of Mississippi.

Blanche K. Bruce

Bruce was nominated for the United States Senate from Mississippi in February 1874. He was elected, becoming the first black person to serve a full term in the United States Senate. Bruce became an outspoken defender of the rights of minority groups, including the Chinese and Indians. He also investigated alleged bank and election frauds and worked for the improvement of navigation on the Mississippi in the hope of increasing interstate and foreign commerce. Bruce also supported legislation aimed at eliminating reprisals against those who had opposed Negro emancipation.

After Bruce completed his term in the Senate, he was named Register of the United States Treasury Department by President James A. Garfield. Bruce held this position until 1885. In 1889, President Benjamin Harrison appointed him recorder of deeds for the District of Columbia. Bruce served as recorder of deeds until 1893, when he became a trustee for the District of Columbia public schools. In 1897, President William McKinley reappointed him to his former post as register of the treasurer. Bruce died on March 17, 1898.

Ralph J. Bunche (1904–1971)
United Nations Undersecretary for Special Political Affairs

The first American black to win the Nobel Peace Prize, Ralph Bunche was an internationally acclaimed statesman whose record of achievement places him among the most significant American diplomats of the twentieth century. Bunche received the coveted award in 1950 for his role in effecting a cease fire in the Arab-Israeli dispute which threatened to engulf the entire Middle East in armed conflict.

Born in Detroit on August 7, 1904, Bunche graduated from UCLA in 1927 summa cum laude and with Phi Beta Kappa honors. A year later he received his M.A. in government from Harvard. Soon thereafter he was named head of the Department of Political Science at Howard University, remaining there until 1932 at which time he was able to resume work toward his doctorate from Harvard. (He later studied at Northwestern University, the London School of Economics, and Capetown University.)

Before World War II broke out in 1939, Bunche did field work with the Swedish sociologist Gunnar Myrdal, author of the widely acclaimed *An American Dilemma*. During the war, he served initially as Senior Social Analyst for the Office of the Coordinator of Information in African and Far Eastern Affairs, and was then reassigned to the African section of the Office of Strategic Services. In 1942, he helped draw up the territories and trusteeship sections ultimately earmarked for inclusion in the United Nations charter.

The single event which brought the name of Ralph Bunche into the international spotlight occurred soon after his appointment in 1948 as chief assistant to Count Folke Bernadotte, U.N. mediator in the Palestine crisis. With the latter's assassination, Bunche was faced with the great challenge of somehow continuing ceasefire talks between Egypt and Israel. After six weeks of intensive negotiations, Bunche worked out the now-famous "Four Armistice Agreements," which brokered an immediate cessation of the hostilities between the two combatants. Once the actual ceasefire was signed, Bunche received numerous congratulatory letters and telegrams from many heads of state and was given a hero's welcome upon his return to the United States.

Bunche served as undersecretary of Special Political Affairs from 1957 to 1967. By 1968, Bunche had attained the rank of undersecretary general, the highest position ever held by an American at the United Nations.

Bunche retired in October 1971 and died on December 9, 1971.

Yvonne Braithwaite Burke (1932–)

United States Representative

Attorney and former California State Assembly Woman Yvonne Braithwaite Burke became the first black woman from California ever to be elected to the House of Representatives in November 1972.

Congresswoman Burke served in the state Assembly for six years prior to her election to Congress. During her final two years there, she was chairman of the Committee on Urban Development and Housing and a member of the Health, Finance and Insurance committees.

As a state legislator, Burke was responsible for the enactment of bills providing for needy children, relocation of tenants and owners of homes taken by governmental action, and one which required major medical insurance programs to grant immediate coverage to newborn infants of the insured.

Prior to her governmental career, Burke was a practicing attorney, during which time she served as a Deputy Corporation Commissioner, a hearing officer for the Los Angeles Police Commissioner, and an attorney for the McCone Commission, which investigated the Watts riots.

Burke's district, created in 1971 by the California legislature, contains low-and middle-income black and integrated neighborhoods plus some white suburban tracts and beach communities, including Venice, which is noted for its "counterculture"

Yvonne Braithwaite Burke at a Washington news conference in 1976.

scene. About 50% of the district's population is black, another 10% of Hispanic and Asian origin. In 1972, the district gave 64% of its vote to Burke.

During Burke's first term in the Senate, she proved to be an ardent spokesperson for the downtrodden. She became a member of the Committee on Appropriations in December 1974 and used her position on this committee to advocate an increase in funding for senior citizen services and community nutrition and food programs. Although her proposal for increased spending was defeated by the House of Representatives, Burke's efforts earned the respect of the African-American community. In January 1977, Burke worked diligently for the passage of the Displaced Homemakers Act, which proposed the creation of counseling programs and job training centers for women entering the work force for the first time.

In 1978, Burke resigned to run for Attorney General in California. She lost that race but, in 1979, she was appointed to the Los Angeles County Board of Supervisors. She resigned from the board in December 1980 and returned to her private law practice. Although she no longer holds public office, Burke remains a prominent figure in California politics. She has also taken on a number of civic responsibilities including serving as a member of the University of California Board of Regents.

Shirley Chisholm (1924–)
Former United States Representative

Chisholm was born November 30, 1924 in New York City. She graduated cum laude from Brooklyn College in 1946 with a B.A. in sociology and with an M.A. in elementary education from Columbia University in

1952. She had an early career in child care and pre-school education culminating in her directorship of the Hamilton-Madison Child Care Center in New York. Leaving that position in 1959 she served until 1964 as a consultant to the Day Care Division of New York City's Bureau of Child Welfare.

In 1964 she was elected New York State Assemblywoman representing the 55th district in New York City. In 1968 she was elected to the United States House of Representatives and represented the 12th district until her retirement in 1982. Throughout her political career Chisholm has been a staunch democrat both in her elected positions and as a delegate to the Democratic National Mid-Term Conference in 1974 and as a Democratic National Committeewoman.

Shirley Chisholm on the steps of the U.S. Capitol in 1969.

After retiring from politics Chisholm taught political science at Mount Holyoke College and in 1985 she was a visiting scholar at Spelman College. In 1984 Chisholm co-founded the National Political Congress of Black Women. She has also written two books *Unbossed & Unbought* (1970) and *The Good Fight* (1973).

Chisholm is a member of the NAACP, the National Association of Colored Women and the League of Women Voters. She has won numerous awards including the Woman of Achievement Award presented by Key Women Inc. (1965) and in 1969 the Sojourner Truth Award given by the Association for the Study of Negro Life and History.

William Clay (1931–)
United States Representative

William Clay

William Clay, the first black man to represent the state of Missouri in the United States Congress, was born in 1931 in the lower end of what is now St. Louis' First District. Clay was educated locally and later took a degree in political science at St. Louis University, where he was one of four blacks in a class of 1,100. After serving in the Army until 1955, Clay became active in a host of civil rights organizations, including the NAACP Youth Council and CORE. During this time he worked as a cardiographic aide, bus driver, and insurance agent, but his heart had already surrendered to politics, at least judging from the number of demonstrations and picket lines he had joined.

In 1959, and again in 1963, Clay was elected alderman of the predominantly black 26th Ward. During his first term, he served nearly four months of a nine-month jail sentence for demonstrations at a local bank. Meanwhile, on the outside, the number of white-collar jobs held by blacks in St. Louis banks began a steady ascent from a low of 16 to a high of 700. In 1964, Clay stepped down from his alderman's post to run for Ward Committeeman, winning handily and being reelected in 1968.

Clay's election platform in 1969 included a number of progressive, even radical, ideas. He advocated that all penal institutions make provisions for the creation of facilities in which married prisoners could set up house with their spouses for the duration of their sentences. He branded most testing procedures and diploma requirements, as well as references to arrest records and periods of unemployment, unnecessary obstacles complicating the path of a prospective employee. In his view, a demonstrated willingness to work and an acceptance of responsibility should be the criteria determining one's selection for a job.

Clay's last job before his election to Congress was as race relations coordinator for Steamfitters Union Local 562. Subjected to considerable criticism from other St. Louis blacks who labeled the union racist, Clay pointed out that dramatic changes in the hiring practices of the union since he had joined it in 1966 were responsible for the employment of 30 black steamfitters in St. Louis—30 more than the union had previously put to work. Still, Clay conceded that the high-paying job had led him to reduce his active involvement with the civil rights struggle to some degree.

As a member of the United States House of Representatives, Clay has proven himself a capable legislator. He has sponsored many pieces of legislation, including the Hatch Act Reform Bill, the City Earnings Tax Bill, and the IRS Reform Bill. Clay has served as chairman of the Subcommittee on Postal Operations and Civil Service, the House Education and Labor Committee and the House Administration Committee. He has also been a member of the board of directors for Benedict College, Tougaloo College, and the Congressional Black Caucus Foundation.

Cardiss Collins (1931–)
United States Representative

Collins was born Cardiss Robertson September 24, 1931 in St. Louis, Missouri and by the time she was ten years old her family had moved to Detroit. After graduating from

Cardiss Collins

Detroit's Commerce High School Collins moved to Chicago where she worked as a secretary for the state's Department of Revenue. She began studying accounting at Northwestern University and was promoted to accountant and then auditor.

In 1973 Collins was elected United States Representative from Illinois' 7th district. She was elected to fill the seat vacated by her husband George Collins who was killed in an airplane crash. She soon became the first African American and the first woman to hold the position of Democratic whip-at-large. Collins has served on congressional sub-committees dealing with consumer protection, national security, hazardous materials and narcotic abuse and control. She has been a proponent of civil rights, pro-bussing and anti-apartheid legislation.

Collins belongs to the NAACP, Chicago Urban League and the National Council of Negro Women. Besides her degree from Northwestern (1967) she has honorary degrees from Barber-Scotia College, Winston-Salem State University, and Spelman College.

John Conyers

John Conyers (1929–)
United States Representative

Conyers was born in Detroit on May 16, 1929 and graduated from Northwestern High School in 1947. In 1950 he enlisted in the United States Army as a private and served in Korea before being honorably discharged as a second lieutenant in 1957. He then attended Wayne State University in Detroit and after studying in a dual program he received a B.A. in 1957 and a law degree in 1958.

Conyers served as a legislative assistant to Congressman John Dingell, Jr. from 1958 to 1961 and was a senior partner in the law firm of Conyers, Bell & Townsend from 1959 to 1961. In that year he took a referee position with the Michigan Workman's Compensation Department and stayed until 1963. In 1964 he won election as a democrat to the United States House of Representatives. Conyers had long been active in the Democratic Party, belonging to the Young Democrats, University Democrats and serving as a precinct delegate to the Democratic Party.

After his election Conyers was assigned to the powerful House Judiciary Committee. From that position he worked for legislation dealing with civil rights, medicare, immigration reform and truth-in-packaging laws. He was an early opponent of United States involvement in Vietnam and an early proponent on the Voting Rights Act of 1965.

Conyers has been vice-chairman of the National Board of Americans for Democratic Action and the American Civil Liberties Union. He is on the executive board of the Detroit Chapter of the NAACP and belongs to the Wolverine Bar Association. He is the recipient of the Rosa Parks Award (1967) and an honorary law degree and an honorary law degree from Wilberforce University (1969).

Ronald V. Dellums (1935–)
United States Representative

Dellums was born in Oakland, California on November 24, 1935. After attending McClymonds and Oakland Technical High Schools Dellum joined the United States Marine Corps in 1954 and was discharged after two years of service. He returned to school, receiving an associate of arts degree from Oakland City College (1958), a B.A. from San Francisco State College (1960) and a masters degree in social work from the University of California at Berkeley (1962).

Ron Dellums

After graduation Dellums was involved in numerous social work positions from 1962 to 1970. He was a psychiatric social worker with the Berkeley Department of Mental Hygiene (1962–1964), program director of the Bayview Community Center (1964–1965), director of the Hunters Point Youth Opportunity Center (1965–1966), consultant to the Bay Area Social Planning Council (1966–1967) and program director for the San Francisco Economic Opportunity Council (1967–1968). From 1968 to 1970 Dellums lectured at San Francisco State College and the University of California's School of Social Work. He also served as a consultant to Social Dynamics Inc.

Dellums was elected to the Berkeley City Council in 1967 and served until his election as a Democrat to the United States House of Representatives in 1971. As a representative he chaired the House Committee on the District of Columbia and served on the House Armed Services Sub-committee on Military Facilities and Installations and the Sub-committee on Military Research and Development. He has been the chairman of the Defense Policy Panel and in 1983 authored *Defense Sense: The Search for a Rational Military Policy.*

Oscar Stanton DePriest (1871–1951)
Former United States Representative

Oscar De Priest was the first black to win a seat in the United States House of Representatives in the twentieth century, and the first to be elected from a northern state.

Born in Florence, Alabama, De Priest moved to Kansas with his family at the age of six. His formal education there consisted of business and bookkeeping classes which he completed before running away to Day-

Ron Dellums and other members of the Congressional Black Caucus meet with former President George Bush, 1989.

ton, Ohio with two white friends. By 1889, he had reached Chicago and become a painter and master decorator.

In Chicago, De Priest amassed a fortune in real estate and the stock market and in 1904 entered politics successfully when he was elected Cook County Commissioner. In 1908, he was appointed an alternate delegate to the Republican National Convention and in 1915 became Chicago's first black alderman. He served on the Chicago City Council from 1915 to 1917 and became Third Ward Committeeman in 1924.

In 1928, De Priest became the Republican nominee for the Congressional seat vacated by fellow Republican Martin Madden. De Priest won the November election over his Democratic rival and an independent candidate to become the first black from outside the South to be elected to Congress.

Following his election to Congress, De Priest became the unofficial spokesman for the 11 million blacks in the United States during the 1920s and 1930s. He proposed that states that discriminated against black Americans should receive fewer Congressional seats. Also, he proposed that a monthly pension be given to ex-slaves over the age of seventy-five. During the early 1930s, with the United States mired in the Depression, De Priest was faced with a difficult dilemma. Although he empathized with the plight of poor black and white Americans, he did not support the emergency federal relief programs proposed by President Franklin Roosevelt. Rather, De Priest and his fellow Republicans believed that aid programs should be created and implemented by individual states or local communities. De Priest's stance on the issue of federal relief programs dismayed many of his constituents. In 1934, he was defeated by Arthur Mitchell, the first black Democrat elected to serve in Congress.

De Priest remained active in public life, serving from 1943 to 1947 as alderman of the Third Ward in Chicago. His final withdrawal from politics came about after a sharp dispute with his own party. De Priest returned to his real estate business, and he died in 1951.

David Dinkins (1927–)
Mayor

In September 1989, David Dinkins surprised political observers by defeating incumbent Mayor Edward I. Koch in New York's Democratic mayoral primary. In the November election, he defeated Rudolph Giuliani, a popular district attorney. Dinkins' victory marked the first time an African American was elected as mayor of New York City. Since assuming this office, Mayor Dinkins has faced the difficult task of leading a racially polarized and financially troubled city. The results of Dinkins' tenure in office are somewhat mixed. Many supporters have cited Dinkins' calm, professional demeanor as having a soothing effect upon New York's festering racial problems. Others have chided Dinkins for not responding forcefully enough to the many fiscal and social challenges facing the city. In general, Dinkins is viewed as a decent man who has done his best to serve the needs of New Yorkers.

David Dinkins was born in Trenton, New Jersey in 1927. His parents separated when he was quite young and he moved to Harlem with his mother and sister. He returned to Trenton to attend high school. He was a fine student and well-liked by his peers. Following a stint in the Marines during World War II, he attended Howard University in Washington D.C. and graduated with a bachelor of science degree in 1950. In 1953, Dinkins enrolled at Brooklyn Law School and graduated in 1956. He became an attorney and, eventually, a partner in the law firm of Dyett, Alexander, Dinkins, Patterson, Michael, Dinkins, and Jones.

David Dinkins speaking at the Democratic National Convention, July 13, 1992.

Mayor Dinkins' first foray into the world of politics occurred in 1965 when he won an election to the New York State Assembly. He served until 1967, but did not seek reelection after his district was redrawn. In 1972, Dinkins was appointed as president of elections for the City of New York and served for one year. Two years later, in 1975, he was appointed as city clerk and served until 1985. Dinkins ran for the office of Manhattan borough president in 1977 and 1981. He lost both elections by a wide margin. Dinkins ran again in 1985 and was elected. As Manhattan borough president, Dinkins was viewed as a mediator who tried to address a myriad of community concerns such as school decentralization, AIDS treatment and prevention services, and pedestrian safety.

Mayor Dinkins' term expires in November 1993. As the 1993 election approached, Dinkins was facing a steady stream of criticism that he had hired incompetent workers to top municipal posts, that he acted reactively rather than proactively, and that, while displaying a talent for pacifying, he lacked the consistently strong leadership and stalwart vision that the city's multifaceted problems demand.

Julian C. Dixon (1934–)
United States Representative

Dixon was born August 8, 1934 in Washington, DC. He received a B.S. in political science from California State University and in 1967 an LL.B. from Southwestern University Law School.

Julian Dixon

In 1972 Dixon was elected on the democratic ticket to the California State Assembly. Staying in that position until 1978 Dixon wrote legislation dealing with criminal justice, education and fair employment. In 1978 he was elected to the United States House of Representatives.

While in the House of Representatives Dixon has served on the House Committee on Standards of Official Conduct, West Point Board of Supervisors, the Appropriations Sub-Committee on Foreign Operations and he chaired the Appropriations Sub-Committee on the District of Columbia. This latter appointment made Dixon the first African American to chair an appropriations subcommittee. Dixon was an original co-sponsor of the Equal Rights Amendment and is active in the Congressional Black Caucus.

Dixon also served in the United States Army from 1957 to 1960.

Sharon Pratt Dixon (1944–)
Mayor

Dixon was born Sharon Pratt in Washington, DC on January 30, 1944. She graduated from Howard University with a B.A. in political science in 1965 and a J.D. from their law school in 1968. She edited the Howard University Law School Journal in 1967.

From 1970 thru 1971 Dixon was the house counsel for the Joint Center for Political Studies in Washington, DC. Between 1971 and 1976 she was an associate in the law firm of Pratt & Queen. During this time she also taught at Antioch Law School. In 1976 Dixon began a 14 year association with the Potomac Electric Power Company. While there she held increasingly responsible positions including associate general counsel

(1976–1979), director of consumer affairs (1979–1983), vice-president of public policy (1986–1990).

In 1990 Dixon left the private sector to win the office of mayor of Washington, DC. In doing so she became the first African-American woman to be mayor of a major American city.

Dixon has long been active in the Democratic Party. In 1976 and 1977 she was general counsel to the Washington, DC Democratic Committee. Between 1985 and 1989 she was treasurer of the Democratic Party and has also sat as a national committeewoman on the Washington, DC Democratic State Committee.

Dixon belongs to the American Bar Association and the Washington, DC Women's Bar Association. She is affiliated with the Legal Aid Society, the American Civil Liberties Union and the United Negro College Fund. Dixon was a Falk Fellow at Howard University (1962–1965) and has received numerous awards including the NAACP's Presidential Award (1983), the United Negro College Fund's Distinguished Leadership Award (1985) and the Distinguished Service Award presented by the Federation of Women's Clubs (1986).

Sharon Pratt Dixon

While in law school she married Arrington Dixon from whom she was divorced in 1982. In 1991 Dixon married James Kelly III.

Michael Espy (1953–)
Cabinet Member, Former Representative

Espy was born November 30, 1953. He received a B.A. from Howard University in 1975 and a J.D. from the Santa Clara School of Law in 1978.

After graduation Espy practiced law in Yazoo City, Mississippi and managed Central Mississippi Legal Services. From 1980 until 1984 he was Director of Public Lands and Elections which is a division of the Mississippi State Secretary's Office. In 1984 Espy left the directorship to become the Chief of the Consumer Protection Division of the State Attorney General's Office.

Espy was then elected to the United States House of Representatives where he served on numerous committees including the House Budget Committee, House Agricultural Committee, Select Committee on Hunger, Sub-Committee on Cotton, Rice & Sugar, Sub-Committee on Conservation, Credit and Rural Development, Consumer Relations & Nutrition Committee and he chaired the Domestic Task Force on Hunger.

In 1993 Espy was appointed Secretary of Agriculture by President Bill Clinton.

In 1977 Espy won the Law School Community Service Award. He is affiliated with

Michael Espy

the American Bar Association, Mississippi Trial Lawyers Association, National Conference of Black Leaders and is on the board of directors of the Jackson Urban League.

Walter E. Fauntroy (1933–)
Former Delegate to the United States House of Representatives

Delegate Walter E. Fauntroy, pastor of New Bethel Baptist Church in Washington, DC, represents the District of Columbia in the House of Representatives. A Yale Divinity School alumnus, he was chairman of the Caucus task force for the 1972 Democratic National Committee and of the platform committee of the National Black Political Convention. Fauntroy was Washington, DC coordinator for the March on Washington for Jobs and Freedom in 1963, coordinator for the Selma to Montgomery march in 1965, and national coordinator for the Poor People's Campaign in 1969. He is also a chairman of the board of directors of the Southern Christian Leadership Conference. Fauntroy was the chief architect of legislation in 1973 that permitted the District of Columbia to elect its own mayor and city council and engineered the passage by both the House and Senate of a constitutional amendment calling for full Congressional representation for District of Columbia residents in the United States Congress. He has strong support from the city's overwhelmingly black population, especially the large population of black civil servants.

Since his election to Congress, he has continued to build a record of achievement by playing key roles in the mobilization of black political power from the National

Black Political Convention in 1972 to the presidential elections of 1972 and 1976. He is a member of the House Select Committee on Narcotics Abuse and Control and co-sponsored the 1988 $2.7 billion anti-drug bill. On Thanksgiving Eve in 1984, Fauntroy and two prominent national leaders launched the "Free South Africa Movement" (FSAM) with their arrest at the South African embassy. He serves as co-chair of the steering committee of the FSAM.

In the 95th Congress Fauntroy was a member of the House Select Committee on Assassinations and Chairman of its Subcommittee on the Assassination of Martin Luther King Jr. He is a ranking member of the House Banking, Finance, and Urban Affairs Committee and chairman of its Subcommittee on Government Affairs and Budget. He is also the first ranking member of the House District Committee.

Gary A. Franks (1953–)
United States Representative

Franks was born February 9, 1953 in Waterbury, Connecticut. He received a B.A. from Yale University in 1975.

Before being elected to the United States House of Representatives Franks was active in local politics and business. He was president of GAF Realty in Waterbury. Franks was also on the Board of Alderman (1986–1990), vice-chairman of the Zoning Board (1986–1987), a member of the Environmental Control Commission (1988–1990), director of the Naugatuck, Connecticut chapter of the American Red Cross (1984–1987), president of the Greater Waterbury Chamber of Commerce (1987–1990), and a member of the Waterbury Foundation (1989–1990).

In 1991 he was elected to the United States House of Representatives and has served on the Armed Services Committee, Small Business Committee and the Select Committee on Aging. Currently, Franks is the only African-American Republican in the United States House of Representatives.

Franks has been named Outstanding Young Man by the Boy's Club and Man of the Year by the Negro Professional Women's Club (1980).

W. Wilson Goode (1938–)
Former Mayor

Goode was born on August 19, 1938 in Seaboard, North Carolina. He received a B.A. from Morgan State University, and a Masters of Public Administration from the University of Pennsylvania's Wharton School in 1968.

Between 1966 and 1978 Goode held a wide variety of positions including probation officer, building maintenance supervisor, insurance claims adjuster and president of the Philadelphia Council for Community Advancement. From 1978 until 1980 Goode

W. Wilson Goode

was chairman of the Pennsylvania Public Utilities Commission, and from 1980 until 1982 he was managing director of the City of Philadelphia. In 1984 Goode was elected first African-American mayor of Philadelphia and held office until 1991.

Goode's term as mayor was marred by a violent and deadly confrontation between the city of Philadelphia and members of MOVE, a Radical "back-to-nature" cult.

Goode also served in the U.S. Army from 1960 to 1962. He left the service with a commendation medal for meritorious service and the rank of captain with the military police.

Patricia Roberts Harris (1924–1985)

Former Ambassador, Former Cabinet Member

As ambassador to Luxembourg, Patricia Harris was the first black woman to hold this diplomatic rank in United States history. Until President Ronald Reagan took office in 1980, Harris served as Secretary of the Department of Health and Human Services and also Secretary of Housing and Urban Development under President Jimmy Carter. She served in these positions from 1977 to 1981.

Born in Mattoon, Illinois, Harris attended elementary school in Chicago, and received her undergraduate degree from Howard University in 1945. While at Howard, Harris also served as vice-chairman of a student branch of the National Association for the Advancement of Colored People (NAACP) and was involved in early nonviolent demonstrations against racial discrimination. Harris worked for the YWCA in Chicago (1946–1949) and served as executive director of Delta Sigma Theta, a black sorority, from 1953 to 1959. After completing post-graduate work at the University of Chicago and at American University, she earned her doctorate in jurisprudence from George Washington University Law School in 1960.

An attorney and professor before she entered politics, Harris was appointed as co-chairman of the National Women's Committee on Civil Rights by President John F. Kennedy and was later named to the Commission on the Status of Puerto Rico. In 1965, Harris was chosen by President Lyndon Johnson to become US ambassador to Luxembourg, the first black woman ever to be named an American envoy.

In 1977, Harris was chosen by President Jimmy Carter to serve as Secretary of Housing and Urban Development. She was also selected as secretary of the Department of Health and Human Services in 1979. Harris remained in these positions until the inauguration of President Ronald Reagan in 1981.

Harris ran an unsuccessful campaign for mayor of Washington, DC in 1982. She became a law professor at George Washington University in 1983 and remained there until her death from cancer in 1985.

Maynard Jackson (1938 –)

Mayor

Jackson was born on March 23, 1938 in Dallas, Texas. At the age of fourteen he was admitted to Morehouse College as a Ford Foundation Early Admissions Scholar. He graduated with a B.A. in 1956 with a concentration in history and political science. After graduation he worked for the Ohio State Bureau of Unemployment Compensation and as a sales manager for P.F. Collier Inc.

In 1964 Jackson received a J.D. from the North Carolina Central University law school and then worked as a lawyer for the National Labor Relations Board. In 1968 and 1969 Jackson was the managing attorney and director of community relations for the Emory Neighborhood Law Office in Atlanta and from 1970 to 1973 he was a senior partner in the law firm of Jackson, Patterson & Parks.

Jackson had been active in Democratic politics and from 1970 to 1974 he was the vice-mayor of Atlanta. In 1974 he was elected mayor, a position he held until 1982. He worked as a bond lawyer before being reelected mayor in 1989.

As mayor, Jackson brought more African Americans into positions of responsibility in city government. His mayoralty however was tarnished by a string of grisly serial murders.

On the federal level Jackson has served as vice-chairman of the White House Committee on Balanced Growth & Economic Development and the White House Committee on the Windfall Profits Tax. Jackson is also the founding chairman of the Atlanta Economic Development Corporation and the chairman of the Atlanta Urban Residential Finance Authority.

Jackson belongs to the Georgia and New York bar associations, the National Conference of Democratic Mayors, the National League of Cities and the National Black Caucus of Local Elected Officials.

Barbara Jordan (1936–)
Former United States Representative

Jordan was born on February 21, 1936 in Houston, Texas. She attended Phyliss Wheately High School where she graduated a member of the Honor Society in 1952. In 1956 Jordan received a B.A. from Texas Southern University in history and political science. She went on to Boston University where she earned a J.D. in 1959.

After teaching at Tuskegee Institute for a year Jordan returned to Houston where she practiced law and was appointed administrative assistant to a Harris County judge. In

Barbara Jordan

1966 Jordan was elected to the Texas Senate. She was the first African American to serve as president pro tem of that body and to chair the important Labor and Management Relations Committee. In 1972 Jordan was elected to the U.S. House of Representatives where she stayed until 1978. While a representative Jordan served on the House Judiciary and Government Operations committees. During her terms in both the Texas Senate and U.S. House, Jordan was known as a champion of civil rights, minorities and the poor.

From 1979 to 1982 she was a professor at the Lyndon Baines Johnson School of Public Affairs at the Austin campus of the University of Texas. In 1982 she was made holder of the Lyndon Baines Johnson Centennial Chair of National Policy.

Jordan has co-authored two books, *Barbara Jordan: A Self-Portrait* (1979), and

The Great Society: A Twenty Year Critique (1986). She has also served on the Democratic Caucus Steering and Policy Committee and in 1976 and 1992 she was the keynote speaker at the Democratic National Convention.

Jordan belongs to the American Bar Association as well as the Texas, Massachusetts, and District of Columbia bars. She has been on the board of directors of the Mead Corporation and the Henry J. Kaiser Family Foundation. Jordan is the recipient of a long list of awards and honors including the Eleanor Roosevelt Humanities Award (1984), Texas Women's Hall of Fame (public service category 1984), Ladies Home Journal "100 Most Influential Women in America", and Time magazine's "Ten Women of the Year" list (1976). Jordan has also received 27 honorary doctorate degrees.

John Mercer Langston (1829–1897)

Former United States Representative

John Mercer Langston, United States Congressman from Virginia, was born in Virginia in 1829.

Upon the death of his father, Ralph Quarles, an estate owner, young Langston was emancipated and sent to Ohio, where he was given over to the care of a friend of his father. Langston spent his childhood there, attending private school in Cincinnati before graduating from Oberlin College in 1849. Four years later, after getting his degree from the theological department of Oberlin, he studied law and was admitted to the Ohio bar in 1854.

Langston began his practice in Brownhelm, Ohio. He was chosen in 1855 to serve as clerk of this township by the Liberty Party. During the Civil War, he was a recruiting agent for Negro servicemen, helping to organize such famed regiments as the 54th and 55th Massachusetts, and the 5th Ohio.

In 1867, Langston served as inspector-general of the Freedmen's Bureau and as dean and vice president of Howard University from 1868 to 1875. In 1877 he was named minister resident to Haiti and chargé d'affaires to Santo Domingo, remaining in diplomatic service until 1885.

Soon after his return to the United States and to his law practice, he was named president of the Virginia Normal and Collegiate Institute. In 1888, he was elected to Congress from Virginia, but was not seated for two years until vote-counting irregularities had been investigated. He was defeated in his bid for a second term. In 1894 Langston wrote an autobiography, *From the Virginia Plantation to the National Capital.* (Eleven years earlier, he had published a volume of his speeches, *Freedom and Citizenship.*)

Langston died in 1897.

George Thomas "Mickey" Leland (1944–1989)

Former United States Representative

Leland was born on November 27, 1944 in Lubbock, Texas. He graduated from Texas Southern University in 1970 with a B.S. in pharmacy and taught clinical pharmacy there for a short time.

Leland had been active in the civil rights movement during his student years and in an effort to affect social change he ran for and was elected to the Texas state legislature in 1973. In 1978 he was elected to the United States House of Representatives filling Barbara Jordan's vacated seat. While a representative Leland served on various committees including Interstate and Foreign Commerce, Post Office and Civil Service and the committee on the District of Columbia.

Mickey Leland

Before entering politics Lewis was associated with numerous social activist organizations including the Student Non-violent Coordinating Committee (1963–66), associate director of the Field Foundation (1966–67), project director of the Southern Regional Council (1967–70) and executive director of the Voter Education Project Inc. beginning in 1970.

In 1982 Lewis was elected Atlanta City Councilman-at-Large and in 1986 voters sent him to the U.S. House of Representatives as a Democrat. While in the House Lewis has served on the Public Works, Interior and Insular Affairs committees. He has also been a member of the Select Committee on Aging.

Lewis is a recipient of the Martin Luther King Jr. Non-Violent Peace Prize and has been named to Ebony's "One of the Nation's Most Influential Blacks" list (1991–92) and

In spite of serving on these committees Leland was devoted to easing the hunger of starving persons in the United States and in other countries, especially African countries. To this end he chaired the House Select Committee on World Hunger and visited starving peoples throughout Africa. In 1989 while traveling to a United Nations refugee camp in Ethiopia the plane Leland was flying on crashed near Gambela, Ethiopia killing all on board.

John Robert Lewis (1940–)
United States Representative

Lewis was born in Troy, Alabama on February 21, 1940. He received a B.S. in 1961 from the American Baptist Theological Seminary and in 1967 another B.A. from Fisk University.

John Lewis

Time magazine's "One of America's Rising Leaders" list (1974). He belongs to the Martin Luther King Jr. Center for Social Change, the National Democratic Institute for International Affairs, Friends of Vista, and the African-American Institute.

Kweisi Mfume (1948–)
United States Representative

Mfume was born Fizzell Gray in Baltimore on October 24, 1948. He received a B.S. from Morgan State University in 1976 and an M.A. from Johns Hopkins University in 1984.

In 1978 Mfume was elected to the Baltimore City Council where he became especially interested in health issues. In 1987 he was elected to the U.S. House of Representatives as a democrat. He had previously been a member of the Maryland Democratic State Central Committee and a delegate to the Democratic National Convention in 1980, 1984 and 1988.

As a House member Mfume has served on the Banking, Finance & Urban Affairs Committee, the Small Business Committee, and the Education & Labor Committee. He is vice-chairman of the Congressional Black Caucus and a member of the Narcotics Abuse & Control sub-committee.

Mfume is also a member of the Caucus for Women's Issues, the Congressional Arts Caucus and the Federal Government Service Task Force. He is a trustee of the Baltimore Museum of Art and the Morgan State University Board of Regents where he previously taught political science and communications.

President Bill Clinton meets with Kweisi Mfume and Senator Carol Moseley Braun.

Arthur Mitchell, 1934.

Arthur W. Mitchell (1883–1968)
Former United States Representative

Born to slave parents in 1883 in Chambers County, Alabama, Mitchell was educated at Tuskegee Institute and at Columbia and Harvard universities. By 1929, he had founded Armstrong Agricultural School in West Butler, Alabama, and become a wealthy landowner and a lawyer with a thriving practice in Washington, DC. When he left the nation's capital that year, it was with the avowed purpose of entering politics and becoming a representative from Illinois.

Mitchell won Democratic approval only after Harry Baker (who had defeated him in the primary) died suddenly, leaving the nomination vacant. Aided by the overwhelming national sentiment for the Democratic party during this period, he unseated Oscar De Priest by the slender margin of 3,000 votes.

Mitchell's most significant victory on behalf of civil rights came, not in the legislative chamber, but in the courts. In 1937, Mitchell brought suit against the Chicago and Rock Island Railroad after having been forced to leave his first class accommodations en route to Hot Springs, Arkansas, and sit in a "Jim Crow" car. He argued his own case before the Supreme Court in 1941, and won a decision which declared "Jim Crow" practices illegal.

Mitchell used his influence in Congress to improve the lot of African Americans. He proposed that states that discriminated against black Americans should receive fewer Congressional seats and advocated strong sanctions against states that practiced lynching. Also, he worked for the elimination of poll taxes to make it easier for black persons to vote. Following the end of World War II, Mitchell held that because blacks fought bravely for the United States, they should be able to vote for their government representatives.

In 1942, Mitchell retired from Congress and continued to pursue his civil rights agenda as a private citizen. He also lectured occasionally and pursued farming on his estate near Petersburg, Virginia, where he died in 1968 at the age of 85.

Eleanor Holmes Norton (1938–)
Delegate to the United States House of Representatives

Norton was born Eleanor Holmes on April 8, 1938 in Washington, DC. She attended Antioch College in Ohio but transferred to Yale University and received an M.A. in American Studies in 1963 and a J.D. from Yale's law school in 1964.

After graduating from law school Norton clerked for a federal judge in Philadelphia before joining the American Civil Liberties

Union in 1965 as a litigator specializing in free speech issues. She stayed with the ACLU until 1970 reaching the position of assistant legal director and successfully arguing a first amendment case before the United States Supreme Court. In 1970 she became chairwoman of the New York City Commission on Human Rights, a post she held until 1977 when she headed the Equal Employment Opportunity Commission. In 1981 she was a senior fellow at the Urban Institute and in 1982 she accepted the position of Professor of Law at Georgetown University. Norton had previously taught black history at Pratt Institute in Brooklyn, New York and law at New York City University Law School.

In 1990 Norton was elected congressional delegate to the United States House of Representatives for the District of Columbia, a non-voting position.

Norton has been named to the Ladies Home Journal "One Hundred Most Important Women" list (1988) and the "One Hundred Most Powerful Women in Washington" list by Washington Magazine (1989). Norton is also a recipient of the Distinguished Public Service Award presented by the Center for National Policy (1985).

Hazel O'Leary (1937–)
Cabinet Member

O'Leary was born Hazel Reid on May 17, 1937 in Newport News, Virginia. She received a B.A. from Fisk College in 1959 and a J.D. from Rutgers University School of Law in 1966.

O'Leary was a utilities regulator under Presidents Ford and Carter and an executive vice-president of the Northern States Power Co. where she functioned as a Washington lobbyist. O'Leary has been a proponent of energy conservation and alternate energy sources. She is a certified Financial Planner and a member of the New Jersey and Washington bars and has been vice-president and general counsel of O'Leary Associates in Washington, DC.

In January of 1993 O'Leary was confirmed as President Bill Clinton's Secretary of Energy.

Clarence McClane Pendleton, Jr. (1930–1988)
Former Civil Rights Commissioner

Pendleton was born in Louisville, Kentucky on November 10, 1930. Raised in Washington, DC he attended Dunbar High School and received a B.S. from Howard University in 1954. Pendleton served three years in the U.S. Army where he was assigned to a medical unit. After his discharge

Clarence M. Pendleton, Jr.

in 1957 Pendleton returned to Howard University where he received a masters degree in 1961 and coached swimming, football, rowing and baseball.

In 1968 Pendleton became the recreation coordinator of the Baltimore Model Cities Program and in 1970 the director of the Urban Affairs Department of the National Recreation and Parks Association. Pendleton soon began attracting national attention and in 1972 he headed San Diego's Model Cities Program and in 1975 he became the director of the San Diego Urban League.

By 1980 however there had been a change in Pendleton's political philosophy. He began to feel that African Americans' reliance on government programs were trapping them in a cycle of dependence and welfare handouts. Pendleton believed that it was in the best interest of African Americans to build strong ties with a strong, expanding private sector and eschew the more traditional ties with liberal bureaucrats and liberal philosophies.

To this end he supported the election of Ronald Reagan to the presidency and in 1981 Pendleton was appointed chairman of the Civil Rights Commission by President Reagan. Pendleton was the first African American to hold this post.

Pendleton's chairmanship was controversial mostly because of his opposition to affirmative action and forced bussing as a means of de-segregating schools. Pendleton retained a more liberal philosophy on other matters however by supporting the Equal Rights Amendment and the Voting Rights Act.

Pendleton died unexpectedly of an apparent heart attack on June 5, 1988 in San Diego.

Pinckney Stewart Pinchback (1837–1921)

Former Lieutenant Governor

Pinchback was born in Macon, Georgia on May 10, 1837. Although his mother had been a slave, by the time Pinchback was born she had been emancipated by Pinchback's father. Moving to Ohio with his mother Pinchback attended high school in Cincinnati in 1847 but in 1848 he began working on riverboats, first as a cabin boy and then as a steward.

At the outbreak of the Civil War Pinchback went to Louisiana and in 1862 he enlisted in the Union Army. He soon began recruiting soldiers for an African-American troop variously known as the Louisiana Native Guards and the Corps d'Afrique. Racial problems soon arose with the military hierarchy and Pinchback resigned his commission in protest.

After the war Pinchback became active in Louisiana politics. He organized a Republican Club in 1867 and in 1868 was a delegate to a state constitutional convention. In that year he was also elected to the state senate and in 1871 he became president pro-tem of that body. He soon became lieutenant governor of Louisiana through the line of succession. For five weeks in late 1872 and early 1873 Pinchback was governor of Louisiana while the elected official underwent impeachment proceedings. In 1872 and 1873 Pinchback was elected to the U.S. Senate and the U.S. House of Representatives. He was refused seating both times when the elections were contested and ruled in favor of his Democratic opponent. He did however receive what would have been his salary as an elected official.

In 1877 Pinchback switched his allegiance to the Democratic Party and in 1882 was appointed surveyor of customs for New Orleans. In 1887 he began attending law school at Straight University in New Orleans and was later admitted to the bar. In 1890 Pinchback moved to Washington, DC where he died December 21, 1921.

Adam Clayton Powell, Jr. (1908–1972)
Former United States Representative

Born in 1908 to Mattie Fletcher and Adam Clayton Powell Sr., Adam Jr. was raised in New York City, attended high school there, and then went to Colgate University where he earned a bachelors degree in 1930. In 1931, Powell graduated from Columbia University with a masters degree in religious education.

The young Powell launched his career as a crusader for reform during the Depression. He forced several large corporations to drop their unofficial bans on employing blacks and directed a kitchen and relief operation which fed, clothed, and provided fuel for thousands of Harlem's needy and destitute. He was instrumental in persuading officials of Harlem Hospital to integrate their medical and nursing staffs, helped many blacks find employment along Harlem's "main stem," 125th Street, and campaigned against the city's bus lines, which were discriminating against Negro drivers and mechanics.

When Powell Sr. retired from Abyssinian Baptist Church in 1936, his son, who had already served as manager and assistant pastor there, was named his successor.

In 1939, Powell served as chairman of the Coordinating Committee on Employment, which organized a picket line before the executive offices of the World's Fair in the Empire State Building and eventually suc-

Adam Clayton Powell

Adam Clayton Powell giving a speech to civil rights demonstrators in 1963.

ceeded in getting employment at the fair for hundreds of blacks.

Powell won a seat on the New York City Council in 1941 with the third highest number of votes ever cast for a candidate in municipal elections. In 1942, he turned to journalism for a second time (he had already been on the staff of the New York *Evening Post* in 1934), and published and edited the weekly *The People's Voice*, which he called "the largest Negro tabloid in the world." He became a member of the New York State Office of Price Administration in 1942 and served until 1944.

In 1944, Powell was elected to Congress and represented a constituency of 300,000, 89% of whom were black. Identified at once as "Mr. Civil Rights," he encountered a host of discriminatory procedures upon his arrival in the nation's capital. He could not rent a room or attend a movie in downtown Washington. Within Congress itself, he was not allowed to use such communal facilities as dining rooms, steam baths, showers, and barber shops. Powell met these rebuffs head on by making use of all such facilities and insisting that his entire staff follow his lead.

As a freshman legislator, Powell engaged in fiery debates with segregationists, fought for the abolition of discriminatory practices at United States military installations, and sought—through the controversial Powell amendment—to deny federal funds to any project where discrimination existed. This amendment eventually became part of the Flanagan School Lunch Bill, making Powell the first black Congressman since Reconstruction to have legislation passed by both houses.

Powell also sponsored legislation advocating federal aid to education, a minimum-wage scale, and greater benefits for the chronically unemployed. He also drew attention to certain discriminatory practices on Capitol Hill and worked toward their elimination. It was Powell who first demanded that a Negro journalist be allowed to sit in the Senate and House press galleries, introduced the first Jim Crow transportation legislation, and the first bill to prohibit segregation in the Armed Forces. At one point in his career, the *Congressional Record* reported that the House Committee on Education and Labor had processed more important legislation than any other major committee. In 1960, Powell, as senior member of this committee, became its chairman. He had a hand in the development and passage of such significant legislation as the Minimum Wage Bill of 1961, the Manpower Development and Training Act, the Anti-Poverty Bill, the Juvenile Delinquency Act, the Vocational Educational Act, and the National Defense Education Act. In all, the Powell committee helped pass forty-eight laws involving a total outlay of fourteen billion dollars.

The flamboyant congressman, however, was accused of putting an excessive number of friends on the congressional payroll, of a high rate of absenteeism from congressional votes, and of excessive zeal for the "playboy's" life.

In 1967, the controversies and irregularities surrounding him led to censure in the House and a vote to exclude him from his seat in the 90th Congress. The House based its decision on the allegation that he had misused public funds and was in contempt of the New York courts due to a lengthy and involved defamation case which had resulted in a trial for civil and criminal contempt. Despite his exclusion, Powell was readmitted to the 91st Congress in 1968. In mid-1969, the Supreme Court ruled that the House had violated the Constitution by excluding him from membership, but left open the questions of his loss of twenty-two years seniority and the chairmanship of the Education and Labor Committee. Also unresolved were the $25,000 fine levied against him and the matter of back pay.

However, rather than return to Congress, Powell spent most of his time on the West Indian island of Bimini, where process servers could not reach him. But photographers did and the ensuing photos of Powell vacationing on his boat while crucial votes were taken in Congress began to affect Powell in his home district. In 1970, he lost the Democratic Congressional primary to Charles Rangel by 150 votes. Powell retired from public office and worked as a minister at the Abyssinian Baptist Church. On April 4, 1972, Powell died in Miami.

Joseph H. Rainey (1832–1887)
Former United States Representative

Joseph H. Rainey, the first black member of the House of Representatives, was born in 1832 in Georgetown, South Carolina. Rainey's father purchased his family's freedom and moved them to Charleston in 1846. During the Civil War, Rainey was drafted to work on Confederate fortifications in Charleston harbor and serve passengers on a Confederate ship. However, Rainey escaped with his wife to the West Indies and remained there until the end of the Civil War in 1865.

Rainey and his wife returned to South Carolina in 1866. In 1868, Rainey was elected as a delegate to the state constitutional convention and was elected to the State Senate in 1870. A year later, he was elected to the House of Representatives.

As a member of Congress, Rainey presented some 10 petitions for a civil rights bill which would have guaranteed blacks full constitutional rights and equal access to public accommodations. On one occasion, Rainey dramatized the latter issue by refusing to leave the dining room of a hotel in Suffolk, Virginia. He was forcibly ejected from the premises. Rainey was a staunch supporter of legislation that prevented racial discrimination in schools, on public transportation, and in the composition of juries. He supported legislation that protected the civil rights of the Chinese minority in California, and advocated the use of federal troops to protect black voters from intimidation by the Ku Klux Klan. Rainey was reelected in 1872 and, during a debate on Indian rights in 1874, became the first black representative to preside over a session of Congress. Rainey gained reelection to Congress in 1874 and 1876.

Rainey retired from Congress in 1879. He was appointed as a special agent for the United States Treasury Department in Washington, DC. He served until 1881, after which he worked for a banking and brokerage firm. Unfortunately, the firm failed and Rainey took a job at a wood and coal factory. In 1886 he returned to Georgetown, where he died in 1887.

Charles Rangel (1930–)
United States Representative

Harlem-born Charles Rangel vaulted into the national spotlight in 1970 when he defeated Adam Clayton Powell for the Democratic nomination in New York's 18th Congressional District. Rangel's upset victory stirred hopes among black leaders that a grassroots political movement generated from within Harlem, rather than stemming from beyond the community, might result in the grooming of an energetic, capable, and untainted successor to the volatile and unpredictable Powell.

Born June 11, 1930, Rangel attended Harlem elementary and secondary schools before volunteering to serve in the United States Army during the Korean war. While stationed in Korea with the 2nd Infantry, he saw heavy combat and received the Purple Heart and the Bronze Star Medal for Valor, as well as United States and Korean Presidential citations. Discharged honorably as a Staff Sergeant, Rangel returned to finish high school and to study at New York University's School of Commerce, from which he graduated in 1957. The recipient of a scholarship, Rangel then attended St. John's Law School, graduating in 1960.

After being admitted to the bar, Rangel earned a key appointment as Assistant United States Attorney in the Southern District of New York in 1961. For the next five years, he acquired legal experience as legal counsel to the New York City Housing and Redevelopment Board, as legal assistant to Judge James L. Watson, as associate counsel to the speaker of the N.Y. State Assembly, and as general counsel to the National Advisory Commission on Selective Service.

In 1966, Rangel was chosen to represent the 72nd District, Central Harlem, in the State Assembly. Since then, he has served as a member of, and secretary to, the New York State Commission on Revision of the Penal Law and Criminal Code.

In 1972, Rangel easily defeated Livingston Wingate in the Democratic primary and went on to an overwhelming victory in November. In 1974, he was elected chairman of the Congressional Black Caucus.

In his first term, he was appointed to the Select Committee on Crime and was influential in passing the 1971 amendment to the drug laws that authorized the President to cut off all military and economic aid to any country that refused to cooperate with the United States in stopping the international traffic in drugs. In 1976, he was appointed to the Select Committee on Narcotics Abuse and Control. Rangel is regarded as one of the leading Congressional experts on the subject.

Representative Rangel served as chairman of the Congressional Black Caucus in 1974–1975 and was a member of the Judiciary Committee when it voted to impeach President Nixon. In 1975, he moved to the Ways and Means Committee, becoming the first black to serve on this committee. Two years later, his colleagues in the New York Congressional delegation voted him the majority whip for New York State.

Rangel is a ranking member of the Ways and Means Committee and chairs the Select Revenue Measures Subcommittee. He is also chairman of the Select committee on Narcotics Abuse and Control and deputy whip for the House Democratic Leadership.

Blacks comprise a majority of the population in Rangel's district while Hispanic Americans are also well represented. His constituency also includes a long stretch of Central Park West and other white middle-class streets of New York's West Side.

Hiram Rhodes Revels (1827–1901)
Former United States Senator

Hiram Rhodes Revels, a native of North Carolina, was the first black to serve in the United States Senate. Revels was elected from his adopted state of Mississippi, and served for approximately one year, from February 1870 to March 1871.

Born in 1827, Revels was educated in Indiana and attended Knox College in Illinois. Ordained a minister in the African Methodist Church, he worked among black settlers in Kansas, Maryland, Illinois, Indiana, Tennessee, Kentucky, and Missouri before settling in Baltimore in 1860. There he served as a church pastor and school principal.

During the Civil War, Revels helped organize a pair of Negro regiments in Maryland, and in 1863 he went to St. Louis to establish a freedmen school and to carry on his work as a recruiter. For a year he served as chaplain of a Mississippi regiment before becoming provost marshal of Vicksburg.

Hiram Rhodes Revels

Revels settled in Natchez, Mississippi in 1866 and was appointed alderman by the Union military governor of the state. In 1870, Revels was elected to the United States Senate to replace Jefferson Davis, the former president of the Confederacy. Revels' appointment caused a storm of protest from white Southerners. However, Revels was allowed to take his seat in the Senate.

As a United States Senator, Revels quickly won the respect of many of his constituents for his alert grasp of important state issues and for his courageous support of legislation which would have restored voting and office-holding privileges to disenfranchised Southerners. He believed that the best way for blacks to gain their rightful place in American society was not through violent means, but by obtaining an education and leading an exemplary life of courage and moral fortitude. He spoke out against the segregation of Washington, DC's public school system and defended the rights of black men who were denied work at the Washington Navy Yard because of their race.

Revels left the Senate in 1871 after serving one full term. He was named president of Alcorn University near Lorman, Mississippi. He left Alcorn in 1873 to serve as Mississippi's secretary of state on an interim basis. He returned to Alcorn in 1876. That year, he became editor of the *South-Western Christian Advocate*, a religious journal. He retired from Alcorn University in 1882.

Revels lived in Holly Springs, Mississippi during his later years and taught theology at Shaw University. He died on January 16, 1901.

Edith Sampson (1951)

Edith Sampson (1901–1979)
Former Alternate Delegate to the United Nations

The first black woman to be named an official representative to the United Nations, Edith Sampson served in this body from 1950 until 1953, first as an appointee of President Harry S. Truman and later during a portion of the Eisenhower administration.

A native of Pittsburgh, Sampson acquired a Bachelor of Laws degree from the John Marshall Law School in Chicago in 1925, and two years later became the first woman to receive a Master of Laws from Loyola University.

A member of the Illinois bar since 1927, one of her cases took her all the way to the Supreme Court in 1934. During the 1930s, she maintained her own private practice, specializing particularly in domestic relations and in criminal law.

After her U.N. appointment, Sampson traveled around the world, often as a lecturer under State Department auspices. She was elected Associate Judge of the Municipal Court of Chicago in 1962, becoming the first black woman ever to sit as a circuit court judge. Sampson presided over divorce courts, traffic courts, and landlord-tenant relations courts. She gained acclaim for her superior mediating powers, her heartfelt sincerity, and her humanistic approach to rendering judgments. In 1978, she retired from Cook County Circuit Court.

Sampson died on October 7, 1979 at Northwestern Hospital in Chicago, Illinois.

Kurt L. Schmoke (1949–)
Mayor

Kurt L. Schmoke was inaugurated as the first black mayor of Baltimore on December 8, 1987. Schmoke grew up and attended public school in Baltimore. He graduated with honors from Baltimore City College high school, and in 1967 won the award as the top scholar-athlete in the City. Schmoke went on to receive his Bachelor of Arts degree from Yale University in 1971, studied at Oxford University as a Rhodes Scholar, and in 1978 earned his law degree from Harvard University.

After graduating from Harvard, Schmoke began his law practice with the prestigious Baltimore firm of Piper & Marbury, and shortly thereafter was appointed by President Carter as a member of the White House Domestic Policy staff.

Schmoke returned to Baltimore as an Assistant United States Attorney where he prosecuted narcotics and white collar crime cases, among others. He then returned to private practice and immersed himself in assorted civic activities.

In November 1982, Schmoke was elected State's Attorney for Baltimore, which is the chief prosecuting office of the city. As State's Attorney, he created a full time Narcotics Unit to prosecute all drug cases, and underscored the criminal nature of domestic violence and child abuse by setting up separate units to handle those cases. Also, Schmoke hired a community liaison officer to make sure that his office was being responsive to neighborhood questions and concerns.

Kurt L. Schmoke

In his inaugural address, Schmoke set the tone and future direction for his administration when he said that he wanted Baltimore to reduce its large high school dropout and teenage pregnancy rates and combat illiteracy. He has overseen the passage of the largest ever increase in the city's education budget, and in partnership with Baltimore businesses and community based organizations, Schmoke developed the Commonwealth Agreement and the College Bound Foundation. These programs will guarantee opportunities for jobs or for college to qualifying high school graduates. Also since taking office, Schmoke has begun major initiatives in housing, economic development, public safety, and proposed educational programs to prepare Baltimore's citizens for high-tech jobs.

In recognition of his commitment to excellence in education and his service to the community, Schmoke has received honorary degrees from several colleges and universities.

Throughout his career, Schmoke has been active in the civic and cultural life of the Baltimore community by serving as a member of numerous boards of trustees.

Robert Smalls (1839–1915)
Former United States Representative

Robert Smalls of South Carolina served a longer period in Congress than any other black Reconstruction congressman. Born a slave in Beaufort, South Carolina in 1839, Smalls received a limited education before moving to Charleston with the family of his owner. While in Charleston, Smalls worked at a number of odd jobs and eventually became adept at piloting boats along the Georgia and South Carolina coasts.

At the outbreak of the Civil War, Smalls was forced to become a crew member on the Confederate ship *Planter*, a transport steamer. On the morning of May 13, 1862, Smalls smuggled his wife and three children on board, assumed command of the vessel, and sailed it into the hands of the Union squadron blockading Charleston harbor. Single-handedly, he was thus responsible for the freedom of his own family and for that of the 12 black crewmen. His daring exploit led President Lincoln to name him a pilot in the Union Navy. He was also awarded a large sum of money for what constituted the delivery of war booty. In December 1863, during the siege of Charleston, Smalls again took command of the *Planter* and sailed it to safety—a feat for which he was promoted to captain, the only black to hold such a rank during the Civil War.

After the war, Smalls was elected to the South Carolina House of Representatives, serving there from 1868 to 1870. In 1870, Smalls became a member of South Carolina's State Senate and served there until 1874. Smalls campaigned for a United States Congressional seat in 1874 against an independent candidate and won the election. He took his seat in Congress on March 4, 1875.

During his tenure in Congress, Smalls consistently supported a wide variety of progressive legislation, including a bill to provide equal accomodations for blacks in interstate travel and an amendment designed to safeguard the rights of children born of interracial marriages. He also sought to protect the rights of black Americans serving in the armed forces.

Smalls won reelection in 1876, an election that was bitterly contested by Smalls' Democratic challenger, George Tillman. Tillman tried unsuccessfully to have Smalls' election to Congress overturned. However, Tillman's supporters were undeterred. In 1877, Smalls was accused of taking a $5,000 bribe while serving as a senator. Although Smalls was exonerated by Governor William D. Simpson, his popularity plummeted. Smalls lost his reelection bid in 1878.

Robert Smalls

Although Smalls was defeated, he did not fade from the political scene. In 1880, Smalls ran again for Congress. He lost the election, but maintained that the results were invalid due to vote-counting irregularities. Smalls' charges were substantiated and he was allowed to take his seat in Congress in July 1882. Two months later, another Congressional election was held and Smalls lost his seat to fellow Republican Edward W.M. Mackey. However, Mackey died in January 1884 and Smalls was allowed to serve the remainder of Mackey's term. In 1886, Smalls' career in Congress was ended when he lost an election to Democratic challenger William Elliott.

Although Smalls was no longer a Congressman, he remained involved in political activities. From 1889 to 1913, Smalls served as collector of the port of Beaufort. He died on February 22, 1915.

Louis Stokes (1925–)
United States Representative

Stokes was born in Cleveland, Ohio on February 23, 1925. He was in the U.S. Army from 1943 until 1946. After leaving the service he attended Case Western Reserve University from 1946 to 1948 and in 1953 was awarded a J.D. from Cleveland Marshall Law School. After 14 years in private practice with the law firm of Stokes, Character, Terry & Perry he was elected as a democrat to the U.S. House of Representatives in 1969.

As Ohio's first African-American representative Stokes has served on a number of committees including Education & Labor, House Internal Security, Appropriations and he has chaired the House Ethics Committee. As part of the House Assassination Committee Stokes has investigated the deaths of Martin Luther King Jr. and President John F. Kennedy.

In 1972 and 1973 Stokes chaired the Congressional Black Caucus and in 1972, 1976 and 1980 he was a delegate to the Democratic National Convention.

Stokes belongs to the Urban League, the American Civil Liberties Union, the American Legion and the African American Institute. He is on the board of trustees of the Martin Luther King Jr. Center for Social Change and in 1965 and 1966 he was vice-president of the Cleveland chapter of the NAACP. He is a recipient of the Distinguished Service Award, the William C. Dawson Award and a Certificate of Appreciation from the United States Commission on Civil Rights of which he was vice-chairman of the Cleveland subcommittee in 1966.

Louis W. Sullivan (1933–)
Former Cabinet Member

On March 1, 1989 Dr. Louis W. Sullivan was confirmed as Secretary of Health and Human Services by the Senate by a vote of 98 to 1, becoming the first African American appointed to a cabinet position in the Bush administration.

Instrumental in the development of the Morehouse School of Medicine as a separate entity from Morehouse College, Dr. Sullivan served as professor of biology and medicine and as dean, director and founder of the

Louis Sullivan

medical education program at Morehouse College. In 1981, he was nominated as Morehouse School of Medicine's first dean and president.

Dr. Sullivan graduated from Morehouse College magna cum laude with a bachelor's of science degree in 1954, and went on to medical school at Boston University, graduating cum laude in 1958. He completed his internship at New York Hospital Cornell Medical Center, and his medical and general pathology residencies at Cornell Medical Center and Massachusetts General Hospital.

He then fulfilled two fellowships and served in a variety of positions with Harvard Medical School, Boston City Hospital, New Jersey College of Medicine, Boston University Medical Center, and the Boston Sickle Cell Center and others.

Described as a "distinguished and dedicated individual who makes things happen," Dr. Sullivan has led an academic and professional life of excellence. He has been involved in numerous educational, medical, scientific, professional, and civic organizations, advisory, consulting, research and academic positions, and has received many professional and public service awards. Dr. Sullivan's research and activities focus on hematology and he has authored and co-authored more than 60 publications on this and other subjects. He is also the founding president of the Association of Minority Health Professions.

On January 20, 1989, Sullivan was nominated by President George Bush for the position of Secretary of Health and Human Services. He was sworn in on March 10, 1989. As Secretary of Health and Human Services,

Harold Washington following his victory in Chicago's mayoral race in 1983.

Sullivan had many responsibilities. He was responsible for ensuring the safety of food, drugs, and medical research and promoting health education. His term expired in January 1993.

Harold Washington (1922–1987)
Former Mayor

Washington was born in Chicago on April 15, 1922. After serving with the Army Air Corp. in the Pacific theatre during World War II he received a B.A. from Roosevelt University in 1949 where he studied political science and economics. Washington then received a J.D. from Northwestern University Law School in 1952.

After graduation Washington worked as an assistant city prosecutor in Chicago from 1954 to 1958 and while establishing a private law practice he was an arbitrator with the Illinois Industrial Commission from 1960 to 1964.

Running on the democratic ticket Washington was elected to the Illinois State House of Representatives (1965–1976) and the Illinois State Senate (1977–1980). While a legislator he helped establish Illinois' Fair Employment Practices Commission and the naming of Martin Luther King Jr.'s birthday as a state holiday. Washington was also concerned with consumer protection legislation and the Illinois Legislative Black Caucus. In 1980 Washington was elected to the U.S. House of Representatives and in 1983 after a tightly contested primary and subsequent election Washington became Chicago's first African-American mayor.

Although Washington's mayoralty was marked by political infighting he did manage to institute some reforms including increased city hiring of minorities, deficit reduction, the appointment of an African-American police commissioner and reduction of patronage influence. Washington died while in office on November 25, 1987.

Maxine Waters (1938–)
United States Representative

Waters was born in St. Louis on August 15, 1938. After graduating from high school she moved to Los Angeles where she worked at a garment factory and for a telephone company. She eventually attended college and received a B.A. in sociology from California State University. She became interested in politics after teaching in a Head Start program and serving as a delegate to the Democratic National Convention in 1972 (she would also attend in the same capacity in 1976, 1980, 1984 and 1988).

In 1976 Waters was elected to the California State Assembly where she served on nu-

Maxine Waters

merous committees including the Ways & Means Subcommittee on State Administration, Joint Committee of Public Pension Fund Investments, Joint Legislative Budget Committee, Judiciary Committee, Joint Committee on Legislative Ethics, Select Committee on Assistance to Victims of Sexual Assault, California Committee on the Status of Women, Natural Resources Committee and the Elections, Reapportionment & Constitutional Amendment Committee.

In 1990 Waters was elected to the U.S. House of Representatives. She has served there on the Banking, Finance & Urban Affairs Committee and the Veterans Affairs and is a vociferous spokesperson for the poor and minorities. She has fought for legislation promoting aid to poor and minority neighborhoods in American cities and combating apartheid in South Africa.

Waters is on the board of directors of Essence magazine and is involved with the National Woman's Political Caucus, the National Steering Committee on Education of Black Youth and the national Steering Committee of the Center for Study of Youth Policy.

Robert Weaver (1907–)
Former Cabinet Member

Robert Weaver became the first black appointed to a presidential cabinet when Lyndon B. Johnson named him to head the newly created Department of Housing and Urban Development (HUD) on January 13, 1966. Previously, Weaver had served as head of the Housing and Home Finance Agency (HHFA) from 1961 to 1966.

Robert Weaver was born on December 29, 1907 in Washington, DC where he attended Dunbar High School and worked during his teens as an electrician. Encountering discrimination when he attempted to join a union, he decided instead to concentrate on economics, and eventually received his Ph.D. in that field from Harvard University. Weaver's grandfather, Dr. Robert Tanner Freeman, was the first black American to earn a doctorate in dentistry at Harvard.

During the 1940s and 1950s, Weaver concentrated his energies on the field of education. He had already been a professor of economics at the Agricultural and Technical College of North Carolina in Greensboro from 1931 to 1932. In 1947, he became a lecturer at Northwestern University and then became a visiting professor at Teachers College, Columbia University and at the New York University School of Education. During this period, he was also a professor of economics at the New School for Social Research.

From 1949 to 1955 he was director of the Opportunity Fellowships Program of the John Hay Whitney Foundation. Weaver also served as a member of the National Selection Committee for Fulbright Fellowships (1952–1954), chairman of the Fellowship Committee of the Julius Rosenwald Fund, and a consultant to the Ford Foundation (1959–1960).

In 1955, Weaver was named Deputy State Rent Commissioner by New York's Governor Averell Harriman. By the end of the year, he had become State Rent Commissioner and the first black to hold state cabinet rank in New York. From 1960 to 1961, he served as vice chairman of the New York City Housing and Redevelopment Board, a three-man body which supervised New York's urban renewal and middle-income housing programs.

Weaver headed the Department of Housing and Urban Development until 1968. From 1969 to 1970, he served as president of Baruch College. Weaver accepted a teaching position at the Department of Urban Affairs

Robert Weaver

at Hunter College in New York in 1971. He retired from Hunter College in 1978.

Lawrence Douglas Wilder (1931–)
Governor

Wilder was born on January 17, 1931 in Richmond, Virginia. He graduated from Virginia Union University in 1951 with a B.S. in chemistry. After graduation he was drafted into the U.S. Army and assigned to a combat infantry unit in Korea. During the Korean War he was awarded a Bronze Star for bravery and valor in combat. After being discharged from the army in 1953 Wilder worked as a chemist in the Virginia State Medical Examiner's Office. In 1959 Wilder graduated with a J.D. from Howard University Law School.

Wilder practiced law in Richmond until he became the first African American elected to the Virginia State Senate since Reconstruction. While there Wilder chaired the important Privileges and Elections committee and worked on legislation supporting fair-housing, union rights for public employees, minority hiring and voted against capital punishment (a position he has since rescinded). In 1985 Wilder was elected lieutenant-governor and in 1989 he became Virginia's first African-American governor winning the election by a razor thin one third of one per cent of the vote.

In 1979 Wilder won the Distinguished Alumni Award presented by Virginia Union University. In succeeding years he was a recipient of the President's Citation (Norfolk State University 1982), Alumnus of the Year (Howard Law School Alumni Association

L. Douglas Wilder announcing his candidacy for the Democratic presidential nomination in 1991.

(1983) and the Distinguished Postgraduate Achievement in Law & Politics Award (Howard University 1985).

Wilder belongs to the Richmond Urban League, Richmond Bar Association, American Judicature Society, American Trial Lawyers Association, Virginia Trial Lawyers Association, National Association of Criminal Defense Lawyers, NAACP and he is vice-president of the Virginia Human Relations Council.

Andrew Young (1932–)
Former Ambassador to the United Nations, Former Mayor

Andrew Young came into national prominence nearly three decades ago and has become a figure of international prominence and stature. Soft-spoken yet eloquent, Young is widely admired for his incisive thinking and his willingness to express his opinion.

Young was born in New Orleans in 1932, and received a B.S. degree from Howard University and a Bachelor of Divinity degree from Hartford Theological Seminary in 1955. He was ordained a minister in the United Church of Christ and then served in churches in Alabama and Georgia before joining the National Council of Churches in 1957. The turning point of his life came in 1961 when he joined Reverend Martin Luther King and became a trusted aide and close confidante. He did much of the negotiating for the Southern Christian Leadership Conference and was respected for his coolness and rationality. He became execu-

Andrew Young announces former President Jimmy Carter at the Democratic National Convention in 1992.

tive vice president of SCLC in 1967 and remained with King until the latter's murder in 1968. During those years with SCLC, Young also developed several programs including antiwar protests, voter registration projects and other major civil rights drives.

In 1970 Young, a Democrat, lost a bid for the United States House of Representatives when Republican Fletcher Thompson beat him by 20,000 votes. In the aftermath of the election, Young was appointed chair of the Community Relations Committee (CRC). Though the CRC was an advisory group with no enforcement powers, Young took an activist role, pressing the city government on many issues, from sanitation and open housing to mass transit, consumer affairs, and Atlanta's drug problem. Young's leadership in the CRC led to a higher public profile and answered critics charges that he was inexperienced in government.

Young launched another bid for the United States Congress in 1972. The campaign was difficult for Young. Blacks comprised only 44% of the voters in Young's congressional district and his Republican opponent, Rodney Cook, was a more appealing candidate than Fletcher Thompson had been in 1970. However, Young captured 23% of the white vote and 54% of the total vote to win by a margin of 8,000 votes. Young was the first black representative to be elected from Georgia since Jefferson Long in 1870.

Thereafter, Young was reelected with ease every two years. He was one of the most vocal supporters of his fellow Georgian Jimmy Carter's campaign for the Presidency in 1976. Following President Carter's inauguration, Young left Congress in 1977 to become America's ambassador to the United Nations.

His tenure there was marked by controversy as well as solid achievement. The controversy resulted from his outspoken manner, which sometimes ruffled diplomatic feathers. His solid achievements were represented primarily in the tremendous improvement he fostered in relations between America and the Third World.

Young's career as a diplomat came to an end in 1979 when he met secretly with a representative of the Palestine Liberation Organization to discuss an upcoming vote in the United Nations. America had a policy that none of its representatives would meet with the PLO as long as it refused to recognize the right of Israel to exist as a state. When the news of Young's meeting leaked out, there was an uproar. Young had originally told the State Department that the meeting was by chance, but later he admitted that it had been planned.

Though the meeting had secured a vote in the United Nations that the United States wanted, the pressure mounted and Young tendered his resignation, which President Carter accepted. The incident badly strained black-Jewish relations because of the feeling within the black community that Jewish leaders were instrumental in Young's removal, a charge that they vehemently denied.

Young became a private citizen, but not for long. When Maynard Jackson was prevented by law from running for his third term of office as mayor of Atlanta in 1981, Young entered the race. Once again, it was not easy. He faced a black candidate and a strong white candidate and was forced into a runoff. Race entered the campaign when the outgoing mayor, himself a black, charged blacks who supported the white candidate, State Legislator Sidney Marcus, with "selling out" the civil rights movement.

Jackson's remarks were widely criticized, and it was feared that they would create a backlash against Young. However, Young ended up with 55% of the total vote. He won 10.6% of the white vote, compared to the 12%

he had won in the primary, and 88.4% of the black vote, up from 61% earlier.

Young took office at a time when Atlanta was going through several economic and social problems. Its population was shrinking, the tax base stagnating, almost a quarter of the city's residents were below the poverty line, and the city was still shaken by the recent murders of 28 black youths and the disappearance of another—even though a man had been convicted of several of the murders.

Some critics doubted Young's ability to deal with Atlanta's problems. He was seen as antibusiness and a weak administrator. However, by 1984, the city had become so successful at attracting new businesses that it was experiencing a major growth spurt. In addition, the crime rate dropped sharply, and racial harmony seemed an established fact. Young was reelected decisively in 1985.

Limited by law to two terms as mayor, Young ran unsuccessfully for governor of Georgia in 1990. He remains very active as president of Young Ideas, a consulting firm he founded. Young is also chair of the Atlanta Committee for the Olympic Games, an organization responsible for preparing Atlanta to host the 1996 Summmber Olympics.

Coleman A. Young (1918–)
Former Mayor

In 1989, Coleman Young won his fifth term as mayor of Detroit. The vote was remarkable because even with the heavy unemployment in Detroit, a shortage of cash, and a high crime rate, the voters returned Young to office.

Part of Young's support stemmed from a sense of revitalization which he breathed into Detroit and the confidence of the voters who believed that though things were rough, the mayor would persevere. A Democrat, and one of the first big-city mayors to support Jimmy Carter's presidential campaign in 1976, Young had a very close relationship with the Carter administration. This relationship proved helpful in securing funds for Detroit.

Young was born in Tuscaloosa, Alabama. His family moved to Detroit's east side in 1926 after the Ku Klux Klan ransacked a neighborhood in Huntsville where his father was learning to be a tailor. In Detroit, he attended Catholic Central and then Eastern High School, graduating from the latter with honors. He had to reject a scholarship to the University of Michigan when the Eastern High School Alumni Association, in contrast to policies followed with poor white students, declined to assist him with costs other than tuition.

Young entered an electrician's apprentice school at the Ford Motor Company. He fin-

Coleman A. Young (1981)

ished first in the program but was passed over for the only available electrician job in favor of a white candidate. He went to work on the assembly line, and soon engaged in underground union activities. One day, a man Young describes as a "company goon" tried to attack him. Young hit him on the head with a steel bar and was fired.

During World War II, he became a navigator in the Army Air Force and was commissioned a second lieutenant. Stationed at Freeman Field, Indiana, he demonstrated against the exclusion of blacks from segregated officers' clubs and was arrested along with 100 other black airmen, among them the late Thurgood Marshall, and Percy Sutton, former president of New York's Borough of Manhattan. Young spent three days in jail. Shortly thereafter, the clubs were opened to black officers.

After the war, Young returned to his union organizing activities and in 1947 was named director of organization for the Wayne County AFL-CIO. However, the union fired him in 1948 when he supported Henry Wallace, candidate of the Progressive Party, in the Presidential election. The union regarded Wallace as an agent of the Communist Party and supported Harry Truman.

Young managed a dry cleaning plant for a few years and, in 1951, founded and directed the National Negro Labor Council. According to Young, the Council was way ahead of its time and successfully prevailed on Sears Roebuck & Co. and the San Francisco Transit System to hire blacks. However, the Council also aroused the interest of the House Un-American Activities Committee, which was then holding hearings around the country at which alleged Communists were required to produce names of people allegedly associated with the Party. Young, who denies he was ever a Communist, refused to name anyone. He emerged from the battle with his self-respect intact, but his Labor Council was placed on the Attorney General's subversive list. In 1956, the Labor Council was disbanded. Charges that Young was a Communist were to be used against him, unsuccessfully, during his first mayoral campaign.

After working at a variety of jobs, Young won a seat on the Michigan Constitutional Convention in 1961. In 1962, he lost a race for state representative but became director of campaign organization for the Democratic gubernatorial candidate in Wayne County (Detroit). He sold life insurance until 1964 when, with union support, he was elected to the State Senate. In the Senate, he was a leader of the civil rights forces fighting for low-income housing for people dislocated by urban renewal and for bars to discrimination in the hiring practices of the Detroit Police Force.

Young declared his candidacy for mayor of Detroit in 1973 and mounted a vigorous campaign for the office. He won the office after a racially divisive campaign. Among his early successes in office were the integration of the Detroit Police Department and promotion of black officers into administrative positions.

12

Population

12

Population

The Size of the African-American Population ■ Regional Distribution ■ Contemporary Demographic Characteristics ■ Population Projections

by Claudette E. Bennett and Kenneth Estell

According to the United States Bureau of the Census, the African-American population of almost 31 million people now constitutes 12.3 percent of the nation's total resident population. Since the 1980 census, the African-American population has grown at a rate faster than has the white population or the total resident population of the United States—an increase of 14.2 percent, as compared to 7.2 percent for the white population and 9.8 percent for the total population. Although immigration rates have been slightly higher for blacks than for whites, due to increased immigration from the Caribbean basin, the growth rate of the African-American population primarily has been the result of increased age-specific fertility rates.

■ THE SIZE OF THE AFRICAN-AMERICAN POPULATION

1619 to 1790

The beginning of America's black population is usually dated to the year 1619, when a small number of colonists and indentured servants landed in Jamestown, Virginia. Historians are uncertain as to the exact number, but between fourteen and twenty black indentured servants were evidently part of this first settlement; within a short time the practice of enslaving newly arrived Africans developed and spread throughout the colonies. By 1630, there were some sixty slaves in the American colonies; by 1660, the number had increased to 2,920.

Within two decades, the colonies were beginning to flourish. The emerging agrarian society demanded a larger labor force, and this labor was supplied by additional slaves. By 1690, seventy years after the first importation of Africans, the total slave population in the American colonies had grown to 16,729. By 1740, the slave population reached 150,000, and 575,000 by 1780. Although a free black population did exist, it grew at a slower rate than the slave population; in 1780, there was only one free black for every nine slaves.

1790 to 1900

In the first official census of the United States, taken in 1790, some 757,208 blacks were counted. At that time, blacks constituted 19.3 percent of the nation's population, of which 9 percent, or some 59,527, were free blacks. (By 1790, Pennsylvania, Massachusetts, Connecticut, Rhode Island, New York, New Jersey, and the Northwest Territory had enacted legislation providing for the gradual emancipation of slaves.) By 1860, there were almost 4,000,000 blacks in the United States, over ninety percent of them in the South; the freed population, most of whom were in the North, numbered under half a million.

Population Growth Since 1900

During the late nineteenth and early twentieth centuries, the white population grew faster than the black population. The primary reasons were the increased European immigration into the United States and the decline and eventual cessation of the slave trade. In 1900, there were 8.8 million blacks in the United States, representing 11.6 percent of the total population. Between 1910 and 1930, the percentage that blacks make up of population declined, reaching a low point in 1930, when blacks constituted only 9.7 percent of the total United States population. Since 1930, however, the African-American population has grown at a rate faster than the national average. According to the 1990 census, the black population constituted 12.1 percent of the population, up from 11.7 percent in 1980. By 1990, the black population in the United States had grown to nearly 30 million.

The growth of the black population since the 1980 census is largely due to natural increase and net immigration. Natural in-

According to the 1990 census, the black population constituted 12.1 percent of the population.

By the year 2010, the median age for blacks in the United States is expected to rise to approximately 30 years.

crease has been the major source of growth. This increase in the number of births over deaths was due mainly to two factors: (1) a young age structure, placing a large percentage of African Americans in the childbearing ages and a smaller percentage in the ages of high mortality risk, and (2) a high age-specific fertility rate for black women under twenty-five years of age.

The African-American population has also grown through immigration—legal as well as illegal. While streams of Asian and Hispanic migrants to the United States have been more highly publicized, black immigration has also increased. The Caribbean basin is one source of black immigration, with immigrants primarily from Jamaica and Haiti entering the United States to look for work. The *Mariel* boatlift in 1980 also brought some blacks from Cuba. Political and economic conditions in Africa itself, in addition, have provided many with incentives to leave for or remain in other countries, and may be associated with the number of African students overstaying their student visas and working in the United States rather than returning home. Estimations of the size and effects of these sources of new population growth are speculative.

The African-American population is likely to continue to grow faster than the national average. The percentage of the total population made up of blacks is also likely to continue to increase—although not at the rate that some other racial and ethnic groups will, including the Asian and Hispanic populations.

One reason for this growth has been the higher than average fertility rates of African Americans. As a result of the higher fertility rates, the black population, with a median age of 28 years, is somewhat younger than the white population, and contains a slightly larger proportion of persons in the prime reproductive ages. A second reason is that blacks have, and for at least the next decade or two are likely to continue to have, higher age-adjusted fertility rates than whites (i.e., higher fertility even when differences in age composition are taken into account).

Reports from 1991 show that the black population is approaching 31,164,000, or approximately 12.4 percent of the nation's total population. This figure is higher than the total populations for many nations. The black population in the United States, for example, is slightly larger than the entire population of Canada. The only African nations with black populations that clearly exceed the United States total are Nigeria (with an estimated 1993 population of 130 million), Ethiopia (56 million), and Zaire (40 million). South Africa had an estimated total population of about 43 million in 1993.

■ REGIONAL DISTRIBUTION

1790 to 1900

From 1790 until 1900, 90 percent or more of the African-American population resided in the South, mostly in rural areas. Even the abolition of slavery following the Civil War had only a minimal short-term impact on the southern, rural character of the black population.

Three men, c.1910.

Early Migration

Episodic migration from the South, nonetheless, did occur during this period. One early exodus occurred in the period 1879 to 1881, when some 60,000 blacks moved into Kansas. The motivation behind this initial

Early settlers of Nicodemus, Kansas

migration was the need for social and economic freedom. The immigration to Kansas strained the resources of the state, and several cities became black refugee camps. One of the towns created by this exodus was Nicodemus, Kansas, which still exists as a small all-black community.

Although other movement by Southern blacks to the Midwest or Northeast have been chronicled, the effect on the regional distribution of the total black population was minor; when the Emancipation Proclamation was signed, under 8 percent of all blacks lived in the Northeast or Midwest. After the Civil War, the percentage of the nation's black population living in the Northeast fell slightly, while the percentage rose in the Midwest. By 1900, only 10 percent of all blacks lived in these two northern regions.

A black family living in rural Georgia.

1900 to 1970

In 1900, almost 90 percent of African Americans still lived in the South. Between 1910 to 1920, however, the percentage of blacks living in the South began to fall. By 1930, more than 21.2 percent of blacks resided outside of the South.

For the next four decades, the percentage of African Americans living in the South steadily fell. In 1970, about 39 percent of blacks were Northerners, 53 percent were Southerners, and about 7.5 percent lived in the West.

The Great Migration

Historians and social scientists have long debated why blacks failed to leave the South in larger numbers at the end of the Civil War. Virtually every migration stream is the product of both push and pull factors—prejudice, discrimination, and a poor economic opportunities in the South obviously provided the strong push factors needed to generate out-migration, while a somewhat

Harlem in the early 1930s.

more open society and the presence of jobs in the industrializing North should have provided the pull to establish a strong South-to-North migration stream. Some blacks did leave the South during the last decades of the nineteenth century, typically following transportation routes directly northward. However, the number of blacks moving North has always seemed smaller than what might be expected given the combined push and pull forces.

European immigration may be one explanation for the relatively slow start of the southern exodus by blacks. As the North industrialized in the late nineteenth and early twentieth centuries, it generated a huge demand for labor, which was met in large part by massive immigration of Europeans. A great many of the urban factory jobs were filled first by Irish and German laborers, and later by immigrants from southern and eastern Europe, particularly Italy. Had northern industries not been able to meet their labor needs through immigration, they might have relied more on domestic sources, including Southern blacks.

As immigration to the United States was curtailed by World War I and restrictive legislation passed in the 1920s, blacks began to leave the South in larger numbers. As a consequence, the proportion of the nation's black population living in the South fell more rapidly during the 1910 to 1920 decade than during the entire period since emancipation.

Although black out-migration from the South was reduced somewhat during the depression of the 1930s, the proportion of blacks living in the South continued to decrease. The greatest volume of out-migration of southern blacks occurred in the 1940 to 1950 decade and was occasioned partly by mobilization for World War II. Therefore, both world wars of the twentieth century provided a powerful impetus for blacks to leave the South.

During the 1940s, 1950s, and 1960s, the net out-migration of blacks from the South totalled about 4.3 million persons. Mechanization of Southern agriculture after World War II decreased the demand for low-wage labor and gave further incentive to leave agricultural areas. The continued exodus of rural blacks decreased the supply of farm labor, thereby giving incentive for Southern farmers to mechanize further and adopt labor-saving methods.

The exodus of blacks from the South, during the thirty years between 1940 and 1970 is one of the major migrations in American history. In volume, it equals the total Italian immigration to the United States during its peak, the thirty–year period from the mid–1890s to the mid–1920s. For most blacks, this journey out of the South meant exchanging a rural, agricultural existence for an urban life based on factory jobs.

Migration Since 1970

By the 1970s, the black migration to the North from the South had ended. Although blacks continued to leave the South, many returned; a few northern-born blacks, the children of earlier migrants, moved to the South in response to the availability of jobs and a change in the political and social climate. In the early 1970s, as many blacks were moving to the region as were leaving it. By the mid-1980s, due to reduced economic growth in some areas of the South, particularly in those areas where economies had been built around the oil and gas industries, black migration to the south had leveled off. The percentage of African Americans living in the western United States has increased from 0.5 percent in 1910 to 9.4 percent in 1990. In the year 2000, about 37 percent of

(In thousands)

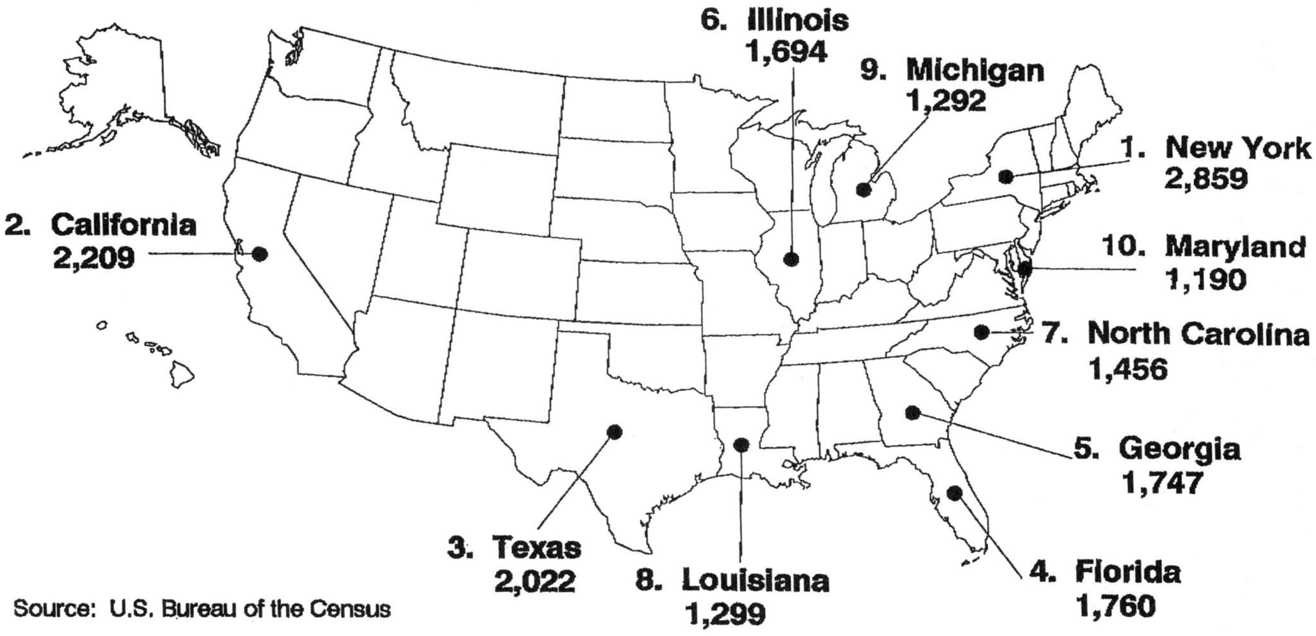

Source: U.S. Bureau of the Census

Ten States with the Largest Black Population, 1990.

blacks are likely to live in the North, 53 percent in the South, and 10 percent in the West.

■ CONTEMPORARY DEMOGRAPHIC CHARACTERISTICS

The Black Population By State

Blacks are most populous in the South, which contains 53 percent of the nation's total black population. In 1990, of the ten states with the largest black populations (New York, California, Texas, Florida, Georgia, Illinois, North Carolina, Louisiana, Michigan, and Maryland), six were in the South. Fifty-eight percent of the black population resided in these states. Six other states had black populations of 1 million or more in 1990: Virginia (1,163,000), Ohio (1,155,000), Pennsylvania (1,090,000), South Carolina (1,040,000), New Jersey (1,037,000), and Alabama (1,021,000).

The Black Urban Population

In 1960, 64.7 percent of the black population resided in metropolitan areas in the United States, 51.4 percent of whom resided in central cities, as opposed to suburban areas and rural areas outside the city. In 1970, 74.3 percent of the black population resided in metropolitan areas, with 58.2 percent living in central cities. By 1990, 83.8 percent of the black population resided in metropolitan areas, while the proportion residing in central cities declined slightly to 57.3 percent.

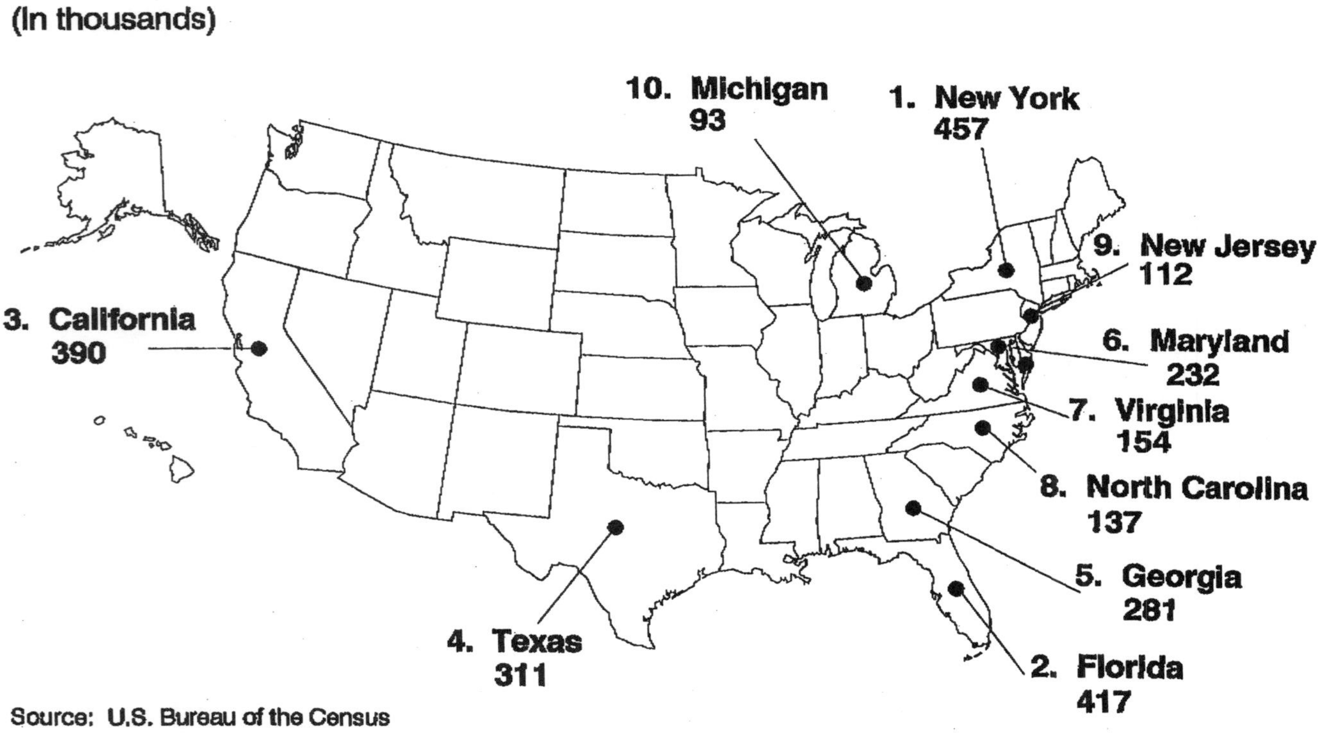

Ten States with the Largest Increases in Black Population, 1980 to 1990.

In 1960, blacks constituted 16.7 percent of all central city residents; by 1970, blacks constituted 20.6 percent. One reason for this increase has been the continued growth (although at a slower rate than in earlier decades) of the black population. A second reason for this change has been the migration of whites out of the central cities to suburban and rural areas.

In 1980, African Americans made up 22.5 percent of the total central city population. However, by 1990 this number fell to 22.1 percent. Like the white population, though in smaller numbers, the black population was migrating out of central cities to suburban and rural areas.

The city of New York, the most populous city in the United States, also has the largest black population in the nation; in 1990, over 2.1 million African Americans resided in Greater New York City. Chicago, Detroit, Philadelphia, and Los Angeles follow, in that order, as cities with the largest black populations.

Among the fifteen cities with the largest black concentrations, Washington, DC and Atlanta had black majorities by 1970. By 1990, four additional cities (Detroit, Baltimore, Memphis, and New Orleans) had black majorities, and five of the eleven largest cities in the nation were more than 50 percent black.

The Black Suburban and Nonmetropolitan Populations

The 1970s marked a turning point in the percentage of African Americans outside of central cities. Between 1980 and 1990, the black population living in suburbs grew faster than did the white suburban population. The white suburban population grew by 9.1 percent, whereas the black suburban population increased by 9.9 percent. In 1980, African Americans constituted 6.1 percent of the suburban population; by 1990, blacks constituted 6.9 percent. In 1960, only 13.3 percent of African Americans residing in metropolitan areas lived in suburban areas. By 1970 this number increased to 16.1 percent, by 1980 to 23.3 percent. In 1990, 26.6 percent of the black metropolitan population resided in suburban areas.

This is an important development since it signifies that for the first time, the number of blacks moving to the suburban areas has become large enough to significantly affect the overall distribution of the black population. The access by African Americans to suburban residences is important for many reasons. One reason is that black suburbanization may further such ideals as an open housing market, freedom of movement, and the ability to choose a neighborhood that balances a family's income and its preferences and needs, such as the availability of quality public schools for children.

Black suburbanization may be beneficial in other ways as well. Since so many jobs have been moving from cities to suburbs, a greater share of blacks living in suburbs might have long-term consequences for improving employment opportunities and occupational mobility. Finally, for many Americans, a move to the suburbs has meant owning a home, a major form of wealth accumulation for middle-class families. African-American households have been less likely than white households to own their

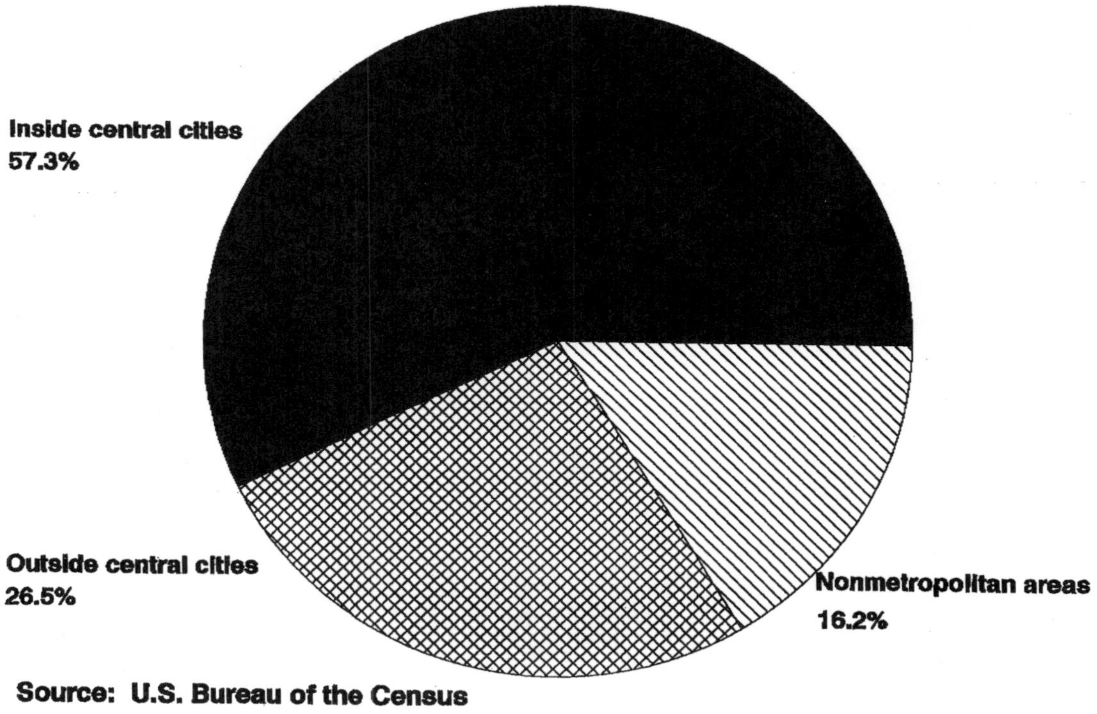

Distribution of the Black Population by Metropolitan and Nonmetropolitan Residence, 1990.

own home, even when income and other socioeconomic characteristics are taken into account. A trend toward suburbanization might offer more blacks the opportunity to build equity in a home and thus help to secure middle-class status and the transmission of that status across generations.

The reasons for the increased movement of blacks to suburbs are doubtlessly heterogeneous. On the one hand, open housing legislation and changing attitudes have contributed to breaking down the barriers to black access to the suburbs. On the other hand, there has been an increase in the number of middle-income black families (often with dual-incomes) who can afford to seek the safety, schools, acreage, and other amenities often cited by those who have chosen to move from the city to the suburbs.

Although the number of African Americans residing in suburban areas has increased, the numbers are still far below those of the white population. According to the Bureau of the Census, in 1991 only 26.7 percent of the African-American population resided in suburbs, compared to 50.7 percent of the white population.

Throughout most of the twentieth century, the African-American population has remained younger than the white population.

Compared with the white population, a greater percentage of the African-American population is under 18 years of age.

Median Age

Although both the black and white populations have aged, the African-American population has remained younger than the white population throughout most of the twentieth century. In 1980, the black population had a median age of 24.8 years, the white population a median age of 30.8 years. In 1991, the black population's median age rose to 28 years, while the median age for the white population rose to 33.9 years.

The aging of the "Baby Boomers" (persons born between the years 1946 and 1964) was the primary reason for the rise in median ages for both the black and white populations. One reason for the difference between the black and white median ages is the differing age structures of the two populations. Compared with the white population, a greater percentage of the African-American population is under 18 years of age, while a smaller percentage of the population is over 65 years. In 1991, 33 percent of the African-American population was under the age of 18, and 8 percent over the age of 65 years. Only 25 percent of the white population was under the age of 18 in this same year, while 13 percent of the population was over the age of 65. By the year 2010, the median age for blacks in the United States is expected to rise to approximately 30 years, and that of whites to 39 years.

■ POPULATION PROJECTIONS

The African-American population is projected to be one of the fastest growing population groups in the nation during the next sixty years. The black population is projected to increase by over 4 million by 2000, almost 9 million by 2010, and over 19 million by 2030. Overall, during the next sixty years, the black population is projected to grow by almost 100 percent, to 62 million. The black share of the total national population is expected to increase from 12 percent in 1992 to 13 percent in 2000, 14 percent in 2010, 15 percent in 2030, and 16 percent in 2050.

State	Slaves	Free
Connecticut	2,759	2,801
Delaware	8,887	3,899
Georgia	29,264	398
Kentucky	11,830	114
Maryland	103,036	8,043
New Hampshire	158	630
New Jersey	11,423	2,762
New York	21,324	4,654
North Carolina	100,572	4,975
Pennsylvania	3,737	6,537
Rhode Island	952	3,469
South Carolina	107,094	1,801
Vermont	17	255
Virginia	293,427	12,766
Ohio Territory	3,417	5,463
Maine	None	538

Black Population by State, 1790.

Black Population Growth

Year	Total	Slave
1790	757,208	697,681
1800	1,002,037	893,602
1810	1,377,808	1,191,362
1820	1,771,656	1,538,022
1830	2,328,642	2,009,043
1840	2,873,648	2,487,355
1850	3,638,808	3,204,313
1860	4,441,830	3,953,760

United States	Number			Percent Distribution		
	1990	1980	1970	1990	1980	1970
Total	248,709,873	226,545,805	203,211,926	100.0	100.0	100.0
White	199,686,070	188,371,622	177,748,975	80.3	83.1	87.5
Black	29,986,060	26,495,025	22,580,289	12.1	11.7	11.1
American Indian, Eskimo and Aleut	1,959,234	1,420,400	827,268 [2]	0.8	0.6	0.4
Asian and Pacific Islander [1]	7,273,662	3,500,439	1,538,721 [3]	2.9	1.5	0.8
Other	9,804,847	6,758,319	516,673	3.9	3.0	0.3
Persons of Hispanic Origin	22,354,059	14,608,673	9,072,602 [4]	9.0	6.4	4.5
Persons Not of Hispanic Origin	226,355,814	211,937,132	194,139,324	91.0	93.6	95.5

Source: U.S. Bureau of the Census

1 In 1970 and 1980 Asian and Pacific Islander groups such as Cambodian, Laotian, and Thai were included in the "other" race category. In sample tabulations, these groups were included in the Asian and Pacific Islander category.

2 Excludes Aleuts and Eskimos in Alaska only.

3 Excludes Koreans and Hawaiians in Alaska.

4 Based on sample.

Resident Population By Race, 1970, 1980, 1990.

Year	Percentage of Blacks Living in: Northeast	North Central	South	West
1850	4.1	3.7	92.1	<0.1
1860	3.5	4.1	92.2	0.1
1870	3.7	5.6	90.6	0.1
1880	3.5	5.9	90.5	0.2
1890	3.6	5.8	90.3	0.4
1900	4.4	5.6	89.7	0.3
1910	4.9	5.5	89.0	0.5
1920	6.5	7.6	85.2	0.8
1930	9.6	10.6	78.7	1.0
1940	10.6	11.0	77.0	1.3
1950	13.4	14.8	68.0	3.8
1960	16.0	18.3	59.9	5.8
1970	19.2	20.2	53.0	7.5
1980	18.3	20.1	53.0	8.5
1990	18.7	19.1	52.8	9.4

Regional Distribution of the Black Population, 1850 to 1990

(Numbers in thousands)

Period	Total Population				Black Population			
	Northeast	Midwest	South	West	Northeast	Midwest	South	West
1990-91								
In-migrants	346	782	1,421	835	44	79	226	72
Out-migrants	932	797	987	668	176	74	112	59
Net migration	(585)*	(15)	433*	167	(132)	4	115	13
1989-90								
In-migrants	461	908	1,428	964	27	64	135	88
Out-migrants	758	1,024	1,198	781	72	78	131	33
Net migration	(297)*	(116)	230*	183	(45)	(14)	4	55
1988-89								
In-migrants	370	777	1,318	791	49	83	157	79
Out-migrants	714	703	1,071	768[r]	123	61	120	63
Net migration	(344)*	74	247*	23[r]	(75)	22	37	16
1987-88								
In-migrants	430	715	1,338	613	21	68	194	79
Out-migrants	671	818	886	721	107	89	75	93
Net migration	(241)*	(103)	452*	(108)	(85)	(21)	120	(14)
1986-87								
In-migrants	398	858	1,374	916	14	62	238	59
Out-migrants	732	969	1,095	750	114	97	90	72
Net migration	(334)*	(111)	279*	166	(100)	(35)[1]	148	(13)[1]
1985-86								
In-migrants	502	1,011	1,355	910	46	133	164	63
Out-migrants	752	996	1,320	710	86	85	148	87
Net migration	(250)*	15	35	200*	(40)	48	16	(24)

Data are from the Current Population Survey.
Note: Numbers in parentheses are negative.
[r] Revised.
* Net flow significant at the 90-percent confidence level.
[1] Not statistically signficant.

Annual In-Migration, Out-Migration, and Net Migration for Regions, 1985 to 1991.

Year	Total Population	Blacks	Whites
1880 [1]	26.3	12.9	28.3
1890 [1]	32.9	17.6	35.1
1900 [1]	37.3	20.5	39.7
1910	46.3	27.4	48.7
1920	51.4	34.0	53.4
1930	56.2	43.7	57.6
1940	56.5	48.6	57.5
1950	64.0	62.4	64.3
1960*	69.9	73.2	69.5
1970	73.5	81.3	72.4
1980	73.7	85.3	71.3
1990	75.2	87.2	71.9

* Denotes first year for which figures include Alaska and Hawaii.

[1] Definition modified to exclude population in incorporated places and New England towns in the 2,500-3,999 size range.

Percentage of Population Living in Urban Territory, 1880 to 1990.

Population Totals

Year	Total Population	Black Population	Percentage
1790	3,929,214	757,208	19.3
1800	5,308,483	1,002,037	18.9
1810	7,239,881	1,377,808	19.0
1820	9,638,453	1,771,656	18.4
1830	12,866,020	2,328,642	18.1
1840	17,069,453	2,873,648	16.8
1850	23,191,876	3,638,808	15.7
1860	31,443,321	4,441,830	14.1
1870 [1]	39,818,449	5,392,172	13.5
1880	50,155,783	6,580,793	13.1
1890	62,947,714	7,488,676	11.9
1900	75,994,575	8,833,994	11.6
1910	91,972,266	9,827,763	10.7
1920	105,710,620	10,463,131	9.9
1930	122,775,046	11,891,143	9.7
1940	131,669,275	12,865,518	9.8
1950	151,325,798	15,044,937	9.9
1960 [2]	179,323,175	18,871,831	10.5
1970	203,211,926	22,580,289	11.1
1980	226,545,805	26,495,025	11.7
1990	248,709,873	29,986,060	12.1

[1] Revised to include adjustments for underenumeration in the Southern states.

[2] Denotes first year for which figures include Alaska and Hawaii.

(Numbers in thousands. Metropolitan areas defined as of June 30, 1984)

Mobility period and type of area	Total Population			Black Population		
	In-migrants	Out-migrants	Net Migration	In-migrants	Out-migrants	Net Migration
1990-91						
Metropolitan areas	1,817	1,700	117	196	92	104
Nonmetropolitan	1,700	1,817	(117)*	92	196	(104)
1989-90						
Metropolitan areas	1,931	1,803	128	123	125	(2)
Nonmetropolitan	1,803	1,931	(128)	125	123	2
1988-89						
Metropolitan areas	1,748	1,537	211	156	121	35
Nonmetropolitan	1,537	1,748	(211)	121	156	(35)
1987-88						
Metropolitan areas	1,820	1,651	169	164	113	51
Nonmetropolitan	1,651	1,820	(169)	113	164	(51)
1986-87[r]						
Metropolitan areas	2,148	1,660	488*	NA	NA	NA
Nonmetropolitan	1,660	2,148	(488)*	NA	NA	NA
1985-86[r]						
Metropolitan areas	2,034	1,731	303*	NA	NA	NA
Nonmetropolitan	1,731	2,034	(303)*	NA	NA	NA

Data are from the Current Population Survey.
Note: Numbers in parentheses are negative.
*Net flow significant at the 90-percent confidence level.
[r]Revised. Revised data for Blacks are not available.

In-Migrants, Out-Migrants, and Net Migration for Metropolitan and Nonmetropolitan Areas by Race, 1985 to 1991.

Area	Black Population			Percent Change in Black Population			Percent Black		
	1990	1980	1970	80 to 90	70 to 80	70 to 90	1990	1980	1970
Central Cities									
New York City	2,102,512	1,784,337	1,668,115	17.8	7.0	26.0	28.7	25.2	21.2
Chicago City	1,087,711	1,197,000	1,102,620	-9.1	8.6	-1.4	39.1	39.8	32.7
Detroit City	777,916	758,939	660,428	2.5	14.9	17.8	75.7	63.1	43.7
Philadelphia City	631,936	638,878	653,791	-1.1	-2.3	-3.3	39.9	37.8	33.6
Los Angeles City	487,674	505,210	503,606	-3.5	0.3	-3.2	14.0	17.0	17.9
Houston City	457,990	440,346	316,551	4.0	39.1	44.7	28.1	27.6	25.7
Baltimore City	435,768	431,151	420,210	1.1	2.6	3.7	59.2	54.8	46.4
Washington, D.C.	399,604	448,906	537,712	-11.0	-16.5	-25.7	65.8	70.3	71.1
Memphis City	334,737	307,702	242,513	8.8	26.9	38.0	54.8	47.6	38.9
New Orleans City	307,728	308,149	267,308	-0.1	15.3	15.1	61.9	55.3	45.0
Dallas City	296,994	265,594	210,238	11.8	26.3	41.3	29.5	29.4	24.9
Atlanta City	264,262	282,911	255,051	-6.6	10.9	3.6	67.1	66.6	51.3
Cleveland City	235,405	251,347	287,841	-6.3	-12.7	-18.2	46.6	43.8	38.3
Milwaukee City	191,255	146,940	105,088	30.2	39.8	82.0	30.5	23.1	14.7
St. Louis City	188,408	206,386	254,191	-8.7	-18.8	-25.9	47.5	45.6	40.9

Black Population Change in 14 Central Cities, 1970 to 1990.

	Total population	Total population in metropolitan areas	Total percent who live in:			Percent of total population in metropolitan areas	Total percent who live in:		
			Central cities of metropolitan areas	Suburbs of metropolitan areas	Outside metropolitan areas		Central cities of metropolitan areas	Suburbs of metropolitan areas	Outside metropolitan areas
ALL RACES									
1960*	179,323,175	112,885,178	58,004,334	54,880,844	66,437,997	63.0	32.3	30.6	37.0
1970	203,211,926	139,418,811	63,796,943	75,621,868	63,793,115	68.6	31.4	37.2	31.4
1980	226,545,805	169,430,623	67,854,344	101,576,279	57,115,182	74.8	30.0	44.8	25.2
1990	248,709,873	192,725,741	77,843,533	114,882,208	55,984,132	77.5	31.3	46.2	22.5
BLACK									
1960*	18,871,831	12,207,231	9,703,584	2,503,647	6,664,600	64.7	51.4	13.3	35.3
1970	22,580,289	16,770,610	13,140,331	3,630,279	5,809,679	74.3	58.2	16.1	25.7
1980	26,495,025	21,477,741	15,297,000	6,180,741	5,017,284	81.1	57.7	23.3	18.9
1990	29,986,060	25,122,054	17,169,430	7,952,624	4,864,006	83.8	57.3	26.5	16.2
WHITE									
1960*	158,831,732	99,687,658	47,653,833	52,033,825	59,144,074	62.8	30.0	32.8	37.2
1970	177,748,975	120,578,729	49,430,443	71,148,286	57,170,246	67.8	27.8	40.0	32.2
1980	188,371,622	138,064,178	46,946,692	91,117,486	50,307,444	73.3	24.9	48.4	26.7
1990	199,686,070	150,863,170	51,452,071	99,411,099	48,822,900	75.6	25.8	50.0	24.4

* Denotes first year for which figures include Alaska and Hawaii.

Distribution of the Total, Black, and White Populations in Central Cities, Suburbs, and Nonmetropolitan Areas, 1960 to 1990.

(Numbers in thousands. Metropolitan areas defined as of June 30, 1984)

Mobility period and type of area	Total Population			Black Population		
	In-migrants	Out-migrants	Net Migration	In-migrants	Out-migrants	Net Migration
1990-91						
Central cities	3,223	5,682	(2,459)*	478	628	(150)
Suburbs	6,021	3,446	2,575*	645	391	254
1989-90						
Central cities	3,692	6,472	(2,780)*	416	928	(512)
Suburbs	6,738	3,830	2,908*	906	396	510
1988-89						
Central cities	3,183	6,138	(2,954)*	435	790	(355)
Suburbs	6,575	3,410	3,165*	754	364	390
1987-88						
Central cities	3,461	6,084	(2,623)*	443	745	(302)
Suburbs	6,421	3,629	2,792*	713	360	353
1986-87[r]						
Central cities	4,342	6,022	(1,680)*	NA	NA	NA
Suburbs	6,378	4,211	2,167*	NA	NA	NA
1985-86[r]						
Central cities	4,222	5,802	(1,580)*	NA	NA	NA
Suburbs	6,168	4,285	1,883*	NA	NA	NA

Data are from the Current Population Survey.
Note: Numbers in parentheses are negative.
*Net flow significant at the 90-percent confidence level.
[r]Revised. Revised data for Blacks are not available.

In-Migrants, Out-Migrants, and Net Migration for Central Cities and Suburbs by Race, 1985 to 1991.

Age	Total	White	Black	American Indian, Eskimo, and Aleut	Asian and Pacific Islander	Other	Persons of Hispanic Origin
All ages	248,709,873	199,686,070	29,986,060	1,959,234	7,273,662	9,804,847	22,354,059
Under 5 years	18,354,443	13,649,490	2,785,902	201,950	589,845	1,127,256	2,387,524
5 to 9 years	18,099,179	13,616,268	2,671,109	199,446	596,133	1,016,223	2,193,852
10 to 14 years	17,114,249	12,853,558	2,601,590	188,000	551,552	919,549	2,001,617
15 to 19 years	17,754,015	13,342,703	2,658,493	180,516	603,761	968,542	2,053,957
20 to 24 years	19,020,312	14,523,912	2,578,953	165,549	632,258	1,119,640	2,304,441
25 to 34 years	43,175,932	33,990,057	5,389,489	346,245	1,417,252	2,032,889	4,403,542
35 to 44 years	37,578,903	30,587,996	4,212,828	276,336	1,242,012	1,259,731	2,944,994
45 to 54 years	25,223,086	21,090,574	2,584,777	173,531	717,241	656,963	1,709,899
55 to 64 years	21,147,923	18,179,539	1,994,368	113,208	469,150	391,658	1,192,950
65 to 74 years	18,106,558	16,026,201	1,503,460	71,980	300,731	204,186	723,029
75 to 84 years	10,055,108	9,037,720	774,908	33,268	123,989	85,223	343,690
85 years and over	3,080,165	2,788,052	230,183	9,205	29,738	22,987	94,564
Median age (years)	32.9	34.4	28.1	26.2	29.8	23.9	25.5
Percent Distribution							
All ages	100.0	100.0	100.0	100.0	100.0	100.0	100.0
Under 5 years	7.4	6.8	9.3	10.3	8.1	11.5	10.7
5 to 9 years	7.3	6.8	8.9	10.2	8.2	10.4	9.8
10 to 14 years	6.9	6.4	8.7	9.6	7.6	9.4	9.0
15 to 19 years	7.1	6.7	8.9	9.2	8.3	9.9	9.2
20 to 24 years	7.6	7.3	8.6	8.4	8.7	11.4	10.3
25 to 34 years	17.4	17.0	18.0	17.7	19.5	20.7	19.7
35 to 44 years	15.1	15.3	14.0	14.1	17.1	12.8	13.2
45 to 54 years	10.1	10.6	8.6	8.9	9.9	6.7	7.6
55 to 64 years	8.5	9.1	6.7	5.8	6.4	4.0	5.3
65 to 74 years	7.3	8.0	5.0	3.7	4.1	2.1	3.2
75 to 84 years	4.0	4.5	2.6	1.7	1.7	0.9	1.5
85 years and over	1.2	1.4	0.8	0.5	0.4	0.2	0.4

Age of the Resident Population by Race and Hispanic Origin, 1990.

13

Employment and Income

13

Employment and Income

Current Employment Trends ■ Factors in Employment and Unemployment Levels ■ Income and Poverty ■ Assessment

by Hayward Derrick Horton

The changing social and economic status of blacks continues to be a major issue in contemporary America. Many point to the increase in the number of blacks in high-status occupations as proof that discrimination is no longer a dominant force in the lives of African Americans.

■ CURRENT EMPLOYMENT TRENDS

In the United States government, the Secretary of Commerce, Secretary of Energy, Secretary of the Veteran's Administration and the Chairman of the Joint Chiefs of Staff are black. There are also a record number of blacks in the House of Representatives and a black woman in the Senate. In the past, blacks in the entertainment world were primarily singers and dancers. Today, many of the biggest stars in the music, television and film industries are black. In addition, blacks are increasingly making strides as producers, directors and screenwriters. Similar success has been experienced by blacks in professional sports. To say that the conditions have not changed in the United States for African Americans is certainly inconsistent with the facts.

Yet, despite the increase in opportunities for the black upper and middle class, blacks as a whole trail whites in every measure of socioeconomic standing. Blacks continue to be disproportionately employed in lower-paying, blue-collar jobs. Unemployment for blacks has consistently been twice that for whites for at least two decades. Black personal and family income continues to be a fraction of that for whites. The poverty rate for African Americans has been three times as high as that for whites for over thirty years. Perhaps the most troubling aspect of these trends is the lack of indication that these measures will improve in the foreseeable future.

In a sense, the story of African Americans has two very different chapters. The first is one of the growing black middle class that is experiencing a greater range of occupational and economic opportunities than ever before. The second part of the story is more somber. It tells of an increasing number of blacks who are disadvantaged and, for all

Blacks continue to be disproportionately employed in blue-collar jobs.

intents and purposes, locked out of the mainstream of American life. This growing schism in the social and economic conditions among blacks has serious implications for the future of the African-American community.

■ FACTORS IN EMPLOYMENT AND UNEMPLOYMENT LEVELS

Unemployment is a major problem in the African-American community. Historically, the levels of unemployment among blacks and their patterns of employment are rooted in the discrimination that they experience in the job market (John Hope Franklin and Alfred A. Moss, Jr. 1988. *From Slavery to Freedom: A History of Negro Americans*). High levels of unemployment among blacks have persisted for several decades. Recent data from the United States Bureau of the Census show that this pattern continues into the 1990s. For example, in 1980 the unemployment rate for blacks was 14.3 percent. The

(in thousands)

	Black		*White*		
Year	*Number*	*Percent*	*Number*	*Percent*	*B/W Ratio*
1980	1,553	14.3	5,884	6.3	2.3
1985	1,864	15.1	6,191	6.2	2.4
1987	1,684	13.0	5,501	5.3	2.5
1988	1,547	11.7	4,944	4.7	2.5
1989	1,544	11.4	4,770	4.5	2.5
1990	1,527	11.3	5,091	4.7	2.4
1991	1,679	12.4	6,447	6.0	2.1

Source: Statistical Abstract of the United States, U.S. Bureau of the Census, 1992, page 383.

Unemployment for Blacks and Whites, 1980–1991.

rate among whites for that year was 6.3 percent. In other words, the rate for blacks was 2.3 times as high as that for whites. Over the decade of the 1980s and into the 1990s, the unemployment rate fluctuated for both blacks and whites. However, in no year did the unemployment rate for blacks drop below 11 percent. Throughout the 1980–1991 period, unemployment rates for blacks were two and one-half times as great as those for whites.

The Effects of Occupational Discrimination

Much of the variance in unemployment rates between blacks and whites is a direct result of discrimination, past and present, in the job market and other spheres of economic opportunity. In fact, until relatively recently, there were many occupations that blacks were not allowed to enter—irrespective of their levels of education (John Sibley Butler. 1991 *Entrepreneurship and Self-Help among Black Americans.*) This has resulted in an occupational structure for blacks that is substantially different from that for whites. These differences remain despite advances due to Civil Rights legislation. Data from the United States Census reveal that, in 1991, 18 percent of all employed blacks held managerial and professional positions, compared to 31 percent of whites. Twenty-two percent of blacks, as compared to 13.2 percent of whites, were employed in the operators, fabricators and labor category.

However, this data becomes more revealing when the occupational categories are subdivided by gender for both groups. This shows that black males are more likely

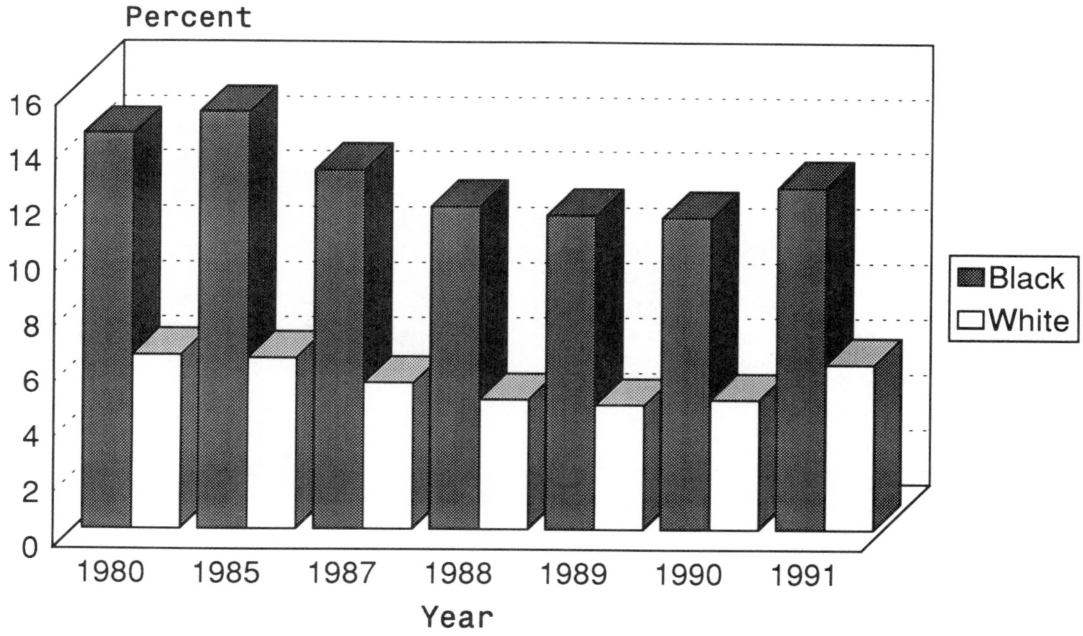

Source: Statistical Abstract of the United States, U.S. Bureau of the Census, 1992, page 383.

Unemployment for Blacks and Whites, 1980–1991.

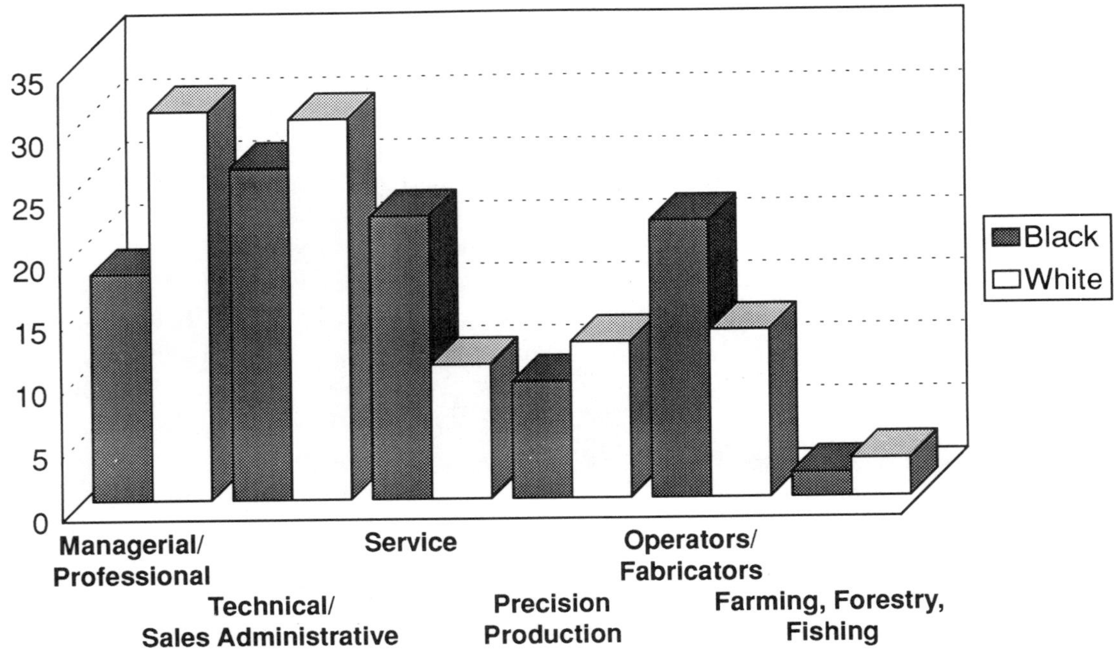

Source: Statistical Abstract of the United States, U.S. Dept. of Commerce, 1992, page 396.

Occupation of Employed Civilians by Race, 1991.

than any other group to be in the most vulnerable occupational category—operators, fabricators and labor. In 1991, 32 percent of all employed black males held these types of jobs. For white males, black females and white females the percentages were 17.7, 12.6 and 7.6, respectively. Also, only 15.3 percent of employed black males held managerial and professional jobs. For white males, this figure was 30.5 percent, representing the largest single category for this group.

Approximately 21 percent of employed black females held professional and managerial jobs. The corresponding figure for employed white females was 31 percent, indicating a level of professional and managerial employment comparable to that of white males. The highest category of employment for both black and white females was the technical/sales and administrative area. Thirty-six percent of black females and 43.2 percent of white females held these types of jobs.

Public Policy on Discrimination in Employment

The above data shows that African Americans continue to experience disadvantage in the labor force. Despite gains by the black upper and middle class, blacks in general have higher levels of unemployment and hold disproportionately more blue-collar jobs.

The Civil Rights Act of 1964 prohibits discrimination on the basis of race, color, gender or national origin. This law formed part of an array of public programs that comprised the "Great Society" legislation of the Kennedy-Johnson administrations. Among these measures was the Economic Recovery Act of 1964, which included the Job Corps, the Manpower Training Programs and many other social interventions. It is generally acknowledged that these programs were important to improving the employment prospects of African Americans.

However, according to many policy experts, the Reagan administrations of the 1980s "turned back the clock" to a time of overt and blatant discrimination toward blacks (James E. Blackwell. 1991. *The Black Community: Diversity and Unity.*). They argue that Reagan attacked many of the social programs that protected the rights of minorities and used the United States Civil Rights Commission to advance his conservative agenda. Indirect support to their claim is the fact that only 4.1 percent of Reagan's appointments were black, as compared to 21 percent for Carter, the previous president. Moreover, experts claim that Reagan's record of recruitment and hiring of blacks was worse than those the previous administrations of Johnson, Nixon and Ford as well. In the estimation of many analysts, furthermore, the Bush administration extended the damaging trends of the Reagan years.

It is still too early to predict the policy direction of the Clinton administration. At this point, neither programs nor policies directed at improving the employment prospects of blacks or other racial/ethnic minorities have materialized. Clinton has initiated efforts at improving the overall employment picture. However, as history has shown, an improvement in employment prospects for whites does not necessarily translate into comparable opportunities for blacks.

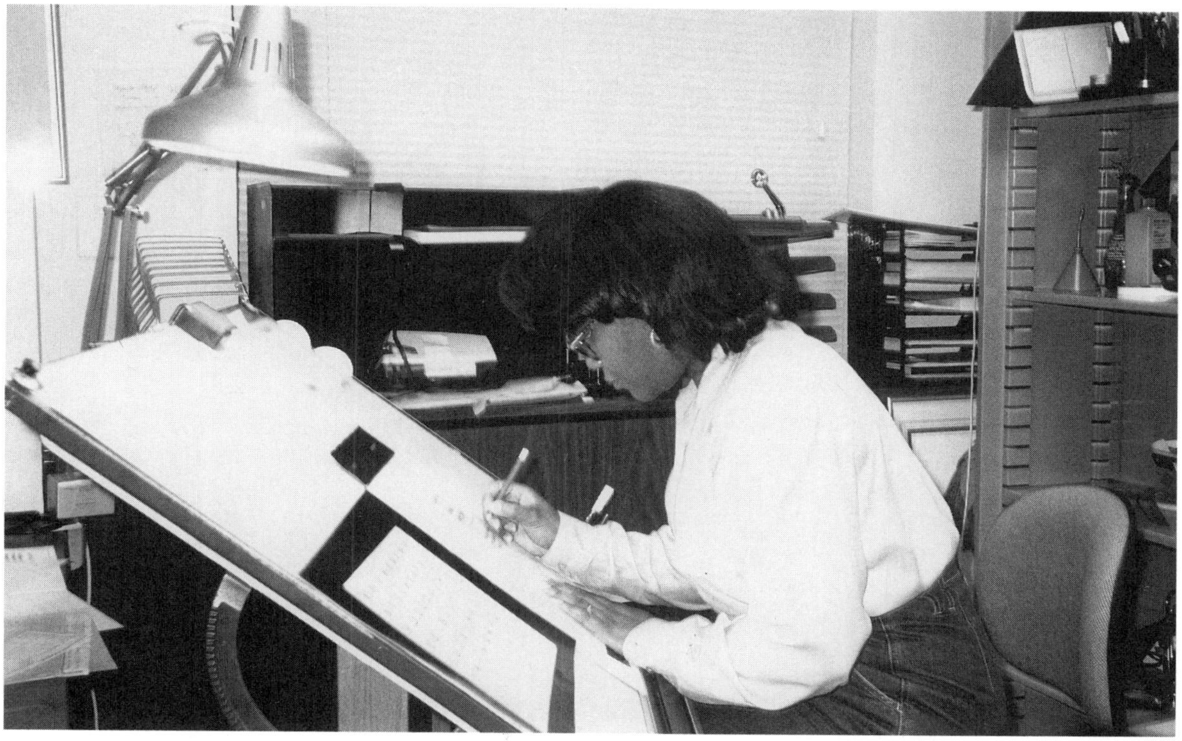

Approximately 21 percent of employed black females held professional and managerial jobs.

INCOME AND POVERTY

Despite gains in occupational status over the last two decades, African-American households have yet to gain equality in income with whites. Recent sociological studies have found that blacks of comparable levels of education, occupation, and experience tend to earn less than their white counterparts (Melvin E. Thomas and Hayward D. Horton. 1992. Race, Class, and Family Structure: The Case of Family Income. *Sociological Perspectives* 35:433–50). Data on household income from the United States Department of Commerce confirm those findings. In 1988, the median income for black families was $19,823, compared to $34,222 for whites. In other words, black families had a median income that was approximately 58 percent of that for whites. In 1989, the essential disparity between black and whites in median family income—$20,911 compared to $36,325—remained unchanged. By 1990, median family income for blacks was still only 59 percent of that for whites, despite an increase in income for black families over the three years. The corresponding increase for white families offset any gains made by blacks during the period.

The Impact of Family Structure on the Income of Black Families

Family structure has a bearing on the incomes of African-American families and how they compare to white families. For instance, black married-couple households had a median income in 1988 of $30,424. This represents 82 percent of the $36,883 median income reported for white married-couple families that year. This figure declined to 78 percent in 1989, but rose again to 84 percent in 1990.

It is important to note that the ratio of black/white income in this category is the highest among the various family types. Single black male householders made only 64 percent as much as single white male householders in 1988; this figure fluctuated to 62 percent in 1989 and 73 percent in 1990. Among racial comparisons based on family-structure types, black single female householders fared the worst. Single black female householders made only 59 percent as much as single white female householders in 1988, and only 60 percent as much in 1990.

The Distribution of Black Family Income

Another perspective on African-American economic life can be gained by examining the income distribution of this group. In 1990, 14.1 percent of all black households had income of less than $15,000. Only 5.2 percent of whites were found in this category. Approximately 52 percent of all black households had income that was less than $20,000. Slightly more than 68 percent of blacks, compared to 50 percent of whites, had less than $30,000 in income in 1990. Eighty-eight percent of all black households had less than $50,000 in income, compared to 75.4 percent of white households. In short, black and white income distributions continue to be disparate in contemporary America. Blacks are still more likely than whites to have households at the lower ends of the income distribution. This trend is consistent with the gap persisting over the years in overall family income for blacks and whites.

Household Size and Black Family Income

Factoring in household size is another way of assessing the degree of economic progress that blacks have made in recent years. Data from the Department of Commerce show that these income differences

Family structure has a bearing on the incomes of African-American families and how they compare to white families.

remain across household size categories. For one-person households, the black median income is $10,156. For four-person households, the black median income is $25,683. For white four-person households, the figure is $43,363. In no household size category does the black median income equal that of whites. Black median income across household sizes ranges from 55 to 66 percent of white median income. A similar pattern is observed when comparing mean incomes across household sizes for blacks and whites.

Regional Differences in Black Family Income

Income for African-American families is likely to vary among different regions of the country. Data from 1990 show that the median family income for blacks was highest in the West, at $27,947, and lowest in the midwest, at $20,512. These two regions also reported the highest and lowest percentages of black-to-white median family income. These differences reflect the variations in regional economies and occupational opportunities for blacks and whites.

Age of Householder and Black Family Income

Age is one of the most important factors to consider when assessing income within the African-American community as it is a reasonably accurate measure of work experience. One fact that is often overlooked when considering black-white income dif-

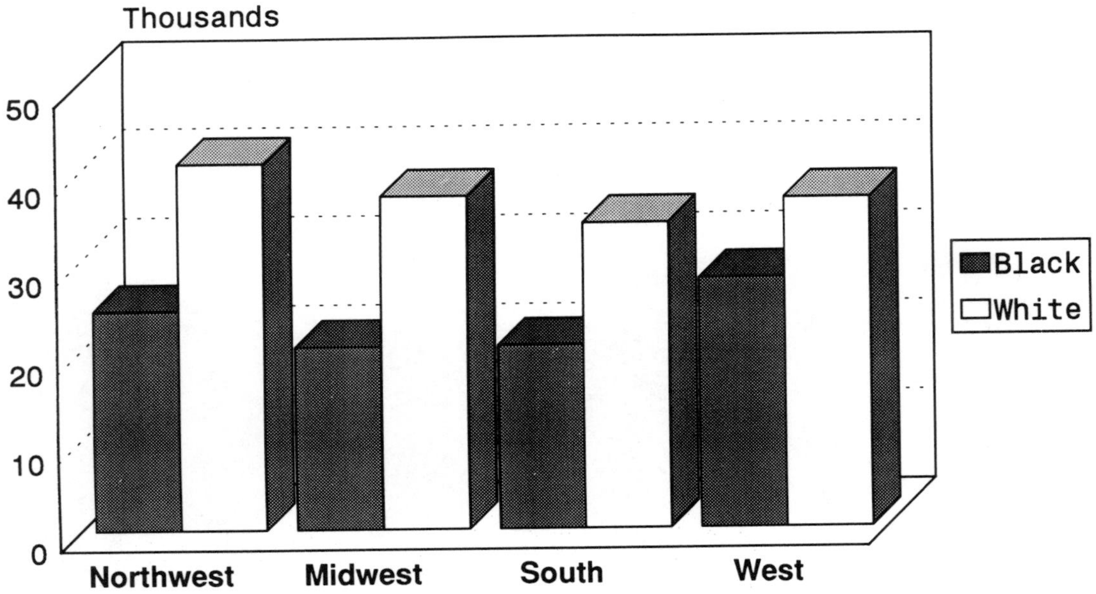

Source: Statistical Abstract of the United States, U.S. Bureau of the Census, 1992, page 383.

Median Income of Families by Region for Blacks and Whites, 1990.

ferences is the significant variation in the age distributions of two groups—variation in itself reflecting sociological factors. In other words, it is necessary to compare blacks and whites in the same age categories to obtain a complete picture of the African-American income situation. Family income data for 1990 from the United States Department of Commerce confirm the relationship between income and age. Generally speaking, family income increases for African Americans as the age of the householder increases. Black householders in the 15 to 24 years category had a median family income of $7,218. For those in the 25 to 34 age category, the median family income was $17,130. Family income gradually rises for blacks until it peaks in the 45 to 54 years category at $30,847. Beyond that age, there is a gradual and expected decline in income as householders withdraw from the labor force. Nonetheless, in no age category do blacks equal whites in median family income. The figures range from 40 percent in the 15 to 24 age group to 72 percent in the 65

Age of Householder	*Black*	*White*	*B/W*
Under 65 years	$22,221	$37,661	.59
15 to 24 years	7,218	18,234	.40
25 to 34 years	17,130	33,457	.51
35 to 44 years	27,025	42,632	.63
45 to 54 years	30,847	49,249	.62
55 to 64 years	25,442	40,416	.63
65 years and over	16,585	25,864	.64
65 to 74 years	20,158	28,027	.72
75 years and over	12,574	21,549	.58

Source: "Money Income of Households, Families and Persons in the United States, 1990," Current Population Reports: Consumer Income, Series P-60, No. 174, Table 13, Pp. 53-54, U.S. Dept. of Commerce, August 1991.

Median Income of Families by Age of Householders, 1990.

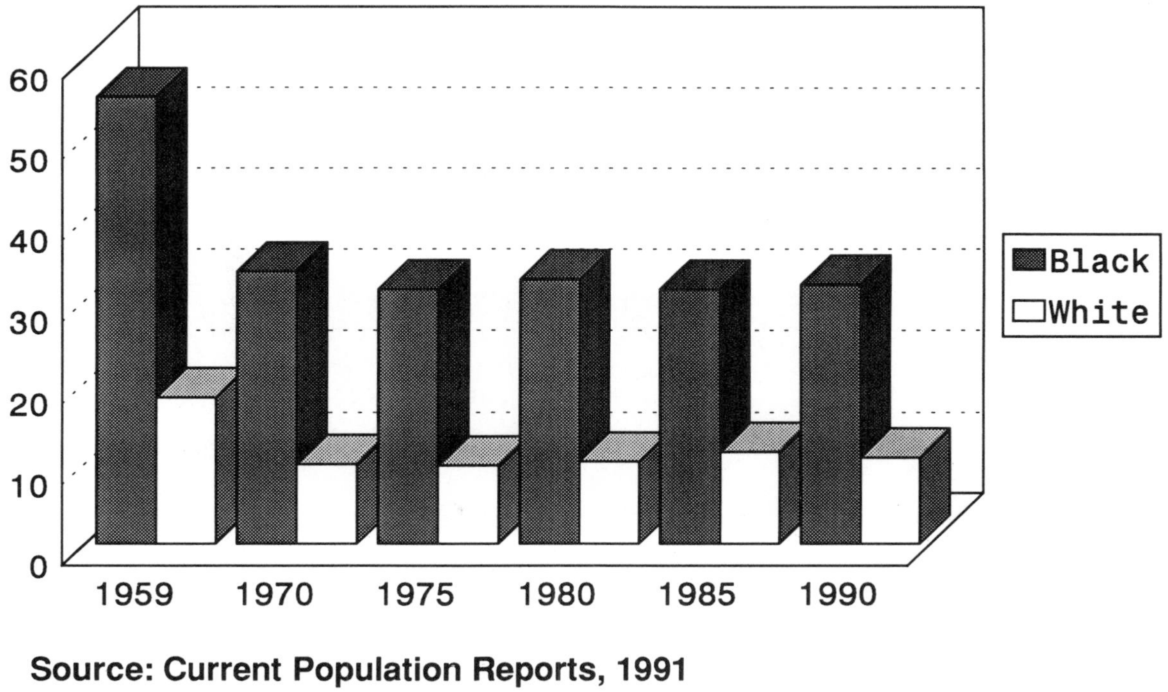

Poverty Status of Blacks and Whites, 1959–1990.

to 74 age group. Overall, black householders under age 65 earn only 59 percent as much as their white counterparts.

	Black		*White*		
Year	Number*	Percent	Number	Percent	B/W
1959	9,927	55.1	28,484	18.1	3.0
1970	7,548	33.5	17,484	9.9	3.4
1975	7,545	31.3	17,770	9.7	3.2
1980	8,579	32.5	19,669	10.2	3.2
1985	8,926	31.3	22,860	11.4	2.8
1990	9,837	31.9	22,326	10.7	3.0

* Number in thousands.

Source: "Poverty in the United State, 1990," Current Population Reports: Consumer Income, Series P-60, No. 175, Table 2, Pp. 16-17, U.S. Dept of Commerce, August 1991.

Poverty Status for Blacks and Whites, 1959–1990.

Poverty and the African-American Community

Employment, unemployment and income all have an impact on the level of poverty that exists in the African-American community. Government statistics on poverty show that, in total numbers, there are nearly as many blacks in poverty in 1990 as there were thirty years ago. In 1959, there were 9.9 million blacks living below the poverty line. In 1990 that figure was 9.8 million. The major difference is between the poverty rates in the two periods. In 1959 the poverty rate was 55.2 percent compared to the 1990 rate of 31.9 percent. One trend that has not changed is the ratio of black to white poverty over the last thirty years. In 1959, the rate of poverty for blacks was three times as great as the rate for whites. In 1990, that ratio was unchanged.

There were 2.2 million African-American families living in poverty in 1990. This represented a poverty rate of 29.3 percent. However, there were important differences in rates of poverty across family types. For instance, black married-couple families had the lowest level of poverty. Black married-couple families without children had a poverty rate of 12.6 percent; those with children had a poverty rate of 14.3 percent. The highest rates were those for female-headed householders. Female-headed householders without children had a poverty rate of 48.1 percent. For those with children, the poverty rate was 56.1 percent. Comparing the poverty rates racially shows that, in every category, black family poverty exceeded that for whites. Black families overall had a poverty rate that was nearly four times the rate for whites. Even in the category that was lowest for blacks, married-couple families without children, the rate of poverty was two and one-half times that for white families of this type.

Poverty and Black Teenage Pregnancy

One problem associated with poverty in the African-American community is that of teenage pregnancy. However, black teenage pregnancy is part of a larger problem of nonmarital births. Rates of pregnancy and nonmarital childbirth are higher for black teenagers than whites, though the gap is closing. Recent studies indicate that the differences between the two groups can be explained by differences in (1) sexual activity; (2) rates of abortion; (3) the use of contraceptives; and (4) rates of marriage before the child's birth (James E. Blackwell. 1991. *The Black Community: Diversity and Unity*).

Irrespective of the causes of black teenage pregnancy, the consequences are dramatic for the African-American community. Generally speaking, teenage mothers are more likely to be poor and are less likely to finish high school. In more cases than not, the fathers are absent or nonsupportive. Thus, it is not unusual for teenage mothers to be dependent on public assistance as a means of support. Teenage mothers tend to be unprepared for the adult responsibilities of parenting. Their children are more likely to be the victims of child abuse and to suffer physical, emotional, and educational problems later on in life.

For well over a decade, black community organizations have addressed the problem of teenage pregnancy. Groups such as the Children's Defense Fund, the National Urban League, Delta Sigma Theta and a host of others have developed teenage pregnancy prevention programs. Often these efforts focus on teenage males as well as females.

Public Programs to Address Poverty and Employment Discrimination

The issue of black teenage pregnancy is only one dimension of the overall problem of poverty within the African-American community. Many of the programs that address the needs of the poor were developed during the Great Society era of the 1960s. Headstart, Medicaid and Medicare, the Food Stamp Program and several other forms of assistance were part of a comprehensive effort referred to as the "War on Poverty." Critics of the Great Society programs argue that these programs were expensive, wasteful, and ineffective. Supporters claim that the programs have not failed, but America's determination to secure a Great Society has.

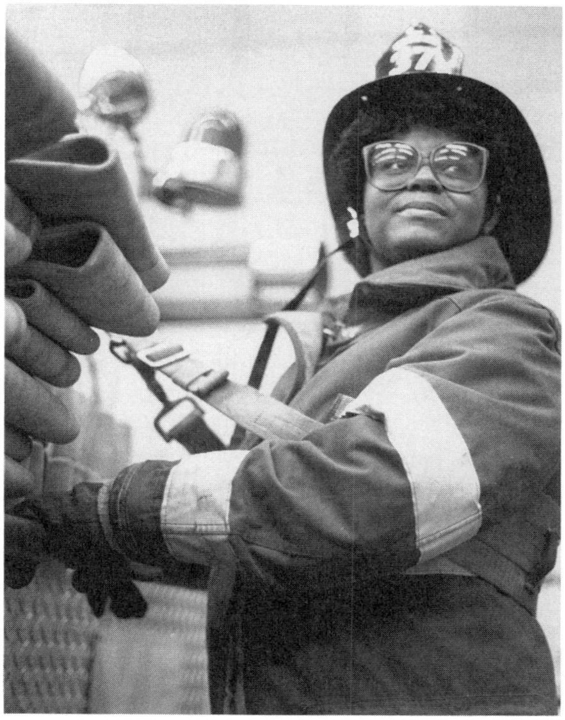

Affirmative action programs call for guidelines and goals in the hiring of underutilized groups.

Certainly the sentiment toward programs that address poverty and employment discrimination has changed. The most controversial program to date is affirmative action. Affirmative action was initiated during the late 1960s by the Nixon administration rather than during the Great Society era of Kennedy and Johnson. Affirmative action programs call for guidelines and goals in the hiring of underutilized groups: racial/ethnic minorities, the handicapped and women. They also require documentation of a good faith effort to hire persons from these groups. Affirmative action programs have been effective in promoting change in hiring practices because they have the weight of the federal government behind them. As a direct result, a broader range of opportunities have become available for blacks in government, the corporate world, and colleges and universities.

Affirmative action programs have their critics. One major criticism is that affirmative action programs do not promote occupational opportunities in general. Recent studies have documented that while whites support the general principle of equality for all, most do not support the idea of programs and social intervention specifically designed to improve the conditions of blacks and other minorities (Herbert J. Gans. 1988. *Middle American Individualism.*). Also, an increasing number of white Americans are of the opinion that social and economic differences between blacks and whites are due to individual factors rather than racial discrimination (James R. Kluegel. 1991. "Trends in White's Explanation of the Black-White Gap in Socioeconomic Status, 1977–1989. *American Sociological Review*) 56:101-16). This backlash is a direct result of the large-scale restructuring of America's economy and the resulting unemployment and underemployment for many white Americans—both working and middle class.

However, affirmative action programs have their share of black critics as well. Many black conservatives argue that affirmative action programs do not help the black disadvantaged. They claim that these programs primarily benefit the black middle class—a group that needs no assistance in achieving its economic goals. In addition, critics of affirmative action argue that it unfairly stigmatizes all blacks. Therefore, the success of African Americans in any field is often dismissed as being due to affirmative action. Whites can also perceive the need for affirmative action as confirming their belief in the inferiority of blacks. (Hayward D. Horton. Population Change and the Employment Status of College-Educated Blacks. *Research in Race and Ethnic Relations*;

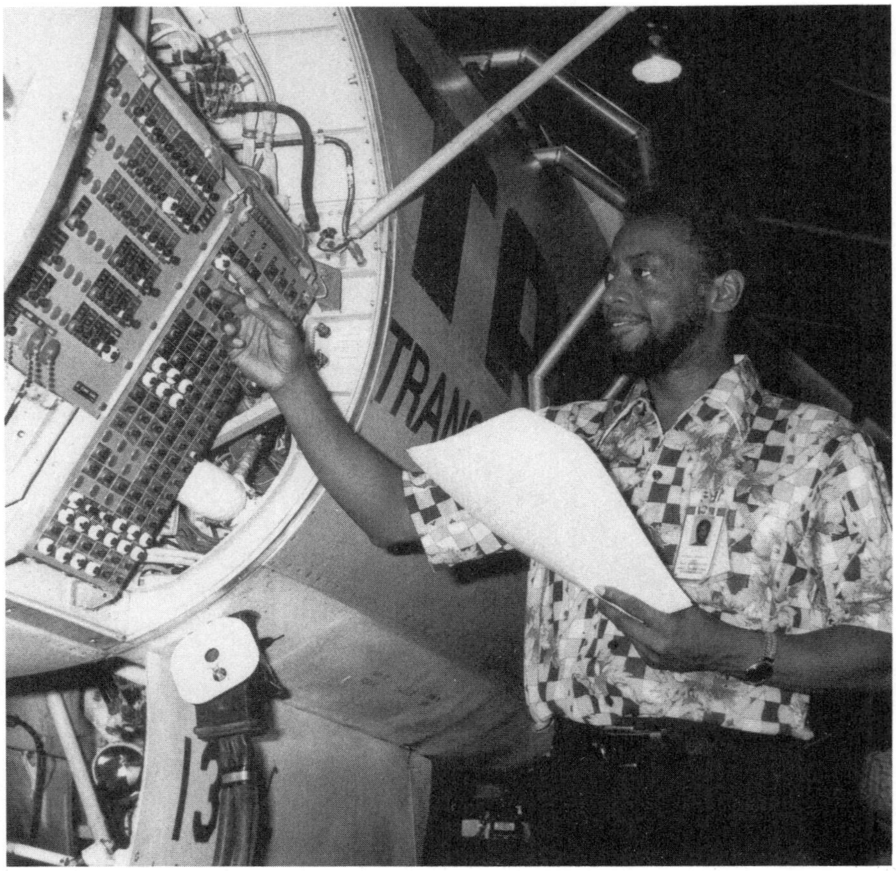

Blacks are holding more higher-status jobs and earning higher incomes than ever before.

Thomas Sowell, *Civil Rights: Rhetoric or Reality*).

The future of affirmative action and other public policies to promote equality is uncertain. At this writing, there are no clear signs from the Clinton administration. Despite the appointment of blacks to key cabinet positions, specific programs to address the problems and concerns of African Americans and other minorities have not been discussed. There have been proposals from the Clinton administration and Congress to make major cuts in federal programs. At this writing, those proposed cuts are approaching $100 billion. It is unlikely that programs that have improved the conditions of African Americans in the past will escape these cutbacks.

■ ASSESSMENT

The issue of the social and economic status of African Americans is complex. It is clear that major change has occurred within the black community as a result of the civil rights movement, civil rights legislation, and affirmative action policies. Blacks are holding more higher-status jobs and earning

The highest category of employment for both black and white females was the technical/sales and administrative area.

higher incomes than ever before. Yet, the number of African Americans who are impoverished is nearly as high as it was 30 years ago. In other words, when one speaks of the conditions or the future of the African-American community, one has to be clear about which segment of the community is referred to. The lifestyles and life chances of the two segments are significantly different. Perhaps one can defensibly state that the interests and concerns of the two groups have likewise become distinct.

Nevertheless, despite the changes that have occurred within the African-American community, one thing has remained the same: blacks have yet to achieve equality with whites on any measure of social and economic standing. Blacks have consistently had rates of unemployment that were at least twice as high as those for whites. Blacks who are employed are more likely than whites to hold blue collar jobs—the type of jobs that are most likely to be eliminated during the current restructuring of the American economy.

The gap between blacks and whites persists in family income as well. Black families still have only a fraction of the income of white families. Neither family size, family structure, age of householder, presence of children, marital status nor regional location fully explains the black-white difference in family income. The gap that remains demonstrates that racial discrimination still plays a part in explaining why the African-American has yet to achieve economic equality with whites. This persisting inequality explains many of the problems that are associated with poverty, such as teenage pregnancy and financially unstable female-headed households.

Many of the programs developed to address poverty and racial discrimination in employment were initiated during the 1960s. Generally speaking, these programs have been instrumental in providing opportunities to African Americans that had been denied long after the emancipation. However, in recent years, whites have increasingly come to resist and resent programs that secure such opportunities for blacks and other racial/ethnic minorities. As opportunities decline for whites, the competition for good jobs in this country is expected to increase. Blacks and other minority populations are growing at rates that far exceed that of whites. As these populations become better educated, the struggle for desirable jobs is expected to intensify.

What do these trends foretell for the future social and economic status of African Americans? The Clinton administration has not committed itself to the development or support of existing programs that address the needs and concerns of the African-American community. What has occurred is an emphasis on general economic issues and proposals for major cuts in federal programs. One potential consequence of these cutbacks is a reversal in some of the gains of the black middle class. Much of the occupational improvement within the African-American community was due to the greater employment opportunities in federal government for the black middle class. Many of these positions were what some sociologists have called soft-money jobs, where black professionals are providing public services to disadvantaged minorities. Therefore, massive federal cutbacks may have a disproportionate impact upon black middle-class workers.

Blacks who are employed are more likely than whites to hold blue collar jobs.

In any case, major social initiatives are not likely to be initiated by the federal government within the near future. Because of the changing social and political environment, many African Americans are advocating a greater emphasis on self-help and internal community development. In a recent study, the first sociological model of black community development was introduced: the Black Organizational Autonomy (BOA) Model (Hayward D. Horton. 1992. A Sociological Approach to Black Community Development. *Journal of the Community Development Society* 25:1–19). This model maintains that viable black communities are those that possess community-based organizations with five basic components: (1) economic autonomy; (2) internally developed and controlled data sources; (3) programs to develop and promote black female leadership; (4) programs that emphasize black history and culture; and (5) socially inclusive in leadership. The model proved successful in a case study in Little Rock, Arkansas of a church-based black community organization. At present, the model is being tested in rural black communities in Iowa and Mississippi. Plans are also underway to adapt the model to rural Hispanic communities in Texas. Whereas it is not known whether the model will eventually be applied nationwide, it has considerable potential for meeting the present and future needs of the African-American community.

The African-American community is undergoing fundamental change. Some of these changes are internal, as blacks with different levels of education and experience are differentially able to take advantage of once-denied opportunities. Some of these changes are external, as the competition for existing jobs increases at a time when government and industry are downsizing their respective labor forces. The history of African Americans provides various examples of how this community has survived challenges faced by no other group in this society. Without doubt, the present and future will continue to be filled with obstacles for African Americans. And no doubt, as in the past, our community will survive.

Occupation of Employed Civilians by Race, 1991.

(in thousands)

	Black		*White*	
Occupation	*Number*	*Percent*	*Number*	*Percent*
Managerial/Professional	1,819	18.0	26,263	31.0
Technical/Sales Administrative	2,664	26.4	25,880	30.3
Service	2,263	22.5	9,040	10.6
Precision Production	929	9.2	10,494	12.3
Operators/Fabricators	2,213	22.0	11,305	13.2
Farming, Forestry, Fishing	190	1.9	2,556	3.0
Total	10,078	100.0	85,538	100.4*

*Number exceeds one hundred due to rounding.

Source: Statistical Abstract of the United States, U.S. Dept. of Commerce, 1992, page 396.

Occupational Distribution by Sex, 1991.

(in thousands)

	Black				*White*			
	Male		*Female*		*Male*		*Female*	
Occupation	Number	Percent	Number	Percent	Number	Percent	Number	Percent
Managerial/Professional	758	15.3	1,061	20.7	14,464	30.5	11,799	31.0
Technical/Sales, Admin.	819	16.5	1,845	36.0	9,425	19.8	16,455	43.2
Service	832	16.7	1,431	27.9	3,449	7.3	5,591	14.7
Precision Production	810	16.3	199	2.3	9,640	20.3	854	2.2
Operators/Fabricators	1,566	32.0	647	12.6	8,396	17.7	2,909	7.6
Farming, Forestry, Fishing	173	3.5	17	.0**	2,109	4.4	447	1.2
Total	4,957	100.3*	5,121	99.5*	47,483	100.0	38,055	99.9*

*Number does not equal one hundred percent due to rounding.

**Number less than .1 percent.

Source: Statistical Abstract of the United States, U.S. Dept. of Commerce, 1992, page 396.

	1988			1989			1990		
	Black	*White*	*B/W*	*Black*	*White*	*B/W*	*Black*	*White*	*B/W*
All Households	$16,407	$28,781	.57	$18,083	$30,406	.59	$18,676	$31,231	.60
Family Households	$19,823	$34,222	.58	$20,911	$36,325	.58	$21,899	$37,219	.59
Married Couple families	$30,424	$36,883	.82	$30,833	$39,328	.78	$33,893	$40,433	.84
Male Householder, no wife present	$19,501	$30,689	.64	$20,044	$32,218	.62	$24,048	$32,869	.73
Female Householder, no husband present	$10,995	$18,685	59	$12,170	$20,164	.60	$12,537	$20,867	.60
Total Number of Households	10,561	79,734	—	10,486	80,163	—	10,671	80,968	—

Source: "Money Income of Households, Families and Persons in the United States; 1990," Current Population Reports: Consumer Income, Series P-60, No. 174, Table 5, Pp. 21-22, U.S. Department of Commerce.

Median Income of Households by Race, 1988–1990.

Total Money Income	*Black* Number (in thousands)	*Black* Percent	*Black* Cumulative Percent	*White* Number	*White* Percent	*White* Cumulative Percent
less than $5,000	1,500	14.1	14.1	4,901	5.2	5.2
$5,000 to $9,999	1,786	16.7	30.8	9,184	9.7	14.9
$12,000 to $14,999	1,240	11.6	42.4	8,925	9.5	24.4
$15,000 to $19,999	1,050	9.8	52.2	8,296	8.8	33.2
$20,000 to $24,999	988	9.3	61.5	8,427	8.9	42.1
$25,000 to $29,999	741	6.9	68.4	7,501	8.0	50.1
$30,000 to $34,999	695	6.5	74.9	7,363	7.8	57.9
$35,000 to $39,999	613	5.7	80.6	6,395	6.8	64.7
$40,000 to $44,999	412	3.9	84.5	5,372	5.7	70.4
$45,000 to $49,999	378	3.5	88.0	4,702	5.0	75.4
$50,000 to $54,999	293	2.8	90.8	4,088	4.3	79.7
$55,000 to $59,999	197	1.9	92.7	3,227	3.4	83.1
$60,000 to $64,999	128	1.2	93.9	2,767	2.9	86.0
$65,000 to $69,999	132	1.2	95.1	2,170	2.3	88.3
$70,000 to $74,999	113	1.1	96.2	1,809	1.9	90.2
$75,000 to $79,999	96	.9	97.1	1,555	1.7	91.9
$80,000 to $84,999	69	.7	97.8	1,204	1.3	93.2
$85,000 to $89,999	51	.5	98.3	98[illegible]	1.0	94.2
$90,000 to $94,999	44	.4	98.7	769	.8	95.0
$95,000 to $99,999	23	.2	98.9	590	.6	95.6
$100,000 and over	122	1.1	100.0	4,085	4.3	99.9*
Total number of households	10,671			94,312		
Median income		$18,676			$29,943	
Mean income		$24,814			$91,403	

Source: "Money Income of Households, Families and Persons in the United States: 1990," Current Population Reports: Consumer Income, Series P-60, No. 174, Table 5, Pp. 21-22, U.S. Department of Commerce.

Income Distribution for Black and White Households, 1990.

	Number of Persons in Household						
	One	*Two*	*Three*	*Four*	*Five*	*Six*	*Seven*
***Black**							
Median	$10,156	$20,122	$21,474	$25,683	$24,342	$26,742	$22,361
Mean	15,193	25,061	27,820	30,573	31,598	33,395	29,790
Income per household member	15,193	11,786	8,933	7,441	6,330	5,479	3,746
White							
Median	15,981	32,561	38,930	43,363	40,715	40,420	40,822
Mean	21,314	40,726	45,837	50,342	48,802	47,331	47,351
Income per household member	21,314	20,107	15,063	12,616	9,786	7,873	6,084
B/W Ratio							
Median	.64	.62	.55	.59	.60	.66	.55
Mean	.71	.62	.61	.61	.64	.71	.63
Income per household member	.71	.59	.59	.59	.65	.70	.62

Source: "Money Income of Households, Families and Persons in the United States, 1990," Current Population Reports: Consumer Income, Series P-60, No. 174, Table 9, Page 40, U.S. Department of Commerce, August 1991.

Total Money Income by Household Size for Blacks and Whites, 1990.

	Black		White		
Family Type	*Number**	*Percent*	*Number*	*Percent*	*B/W*
With & Without Children Under 18 Years					
All Families	2,193	29.3	4,622	8.1	3.6
Married Couple Families	448	12.6	2,286	5.1	2.5
Male Householder, no wife present	97	20.6	226	9.9	2.1
Female householder, no husband present	1,648	48.1	2,010	26.8	1.8
With Children Under 18 Years of Age					
All Families	1,887	37.2	3,553	12.6	3.0
Married Couple Families	301	14.3	1,572	7.1	2.0
Male householder, no wife present	73	27.3	167	16.0	1.7
Female householder, no husband present	1,513	56.1	1,814	37.9	1.5

* Number in thousands.

Source: "Poverty in the United States, 1990," Current Population Reports: Consumer Income, Series P-60, No. 175, Table 4, Pp. 21-22, U.S. Dept. of Commerce, August 1991.

Poverty Status of Families by Type of Family, 1990.

14

Entrepreneurship

14

Entrepreneurship

Pre-Civil War Entrepreneurship in the Black Community ■ Post-Civil War Entrepreneurship in the Black Community ■ Black Entrepreneurs in the Post-Civil Rights Era ■ Recent Trends ■ Notable Business Executives and Entrepreneurs

Essay by Michael D. Woodard

African Americans have a long and rich history of entrepreneurship in America; blacks have been in business since before the Civil War and continue their entrepreneurial tradition today. Segments of the African-American population have exhibited the same entrepreneurial spirit as segments of other ethnic groups who have migrated to this country. Very often, however, the history of black entrepreneurship has been either overlooked or misconstrued.

■ PRE-CIVIL WAR ENTREPRENEURSHIP IN THE BLACK COMMUNITY

As the United States began to take shape, a number of people of African origin were successful in their attempt to carve out an economic stake for themselves. Anthony Johnson, who accumulated substantial property in Jamestown, Virginia, is believed to be the first person of African descent to have become an entrepreneur in America. Jean Baptist Du Sable, a wholesaler and merchant who established the first settlement in Chicago in the early 1770s, was another pre-Civil War era entrepreneur.

Prior to the Civil War, nonetheless slavery defined the existence of most African Americans. Thus, two categories of business persons were able to develop and sustain business enterprises. The first group was composed of free African Americans, numbering approximately 60,000, who could accumulate the capital to generate business activity. They developed enterprises in almost every area of the business community, including merchandising, real estate, manufacturing, construction, transportation, and extractive industries.

The second group consisted of slaves who—as a result of thrift, ingenuity, industry, and/or the liberal paternalism of their masters—were able to engage in business activity. Although the constraints of slavery were such that even highly skilled slaves could not become entrepreneurs in the true sense of the word, slaves did, during their limited free time, sell their labor and create products to sell.

Slaves did, during their limited free time, sell their labor and create products to sell.

The fact that African-American entrepreneurship existed at all during the era of slavery is testimony to an entrepreneurial spirit and the determination of a people to achieve economic freedom even under the harshest conditions.

If it was all but impossible for slaves to engage in private enterprise, it was also hazardous for "free" blacks to do so, since they were effectively only half free. Free blacks lived under a constant fear of being labeled as "run-away" slaves and being sold into slavery. In addition, in areas where free blacks lived, laws were passed to restrict their movement and thus their economic freedom. This was one intention, for example, of the laws Virginia, Maryland, and North Carolina had passed by 1835 forbidding free blacks to carry arms without a license. The right of assembly was also denied blacks throughout the south—leaving it illegal for black civic, business, or benevolent organizations to convene. In addition to reflecting white slaveowners' fears of an African-American uprising, such legal restriction had the purpose and effect of making it difficult for free blacks to earn a living.

However, the Southern economic exploitation of blacks indirectly had a positive impact on black entrepreneurship: the development of business enterprise by African Americans in the North. In 1838, for example the *Register of Trades of Colored People* in the city of Philadelphia listed eight bakers, twenty-five blacksmiths, three brass founders, fifteen cabinet makers and carpenters, five confectioners, two caulkers, two chair bottomers, fifteen tailoring enterprises, thirty-one tanners, five weavers, and six wheelwrights.

The Philadelphia business register also listed businesses run by African-American women. Among these were eighty-one dressmakers and tailors, four dyers and scourers, two fullers, and two glass and paper makers. The ninety-eight hairdressers registered, comprising the largest trade group, operated some of the most lucrative enterprises.

Another profitable business controlled by African Americans in Philadelphia during the 1820s and 1830s was sail-making. Nineteen sail-makers were recorded in the business register of 1838. James Forster, who lived between 1766 and 1841, ran a major manufacturing firm that made sails; in 1829, Forster employed forty workers, black and white.

Although several individuals succeeded in the manufacturing trades, the business enterprise that brought prosperity to the largest number of African Americans in Philadelphia was catering. Robert Boyle, a black waiter, is believed to have developed the idea of contracting to provide formal dinners to serve in domestic entertaining. Catering quickly spread across the developing country, but it was in Philadelphia, the city of its birth, that catering was king.

Significantly, most of the businesses discussed thus far involved the craft or service trades. These were small enterprises that required only a modest capital investment and allowed African Americans to develop a niche without threatening larger white-owned businesses.

POST-CIVIL WAR ENTREPRENEURSHIP IN THE BLACK COMMUNITY

The promise of freedom and political enfranchisement held out by Lincoln's Emancipation Proclamation of 1862 was soon undermined by racist judicial rulings. In 1878, in *Hall v. DeCuir*, the United States Supreme Court ruled that a state could not prohibit segregation on a common carrier. In 1896, with the *Plessy v. Ferguson* ruling, "separate but equal" became the law of the land. Following these decisions, a pattern of rigid segregation of the races was established that remained the norm until the advent of the civil rights movement in the 1960s.

Nevertheless, even within the context of disenfranchisement and segregation, Booker T. Washington saw the possibility of securing African-American economic stability through business development. In 1900, Washington spearheaded the development of the National Negro Business League to encourage black enterprise. During the organization's first meeting, the delegates concluded that:

> a useless class is a menace and a danger to any community, and . . . when an individual produces what the world wants, whether it is a product of the hand, heart, or head, the world does not long stop to inquire what is the color of the skin of the producer. . . . [I]f every member of the race should strive to make himself the most indispensable man in his community, and to be successful in business, however humble that business might be, he would contribute much toward soothing the pathway of his own and future generations. (John Sibly Butler. 1991. *Entrepreneurship and Self-Help Among Black Americans*. New York: State University of New York Press, pp. 67–68.)

During the early 1900s, although services continued to be the cornerstone of the black business community, blacks found it easier to raise capital and ventured into more entrepreneurial endeavors.

Booker T. Washington

In 1905, for example, Madame C. J. Walker developed a hair care system that gave dry hair a soft texture; millions of women, both black and white, became customers for Madame Walker's products. Before her death in 1919, Madame Walker had more than 2000 agents marketing her ever expanding line of products, which made her America's first black female millionaire.

Madame C. J. Walker

Durham, North Carolina: A Special Case

Turn of the century Durham, North Carolina represented a special case of enterprise and economic resilience. In publications of the time, Durham was referred to as "The Wall Street of Negro America." By the late 1940s, more than 150 businesses owned by African Americans flourished in Durham. Among these businesses were traditional service providers, such as cafes, moviehouses, barber shops, boarding houses, pressing shops, grocery stores, and funeral parlors. What distinguished Durham, however, was the presence of large black businesses.

One of the largest and most successful black businesses in the nation was the North Carolina Mutual Life Insurance Company. Surrounding the North Carolina Mutual Life Insurance Company were the Banker's Fire Insurance Company, the Mutual Building and Loan Association, the Union Insurance and Realty Company, the Durham Realty and Insurance Company, the People's Building and Loan Association, the Royal Knights Savings and Loan Association, T. P. Parham and Associates (a brokerage corporation), and the Mortgage Company of Durham (Butler, *Entrepreneurship and Self-Help Among Black Americans*, p. 175). Such businesses established a "city of enterprise" for African Americans.

Although Durham was a success, external economic pressure and racial hostility made it impossible for blacks, on a large scale, to develop stores that could compete in the larger economy. As a result of Jim Crow laws and segregation, most black-owned businesses were forced to limit their market to their own community. A partial exception was the Durham textile mill, at the time the only hosiery mill in the world owned and operated by African Americans. It operated eighteen knitting machines and did business in the open market; their salesman, who traveled mostly in North Carolina, Indiana, Georgia, South Carolina and Alabama, were white. This manufacturing firm was exceptional in the sense that it was perhaps the first large-scale black-owned enterprise to hire whites.

Nevertheless, race relations in Durham during this time were such that the most successful retail and service businesses tended to generate a white clientele. For example, in 1940 Smith's Fish Market, established by the former postal clerk Freeman M. Smith, supplied Durham's largest white-operated hotel, the Washington Duke. Smith was also the major supplier for smaller white and black-owned businesses. In 1940, Smith grossed more than $90,000 and opened four other outlets throughout the city. Similarly, Rowland and Mitchell established a tailor shop in 1930 where they did work for "exclusive whites and department stores." It was estimated that 80 percent of their customers were white. Among other successful businesses was Thomas Baily & Sons, a meat and grocery store that opened in 1919 and grossed $80,000 a year by 1940. The Home Modernization and Supply Company, founded in 1938 by the brothers U. M. and R. S. George, grossed more than $100,000 in constructing 500 homes in the Durham area and employed thirty-five people by 1948.

Many people came to Durham to learn the beautician trade by attending the commercial hair care school established by Jacqueline DeShazor. Beginning in three rooms, she expanded in 1945 to thirty-six rooms in a three-story building, which she purchased for $42,500.

African-American businesses were so stable and looked so promising for the future that, in 1924, Durham was chosen as the location for the headquarters of the National Negro Finance Corporation, which was capitalized at $1 million. The organization was started to provide working capital to individuals, firms, and corporations in all parts of the country. Durham, from the turn of the century until the 1950s, remained unrivaled as the black business capital of America.

Present-Day Durham

Today, 150 or so black entrepreneurs and professionals are still held together by the Durham Business and Professional Chain, an organization founded fifty-two years ago. It would be difficult, however, to replicate the entrepreneurial excitement that existed in Durham between 1900 and 1950. Indeed, scholars have noted that grass roots entrepreneurship tends to develop quickly by groups who newly enter the economy of a country, as did African Americans after the abolition of slavery. However, from generation to generation, there is typically a decrease in the number or rate of entrepreneurs. In the case of African Americans, a full blown civil rights movement was required to create another surge in the entrepreneurial spirit.

■ BLACK ENTREPRENEURS IN THE POST-CIVIL RIGHTS ERA

The civil rights movement prompted the development of legislation and a number of government agencies to ensure the social, political, and economic rights of African Americans. Perhaps the greatest boost to black entrepreneurship came in 1967 with the establishment of the Small Business Administration (SBA) Section 8 (a) program. Under Section 8 (a) of the Small Business Act Amendments (Pub.L. 90-104), the SBA is authorized to enter into contract with federal agencies on behalf of small and disad-

Freedom National Bank, Harlem's first black commerical bank, was founded in 1965.

vantaged businesses. Entry into the 8 (a) program is contingent upon SBA approval of the business plan prepared by prospective firms. The total dollar value of contracts processed through Section 8 (a) has grown from $8.9 million in 1969 to $2.7 billion in 1985. Through the program, many small and black-owned businesses have been able to stabilize and grow.

Another product of the civil rights movement has been the 1977 Public Works Employment Act (Pub.L. 95-28). Supplementing the SBA 8 (a) Program, the Public Works Act requires that all general contractors bidding for public works projects allocate at least 10 percent of their contracts to minority subcontractors.

During the early 1980s, the SBA Section 8 (a) program was criticized because less than 5 percent of the firms have achieved open-market competitiveness, which implies that the program is in effect assisting the marginal entrepreneur, as opposed to the promising self-employed minority business-person.

The fundamental concept of set-aside minority assistance programs was called into question during the height of the Reagan-Bush era. In 1989, the landmark United States Supreme Court ruling in *City of Richmond v. Croson* struck down as unconstitutional under the Fourteenth Amendment a city ordinance of Richmond, Virginia requiring that 30 percent of each public construction contract to be set aside for minority businesses. The Supreme Court did make a distinction between local/state and federally enacted business development programs, holding that the United States Congress has far more authority than the states in formulating remedial legislation.

The *Croson* decision has had a devastating impact on minority businesses. In Richmond, during the month of July 1987 when a lower court first ruled against the city's set-aside program, 40 percent of the city's total construction dollars were allocated for products and services provided by minority-owned construction firms. Immediately following the court's decision, the minority businesses' share of contracts fell to 15 percent, dropping to less than 3 percent by the end of 1988. In Tampa, Florida the number of contracts awarded to black-owned companies decreased 99 percent, and contracts with Latino-owned firms fell 50 percent, after *Croson*. Such dramatic decreases in contracts awarded to minority businesses occurred throughout the country. More than thirty-three states and political subdivisions have taken steps to dismantle their racial/ethnic set-aside programs; more than seventy jurisdictions are conducting studies and/or holding hearings to review and evaluate their programs in light of *Croson*.

Growth Industries

Historically, African-American businesses have been restricted to the narrow range of service enterprises. They have tended to establish businesses that require relatively limited capital and technical expertise—personal services, and small-scale retailing. These firms have had to rely heavily on the African-American community as their market for goods and services.

Recent business initiation trends indicate increasing diversity among black businesses. An examination of the nation's largest black owned corporations reveals considerable diversity.

The location of corporate headquarters in urban areas has provided increased business opportunity for black business service enterprises. Large cities have become areas where administrative and service functions are the dominant economic activities. The growth in corporate and government administration in central city business districts has created a need for complementary advertising, accounting, computer, legal, temporary secretarial, and maintenance business services. Employment in such business firms owned by African Americans grew by 224 percent between 1972 and 1987; the number of firms increased nearly five times, and gross receipts grew by 700 percent.

■ RECENT TRENDS

Since 1962, the Bureau of the Census has published a survey of minority-owned businesses every five years. The most recent survey, from 1987, indicates that African Americans owned 427,165 businesses, a 37.6 percent increase from 308,260 in 1982, and nearly an 85 percent increase from the 1977 total of 231,203. The 37.6 percent increase between 1982 and 1987 is greater than the 26.2 percent increase for all United States forms for this time period. These numbers indicate that African Americans are starting business enterprises at a greater rate than Americans in general.

Gross Receipts and Legal Organization

According to the Bureau of the Census, the overwhelming majority of black-owned firms, 94.4 percent or 400,339 firms, operated as sole proprietorships in 1987; this is consistent with 1982 and 1977 statistics in which 95 percent and 94.3 percent of black-owned firms were sole proprietorships. Partnerships represented 2.7 percent or 11,261 firms in 1987, and 3.3 percent in 1982. Subchapter S corporations (corporations with fewer than thirty-five stockholders, which are not taxed as regular corporations, but provide legal liability protection to shareholders) accounted for 3 percent of the total number of black-owned firms in 1987.

By 1987, the total gross receipts (the total amount of money received before deductions for expenses and taxes) for African-American businesses also increased. From 1982 to 1987, receipts increased by 105 percent, from $9.6 billion to $19.8 billion. However, gross receipts were unevenly distributed among firms in 1987. Only 0.5 percent of the total number of black-owned firms grossed $1 million or more; these firms accounted for 37 percent of the total gross receipts. Slightly more than a third (35 percent) of the firms had gross receipts of less than $5,000; the average annual gross receipt for a black-owned business was approximately $47,000.

Historically, black-owned firms have been concentrated in a narrow range of service businesses, including small restaurants.

The growth in corporate and government administration has created a need for complementary advertising, accounting, computer, legal, and temporary secretarial services.

There is a direct correlation between the organizational structure of black businesses and receipts. Sole proprietorships earned relatively less money. Sole proprietorship accounted for 50.9 percent of gross receipts in 1987, compared to 68.4 percent in 1982 and 55.7 percent in 1977. Partnerships accounted for 10 percent of the gross receipts in 1987, down from 13.7 percent in 1982.

In contrast, while Subchapter S corporations accounted for only 3 percent of the total number of firms, such corporations accounted for 39.2 percent of the gross receipts. This is up from 1.7 percent of the firms and 17.2 percent of the gross receipts in 1982. Thus, the real increase in gross receipts among black-owned businesses has occurred among subchapter S corporations.

Geographic Distribution of Black Businesses

The geographic concentration of black firms coincides with the African-American population concentration. California had the greatest number of black-owned firms in 1987, with 47,728. California firms' gross receipts were $2.4 billion. New York was second with 36,289 firms and $1.9 billion in gross receipts. Slightly less than 44 percent of black-owned firms and 44.7 percent of gross receipts (185,563 firms and $8.8 billion in gross receipts) were concentrated in California, New York, Texas, Florida, Georgia, and Illinois.

The next tier of states includes Michigan with 13,708 firms that grossed $701.3 million; Maryland, with 21,678 businesses and nearly $720 million in receipts; and Pennsylvania, with 11,728 businesses that grossed $747.5 million.

The District of Columbia had the greatest share of firms owned by African Americans, with 28.3 percent of the firms and 6.3 percent of the gross receipts in that city. Black-owned firms had the smallest share of business in Montana, with 0.1 percent of the firms and gross receipts.

Size of Firm and Industry Characteristics

Only a modest portion of firms owned by African Americans have paid employees; in 1987, 83.3 percent of black-owned firms had no paid employees. The 16.7 percent of black-owned firms with paid employees, however, accounted for 71.5 percent of the gross receipts. There were 189 firms with 100 or more employees, which accounted for $2 billion in gross receipts, or 14.2 percent of the total receipts of black-owned employer firms.

Historically, black-owned firms have been concentrated in a narrow range of service businesses including small restaurants, cleaning establishments, funeral parlors, shoe shops, hair salons, and gas stations. The trend, by and large, continued throughout the late 1980s. Service industries accounted for 49 percent of all black-owned firms, and 31 percent of the gross receipts. Retail trade comprised the next greatest concentration of black-owned firms, with 15.6 percent of the firms and 29.8 percent of the gross receipts. The industry that grossed the greatest total receipts in 1987 was automobile dealers and service stations, with nearly $2.2 billion in earnings.

NOTABLE BUSINESS EXECUTIVES AND ENTREPRENEURS

Wally Amos (1937–)
Entrepreneur

Born Wallace Amos, Jr. in Tallahassee, Florida in 1937, he achieved success as the first African-American talent agent for the William Morris Agency. Starting there as a mail clerk he quickly worked his way up to executive vice-president. While there he "discovered" Simon & Garfunkel for the agency and has been the agent for such well known acts and entertainers as the Supremes, the Temptations, Marvin Gaye, Dionne Warwick and Patti Labelle.

In 1975 Amos founded Famous Amos Chocolate Chip Cookies. Based on his Aunt Della's recipe, the cookies became a nationwide success as they spread across the

Wally Amos

country from his original store on Sunset Boulevard in Los Angeles. By 1980 Amos was selling 5 million dollars worth of cookies each year and his operation had expanded to include a large production facility in Nutley, New Jersey. Amos' success and expansion was enhanced by the backing of such well known entertainers as Bill Cosby and Helen Reddy. In 1985 Amos became vice-chairman of the company.

Amos had previously spent four years in the United States Air Force where he served as a cook and radio technician. He has a high school diploma and Chef's Hat from the New York Food Trades High School. Amos has donated personal items to the Business Americana Collection at the Smithsonian's Collection of Advertising History and has received the Excellence award from President Ronald Reagan. Amos' company is presently headquartered in San Francisco.

Dave Bing

Dave Bing (1943–)
Business Executive, Former Professional Basketball Player

Bing was born November 29, 1943 in Washington, DC, where he played basketball at Springarn High School. He was named to play on a national All-Star team and was voted most valuable player on the tour. Bing attended Syracuse University on a basketball scholarship graduating in 1966 with a B.A. in economics. He was the second overall pick in the 1966 National Basketball Association draft and was chosen by the Detroit Pistons.

During his first season he was the league's top rookie and the league's high scorer his second year. In the 1974–1975 season Bing played for the Washington, DC Bullets and in the 1977–1978 season he was with the Boston Celtics. Bing was voted the league's Most Valuable Player in 1976 and played in seven NBA All-Star games. The Professional Basketball Writer's Association of America gave him their Citizenship Award in 1977. In 1989 he was elected to the Naismith Memorial Basketball Hall of Fame.

After being associated with management programs at the National Bank of Detroit, Chrysler Corporation and Paragon Steel, Bing formed Bing Steel Inc. in Detroit, a steel supplier to the automobile industry.

Earl G. Graves (1935–)
Publisher and Media Executive

See Media.

George E. Johnson (1927–)
Business Executive

Johnson was born in Richton, Mississippi on June 16, 1927. He attended Wendell Phillips High School in Chicago then went to work as a production chemist for a firm that produced cosmetic products for African Americans. While there he developed a hair straightener for men and began marketing it himself in 1954. By 1957 he had formed Johnson Products and was selling products under the Ultra-Sheen label. The company prospered and by 1971 its stock was being traded on the American Stock Exchange. Johnson Products was the first African-American owned company to trade on a major stock exchange. In June 1993 Joan B. Johnson, chair and CEO of Johnson Products, announced the sale of the company.

Johnson has served as a director of the Independence Bank of Chicago, the United States Postal Service and the Commonwealth Edison Co. Johnson also is responsible for the George E. Johnson Foundation which funds charitable and educational programs for African Americans.

Johnson has received the Abraham Lincoln Center's Humanitarian Service Award (1972), *Ebony* magazine's Black Achievement Award (1978) and the public service award presented by the Harvard Club of Chicago. He has also been awarded the Horatio Alger Award (1980) and the Babson Medal (1983).

Johnson has received honorary degrees from many institutions of learning including Chicago State University (1977), Fisk University (1977) and the Tuskegee Institute (1978).

George E. Johnson

John H. Johnson (1918–)
Publisher, Media Executive

See Media.

Reginald F. Lewis (1942–1993)
Business Executive

Lewis was born December 7, 1942 in Baltimore, Maryland. He received an A.B. from Virginia State College in 1965 and a law degree from Harvard Law School in 1968. He first worked with the firm of Paul, Weiss, Rifkind, Wharton and Garrison until 1970. He was a partner in Murphy, Thorpe & Lewis, the first African-American law firm on Wall Street until 1973. Between 1973 and 1989 Lewis was in private practice as a corporate lawyer. In 1989 he became president and CEO of TLC Beatrice International Holdings Inc. With TLC's leveraged acquisition of the Beatrice International Food Co. Lewis became the head of the largest African-American owned business in the United States. TLC Beatrice had revenues of $1.54 billion in 1992.

Lewis was a member of the American and National Bar Associations and the National

Reginald Lewis

Conference of Black Lawyers. He was on the board of directors of the New York City Off-Track Betting Corp., the Central Park Conservance, the NAACP Legal Defense Fund and WNET-Channel 13, the public television station in New York. He was the recipient of the Distinguished Service Award presented by the American Association of MESBIC (1974) and the Black Enterprise Achievement Award for the Professions.

Lewis died unexpectedly January 19, 1993 in New York.

James B. Llewellyn (1927–)
Business Executive

Llewellyn was born July 16, 1927 in New York City and earned a B.S. from City College of New York. He attended Columbia University's Graduate School of Business and New York University's School of Public Administration before receiving a degree from New York Law School.

Before attending law school Llewellyn was the proprietor of a retail liquor store. While attending law school he was a student assistant in the District Attorney's Office for New York County from 1958 to 1960. After graduating he practiced law as part of Evans, Berger & Llewellyn. Between 1964 and 1969 he worked in a variety of professional positions for various governmental agencies including the Housing Division of the Housing and Re-Development Board (1964–1965), Small Business Development Corporation (1965) and the Small Business Administration (1965–1969).

In 1969 as part of a syndicate buyout he became president of Fedco Food Stores of New York. By 1975 the company had grown

J. Bruce Llewellyn

from 11 to 14 stores and had annual revenues of $30 million and 450 employees.

Llewellyn has served on the boards of the City College of New York and its Graduate Center, American Can Co., American Capital Management Research and the Freedom National Bank. He has belonged to the Harlem Lawyers Association, the New York Interracial Council for Business Opportunity and the New York Urban Coalition and its Venture Capital Corporation.

Llewellyn has honorary doctorates from Wagner College, City University of New York and Atlanta University. He spent four years in the United States Army Corps of Engineers from 1944 to 1948. He is currently CEO of Queen City Broadcasting Inc.

Henry G. Parks (1916–   )
Entrepreneur, Business Executive

Parks was born September 20, 1916 in Atlanta, Georgia. He received a B.S. from Ohio State University and did graduate work there in marketing.

After graduating Parks worked at the Resident War Production Training Center in Wilberforce, Ohio where he was associated with Dr. Mary McLeod Bethune. In 1939 he was a national sales representative for the Pabst Brewing Co. In addition he has been involved in a variety of enterprises including theatrical bookings in New York City, a failed attempt at marketing a beverage with Joe Louis, the former heavyweight boxing champion (now deceased), real estate, drug store operations and cement block production, mostly in Baltimore, Maryland.

Parks ultimately bought into Crayton's Southern Sausage Company of Cleveland, Ohio. After becoming familiar with the meat packing industry he sold his interest in the company for a profit. In 1951 he started H.G. Parks Inc., a sausage packer and distributor with the aid of a group of investors. By 1971 the company had annual revenues of $10.4 million dollars and was distributing its products to over 12,000 east coast stores.

Parks has also been vice-president of the Chamber of Commerce of Metropolitan Baltimore, served on the board of directors of Magnavox, held a seat on the Baltimore City Council and has an interest in Tuesday Publications.

Naomi R. Sims (1949–   )
Business Executive, Model

Sims was born March 30, 1949 in Oxford, Mississippi. She attended New York University (where she studied psychology) and the Fashion Institute of Technology, both on scholarships.

Naomi Sims

Sims was a fashion model with the Ford Agency in New York from 1970 to 1973. She was the first African-American woman to be a high fashion model and the first to appear in a television commercial. She also appeared on the cover of *Life* Magazine.

In 1970 Sims also started lecturing and writing fashion and beauty articles on a freelance basis. In 1973 she co-developed a new fiber for her line of wigs and founded the Naomi Sims Collection which by 1977 had annual revenues of $4 million. Sims has also written a number of books including, *All About Health and Beauty for the Black Woman* (1975), *How to Be a Top Model* (1979), *All About Hair Care for the Black Woman* (1982), and *All About Success for the Black Woman.*

In 1969 and 1970 Sims was voted Model of the Year by International Mannequins and won the *Ladies Home Journal* Women of Achievement Award. For her work with underprivileged children in Bedford-Stuyvesant she also won an award from the New York City Board of Education. In 1977 Sims was voted into the Modeling Hall of Fame by International Mannequins and made the International Best Dressed List 1971–73, 1976–77. Sims has also received recognition for her fund raising efforts for sickle cell anemia and cancer research. She belongs to the NAACP and works closely with drug rehabilitation programs.

She is currently with Naomi Sims Beauty Products Limited in New York City.

Percy E. Sutton (1920–)
Business Executive, Attorney

Sutton was born November 24, 1920 in San Antonio, Texas. He graduated from the Phillis Wheatley High School and attended a number of colleges including Prairie View College, Tuskegee Institute and the Hampton Institute. His education was interrupted by World War II when Sutton enlisted in the United States Army Air Corps. He was promoted to captain and served as a combat intelligence officer in the Italian and Mediterranean Theaters. He was decorated with Combat Stars for his service.

Percy Sutton

After his discharge Sutton attended law school on the G.I. Bill, first at Columbia University in New York, and then Brooklyn Law School where he received an LL.B. in 1950. During the Korean conflict Sutton re-enlisted in the USAF and served as an intelligence officer and a trial judge advocate.

Returning to civilian life he opened a law office in Harlem with his brother and another attorney. In 1964 he was elected to the New York State Assembly where he served until 1966. In 1966 he was appointed and later elected to the office of president of the

Borough of Manhattan, a post he held until 1977.

Sutton then founded the Inner City Broadcasting Corporation from which he is now retired.

Sutton has been a civil rights advocate both as an attorney and a politician. He was a national director of the Urban League and a past president of the New York branch of the NAACP. He was voted Assemblyman of the Year by the Intercollegiate Legislative Assembly in 1966. Sutton has also served as a director of the Museum of the City of New York and the American Museum of Natural History.

Madame C. J. Walker (1867–1919)
Entrepreneur

Walker was born Sarah Breedlove near Delta, Louisiana in 1867. She was orphaned as a child, raised by a sister in Vicksburg, Mississippi, married at the age of fourteen and widowed in 1887 at the age of twenty.

Walker moved with her daughter to St. Louis where she earned a living by taking in laundry and sewing. By 1905 she had become interested in hair care products for African-American women and began working on a hot comb and her "Wonderful Hair Grower." In 1906 she moved to Denver and with $1.50 in her pocket started a hair preparations company. She soon married C. J. Walker, a newspaperman who taught her the fundamentals of advertising and mail order promotion. In 1908 she moved with her daughter to Pittsburgh where she founded a beauty school which trained cosmetologists in the use of her products.

In 1910 with a more central location in mind she moved to Indianapolis, Indiana where she established a laboratory and factory and developed a nationwide network of 5000 sales agents, mostly African-American women.

Her business prospered and Walker became very wealthy. She had a townhouse in Harlem and a custom built mansion on the Hudson River near Irvington, New York. She died in New York on May 25, 1919.

Walker was a strong believer in self-reliance and education. She was proud of her accomplishments, especially of providing employment for thousands of African Americans who might otherwise have less meaningful jobs. Walker was also a genius at marketing, promotion, and mail order sales. Beneficiaries of her estate included Mary McLeod Bethune's school in Daytona, Florida and other African-American schools, the NAACP and the Frederick Douglass home restoration project in Florida.

Maggie Lena Walker (1867–1934)
Banker

Walker was born on or around July 15, 1867 in Richmond, Virginia. She was the daughter of Elizabeth Draper, a former slave, and Eccles Cuthbert, a New York journalist of Irish extraction.

Walker attended Richmond public schools including Armstrong Normal School which functioned as a high school. After graduating in 1883 she taught in the Richmond schools for three years before marrying building contractor Armstead Walker in 1886.

While she had been in school, Walker joined the Grand United Order of Saint Luke, a mutual aid society that served as an insurance underwriter for African Americans. Walker became active in the organization and held a number of lesser positions before becoming the Right Worthy Grand Secretary in 1899. She soon changed the name of the organization to the Independent

Maggie L. Walker

Order of Saint Luke and moved its headquarters to Richmond.

In 1903 she became the head of the Saint Luke Penny Bank and the first woman in the United States to hold such a position. Although legally separate, the bank had a close financial association with the Independent Order of Saint Luke. The bank later became the Saint Luke Bank and Trust Company and finally the Consolidated Bank and Trust Company.

By 1924 under Walker's guidance, the Order had a membership of 100,000, a new headquarters building, over 200 employees and its own newspaper—the *Saint Luke Herald*.

Walker was active in many other organizations including the National Association of Colored Women, the Virginia Federation of Colored Women's Clubs and its Industrial School for Colored Girls. In 1912 she founded the Richmond Council of Colored Women and was a founding member of the Negro Organization Society, a blanket association for African-American clubs and organizations.

She was a board member of the NAACP from 1923 to 1934 and the recipient of an honorary degree from Virginia Union University. In 1927 she received the Harmon Award for Distinguished Achievement. Walker died December 15, 1934.

	Company/Location	Chief Executive	Year Started	Assets*	Capital*	Deposits*
1	Carver Federal Savings Bank, New York, NY	Richard T. Greene	1948	320.862	13.741	252.684
2	Independence Federal Savings Bank, Washington, DC	William B. Fitzgerald	1968	239.223	12.852	181.708
3	Seaway National Bank of Chicago, Chicago, IL	Walter E. Grady	1965	202.093	14.136	168.076
4	Industrial Bank of Washington, Washington, DC	B. Doyle Mitchell Jr.	1934	186.808	12.299	173.807
5	Family Savings Bank, FSB, Los Angeles, CA	Wayne-Kent Bradshaw	1948	140.113	7.279	114.806
6	Independence Bank of Chicago, Chicago, IL	Alvin J. Boutte	1964	137.278	10.593	121.726
7	Citizens Trust Bank, Atlanta, GA	William L. Gibbs	1921	128.152	8.543	117.401
8	Drexel National Bank, Chicago, IL	Alvin J. Boutte	1989	127.754	8.463	118.482
9	First Texas Bank, Dallas, TX	William E. Stahnke	1975	110.314	9.672	99.709
10	Mechanics and Farmers Bank, Durham, NC	Julia W. Taylor	1908	107.154	11.156	94.584
11	Illinois Service/Federal S&L Assn. of Chicago, Chicago, IL	Thelma J. Smith	1934	104.347	5.940	97.027
12	Broadway Federal Savings and Loan Assn., Los Angeles, CA	Paul C. Hudson	1946	97.784	4.345	91.976
13	Consolidated Bank and Trust Co., Richmond, VA	Vernard W. Henley	1903	94.495	5.550	88.000
14	Liberty Bank and Trust Co., New Orleans, LA	Alden J. McDonald Jr.	1972	89.977	5.746	82.070
15	Boston Bank of Commerce, Boston, MA	Ronald A. Homer	1982	85.636	4.447	75.402
16	First Independence National Bank of Detroit, Detroit, MI	Richard W. Shealey	1970	81.480	3.306	73.900
17	Citizens Federal Savings Bank, Birmingham, AL	Bunny Stokes Jr.	1957	76.745	6.156	69.199
18	Founders National Bank of Los Angeles, Los Angeles, CA	John P. Kelly Jr.	1991	74.201	5.201	61.725
19	Tri-State Bank of Memphis, Memphis, TN	Jesse H. Turner Jr.	1946	73.836	7.829	65.307
20	City National Bank of New Jersey, Newark, NJ	Louis Prezeau	1973	61.911	3.356	57.853
21	The Harbor Bank of Maryland, Baltimore, MD	Joseph Haskins Jr.	1982	56.575	4.046	52.037
22	Mutual Community Savings Bank, SSB, Durham, NC	Ferdinand V. Allison Jr.	1921	47.174	4.125	42.053
23	North Milwaukee State Bank, Milwaukee, WI	James Jackson	1971	36.908	2.279	34.497
24	First Tuskegee Bank, Tuskegee, AL	James W. Wright	1894	36.424	3.244	25.000
25	Mutual Federal Savings & Loan Assn. of Atlanta, Atlanta, GA	Hamilton Glover	1925	35.912	2.244	31.618

* In millions of dollars. As of December 31, 1992.

Largest Financial Companies

	Company/Location	Chief Executive	Year Started	Assets	Statutory Reserves*	Insurance Premium in Force*	Income*
1	North Carolina Mutual Life Insurance Co., Durham, NC	Bert Collins	1899	220.133	134.820	9,406.671	55.091
2	Atlanta Life Insurance Co., Atlanta, GA	Jesse Hill Jr.	1905	163.093	123.294	3,223.000	25.672
3	Golden State Mutual Life Insurance Co. Los Angeles, CA	Larkin Teasley	1925	105.171	73.706	5,855.082	15.177
4	Universal Life Insurance Co. Memphis, TN	Gerald P. Howell	1923	63.970	56.061	760.873	21.644
5	Chicago Metropolitan Assurance Co. Chicago, IL	Anderson M. Schweich	1927	58.511	35.778	2,664.238	17.856
6	Booker T. Washington Insurance Co. Birmingham, AL	Louis J. Willie	1932	40.986	33.543	945.332	10.965
7	Protective Industrial Ins. Co. of Alabama Inc. Birmingham, AL	Paul E. Harris	1923	14.637	10.286	72.622	3.102
8	Golden Circle Life Insurance Co. Brownsville, TN	William D. Rawls Sr.	1958	9.072	4.125	23.632	1.554
9	Winnfield Life Insurance Co. Natchitoches, LA	Ben D. Johnson	1936	8.173	6.840	50.643	1.734
10	Williams-Progressive Life & Accident Insurance Co. Opelousas, LA	Borel C. Dauphin	1947	5.892	4.843	35.791	1.283
11	Wright Mutual Insurance Co. Detroit, MI	Wardell C. Croft	1942	4.686	1.133	39.477	1.088
12	Reliable Life Insurance Co. Monroe, LA	Joseph H. Miller Jr.	1940	4.500	3.631	30.883	1.456
13	Gertrude Geddes Willis Life Insurance Co. New Orleans, LA	Joseph O. Misshore Jr.	1941	4.421	3.885	40.500	1.156
14	Benevolent Life Insurance Co. Inc. Shreveport, LA	Granville L. Smith	1934	3.782	1.977	16.547	0.643
15	Majestic Life Insurance Co. New Orleans, LA	Cecilia Roberts	1947	3.089	0.885	9.989	0.414

*In millions of dollars. As of December 31, 1992.

Largest Insurance Companies

	Company/Location	Chief Executive	Year Started	Staff	Type of Business	Sales*
1	TLC Beatrice International Holdings Inc., New York, NY	Jean S. Fugett Jr.	1987	5,000	Food processor/distributor	1,665.000
2	Johnson Publishing Co. Inc., Chicago, IL	John H. Johnson	1942	2,785	Media; cosmetics/hair care	274.197
3	Philadelphia Coca-Cola Bottling Co. Inc., Phil., PA	J. Bruce Llewellyn	1985	1,000	Soft-drink bottler	266.000
4	H.J. Russell & Co., Atlanta, GA	Herman J. Russell	1952	825	Construction; food services	145.610
5	The Anderson-Dubose Co., Solon, OH	Warren Anderson	1991	80	Food distributor	110.000
6	RMS Technologies Inc., Marlton, NJ	David W. Huggins	1977	1,176	Computer & technical services	103.300
7	Gold Line Refining Ltd., Houston, TX	Earl Thomas	1990	51	Oil refining	91.880
8	Soft Sheen Products Inc., Chicago, IL	Edward G. Gardner	1964	547	Hair care products	91.700
9	Garden State Cable TV, Cherry Hill, NJ	J. Bruce Llewellyn	1989	300	Cable TV operator	91.000
10	Threads 4 Life Corp., Los Angeles, CA	Carl Jones	1990	250	Apparel manufacturer	89.000
11	Barden Communications Inc., Detrtoit, MI	Don H. Barden	1981	328	Communications; real estate	78.600
12	The Bing Group Detroit, MI	David Bing	1980	210	Steel processing	77.634
13	Burrel Communications Group, Chicago, IL	Thomas J. Burrell	1971	115	Advertising; public relations	77.007
14	Unworld Group Inc., New York, NY	Byron E. Lewis	1969	85	Advertising	72.419
15	Pulsar Systems Inc., New Castle, DE	William W. Davis Sr.	1982	65	Systems integration	67.000
16	Stop Shop and Save, Baltimore, MD	Henry T. Baines Sr.	1978	600	Supermarkets	66.000
17	Black Entertainment Television Holdings, Washington, DC	Robert Johnson	1980	328	Media	61.655
18	Mays Chemical Co. Inc., Indianapolis, IN	William G. Mays	1980	75	Industrial chemicals	60.800
19	Essence Communications Inc., New York, NY	Edward Lewis	1969	87	Media	56.345
20	Community Foods Inc., Baltimore, MD	Oscar A. Smith Jr.	1970	400	Supermarkets	47.500
21	Technology Applications Inc., Alexandria, VA	James I. Chatman	1977	525	Systems integration	46.500
22	Surface Protection Industries Inc., Los Angeles, CA	Robert C. Davidson Jr.	1978	200	Paint & specialty coatings	46.200
23	Johnson Products Co. Inc., Chicago, IL	Joan B. Johnson	1954	215	Hair & personal care products	46.000
23	Luster Products Co., Chicago, IL	Jory Luster	1957	315	Hair care products	46.000
25	The Maxima Corp., Lanham, MD	Joshua I. Smith	1978	752	Systems engineering	45.098
26	Wesley Industries Inc., Fllint, MI	Delbert W. Mullens	1983	395	Industrial coatings	45.000
27	Pepsi-Cola of Washington, DC, L.P, Washington, DC	Earl G. Graves	1990	138	Soft-drink distributor	43.869
28	Integrated Systems Analysts Inc., Arlington, VA	C. Michael Gooden	1980	595	Systems engineering	43.600
29	Granite Broadcasting Corp., New York, NY	W. Don Cornwell	1988	364	Media	43.108
30	The Mingo Group, New York, NY	Samuel J. Chisholm	1977	40	Advertising & public relations	42.733
31	Crest Computer Supply, Skokie, IL	Gale Sayers	1984	60	Computer hardware & software	42.000
32	Beauchamp Distributing Co., Compton, CA	Patrick L. Beauchamp	1971	100	Beverage distributor	40.200
33	Rush Communications, New York, NY	Russell Simmons	1990	65	Music publishing; media	40.000
34	Grimes Oil Co. Inc., Boston, MA	Calvin M. Grimes	1940	18	Petroleum products	38.700
35	Westside Distributors, South Gatae, CA	Edison R. Lara Sr.	1974	115	Beer & snack foods	37.131
36	Pro-Line Corp., Dallas, TX	Comer J. Cottrell Jr.	1970	236	Hair care products	36.874
37	Thacker Engineering Inc., Atlanta, GA	Floyd Thacker	1970	140	Construction; engineering	36.500
38	Calhoun Enterprises, Montgomery, AL	Greg Calhoun	1984	578	Supermarkets	36.479
39	The Gourmet Cos., Atlanta, GA	Nathaniel R. Goldston III	1975	813	Food services	36.200
40	Capsonic Group, Division of Gabriel Inc., Elgin, IL	Jim Liautaud	1968	232	Electrical components	36.000
40	Trumark Inc., Lansing, MI	Carlton L. Guthrie	1985	300	Metal stamping; welding	35.300
43	Network Solutions Inc., Herndon, VA	Emmit J. McHenry	1979	380	Systems integration	35.000
44	Am-Pro Protective Agency Inc., Columbia, SC	John E. Brown	1982	1,082	Security guard services	32.127
45	Metters Industries Inc., McLean, VA	Samuel Metters	1981	494	Systems engineering	31.597
46	Input Output Computer Services Inc., Waltham, MA	Thomas A. Farrington	1969	200	Computer software	31.000
47	Advantage Enterprises Inc., Toledo, OH	Levi Cook Jr.	1980	250	Project integrator	30.134
48	Automated Sciences Group Inc., Silver Spring, MD	Arthur Holmes Jr.	1974	300	Sensor technologies	30.000
48	Dudley Products Inc., Greensboro, NC	Joe Louis Dudley Sr.	1968	501	Beauty products	30.000

Largest Industrial/Service Companies

	Company/Location	Chief Executive	Year Started	Staff	Type of Business	Sales*
50	Brooks Sausage Co. Inc., Kenosha, WI	Frank B. Brooks	1985	148	Sausage manufacturer	29.000
51	Inner City Broadcasting Corp., New York, NY	Pierre Sutton	1972	200	Media	28.000
51	Yancy Minerals, Woodbridge, CT	Earl Yancy	1977	8	Industrial metals & minerals	28.000
53	Cimarron Express, Inc., Genoa, OH	Glenn G. Grady	1984	85	Interstate trucking	27.773
54	Queen City Broadcasting Inc., Buffalo NY	J. Bruce Llewellyn	1985	130	Media	26.000
55	Premium Distributors Inc. of Washington, DC,	Henry Neloms	1984	75	Beer distributor	26.000
55	Integrated Steel Inc., Detroit, MI	Geralda L. Dodd	1990	305	Automotive stamping	26.000
57	African Development Public Invest. Corp., Hollywood, CA	Dick Griffey	1985	12	African commodities	25.500
58	Restoration Supermarket Corp., Brooklyn, NY	Roderick B. Mitchell	1977	178	Supermarkets & drugstores	25.457
59	Navcom Systems Inc., Manassas, VA	Elijah "Zeke" Jackson	1986	139	Electronic engineering	25.000
60	Lockhart & Pettus, New York, NY	Keith E. Lockhart	1977	32	Advertising	24.893
61	Parks Sausage Co., Baltimore, MD	Raymond V. Haysbert Sr.	1951	230	Sausage manufacturer	24.800
62	Dick Griffey Productions, Hollywood, CA	Dick Griffey	1975	78	Entertainment	24.200
63	R.O.W. Sciences Inc., Rockville, MD	Ralph Williams	1983	365	Biomendical & health research	24.000
64	American Development Corp., N. Charleston, SC	W. Melvin Brown Jr.	1972	175	Sheet metal fabrication	23.000
65	Sylvest Management Systems Corp., Lanham, MD	Gary S. Murray	1987	42	Computer systems	22.600
66	Regal Plastics Co. Inc., Roseville, MI	William F. Pickard	1985	222	Plastic injection molding	21.711
67	Simmons Enterprises Inc., Cincinnati, OH	Carvel Simmons Inez Simmons	1970	52	Trucking; farm operations	21.475
68	Earl G. Graves Ltd., New York, NY	Earl G. Graves	1970	65	Magazine publishing	21.418
69	H.F. Henderson Industries Inc., West Caldwell, NJ	Henry F. Henderson Jr.	1954	150	Industrial process controls	20.662
70	Stephens Engineering Co. Inc., Lanham, MD	Wallace O. Stephens	1979	140	System integration	20.500
71	D-Orum Hair Products, Gary, IN	Ernest Daurham Jr.	1979	150	Hair cair products	20.000
72	Bronner Brothers, Atlanta, GA	Nathaniel Bronner Sr.	1947	250	Hair care products	19.500
73	Dual Inc., Arlington, VA	J. Fred Dual Jr.	1983	241	Engineering services	19.306
74	C.H. James & Co., Charleston, WV	Charles H. James III	1883	22	Wholesale food distribution	18.702
75	Consolidated Beverage Corp., New York, NY	Albert N. Thompson	1978	24	Beverage exporter & importer	18.500
76	Watiker & Son Inc.,	Al Watiker Jr.	1973	200	Construction; reclamation	18.000
77	Terry Manufacturing Co. Inc., Roanoke, AL	Roy Terry	1963	300	Apparel manufacturer	17.500
78	J.E. Ethridge Construction Inc., Fresno, CA	John E. Ethridge	1971	25	Construction	17.300
79	Burns Enterprises, Louisville, KY	Tommie Burns Jr.	1969	460	Janitorial services; supermarkets	17.000
79	Ozanne Construction Co. Inc., Cleveland, OH	Leroy Ozanne	1956	130	Construction	17.000
81	UBM Inc., Chicago, IL	Sandra Dixon Jiles	1975	53	Contracting & construction	16.674
82	AMSCO Wholesalers Inc., Norcross, GA	Thurmond B. Woodard	1990	86	Wholesale distributor	16.200
83	Systems Engineering & Mgmt Assocs. Inc., Alexandria, VA	James C. Smith	1985	260	ADP support services	16.000
84	Mid-Delta Home Health Inc., Belzoni, MS	Clara Taylor Reed	1978	345	Medical equipment & supplies	15.000
84	Urban Constructors Inc., Miami, FL	Jacque E. Thermilus	1988	60	Contracting & construction	15.000
84	American Urban Radio Networks, New York, NY	Sydney Small	1973	65	Media; telemarketing	15.000
87	Specialized Packaging International Inc., Hamden, CT	Carlton L. Highsmith	1983	7	Packaging design; brokerage	14.860
88	A Minority Entity Inc., Norco, LA	Burnell K. Moliere	1978	1,200	Janitorial & food services	14.753
89	TRESP Associates Inc., Alexandria, VA	Lillian B. Handy	1981	220	Logistics; systems engineering	14.000
90	Solo Construction Corp., N. Miami Beach, FL	Randy Pierson	1978	46	Engineering construction	13.959
91	RPM Supply Co. Inc., Philadelphia, PA	Robert P. Mapp	1977	20	Electrical components	13.891
92	Powers & Sons Construction Co. Inc., Gary, IN	Mamon Powers Sr.	1967	60	Construction	13.721
93	Williams-Russell and Johnson Inc., Atlanta, GA	Pelham Williams	1976	125	Engineering/construction	13.600
94	Black River Mfg. Inc., Port Huron, MI	Isaac Lang Jr.	1977	77	Auto parts manufacturer	13.400
95	Eltrex Industries, Rochester, NY	Matthew Augustine	1968	155	Office furniture	12.976
96	Advanced Systems Technology Inc., Atlanta, GA	Wayne H. Knox	1981	200	Nuclear technology	12.700
97	Advanced Consumer Marketing Corp., Burlingame, CA	Harry W. Brooks	Jr.	1984	35 Information systems	12.380
98	Spiral Distribution Inc., Phoenix, AZ	Reggie Fowler	1987	24	Packaging supplier	12.300
99	Wise Construction Co. Inc., Dayton, OH	Warren C. Wise	1983	75	Construction	12.000
99	Systems Management American Corp., Norfolk, VA	Herman Valentine	1970	130	Systems integration	12.000

*In millions of dollars. As of December 31, 1992.

Largest Industrial/Service Companies (continued)

	Company/Location	Chief Executive	Year Type	Sales*
1	Trainer Oldsmobile-Cadillac-Pontiac-GMC Truck Inc., Warner Robbins, GA	James E. Trainer	1991 GM	254.574
2	Shack-Woods & Associates, Long Beach, CA	William E. Shack Jr.	1977 Ford-Volkswagen	228.300
3	Pavilion Lincoln-Mercury Inc., Austin, TX	J. Michael Chargois	1988 Ford	223.788
4	Peninsula Pontiac-Oldsmobile Inc., Torrance, CA	Cecil B. Willis	1979 GM	128.912
5	Mel Farr Automotive Group, Oak Park, MI	Mel Farr	1975 Ford-Toyota	118.000
6	S & J Enterprises, Charlotte, NC	Sam Johnson	1973 Ford-Subaru	112.199
7	The Baranco Automotive Group, Decatur, GA	Gregory T. Baranco	1978 GM-Acura-Ford	69.292
8	Avis Ford Inc., Southfield, MI	Walter E. Douglas Sr.	1986 Ford	66.384
9	Rountree Cadillac-Oldsmobile Co. Inc., Shreveport, LA	Lonnie M. Bennett	1991 GM	47.000
10	Tropical Ford Inc., Orlando, FL	Hamilton W. Massey	1985 Ford	46.665
11	Alan Young Buick-GMC Truck Inc., Fort Worth, TX	Alan Young	1979 GM	45.661
12	Martin Automotive Group, Bowling Green, KY	Cornelius A. Martin	1985 GM-Chrysler-Isuzu	44.994
13	Metrolina Dodge Inc., Charlotte, NC	Reginald T. Hubbard	1986 Chrysler	43.466
14	Sidney Moncrief Pontiac-Buick-GMC Truck Inc., Sherwood, AR	Sidney A. Moncrief	1987 GM	42.018
15	Bob Ross Buidk-Mercedes-GMC Inc., Centerville, OH	Robert P. Ross	1974 GM-Benz	41.407
16	Southside Ford Truck Sales Inc., Chicago, IL	Carl Statham	1984 Ford	41.172
17	Leader Motors Inc., St. Louis, MO	Jesse Morrow	1983 Ford	37.823
18	Dick Gidron Cadillac & Ford Inc., Bronx, NY	Richard D. Gidron	1972 GM-Ford	37.500
19	32 Ford Mercury Inc., Batavia, OH	Clarence Warren	1990 Ford	35.118
20	Gulf Freeway Pontiac-GMC Truck, Houston, TX	Carl L. Barnett Sr.	1991 GM	32.298
21	Shelby Dodge Inc., Memphis, TN	H. Steve Harrell	1987 Chrysler	31.563
22	Varsity Ford-Lincoln-Mercury Inc., Bryan, TX	Tony Majors	1988 Ford	30.134
23	Conyers Riverside Ford Inc., Detroit, MI	Nathan G. Conyers	1970 Ford	30.100
24	Al Johnson Cadillac-Avanti-Saab Inc., Tinley Park, IL	Albert W. Johnson Sr.	1967 GM-Saab-Avanti	29.800
25	Campus Ford Inc., Okemos, MI	Wendell Barron	1986 Ford	29.792
26	Olympia Fields Ford Sales Inc., Olympia Fields, IL	Nathaniel K. Sutton	1989 Ford	29.244
27	Jim Bradley Pontiac-Cadillac-GMC Inc., Ann Arbor, MI	James H. Bradley Jr.	1973 GM	29.192
28	Team Ford Inc., Sioux City, IA	Arthur P. Silva	1986 Ford	29.056
29	Bob Johnson Chevrolet Inc., Rochester, NY	Robert Johnson	1981 GM	28.855
30	Northwestern Dodge Inc., Ferndale, MI	Theresa Jones	1980 Chrysler	28.791
31	Quality Ford Inc., W. Des Moines, IA	Franklin D. Greene	1989 Ford	28.714
32	North Seattle Chrysler-Plymouth Inc., Seattle, WA	William E. McIntosh Jr.	1985 Chrysler	28.000
33	Duryea Ford Inc., Brockport, NY	Jesse Thompson	1985 Ford-Toyota	27.431
34	University Ford of Peoria Inc., Peoria, IL	James L. Oliver	1985 Ford	26.612
35	Deerbrook Forest Chrysler-Plymouth Inc., Kingwood, TX	Ezzard Dale Early	1987 Chrysler	26.443
36	River LView Ford-Mercury Inc., Columbia, IL	John Carthen Sr.	1988 Ford	26.260
37	Spalding Ford-Lincoln-Mercury Inc., Griffin, GA	Alan M. Reeves	1981 Ford	26.057
38	Republic Ford Inc., Republic, MO	Franklin D. Greene	1983 Ford	25.939
39	Empire Ford Inc., Spokane, WA	Nathaniel D. Greene	1986 Ford	25.600
40	Coastal Ford Inc., Mobile, AL	Delmont O. Dapremont Jr.	1984 Ford	25.000
41	Fairway Ford of Augusta Inc., Augusta, GA	James H. Brown	1989 Ford	24.743
42	Kemper Dodge Inc., Cincinnati, OH	Paul C. Keels	1986 Chrysler	24.167
43	Chino Hills Ford Sales Inc., Chino, CA	Timothy L. Woods	1982 Ford	23.042
44	R.H. Peters Chevrolet Inc., Hurricane, WV	R.H. Peters Jr.	1982 GM	22.663
45	University Motors, Athens, GA	Ronald Hill	1991 Ford-Mazda	22.082
46	Fred Jones Pontiac-GMC Truck Inc., Brookfield, WI	Fredrick E. Jones	1984 GM	22.079
47	Hill Top Chrysler Plymouth Inc., Lancaster, TX	Eric V. Wilkins	1991 Chrysler	22.000
48	Southwest Ford Sales Inc., Oklahoma City, OK	Roger L. Williams	1990 Ford	21.856
49	Prestige Pontiac-Oldsmobile Inc., Mt. Morris, MI	Freddie J. Poe	1989 GM	21.772
50	Broadway Ford Inc., Edmond, OK	LeMon Henderson	1981 Ford	21.500
50	Ferndale Honda Inc., Ferndale, MI	Barbara J. Wilson	1983 Honda	21.500

Largest Auto Dealers

	Company/Location	Chief Executive	Year Type	Sales*
52	Heritage Cadillac Inc., Forest Park, GA	Ernest M. Hodge	1991 GM	21.403
53	Noble Ford-Mercury Inc., Indianola, IA	Dimaggio Nichols	1985 Ford	21.138
54	Barron Chevrolet-GEO Inc., Danvers, MA	Reginald Barron	1984 GM	20.468
55	Utica Chrysler-Plymouth Inc., Yorkville, NY	William E. Norris	1986 Chrysler	20.373
56	Winter-Haven Ford Inc., Winter Haven, FL	Johnny Mac Brown	1989 Ford	20.247
57	Hayes-Franklin Ford Inc., Crosby, TX	Elvin E. Hayes	1991 Ford	20.000
57	Al Meyer Ford Inc., Lufkin, TX	Alton J. Meyer	1987 Ford	20.000
59	Beddingfield Buick-GMC Truck-BMW Inc., Decatur, IL	Edward C. Beddingfield	1989 GM-BMW	19.865
60	Highland Lincoln-Mercury Inc., Highland, IN	Nathan Z. Cain	1991 Ford	19.830
61	Pasadena Lincoln-Mercury Inc., Pasadena, CA	Lester C. Jones	1991 Ford	19.487
62	Thomas A. Moorehead Buick Inc., Omaha, NB	Thomas A. Moorehead	1988 GM-Isuzu	19.288
63	Cardinal Dodge Inc., Louisville, KY	Winston R. Pittman Sr.	1988 Chrysler	19.232
64	Brandon Dodge Inc., Tampa, FL	Sanford L. Woods	1989 Chrysler	18.894
65	Smokey Point Sales & Service Inc., Arlington, WA	Henry F. Taylor	1981 GM	18.773
66	Red Bluff Ford-Mercury Inc., Red Bluff, CA	Phillip G. Price	1989 Ford	18.315
67	Southland Chrysler-Plymouth Inc., Memphis, TN	John Willie Roy	1986 Chrysler	17.920
68	Mike Pruitt's Lima Ford Inc., Lima, OH	Michael Pruitt	1990 Ford	17.600
69	Wilson Buick-Pontiac-GMC-Truck Inc., Jackson, TN	Sidney Wilson Jr.	1990 GM-Hyundai	17.577
70	Gresham Dodge Inc., Gresham, OR	Dorian S. Boyland	1987 Chrysler	17.520
71	Heritage Lincoln-Mercury Inc., Hackensack, NJ	T. Errol Harper	1983 Ford	17.518
72	Conway Ford Inc., Conway, SC	Samuel H. Frink	1986 Ford	17.493
73	Midfield Dodge Inc., Midfield, AL	Jordan A. Frazier	1989 Chrysler	17.477
74	West Covina Lincoln-Mercury Inc., West Covina, CA	Boyd Harrison Jr.	1986 Ford	17.112
75	Puget Sound Chrysler-Plymouth Inc., Renton, WA	B. Edward Fitzpatrick	1986 Chrysler	17.000
76	Mountain Home Ford-Lincoln-Mercury Inc., Mountain Home, ID	Robert E. Montgomery	1988 Ford	16.998
77	Macon Chrysler-Plymouth Inc., Macon, GA	James B. Jones	1988 Chrysler	16.967
78	All American Ford Inc., Saginaw, MI	Laval Perry	1988 Ford	16.500
79	Vision Ford-Lincoln-Mercury Inc., Alamagordo, NM	Wayne Martin	1989 Ford	16.235
80	Bay City Chrysler-Plymouth Inc., Green Bay, WI	Larry L. Hovell	1987 Chrysler	16.046
81	Shamrock Lincoln-Mercury-Nissan-Saab Inc., Mishawaka, IN	Theodore Williams Jr.	1988 Ford-Saab-Nissan	16.000
82	Freedom Ford-Lincoln-Mercury Inc., Wise, VA	Bobby H. Dawson	1990 Ford	15.889
83	Gresham Chrysler-Plymouth Inc., Gresham, OR	Clarence E. Parker	1991 Chrysler	15.860
84	Mike Branker Buick Inc., Lincoln, NB	Julian Michael Branker	1985 GM-Hyundai	15.750
85	Mission Blvd. Lincoln-Mercury Inc., Hayward, CA	Austin O. Chuks-Orji	1986 Ford	15.349
86	George Hughes Chevrolet Inc., Freehold, NJ	George Hughes	1978 GM	15.025
87	Pittsburg Ford Inc., Pittsburg, CA	Laroy S. Doss	1974 Ford	14.919
88	Ross Park Dodge Inc., Pittsburgh, PA	David A. Eaton	1987 Chrysler	14.916
89	Shoals Ford Inc., Muscle Shoals, AL	Fred D. Lee Jr.	1986 Ford	14.786
90	Ray Wilkinson Buick-Cadillac-Isuzu Inc., Racine, WI	Raymond M. Wilkinson Jr.	1984 GM-Isuzu	14.775
91	Classic Cadillac-GMC Truck Inc., Winston-Salem, NC	Chandler B. Lee	1991 GM	14.749
92	Gene Moon Buick-Pontiac Inc.-Signature Toyota Inc., Paw Paw, MI	Gene E. Moon	1976 GM-Toyota	14.593
93	Courtesy Ford-Lincoln-Mercury Inc., Danville, IL	G. Michael McDonald	1987 Ford	14.550
94	Huntsville Dodge Inc., Huntsville, AL	Ellenae L. Henry-Fairhurst	1990 Chrysler	14.486
95	Southland Chrysler Products Inc., Marion, OH	Eugene Turner	1985 Chrysler	13.798
96	Vicksburg Chrysler-Plymouth-Dodge Inc., Vicksburg, MI	Monti M. Long	1990 Chrysler	13.792
97	Prestige Ford Inc., Eustis, FL	Irving J. Matthews	1991 Ford	13.661
98	Auburn Ford-Lincoln-Mercury Inc., Auburn, AL	Andrew L. Ferguson	1985 Ford	13.580
99	Dyersburg Ford Inc., Dyersburg, TN	George L. Mitchell	1985 Ford	13.354
100	Plaza Ford-Lincoln-Mercury Inc., Lexington, NC	Archie Kindle	1987 Ford	13.226

*In millions of dollars. As of December 31, 1992.

Largest Auto Dealers (continued)

15

The Family

15

The Family

Family Structure and Stability ■ Marriage ■ Fertility and Births ■ Children ■ Health ■ Life Expectancy ■ Assessment

by Faustine C. Jones-Wilson

The family, as defined by the United States Bureau of the Census, is a group of two or more persons (one of whom is the householder) who are related by birth, marriage, or adoption, and who reside together. In everyday social usage, this definition is usually refined to include diverse family pattern variations; however, the American value system has traditionally embraced the concept of lifetime monogamous marriage and prized the "nuclear" family pattern of husband and wife living with their own children in the same household. Yet, with divorce rates currently hovering at about 50 percent, the prevalence of this prized pattern has diminished. Fewer than 50 percent of existing American families conform to this "norm." Remarriages have created increasing numbers of "blended" families comprised of various configurations of stepparents and stepchildren. Formal adoptions of stepchildren and increasing adoptions of children from other countries are also more common today than in the past. The growth in the numbers of single-parent families headed by women has been called "one of the most startling social developments of the past quarter century."

■ FAMILY STRUCTURE AND STABILITY

The black family's structure and status have changed dramatically over the last forty years, and its configuration, while following the majority population's general post-World War II trends, reflects historical inequities between the races that make the African American family's security especially tenuous as the nation prepares to enter the twenty-first century. The same forces that have molded the United States into what it is today have been at work on all facets of African American family life and culture. In that sense, the fortunes of African Americans ebb and flow with the tide of the general economic and social conditions of the nation. The African-American family also faces dilemmas that emanate from its unique position and identity within American society. African Americans experience problems related to their general minority group status as well as to their unique historical experiences of slavery, oppression, second-class citizenship, and the continuing stigma related thereto.

Census data reveal that since the late 1960s the black unemployment rate has been twice as high as the white unemployment rate—no matter what the economic condition of the country. The 1970s and 1980s, however, were periods of severe economic instability and recession in the United States. African-American males were particularly hard-hit by joblessness and/or underemployment during these decades due to the decline of the manufacturing industries in which many African-American males were employed (the automobile and steel industries, for example). This combination of double-digit inflation and high levels of unemployment over the past two decades—"stagflation"—disproportionately eroded the purchasing power of African-American families (Robert Hill. "Critical Issues for Black Families by the Year 2000." *The State of Black America 1990.* 1989).

Photographs of two Black Families taken around the turn of the Century.

While disproportionate segments of the black family are poor, there has been significant growth in the number of middle-class and affluent African-American families at the upper end of the family spectrum, particularly of younger, college-educated, dual-income, married-couple families. This growth has occurred since the opening of the opportunity structure in the mid-1960s with the passage of the Civil Rights Act of 1964 and the Voting Rights Act of 1965. Less research has been focused on these upper-strata families than on low-income black families; as a result, less is known about African-American families that are prospering in the current economic climate.

African-American families in the lower economic strata are plagued by the proliferation of their numbers headed by poor, single, never-married black females; teenage pregnancies; the shortage of marriageable, employed black males; disparities between African-American and white earning power; inadequate housing and social services; chronic unemployment and underemployment; and rising welfare dependency. Some of the social and psychological costs of these phenomena are the crime, violence, drug abuse, and despair that are frequently endemic in many low-income communities, along with the disproportionate levels of imprisonment of black males from those communities. As was indicated in the previous edition of this publication, unprecedented levels of crime and gang violence have also destabilized African-American families. With drug trafficking rampant in most inner-city areas, drug-related homicides among African Americans have reached record levels. These activities continue to have very negative impacts on black families and communities.

Some analysts place the primary blame for the deterioration of inner-city black families on public policies that are inimical to

In recent years there has been significant growth in the number of middle-class and affluent African-American families.

these families, or on the absence of public policies that provide corrective measures (incentives) that could empower them to help themselves. Representative of those analysts is Robert B. Hill, who in his article "Economic Forces, Structural Discrimination, and Black Family Instability" (1990), contends that "the key economic policies that undermined black family stability have been anti-inflation fiscal and monetary policies, trade policies, plant closings, social welfare, block grants, and federal per capita formulas for allocating funds to states and local areas that have not been corrected for the census undercount."

Particularly crippling in Hill's view is the absence of policy to provide affordable housing for moderate and low-income families, an absence that has a greater impact on African-American families because of their unique employment and income problems. One consequence of this shortage is a return to traditional black extended or augmented family arrangements as dispossessed family members seek temporary housing with relatives and as friends share their abodes with the less-fortunate. Another consequence is that increasing numbers of black families are homeless. Hill estimated the number of homeless individuals and families in 1989 at two to three million (Hill, "Critical Issues for Black Families by the Year 2000." 1989). Many of these families, but not all, were single-parent families headed by women.

K. Sue Jewell maintains that "policies, procedures, and assumptions underlying social and economic programs in the 1960s and 1970s, the Great Society years, contributed to the disintegration of black two-parent and extended families and to an increase in black families headed by women." Jewel asserts that "social and economic programs and civil rights legislation could not effectively remove social barriers, which prevent black families from participating fully in mainstream American society." In her view, the liberal social policy of the Great Society era resulted in modest, not substantial, gains for middle-class African-American families (K. Sue Jewell, *Survival of the Black Family: The Institutional Impact of U.S. Social Policy*, 1988).

Other scholars, many of them neoconservative or conservative in their sociopolitical orientation, continue to attribute the marked erosion in the social and economic stability of African-American families to internal factors within the families themselves, to the welfare system, and to the "Great Society" programs. For example, Irving Kristol ("Family Values: Not a Political Issues." *On the Issue* No. 55. 1992) notes that, while illegitimate births have increased startlingly since World War II, among blacks the rate had risen to 66 percent in 1992. Kristol decries the decline in "family values" among these "single moms" who, after having one illegitimate child, opt for and remain on public welfare support as they continue to produce additional children. Daniel Patrick Moynihan ("How the Great Society Destroyed the American Family." *The Public Interest* 108 (1992):53–64) alleges that "Great Society" programs destroyed the inner-city black family structure, largely through welfare policies, and argues that social scientists still do not know what public policies will reverse the downward spiral of life conditions of inner-city black families. Moynihan enjoys reminding his readers that he had forecast the crisis in the

Extended families have long been a strong support system within the African-American community.

social structure of inner-city black families in March 1965 in his United States Department of Labor paper entitled "The Negro Family: The Case for National Action." Central to Moynihan's analysis and that of his neoconservative successors who have sought to understand changes in African-American community and family relations are the relationships between black family stability and male employment, unemployment, and labor force nonparticipation rates. In 1965, Moynihan and his staff reported strong indicators of change in behaviors of the black urban poor, including a rise in Aid to Families with Dependent Children (AFDC) even as the black unemployment rate declined, and an increase in the percentage of non-white married women separated from their husbands. As a result of these factors, Moynihan argued, the black community had become immersed in "a tangle of pathology" that included family breakdown. Many prominent African Americans disputed Moynihan's conclusions and accused him of "blaming the victims" of social conditions rather than looking at the causes of their problems (i.e., racism, segregation, economic inequities).

The Extended and Augmented Family

One family pattern, that has historically been common among African Americans, is that of the "extended" family. This family grouping includes other relatives such as grandparents, aunts, uncles, cousins, nieces, nephews, or other relatives, formally or informally adopted, who share the household temporarily or for a longer time period with a nuclear family. Extended families have long been a strong support system within the African-American community. Today, members of extended families may not all live in the same household, because of the migratory patterns of family members, but they nonetheless function as a supportive intergenerational kinship unit.

Andrew Billingsley, in his now-classic work, *Black Families in White America* (1968), identifies an additional category of families called "augmented" families, which include unrelated persons. In a more recent publication, "Understanding African-American Family Diversity," Billingsley describes these supportive, dependable, family-like networks of relationships. Another classification, "fictive kin" (as Carol Stack calls them), includes "play" mothers, brothers, sisters, and so on, who usually do not live together. In some communities, these friendship networks resemble and substitute for extended family networks that may no longer exist. Foster families are also a growing phenomenon in the African-American community, and the increase in single-female headed households is more characteristic of the black population than of any other American racial or ethnic grouping today.

As Billingsley contends, diversity is and always has been characteristic of African-American family life. African-American households presently fall into the following categories: (1) married couples with children, (2) married couples without children, (3) extended families (usually those including grandparents), (4) blended families, (5) single-parent families (usually but not always headed by women), (6) cohabitating adults (with or without children), (7) single-person households (predominantly female).

Number and Size of Families

According to Census reports, there were 10.7 million African-American households in the United States in 1991, up from 4.8 million in 1960. However, the average size of black households declined to 2.9 persons in 1991, compared to 2.6 persons for whites and 3.5 persons for Hispanics. The period from 1980 to 1991 experienced the greatest growth (44 percent) in the number of black households. This growth is attributable to the increase in the number of never-married, separated, and divorced black householders, particularly in the proportion of never-married black female householders (not all of whom have borne children), which jumped from 9 percent in 1950 to 41 percent in 1991. Sixteen percent of these female householders were separated, 23 percent were divorced, and 17 percent were widowed. Male-headed households with no spouse present represented a mere 6 percent of black families in 1991.

In 1991, the number of African-American families increased to 7.5 million, up from 3.4 million in 1950. This increase was most evident in the number of married-couple families and female-headed families black with no husband present. In 1991, married-couple families comprised only 48 percent of all African-American families, contrasted with 1950 when they comprised 78 percent. Forty-six percent of African-American families in 1991 were headed by a female householder with no husband present, quite an increase from the 1950 proportion of 18 percent. This proportion is moving swiftly toward being equal with the percentage of married-couple families. The increase in black female-headed families can be attributed to a multiplicity of factors: the shortage of eligible black males, the shorter life expectancy of black males, increasing separation and divorce rates among African Americans, the rising rate of out-of-wedlock parenthood, increasing societal permissiveness regarding sexuality, and the wider availability of welfare assistance to aid father-absent families with dependent children.

Year and Race	Number of households (thousands)	Percent change over preceding date	Average size of household
BLACK			
1960	4,779	(X)	3.8
1970	6,180	29.3	3.5
1980	7,262	17.5	3.3
1990	10,486	44.4	2.9
1991	10,671	1.8	2.9
WHITE			
1960	47,868	(X)	3.2
1970	56,529	18.1	3.1
1980	62,945	11.3	2.9
1990	80,163	27.4	2.6
1991	80,968	1.0	2.6

NOTE: 1960 and 1970 data are from the decennial censuses.

Source: U.S. Bureau of the Census, Current Population Reports, The Black Population in the United States: March 1991, Washington, DC, 1992. p.6.

Number of Households and Average Size by Race, 1960 to 1991.

Families in Poverty

Proportionally many more black than white families were in poverty in 1990, 29.3 percent, compared with 8.1 percent of white families. African-American families were more than 3½ times more likely to be poor than were white families, a situation which has not changed measurably since 1967 (United States Bureau of the Census). Of 7,471,000 black families in 1990, 2,193,000 were below poverty level, whereas only 4,622,000 of 56,803,000 white families were in similar circumstances. In absolute numbers, more white families than black ones were poor, but the proportions of poor families was racially lopsided.

Seventy-five percent of the African-American families in poverty in 1990 were maintained by women alone, 20 percent were maintained by married couples, and the remainder by men alone. For the past twenty-three years, the poverty rate for female-headed black families has been consistently higher than the rate for other African-American family types.

Thirty-seven percent of all black families with related children under eighteen years old were poor in 1990. This was not statistically different from the 1967 level of 39 percent or the 1982 level of forty-one percent (United States Bureau of the Census). Fifty-six percent of black families maintained by women with children under eighteen years old were poor in 1990, less than the 64 percent in 1982 at the end of the 1981–82 recession (United States Bureau of the Census).

In 1990, 34 percent of elderly black individuals (sixty-five years old and over) were poor. While this marks an improvement over the 1967 figure of 53 percent, proportionally more elderly blacks than whites were poor in both comparison years—10 percent of elderly whites were poor in 1990 and 28 percent in 1967 (United States Bureau of the Census). Despite the presence of policies such as Social Security, Medicare, and Supplemental Security Income (SSI), designed to help all elderly Americans, elderly African Americans were twice as likely as elderly whites to be poor in 1967, and in 1990 they were three times more likely to be poor (United States Bureau of the Census).

The Rural Underclass

The findings of O'Hare and Curry-White's (1992) study of rural, inner-city, and suburban underclass populations reveals that there were approximately 3 million underclass adults in these areas in 1990. Using 1990 Current Population Survey (CPS) data on adults aged nineteen to sixty-four, they reported that underclass characteristics were much more prevalent in central cities and rural areas than in the suburbs, noting that 2.4 percent of the underclass lived in rural areas and 3.4 percent lived in central cities, yet only 1.1 percent lived in suburban areas. Approximately 32 percent (almost a third) of the rural underclass was found to be black in 1990, compared to 49 percent (almost half) of the inner-city underclass. The rate of black underclass membership was also higher in rural areas—9.1 percent—compared to 7.5 percent in central cities. A sizable body of impoverished rural African Americans lived in the South. Blacks in the rural South have higher underclass rates (about 1 in 10) than do blacks in large northern cities.

■ MARRIAGE

In 1991, only 38.4 percent of African-American women, fifteen years of age and over, were married, compared to 60.3 percent in 1960. The corresponding percentages for African-American men were 44.8 percent in 1991 and 63.3 percent in 1960. More research must be done to reveal the causes for this very drastic change in marriage patterns among African Americans in the last thirty years. For females some non-male-related causative factors may be: increased earnings of women in the labor market, increased opportunity to be employed, heightened desire to work, and the increased availability of government welfare payments for female householders (David T. Ellwood & Johnathan Crane. 1990. "Family Change Among Black Americans: What Do We Know?" *Journal of Economic Perspectives* 4(4):65–84).

Shortage of Black Men

The population of black males aged fifteen years old and over in 1990 stood at

Male-headed households with no spouse present represented a mere 6 percent of black families in 1991.

10,074,000, compared to 12,124,000 black females in the same age grouping. The resulting ratio of approximately 83 males to every 100 females makes the matching of every black female with a same-race male for the traditionally valued lifetime monogamous marriage a numerical impossibility—there simply are not enough African-American men alive. When one also removes from consideration those males who are gay, the proportion of eligible black men for black women dwindles even more. Further, when one counts the number of black males who are poorly educated and therefore educationally mismatched for marriage to their relatively more highly educated black female counterparts, the pool of eligible men shrinks even lower. High black male unemployment rates further compound the problem. These factors also help to explain the increasing numbers of never-married black females.

Reportedly, many of today's young black men delay marriage or never marry because of their unemployment or underemployment status, the rationale being that lack of a job or small earnings will not enable them to support families. However, well-educated black men who are employed at good salaries are also less likely to be married than their white counterparts (David T. Ellwood & Johnathan Crane. 1990.) Documentation of their reasons for not marrying is lacking; additional research is needed.

Interracial Marriage

Marriage outside the race further reduces the number of black men available for marriage to black women. In 1991, there were 156,000 marriages of black men to white women, compared to 75,000 marriages of white men to black women. This represented the "loss" of another 81,000 marriageable black men.

Incarcerated Black Men

]Incarcerated single black men are also unavailable as marriage partners, and black men in prison who are married are unavailable to be at home with their families and/or provide for them. Data from *Statistical Abstract* provide only partial figures on incarcerated black men because federal prisoners are not itemized by race or sex. Among inmates of state prisons there were 211,021 black men in 1986, or 46.9 percent of the total state prison population. In 1990, there were 174,335 black male prison inmates (not including those in federal and state prisons or juvenile institutions).

■ FERTILITY AND BIRTHS

Fertility Rates

In 1989, there were 90.4 live births per 1,000 black women aged fifteen to forty-four years old, and 64.7 such live births to comparable white women. There were 673,124 live births to black females that year, approximately 17 percent of all births nationwide. Black women have had higher fertility rates than white women for the past two centuries; however, birth rates are similar for black and white women with the same level of educational attainment (William P. O'Hare, et al. 1991. "African Americans in the 1990s." *Population Bulletin* 46(1)).

Teenage Pregnancy

For a number of years Marian Wright Edelman of the Children's Defense Fund has stressed that teenage pregnancy is a special problem among poor and minority groups who usually have limited opportunities to offer their offspring ("Address to the National Conference on Educating Black Children." *Education Black Children: America's Challenge.* 1987). Joyce Ladner has explained that the causes of teenage pregnancy range from attempts to find emotional fulfillment and the desire to achieve "womanhood" to ignorance of contraceptives (1987. "Black Teenage Pregnancy: A Challenge for Educators." *The Journal of Negro Education* 56(1): 53–63). Political conservatives and neoconservatives maintain that poor teenagers view welfare programs such as Aid to Families with Dependent Children (AFDC) as a viable source of economic support and consequently perceive pregnancy as a means of tapping into the welfare system at an early age (Irving Kristol, 1992).

Teenage pregnancy is both a national problem and a African-American problem. Data from the National Center for Health Statistics reveal that in 1989 the birth rate for all teenagers aged fifteen to seventeen years old was 36.5 live births per 1,000. African-American girls in that age group were almost 3 times more likely than white girls to give birth (80.0 compared with 28.3 per 1,000). Among girls younger than fifteen years old, the birth rate was seven times higher among blacks than whites. Further, in 1989, African-American girls in the fifteen to seventeen year-old age group were almost five times more likely to have a second baby and seven times more likely to have a third baby as white girls in this age group. This state of affairs and its moral, economic and political ramifications cause great consternation in the African-American community as well as in the larger society. Teenage childbearing exacerbates such social problems as high infant mortality, maintaining good physical and mental health, educational insufficiencies, long-term welfare dependency, and poverty. Many teenage mothers do not complete high school, the basic educational expectation in this country; as a result, they are often seriously undereducated and lack marketable skills. Others do not know how or know enough to care adequately for their children. By and large, their children will not have the same opportunities and life-chances as their more advantaged counterparts in any race or ethnic group.

Various efforts have been aimed at stemming the tide of teenage pregnancy. At the bureaucratic level, some states have decreed punitive measures such as sterilization and/or reduced welfare payments for girls and women on public assistance who have more than one out-of-wedlock birth. Black sororities, fraternities, churches, and civil groups have initiated programs to work directly with African-American teenagers. The Children's Defense Fund continues to enlighten the public via a multimedia campaign that urges black males as well as females to be more responsible for their sexual behavior.

Births of Mixed Racial Parentage

According to the Population Reference Bureau's December 1992 report, the proportion of mixed-race births for which the race of both parents was known increased from 1 percent to 3.4 percent between 1968 and 1989; births of children with a black and a white parent increased from 8,700 in 1968 to 45,000 in 1989. This increase was described as "a striking sign of social change" with respect to attitudes about interracial marriage (Susan Krafft. 1991. "Black Death: the Demographic Difference." *American Demographics* 13(12):12–13).

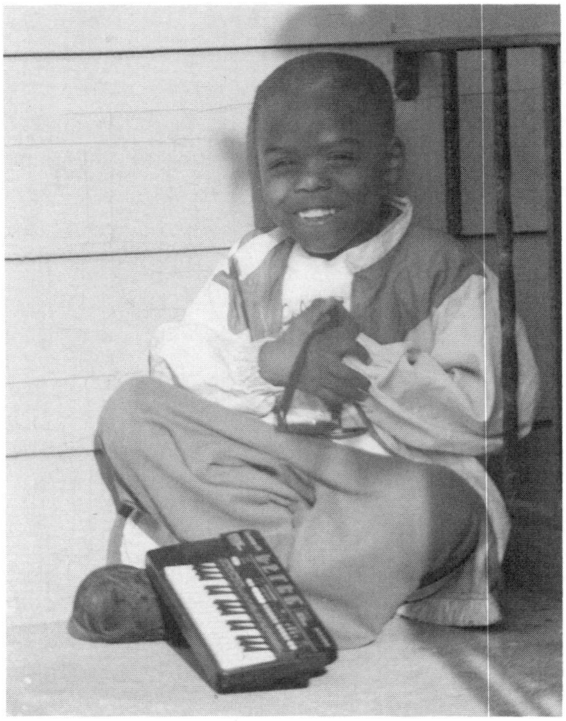

In 1991, only 36 percent of African-American children lived with both parents.

■ CHILDREN

Living Arrangements of Children

In 1991, only 36 percent of African-American children lived with both parents, compared to 67 percent in 1960 and 58.5 percent in 1970. This dramatic decline roughly parallels the changes in living arrangements of African-American adults resulting from increased divorce and separation rates as well as increases in births to never-married females. By contrast, 78.5 percent of white children were living with both their parents in 1991, down from 90.9 percent in 1960 and 89.5 percent in 1970. In 1990, 12 percent of black children lived with their grandparents, compared to 4 percent of whites and 6 percent of Hispanics (William P. O'Hare, et. al. 1991). Black grandparents, particularly grandmothers, are more likely to care for their grandchildren than are whites or Hispanics. Also in 1990, 6.5 percent of black children lived with other relatives, and 1 percent lived with non-relatives.

In 1991, 67 percent of black female-headed families had one or more children under eighteen years old present in the household; 56 percent had two or more. These families were more likely to be poor than were married-couple families. They were also more likely to live in inner cities; about 30 percent lived in public housing. Many economic analysts maintain that there is a very strong probability that children from such households will grow up poor and on welfare, be environmentally disadvantaged compared to their middle class counterparts, may drop out of school, have one or more out-of-wedlock births themselves, and be unemployed or unemployable in their adult lives (David T. Ellwood & Johnathan Crane. 1990).

Child Support

It is customary for parents to support their children. In years past, when parents could not do so, extended family members were expected to assist in the process. In today's dismal economic climate, many more mothers than in the past are working in the paid labor force and contributing a larger share of their earned income to their families. Grandparents continue to do and provide what they can, including providing child care while the parent or parents work. Poor families are supported by the welfare system. Many families have been forced to accept unemployment compensation as their support base when one or more member loses a job.

When African-American parents divorce or are separated, how many former wives receive child support from their estranged mates? In 1989 there were 2,770,000 ever-divorced and currently separated black women. Child support payments were court-awarded to only 955,000 (35 percent) of these women. Of the 791,000 who were supposed to receive child support, only 70 percent actually received payment. The mean child support amount received was $2,263.00, or 16 percent of total household income. As these figures reveal, in the event of divorce or separation, African-American women were primarily responsible for the support of their children.

In terms of dollars received, African-American women with incomes below the

In 1991, 67 percent of black female-headed families had one or more children under eighteen years old present in the household.

Living arrangement	1960	1970	1980	1990	1991
BLACK					
Total, children under 18	8,650	9,422	9,375	10,018	10,209
Percent living with both parents	67.0	58.5	42.2	37.7	35.9
WHITE					
Total, children under 18	55,077	58,790	52,242	51,390	51,918
Percent living with both parents	90.9	89.5	82.7	79.0	78.51

Children Under 18 Years Living with both Parents.

poverty level fared worse than the average in 1989. Of 325,000 such women who were supposed to receive child support, 70 percent actually received payment. Their mean child support sum, a mere $1,674.00, nevertheless amounted to 32 percent of their total household income.

■ HEALTH

Medicaid

Many American families receive health care through the federally funded Medicaid program. Disproportionately high percentages of these families are black. The total number of Medicaid recipients in the United States increased from 17.6 million in 1972 to 25.3 million in 1990. In 1990, 44.4 percent of the recipients were children in AFDC families, for whom health care vendors received an average payment of $811.00 each. That same year, 23.8 percent of Medicaid recipients were adults in AFDC families; vendors received $1,429 each for serving them (United States Department of Health and Human Services, 1992). In 1990, 7,809,000 black persons were covered by Medicaid; 5,686,000 of these had incomes below the poverty line and 2,123,000 had incomes above it.

Child Health

Thousands of children are not being immunized, although our society knows that the spread of communicable diseases can be prevented thereby. In 1990, only about half of inner-city young children had been immunized against measles, mumps, and rubella (National Commission on Children, 1991). The government suspended data collection on polio and whooping cough in 1985, so data on those communicable diseases are not available. Measles outbreaks have erupted in many American cities in the 1990s; most were among poor, inner-city children. Nearly 100 deaths from measles were reported in 1990 (National Commission on Children, 1991).

A new and growing population of children are born of mothers who used drugs (including alcohol) during their pregnancies. Many of these children experience after-birth withdrawal problems from drugs that affected them *in utero*; they are later more prone to physical and mental disabilities, followed by behavioral problems and learning impairments when they arrive in the nation's schools. Infants whose mothers drink alcoholic beverages during pregnancy are at risk of Fetal Alcohol Syndrome. Each year, Acquired Immune Deficiency Syndrome (AIDS) afflicts a growing number of children, who usually contract the disease from their mothers before or at birth. Urban children who live in old and/or poor housing also remain at risk of being exposed to high levels of lead. It has been estimated that 12 million American children, primarily those who are poor, are at risk of lead poisoning and potentially will have their intellectual growth stunted because of exposure to lead (National Commission on Children, 1991). Like black adults, and perhaps due to their affiliation with them, black children are also at greater risk of accidents, physical abuse, and other violence that may result in disability or death.

AIDS

African Americans suffer disproportionately from Acquired Immune Deficiency Syndrome (AIDS), the final stage of a disease caused by the Human Immunodeficiency Virus (HIV). The HIV virus severely weakens the body's immune system, leaving HIV-infected people vulnerable to other infections of various kinds. At this writing, there is no cure for AIDS—although the life expectancy of its victims varies, it is 100 percent fatal. Though African Americans represent only 12 percent of the United States population, 31 percent of all new AIDS cases in 1989 were black. A new report, "The Challenge of HIV/AIDS in Communities of Color," stated that blacks and Hispanics, representing 21 percent of the population, accounted for 46 percent of all AIDS cases in September 1992 ("AIDS and Race," *Washington Post*, January 25, 1993). Unknown is the number of such persons infected with HIV who have not as yet experienced symptoms of the disease.

Data from the United States Department of Health and Human Services show that in 1989 the age-adjusted HIV death rate for African-American men was three times higher than that for white men (40.3 and 13.1 deaths per 100,000). The death rate for African-American women was nine times that for white women (8.1 and 0.9 deaths per 100,000). The Population Reference Bureau's analysis shows that, between 1987 and 1989, the number of black AIDS cases escalated 59 percent, compared to a 38 percent increase in its incidence among white gay or bisexual men. The disease is expected to spread even faster among African Americans in the future.

AIDS is spread by viral passage during unprotected sexual intercourse, intravenous drug use, or blood transfusions; it can also be transmitted from mother to child *in utero* or during birth. It is estimated that 52 percent of the AIDS cases among African Americans in 1989 resulted from intravenous drug use. While AIDS is fatal, it is preventable if sexually active adults and teenagers engage in "safe sex" practices such as using condoms and avoid behaviors that put them at risk of AIDS infection such as promiscuity, having multiple sex partners, using drugs, and exchanging drug paraphernalia. The African-American community and the larger society are saturating the public with information about AIDS in the hope that education will cause people to behave differently and thereby slow the progress of the disease.

Cigarette, Alcohol, and Drug Use

The use and abuse of cigarettes, alcohol, marijuana, and cocaine (including addiction thereto) is a serious social problem in contemporary American society. The National Center for Health Statistics reports that, in a given month in 1991, 4 percent of black youth twelve to seventeen years old smoked cigarettes, compared with 13 percent of whites and 9 percent of Hispanics of the same age. Cigarette smoking has been identified as a major risk factor in lung cancer, cardiovascular disease, and chronic obstructive lung disease. Twenty percent of blacks, 20 percent of whites and 23 percent of Hispanics in this same age group had used alcohol; 5 percent of African Americans and

Hispanics but 4 percent of whites had used marijuana; and 0.5 percent of blacks, 0.3 percent of whites, and 1.3 percent of Hispanic youths had used cocaine. In the eighteen to twenty-five year-old group in the given month, 22 percent of blacks had smoked cigarettes, compared to 36 percent of whites and 25 percent of Hispanics; and 56 percent of blacks had used alcohol, compared to 67 percent of whites and 53 percent of Hispanics. Fifteen percent of blacks, compared to 14 percent of whites and 9 percent of Hispanics had used marijuana; and 3.1 percent of blacks had used cocaine, compared to 1.7 percent of whites and 2.7 percent of Hispanics. It is clear that youth are using these substances as early as age twelve and that usage increases through the young adult period. These percentages represent large numbers of young people.

Sickle Cell Anemia

Sickle Cell Anemia (SCA) is a chronic inherited affliction caused by a defect in the hemoglobin component of the blood. It occurs as a result of the mating of two people, each of whom carries the gene for the defective trait, which is passed on to their children. The presence of this abnormal hemoglobin trait can cause distortion (sickling) of the red blood cells and a decrease in their number. The source of SCA seems to be malarious countries; people with sickle cell disease are almost always immune to malaria, so it appears that the sickle cell is a defense mechanism against malaria.

Sickled red blood cells have been found in 1 of every 12 American blacks; but the active disease occurs about once in every 600 American blacks and once in every 1,200 American whites. It is estimated that about 50,000 persons in the United States suffer from the disease. Persons of other races and nationalities are affected by the trait and the anemia including people from Southern India, Greece, Italy, Syria, Caribbean Islands, South and Central America, Turkey, and other countries.

The disease is diagnosed through microscopic and electrophoretic analysis of the blood. The first symptoms of SCA usually appear in children with the disease at about six months of age. Because SCA is a chronic disease, medical management is directed toward both the quiescent and active periods (called "crises") of the malady. Good medical and home care may make it possible for persons with SCA to lead reasonably normal lives. When crises occur, they experience fever, pain, loss of appetite, paleness of the skin, generalized weakness, and sometimes a striking decrease in the number of red blood corpuscles. Complications and infections from these crises can be controlled with antibiotic drugs. A new drug, hydroxyurea, has been developed to stimulate fetal hemoglobin to produce more red blood cells and thereby ameliorate SCA crises. However, hydroxyurea is very toxic, and thus far has only been tested on adults with SCA. In other efforts, a female SCA sufferer, also stricken with leukemia, recently received a radical bone-marrow transplant from her brother. Since the transplant, she has been free of symptoms from both diseases. This case, the first of its kind, is being closely monitored to determine the mechanisms by which the patient's remission occurred and to see if the results of this procedure can be duplicated with other persons with SCA.

African-American people who intend to have children are advised to undergo blood tests to determine whether they are carriers of the sickle cell gene. Two such carriers should agree not to produce children, since half the children will have the trait and one in four the anemia. There is only one chance in four that their child will be free of the disease. Some jurisdictions (Washington,

DC, for example) have enacted laws mandating that newborns be screened for sickle cell anemia, along with other diseases. As a result of such legislation, newborns found to be afflicted with SCA can be cared for from birth.

■ LIFE EXPECTANCY

Life expectancy at birth increased substantially during the first ninety years of this century, from 33 years for African Americans of both sexes in 1900 to 70.3 years in 1990. Corresponding figures for both sexes of all races are 47.3 years in 1900 and 75.4 years in 1990. Provisional data of the National Vital Statistics System project a life expectancy of 66 years for black males born in 1990 and 74.5 years for black females born that year, an average of 70.3 years for both sexes. Corresponding life expectancy projections for white males and females born in 1990 are 72.6 and 79.3 years, averaged at 76.0 years. That black babies born in one of the most affluent countries in the world in this last decade of the twentieth century should have a lower life expectancy at birth than their white counterparts is an ignominious social problem.

At the other end of the age continuum, black males aged sixty-five years old in 1990 are projected to live 14.2 more years, and black females 17.6 additional years, averaged for both sexes at 16.1 years. This compares with 15.3 more years for white males, and 19 additional years for white females, averaged for both sexes at 17.3 years. Thus the same pattern holds: white people in the United States continue to have longer life expectancy than African Americans.

These black/white differences can be attributed to a number of factors. African Americans have higher death rates due to the following major causes: accidents, homicides, suicides, heart disease, strokes, liver disease, cancer, diabetes, and AIDS. It is also true that whites, more than blacks, have health insurance coverage of some kind and sufficient personal income to partake of higher-quality health care, both preventive and curative. whites' higher education and income levels also assure them the greater likelihood of eating nutritionally balanced, healthy meals. Dietary patterns and food choices of low-income blacks include too many fats and sweets, factors that contribute to obesity and high blood pressure, which carry their own sets of health risks.

Homicide and Death by Accident

Homicide among African-American men is a primary cause for the drop in their life expectancy. In 1989, 61.1 percent of all black male deaths and 12.9 percent of all black female deaths from accidents and violence were due to homicide. Some social theorists claim that the increasing numbers of African Americans who are poor and hopeless, added to those who are involved in drugs or other substance abuses, account for the homicide rates among African Americans. Motor vehicle deaths and other accidents also accounted for many deaths among black males since 1970.

Suicide

Suicide rates are lower among African Americans than whites, but black suicide rates are on the rise, a most undesirable form of parity. In 1985, the suicide rate for white males exceeded that for black males by 70 percent; by 1989, the difference had narrowed to 40 percent. Data from the National Center for Health Statistics show that more than 30,000 lives are lost through suicide annually. Among all Americans, the age-adjusted death rate by suicide in 1989 was 11.3 deaths per 100,000. For black males, the rate was 12.5 per 100,000, and for black females, it was 2.4 per 100,000. Among black adolescents and young adults aged 15 to 24 years old, the suicide rate for males was 16.7 per 100,000, and 2.8 per 100,000 for black females, increases of 49 percent (from 1984 to 1989) and 40 percent (from 1986 to 1989), respectively.

Infant Mortality

Infant mortality rates for African Americans remain more than double that of whites. In 1989, 17.7 deaths per 1,000 live births were reported for black infants, compared to 8.2 deaths per 1,000 live births for whites. The black/white infant death ratios have not changed appreciably since 1950, when the black infant mortality rate was 43.9 deaths per 1,000 live births, and the white rate was 26.8 deaths per 1,000. Some progress has been made since 1950, however, as the infant mortality statistics have improved for both races. Nonetheless, the infant mortality rate in the United States is higher than those of twenty-one other industrialized countries.

African-American women are more likely than whites to give birth to low-weight babies, many of whom fall victim to serious health problems or die during their first year. These babies are particularly susceptible to Sudden Infant Death Syndrome (SIDS), respiratory distress syndrome, infections, and injuries. This phenomenon occurs because disproportionate numbers of babies are born to low-income, less-educated, and/or teenage mothers who have inadequate prenatal care and poor nutrition, and who smoke, use drugs, or otherwise fail to take care of themselves properly during their pregnancies.

■ ASSESSMENT

In early 1993, there is growing economic differentiation among America's black families. Approximately one-third are prospering. Indeed, some African-American families—primarily married-couple families headed by highly educated spouses with two or more fully employed year-round earners—are becoming more affluent. These families, who tend to live in suburban areas, are primarily nuclear families, though some are blended units. They may also be part of supportive friendship networks.

Affluent black families have benefitted from the abolition of segregation and other legal barriers to blacks' social, educational, occupational, and residential access and equity. Many of them are headed by persons who are second-, third-, and even fourth-generation college graduates, the beneficiaries of a heritage of education, motivation, and hard work. Nonetheless, such affluent African Americans continue to face "glass ceilings" and attitude-related barriers in many places of employment as they seek to move upward in corporate or government hierarchies.

Another third of black families, the working (middle) class, is comprised of families that are struggling to maintain themselves and provide support systems for their young in the face of reductions in force (RIFs), layoffs, or terminations as the corporations upon which they depend for their livelihood have downsized, moved to different regions of this country, gone out of business, or exported jobs to other countries. The extended or augmented family structure is visible in many of these homes. "Fictive kin" often are part of these family relationships.

The final third includes the nation's poorer black families. This grouping includes (1) former working-class families who have fallen on hard times; (2) the "working poor," who are employed daily but

In 1991, married-couple families were only 48 percent of all African-American families.

at minimum wages that do not permit secure or dependable livelihoods; and (3) families of the "underclass," poorest of the poor, most of which are headed by females alone. Many of this latter group have been supported by the welfare system for one or more generations.

In 1991, married-couple families were only 48 percent of all African-American families. Forty-six percent of African-American families were headed by a female householder with no husband present. Overwhelmingly, the nation's poor black families fell into this latter category.

What do African-American families need to improve their overall condition? Like other American families, they need federal, state, and local policies that are designed to strengthen all families regardless of race, class, or composition. Gun-control laws could solve some of the problems related to family violence and homicides (most of which involve family members or other closely related persons). Law enforcement related to drugs and alcohol is an urgent priority. Blacks and other Americans also need universal health care policies, jobs that pay cost-of-living wages, and affordable housing in safer neighborhoods. Education of quality and substance is critically needed by the children and adults in many of these families. Recreational and other leisure-time outlets must also be made available to the youth

Recreational and other leisure-time outlets must be made available to the youth and children in cities.

and children in cities. Middle- and upper-income black families would benefit from an end to discriminatory employment and promotion policies designed to limit their upward mobility.

Within the African-American community itself, certain attitudinal and behavioral changes are essential. For example, more highly educated young black men must decide to marry and to produce and maintain families. Family planning information, including sex education and intervention programs, must be disseminated among teenage males and females, so that the out-of-wedlock birth rate can be dramatically reduced. Substance abuse must be curtailed; people who have hope for the future and who feel that they have some power and control over their lives are less likely to "escape" through drugs or alcohol. Children and youth need more adult interaction and supervision in their lives, whether it comes from family members or "significant others" such as mentors provided by organizations like Concerned Black Men, Inc., or other community service-minded groups.

So many of the problems faced by African-American and other low-to-moderate-income families are systemic and interlocking. Action on only one problem will not solve the network of family woes that our society has allowed to accumulate. Once again, the National Urban League has called for a "Marshall Plan for the Cities" to address the totality of current problems (Tidwell, 1992). If our society wants to save its cities and a significant portion of its human capital—of which these families comprise a significant part—it must give serious consideration to the formation and implementation of such a plan in both the cities and the rural areas. By so doing, the nation can help all its citizens become productive workers, consistent taxpayers, meritorious parents, and contributing members of stable families.

Year and race	Black					White				
	All families (thous.)	Percentof all families				All families (thous.)	Percent of all families			
		Total	Married-couple	Male house-holder, no spouse present	Female house-holder, no spouse present		Total	Married-couple	Male house-holder, no spouse present	Female house-holder, no spouse present
UNITED STATES										
19501	3,432	100.0	77.7	4.7	17.6	35,021	100.0	88.0	3.5	8.5
1960	3,950	100.0	74.1	4.1	21.7	40,873	100.0	89.2	2.7	8.1
1970	4,856	100.0	68.3	3.7	28.0	46,166	100.0	88.9	2.2	8.9
1980	6,184	100.0	55.5	4.1	40.3	52,243	100.0	85.7	2.8	11.6
1990	7,470	100.0	50.2	6.0	43.8	56,590	100.0	83.0	4.1	12.9
1991	7,471	100.0	47.8	6.3	45.9	56,803	100.0	82.8	4.0	13.2
SOUTH										
19501	2,205	100.0	77.9	4.6	17.5	9,348	100.0	88.7	3.0	8.3
1960	2,290	100.0	74.1	4.3	21.6	11,189	100.0	89.4	2.3	8.3
1970	2,533	100.0	69.4	4.0	26.6	13,571	100.0	89.4	1.9	8.7
1980	3,202	100.0	57.9	3.9	38.2	16,773	100.0	87.2	2.5	10.4
1990	4,147	100.0	52.3	5.5	42.2	18,746	100.0	84.5	3.6	11.9
1991	4,169	100.0	50.6	6.5	43.0	18,764	100.0	83.8	3.4	12.7
NORTH AND WEST										
19501	1,227	100.0	77.3	4.9	17.8	25,674	100.0	87.8	3.7	8.5
1960	1,660	100.0	74.2	4.0	21.8	29,683	100.0	89.1	2.9	8.0
1970	2,323	100.0	67.1	3.4	29.4	32,595	100.0	88.7	2.4	8.9
1980	2,982	100.0	53.0	4.4	42.7	35,470	100.0	85.0	3.7	12.2
1990	3,323	100.0	47.5	6.5	45.9	37,845	100.0	82.3	4.3	13.4
1991	3,301	100.0	44.2	6.1	49.6	38,038	100.0	82.2	4.3	13.5

NOTE: 1950 and 1960 data are from the decennial censuses.

[1] Data include families of "Other races" for Black.

Source: U.S. Bureau of the Census, Current Population Reports, The Black Population in the United States: March 1991, Washington, DC, 1992. p. 8.

Percent Distribution of Families by Type, Region, and Race, 1950 to 1991.

(Numbers in thousands)

Characteristic	Black 1950[1]	1960[1]	1970	1980	1990	1991	White 1950[1]	1960[1]	1970	1980	1990	1991
AGE												
Female householder, no spouse present	605	843	1,382	2,495	3,275	3,430	2,966	3,297	4,165	6,052	7,306	7,512
Percent	100.0	100.0	100.0	100.0	100.0	100.0	100.0	100.0	100.0	100.0	100.0	100.0
15 to 34 years	26.0	29.0	35.2	44.0	42.3	39.6	12.0	15.0	20.8	30.8	30.3	31.0
35 to 64 years	59.0	58.0	53.0	46.4	48.6	51.2	61.0	59.0	56.2	52.6	54.1	53.9
65 years and over	15.0	13.0	11.9	9.6	9.2	9.2	27.0	26.0	23.0	16.7	15.6	15.1
PRESENCE OF OWN CHILDREN UNDER 18 YEARS												
Female householder, no spouse present	605	890	1,382	2,495	3,275	3,430	2,966	3,306	4,165	6,052	7,306	7,512
Percent	100.0	100.0	100.0	100.0	100.0	100.0	100.0	100.0	100.0	100.0	100.0	100.0
With own children	47.0	56.0	66.0	71.9	68.2	66.9	33.0	42.0	47.9	58.8	57.5	57.7
With 2 or more own children	59.0	70.0	71.4	63.4	56.0	56.1	50.0	54.0	60.9	52.2	48.1	48.7
With no own children	53.0	44.0	34.0	28.1	31.8	33.1	67.0	58.0	52.1	41.2	42.5	42.3
MARTIAL STATUS												
Female householder, no spouse present	612	843	1,382	2,495	3,275	3,430	2,960	3,297	4,165	6,052	7,306	7,512
Percent	100.0	100.0	100.0	100.0	100.0	100.0	100.0	100.0	100.0	100.0	100.0	100.0
Separated or divorced	35.0	40.0	48.0	48.7	42.0	39.2	21.0	28.0	36.6	53.7	56.2	56.3
Separated	27.0	29.0	33.9	26.8	18.9	16.4	8.0	10.0	11.3	13.9	13.6	14.2
Divorced	8.0	11.0	14.2	21.9	23.1	22.9	13.0	18.0	25.3	39.8	42.6	42.1
Other	65.0	60.0	51.8	51.3	58.0	60.7	79.0	72.0	63.4	46.3	43.8	43.8
Single (never married)	9.0	12.0	16.0	27.3	39.4	41.0	12.0	11.0	9.2	10.6	15.0	16.5
Widowed	51.0	42.0	30.2	22.2	16.6	16.9	61.0	53.0	47.1	32.7	26.1	23.6
Husband temporarily absent	5.0	6.0	5.6	1.8	2.0	2.9	5.0	8.0	7.2	3.0	2.8	3.7

NOTE: Totals for female family heads 1950 and 1960 may not agree in some cases because data are from different tabulations.

[1] Data for 1950 and 1960 are from previously published tables where percents were rounded to the nearest whole number. (1050 and 1960 data are from the decennial censuses.)

Source: U.S. Bureau of the Census, Current Population Reports, *The Black Population in the United States*: March 1991, Washington, DC, 1992. p. 9.

Selected Characteristics of Families Maintained by Women with no Spouse Present, 1950 to 1991.

Characteristic	1967		1971		1976		1981	
	Black	White	Black	White	Black	White	Black	White
TYPE OF FAMILY								
All families	4,589	44,813	5,157	47,641	5,804	50,083	6,413	53,269
Number below poverty level	1,555	4,056	1,484	3,751	1,617	3,560	1,972	4,670
Percent below poverty level	33.9	9.1	28.8	7.9	27.9	7.1	30.8	8.8
Married-couple families	3,118	39,821	3,289	42,039	3,406	43,397	3,535	45,007
Number below poverty level	(NA)	(NA)	(NA)	(NA)	450	2,071	543	2,712
Percent below poverty level	(NA)	(NA)	(NA)	(NA)	13.2	4.8	15.4	6.0
Female householder, no husband present	1,272	4,008	1,642	4,489	2,151	5,467	2,605	6,620
Number below poverty level	716	1,037	879	1,191	1,122	1,379	1,377	1,814
Percent below poverty level	56.3	25.9	53.5	26.5	52.2	25.2	52.9	27.4
Male householder, no wife present	199	984	226	1,113	247	1,219	273	1,642
Number below poverty level	(NA)	(NA)	(NA)	(NA)	45	110	52	145
Percent below poverty level	(NA)	(NA)	(NA)	(NA)	18.2	9.0	19.1	8.8
Families with related children under 18 years	3,200	25,531	3,660	26,745	4,047	26,812	4,455	27,223
Number below poverty level	1,261	2,276	1,261	2,372	1,382	2,566	1,652	3,362
Percent below poverty level	39.4	8.9	34.5	8.9	34.2	9.6	37.1	12.4
Married-couple families	(NA)	(NA)	(NA)	(NA)	2,146	22,872	2,202	22,334
Number below poverty level	(NA)	(NA)	(NA)	(NA)	311	1,242	357	1,723
Percent below poverty level	(NA)	(NA)	(NA)	(NA)	14.5	5.4	16.2	7.7
Female householder, no husband present	(NA)	(NA)	1,369	2,664	1,781	3,456	2,118	4,237
Number below poverty level	(NA)	(NA)	821	982	1,043	1,260	1,261	1,564
Percent below poverty level	(NA)	(NA)	60.0	36.9	58.6	36.4	59.5	36.9
Male householder, no wife present	(NA)	(NA)	(NA)	(NA)	120	484	135	652
Number below poverty level	(NA)	748	(NA)	(NA)	28	64	34	75
Percent below poverty level	(NA)	34.9	(NA)	(NA)	23.3	13.2	25.0	11.6
Householder 65 years old and over	(NA)	(NA)	632	6,794	695	7,362	763	8,511
Number below poverty level	265	1,246	211	842	191	515	227	611
Percent below poverty level	48.4	19.2	33.4	12.4	27.4	7.0	29.7	7.2

Characteristic	1982		1986		1989		1990	
	Black	White	Black	White	Black	White	Black	White
TYPE OF FAMILY								
All families	6,530	53,407	7,096	55,676	7,470	56,590	7,471	56,803
Number below poverty level	2,158	5,118	1,987	4,811	2,077	4,409	2,193	4,622
Percent below poverty level	33.0	9.6	28.0	8.6	27.8	7.8	29.3	8.1
Married-couple families	3,486	45,252	3,742	46,410	3,750	46,981	3,569	47,014
Number below poverty level	543	3,104	403	2,591	443	2,329	448	2,386
Percent be low poverty level	15.6	6.9	10.8	5.6	11.8	5.0	12.6	5.1
Female householder, no husband present	2,734	6,507	2,967	7,227	3,275	7,306	3,430	7,512
Number below poverty level	1,535	1,813	1,488	2,041	1,524	1,858	1,648	2,010
Percent below poverty level	56.2	27.9	50.1	28.2	46.5	25.4	48.1	26.8
Male householder, no wife present	309	1,648	388	2,038	446	2,303	472	2,277
Number below poverty level	79	201	96	179	110	223	97	226
Percent below poverty level	25.6	12.2	24.9	8.8	24.7	9.7	20.6	9.9
Families with related children under 18 years	4,470	27,118	4,806	27,929	5,031	27,977	5,069	28,117
Number below poverty level	1,819	3,709	1,699	3,637	1,783	3,290	1,887	3,553
Percent below poverty level	40.7	13.7	35.4	13.0	35.4	11.8	37.2	12.6
Married-couple families	2,093	22,390	2,236	22,466	2,179	22,271	2,104	22,289
Number below poverty level	360	2,005	257	1,692	291	1,457	301	1,572
Percent below poverty level	17.2	9.0	11.5	7.5	13.3	6.5	14.3	7.1
Female householder, no husband present	2,199	4,037	2,386	4,522	2,624	4,627	2,698	4,786
Number below poverty level	1,401	1,584	1,384	1,812	1,415	1,671	1,513	1,814
Percent below poverty level	63.7	39.3	58.0	39.8	53.9	36.1	56.1	37.9
Male householder, no wife present	178	692	185	911	228	1,079	267	1,042
Number below poverty level	58	120	58	132	77	162	73	167
Percent below poverty level	32.7	17.4	31.5	14.5	33.8	15.0	27.3	16.0
Householder 65 years old and over	813	8,635	886	9,201	880	9,643	923	9,797
Number below poverty level	239	632	196	498	173	510	224	443
Percent below poverty level	29.4	7.3	22.1	5.4	19.6	5.3	24.2	4.5

Source: U.S. Bureau of the Census, Current Population Reports, The Black Population in the United States: March 1991, Washington, DC, 1992. p. 26.

Selected Characteristics of Families Below the Poverty Level.

Marital status, sex, and race	1960[1]	1970	1980	1990	1991
BLACK					
Men					
Total, 15 years and over	5,713	6,936	8,292	9,948	10,074
Percent	100.0	100.0	100.0	100.0	100.0
Never married	29.6	35.6	41.1	43.4	44.8
Married	63.3	56.9	48.9	45.1	43.1
Widowed	4.6	4.4	3.7	3.4	3.3
Divorced	2.4	3.1	6.3	8.1	8.8
Women					
Total, 15 years and over	6,375	8,108	10,108	11,966	12,124
Percent	100.0	100.0	100.0	100.0	100.0
Never married	21.7	27.7	33.7	36.9	38.7
Married	60.3	54.0	44.6	40.2	38.4
Widowed	14.3	13.8	13.0	11.6	11.9
Divorced	3.7	4.4	8.7	11.2	11.0
WHITE					
Men					
Total, 15 years and over	55,080	62,868	71,887	78,908	79,555
Percent	100.0	100.0	100.0	100.0	100.0
Never married	24.4	27.2	28.1	28.0	28.0
Married	70.3	68.0	65.0	62.7	62.4
Widowed	3.3	2.7	2.3	2.4	2.5
Divorced	2.1	2.1	4.7	6.8	7.1
Women					
Total, 15 years and over	58,040	68,888	77,882	84,508	85,012
Percent	100.0	100.0	100.0	100.0	100.0
Never married	18.6	21.3	21.0	20.6	20.8
Married	66.7	62.8	60.7	59.2	59.0
Widowed	11.9	12.4	11.9	11.6	11.2
Divorced	2.8	3.4	6.4	8.6	8.9

NOTE: 1960 and 1970 data are from the decennial censuses.

[1] Data for 1960 are for persons 14 years old and over.

Source: U.S. Bureau of the Census, Current Population Reports, The Black Population in the United States: March 1991, Washington, DC, 1992. p. 5.

Marital Status of the Population 15 years Old and Over.

ITEM	NUMBER (1,000)			PERCENT		
	1980	1990	1991	1980	1990	1991
Total married couples	49,714	53,256	53,227	100.0	100.0	100.0
Black-White married couples, total	167	211	231	0.3	0.4	0.4
Husband Black, wife White	122	150	156	0.2	0.3	0.3
Wife Black, husband White	45	61	75	0.1	0.1	0.1

Source: U.S. Bureau of the Census, Statistical Abstract of the United States: 1992 (112th edition) Washington, DC, 1992. p. 45.

Black-White Married Couples, 1980 to 1991.

POVERTY STATUS	1980	1985	1988	1990							
				Total[1]	White	Black	Hispanic[2]	Under 18 years old	18-44 years old	45-64 years old	65 years and over
Persons covered, total	18,966	19,204	21,185	24,261	15,078	7,809	3,912	12,094	7,284	2,302	2,582
Below poverty level	11,113	12,652	13,325	15,175	8,758	5,686	2,686	8,313	4,490	1,261	1,112
Above poverty level	7,854	6,552	7,860	9,086	6,320	2,123	1,226	3,781	2,794	1,041	1,470
Percent of total population	8.4	8.1	8.6	9.7	7.2	25.3	18.3	18.5	6.8	4.9	8.6
Below poverty level	39.1	39.7	42.3	45.2	39.2	57.8	44.7	61.9	36.1	31.0	30.4
Above poverty level	4.0	3.2	3.7	4.2	3.4	10.2	7.9	7.3	3.0	2.4	5.6

[1] Includes other races not shown separately. [2] Persons of Hispanic origin may be of any race.

Source: U.S. Bureau of the Census, Statistical Abstract of the United States: 1992 (112th edition) Washington, DC, 1992. p.103.

Selected Characteristics of Persons Covered by Medicaid, 1980 to 1990.

Specified age and year	All races Both sexes	All races Male	All races Female	White Both sexes	White Male	White Female	Black Both sexes	Black Male	Black Female
At birth				Remaining life expectancy in years					
1900[1,2]	47.3	46.3	48.3	47.6	46.6	48.7	333.0	332.5	333.5
1950[2]	68.2	65.6	71.1	69.1	66.5	72.2	60.7	58.9	62.7
1960[2]	69.7	66.6	73.1	70.6	67.4	74.1	63.2	60.7	65.9
1970	70.9	67.1	74.8	71.7	68.0	75.6	64.1	60.0	68.3
1975	72.6	68.8	76.6	73.4	69.5	77.3	66.8	62.4	71.3
1980	73.7	70.0	77.4	74.4	70.7	78.1	68.1	63.8	72.5
1981	74.2	70.4	77.8	74.8	71.1	78.4	68.9	64.5	73.2
1982	74.5	70.9	78.1	75.1	71.5	78.7	69.4	65.1	73.7
1983	74.6	71.0	78.1	75.2	71.7	78.7	69.6	65.4	73.6
1984	74.7	71.2	78.2	75.3	71.8	78.7	69.7	65.6	73.7
1985	74.7	71.2	78.2	75.3	71.9	78.7	69.5	65.3	73.5
1986	74.8	71.3	78.3	75.4	72.0	78.8	69.4	65.2	73.5
1987	75.0	71.5	78.4	75.6	72.2	78.9	69.4	65.2	73.6
1988	74.9	71.5	78.3	75.6	72.3	78.9	69.2	64.9	73.4
1989	75.3	71.8	78.6	76.0	72.7	79.2	69.2	64.8	73.5
Provisional data:									
1988[2]	74.9	71.4	78.3	75.5	72.1	78.9	69.5	65.1	73.8
1989[2]	75.2	71.8	78.5	75.9	72.6	79.1	69.7	65.2	74.0
1990[2]	75.4	72.0	78.8	76.0	72.6	79.3	70.3	66.0	74.5
At 65 years									
1900-1902[1,2]	11.9	11.5	12.2	—	11.5	12.2	—	10.4	11.4
1950[2]	13.9	12.8	15.0	—	12.8	15.1	13.9	12.9	14.9
1960[2]	14.3	12.8	15.8	14.4	12.9	15.9	13.9	12.7	15.1
1970	15.2	13.1	17.0	15.2	13.1	17.1	14.2	12.5	15.7
1975	16.1	13.8	18.1	16.1	13.8	18.2	15.0	13.1	16.7
1980	16.4	14.1	18.3	16.5	14.2	18.4	15.1	13.0	16.8
1981	16.7	14.3	18.6	16.7	14.4	18.7	15.5	13.4	17.3
1982	16.8	14.5	18.7	16.9	14.5	18.8	15.7	13.5	17.5
1983	16.7	14.5	18.6	16.8	14.5	18.7	15.5	13.4	17.3
1984	16.8	14.6	18.6	16.9	14.6	18.7	15.5	13.5	17.2
1985	16.7	14.6	18.6	16.8	14.6	18.7	15.3	13.3	17.0
1986	16.8	14.7	18.6	16.9	14.8	18.7	15.4	13.4	17.0
1987	16.9	14.8	18.7	17.0	14.9	18.8	15.4	13.5	17.1
1988	16.9	14.9	18.6	17.0	14.9	18.7	15.4	13.4	16.9
1989	17.2	15.2	18.8	17.3	15.2	19.0	15.5	13.6	17.0
Provisional data:									
1988[2]	16.9	14.8	18.6	17.0	14.9	18.7	15.5	13.6	17.1
1989[2]	17.2	15.2	18.8	17.3	15.2	18.9	15.8	13.8	17.4
1990[2]	17.3	15.3	19.0	17.3	15.3	19.0	16.1	14.2	17.6

Life Expectancy According to Race and Sex for Selected Years.

Sex, race, and cause of death	1985	1986	1987	1988	1989	1985	1986	1987	1988	1989
All races	Number					Rank				
All causes	2,086,440	2,105,361	2,123,232	2,167,999	2,150,466	—	—	—	—	—
Diseases of heart	771,169	765,490	760,353	765,156	733,867	1	1	1	1	1
Cerebrovascular diseases	153,050	149,643	149,835	150,517	145,551	3	3	3	3	3
Malignant neoplasms	461,563	469,376	476,927	485,048	496,152	2	2	2	2	2
Chronic obstructive pulmonary diseases	74,662	76,559	78,380	82,853	84,344	5	5	5	5	5
Pneumonia and influenza	67,615	69,812	69,225	77,662	76,550	6	6	6	6	6
Chronic liver disease and cirrhosis	26,767	26,159	26,201	26,409	26,694	9	9	9	9	9
Diabetes mellitus	36,969	37,184	38,532	40,368	46,833	7	7	7	7	7
Nephritis, nephrotic syndrome, and nephrosis	21,349	21,767	22,052	22,392	21,118	11	11	11	10	12
Septicemia	17,182	18,795	19,916	20,925	19,333	14	13	13	13	14
Atherosclerosis	23,926	22,706	22,474	22,086	19,357	10	10	10	11	13
Human immunodeficiency virus infection	—	—	13,468	16,602	22,082	—	—	15	15	11
Accidents and adverse effects	93,457	95,277	95,020	97,100	95,028	4	4	4	4	4
Suicide	29,453	30,904	30,796	30,407	30,232	8	8	8	8	8
Homicide and legal intervention	19,893	21,731	21,103	22,032	22,909	12	12	12	12	10
Black male										
All causes	133,610	137,214	139,551	144,228	146,393	—	—	—	—	—
Diseases of heart	38,982	39,076	38,934	39,584	38,321	1	1	1	1	1
Cerebrovascular diseases	8,000	7,938	7,852	8,098	7,739	4	4	4	5	5
Malignant neoplasms	29,028	29,363	29,928	30,321	31,452	2	2	2	2	2
Chronic obstructive pulmonary diseases	3,154	3,302	3,319	3,644	3,593	8	8	8	9	9
Pneumonia and influenza	3,664	3,836	3,795	4,047	4,168	6	6	6	7	7
Chronic liver disease and cirrhosis	2,616	2,404	2,574	2,476	2,517	9	9	10	11	11
Diabetes mellitus	2,230	2,295	2,388	2,640	3,072	10	10	11	10	10
Nephritis, nephrotic syndrome, and nephrosis	1,935	1,963	1,905	1,908	2,047	11	11	12	12	12
Septicemia	1,595	1,697	1,760	7,729	1,643	12	12	13	13	14
Atherosclerosis	758	756	680	739	547	16	15	17	17	17
Human immunodeficiency virus infection	—	—	3,301	4,202	5,475	—	—	9	6	6
Accidents and adverse effects	8,752	9,035	9,159	9,608	9,503	3	3	3	3	3
Suicide	1,481	1,537	1,635	1,648	1,771	13	13	14	14	13
Homicide and legal intervention	6,616	7,634	7,518	8,314	8,888	5	5	5	4	4
Black female										
All causes	110,597	113,112	115,263	119,791	121,249	—	—	—		
Diseases of heart	37,702	38,650	38,813	39,882	39,110	1	1	1	1	1
Cerebrovascular diseases	10,341	10,014	10,055	10,381	10,240	3	3	3	3	3
Malignant neoplasms	21,878	22,616	23,099	23,647	24,112	2	2	2	2	2
Chronic obstructive pulmonary diseases	1,505	1,554	1,733	1,832	2,078	11	11	11	11	9
Pneumonia and influenza	2,674	2,864	2,770	3,144	3,417	7	6	6	6	6
Chronic liver disease and cirrhosis	1,439	1,341	1,342	1,427	1,334	12	12	12	12	12
Diabetes mellitus	3,874	4,004	4,109	4,332	4,883	4	4	4	4	4
Nephritis, nephrotic syndrome, and nephrosis	2,109	2,057	2,070	2,249	2,119	8	8	8	8	8
Septicemia	1,662	1,720	1,988	2,011	1,912	10	10	9	10	11
Atherosclerosis	1,022	964	942	955	889	13	15	15	15	16
Human immunodeficiency virus infection	—	—	739	995	1,320	—	—	16	14	13
Accidents and adverse effects	3,455	3,550	3,618	3,879	3,901	5	5	5	5	5
Suicide	314	355	328	374	382	19	19	19	20	19
Homicide and legal intervention	1,666	1,861	1,969	2,089	2,074	9	9	10	9	10

NOTES: For data years shown, the code numbers for cause of death are based on the International Classification of Diseases, Ninth Revision, described in Appendix II, table V. Categories for the coding and classification of human immunodeficiency virus infection were introduced in the United States beginning with mortality data for 1987.

Source: National Center for Health Statistics. Health United States, 1991. Hyattsville, MD: Public Health Service, 1992. p. 158-160.

Number of Deaths and Rank for Selected Causes of Death, 1958 to 1989.

Race and year	Infant mortality rate[1] Total	Neonatal Under 28 days	Neonatal Under 7 days	Postneonatal	Fetal death rate[2]	Late fetal death rate[3]	Perinatal mortality rate[4]
Race of mother[7]: Black	Deaths per 1,000 live births						
1980	22.2	14.6	12.3	7.6	15.0	9.3	21.5
1981	20.8	14.0	11.8	6.8	14.3	8.5	20.2
1982	20.5	13.6	11.6	6.9	14.3	8.5	19.9
1983	20.0	12.9	11.1	7.0	14.0	8.0	19.0
1984	19.2	12.3	10.6	6.8	13.3	7.6	18.1
1985	19.0	12.6	10.8	6.4	13.1	7.4	18.1
1986	18.9	12.3	10.6	6.6	13.1	7.3	17.8
1987	18.8	12.3	10.5	6.4	13.5	7.3	17.7
1988	18.5	12.1	10.3	6.5	13.4	7.2	17.4
1989	18.6	11.9	10.1	6.7	13.5	7.1	17.1

[1] Infant mortality rate is number of deaths of infants under 1 years per 1,000 live births. Neonatal deaths occur within 28 days of birth; postneonatal death occur 28-365 days after birth. Deaths within 7 days are early neonatal deaths.

[2] Number of deaths of fetuses of 20 weeks or more gestation per 1,000 liver births plus fetal deaths.

[3] Number of fetal deaths of 28 weeks or more gestation per 1,000 liver births plus fetal deaths.

[4] Number of late fetal deaths plus infant deaths within 7 day of birth per 1,000 liver births plus late fetal deaths.

[5] Includes births and deaths of nonresidents of the United States.

[6] Deaths are tabulated by race of descendants; live births are tabulated by race of child (see Appendix II).

[7] Deaths are tabulated by race of descendants; live births are tabulated by race of mother (see Appendix II).

Source: National Center for Health Statistics. Health United States, 1991. Hyattsville, MD: Public Health Service, 1992. pp. 141-42.

Infant Mortality Rates, Fetal Death Rates, and Perinatal Mortality Rates for Selected Years.

16

Education

16

Education

The Origins of Black Educational Institutions ■ Toward African-Centered Education ■ Administrators, Educators, and Scholars ■ Historically and Predominantly Black Colleges and Universities ■ Research Institutions

Essays by Kenneth Estell and Kwame Kenyatta

The Origins of Black Educational Institutions

by Kenneth Estell

Since the first arrival of Africans in America, the African-American community has worked to sustain a system for educating its youth. In addition to the efforts of individuals, churches and charitable organizations have also played an important role in the creation of educational institutions for blacks in this country.

Early Christian Missionary Endeavors

Early attempts at educating blacks in America can be traced back to efforts by Christian churches. Although the primary goal of these missionaries was to convert Africans to Christianity, the process often involved general education.

French Catholics in Louisiana were probably the earliest group to begin providing instruction to black laborers in the early 1600s. The French code noir, a system of laws, made it incumbent upon masters to educate slaves.

Pennsylvania Quakers, who were in opposition to the institution of slavery, during the early 1700s organized monthly educational meetings for blacks, so they might have the opportunity for improvement. One such Quaker, Anthony Benezet, in 1750 established an evening school in his home which remained successful until 1760. In 1774 Quakers in Philadelphia joined together to open a school for blacks.

The Society for the Propagation of the Gospel in Foreign Parts, organized by the Church of England in 1701 for the purpose of converting African slaves to Christianity, was another organization which provided educational opportunities to blacks. In 1751 the Society sent Joseph Ottolenghi to convert and educate blacks in Georgia. Ottolenghi "promised to spare no pains to improve the young children."

African Free Schools in New York and Philadelphia

Like the Church, the anti-slavery movement played an important part in the creation of schools. In 1787 the Manumission Society founded the New York African Free School; by 1820 more than 500 black children were enrolled. Support increased as other African Free Schools were established in New York, until 1834 when the New York Common Council took over control of the schools.

In 1804 African Episcopalians in Philadelphia organized a school for black children. In 1848 a black industrial training school opened in Philadelphia at the House of Industry. Other schools in operation in Philadelphia included the Corn Street Unclassified School (1849), the Holmesburg Unclassified School (1854), and the Home for Colored Children (1859). By the mid-1860s there were 1,031 pupils in the black public schools of Philadelphia; 748 in the charity schools; 211 in the benevolent schools, and 331 in private schools.

Freedmen's Organizations and Agencies

At the close of the Civil War hundreds of thousands of free blacks were left without homes and adequate resources. As a means for providing temporary assistance to the newly freed slaves, numerous organizations were formed.

The New England Freedmen's Aid Society, organized in Boston on February 7, 1862, was founded to promote education

An engraving depicting an early black schoolroom.

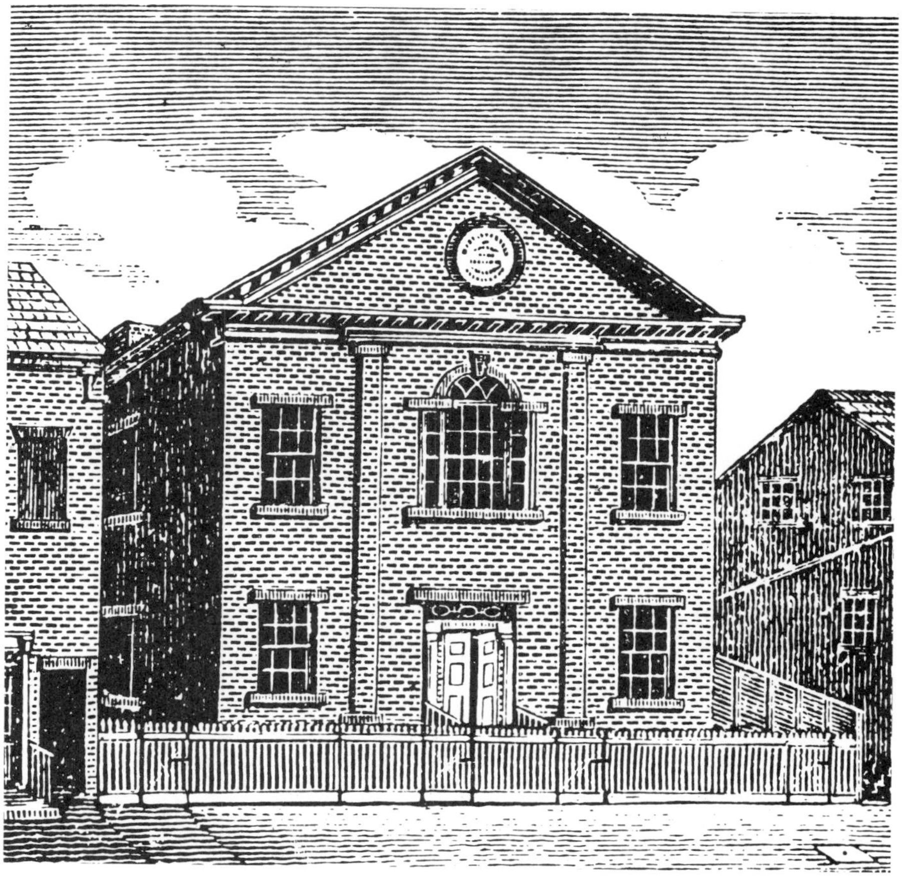

New York's African Free School No. 2.

among free African Americans. Supporters of the organization included Edward Everett Hale, Samuel Cabot, Charles Bernard, William Lloyd Garrison, and William Cullen Bryant. In New York a similar organization was founded, the National Freedmen's Relief Association on February 20, 1862. This was followed by the Port Royal Relief Committee, later known as the Pennsylvania Freedmens Relief Association, founded in Philadelphia on March 3, 1862. In 1863 several of these organizations merged to form the United States Commission for the Relief of the National Freedmen, which, in 1865, became the American Freedmen's Aid Union.

During the 1860s Congress passed several Freedmen's Bureau Acts, creating and financing an agency designed to provide temporary assistance to newly freed slaves. Under the acts, the bureau's chief functions were to provide food, clothing, and medical supplies. Working in conjunction with various benevolent organizations, bureau Commissioner General Oliver Otis Howard established and maintained schools, and managed to provide provisions for teachers. By 1870 the bureau operated over 2,600 schools in the South with 3,300 teachers educating 150,000 students; almost 4,000 schools were in operation prior to the abolition of the agency.

School-aged children in the rural South, c.1865.

A freedman's school in Beaufort, South Carolina, 1862

Independent Schools in the Late-Nineteenth Century

The education of African Americans has been largely a function of independent schools, private institutions founded to meet the educational and employment needs of African Americans.

One of the earliest surviving black independent schools, Tuskegee Normal and Industrial Institute (now Tuskegee Institute) was established in 1881 by an act of the Alabama general assembly. Booker T. Washington, the school's organizer and first principal, established at the school a curriculum which was to provide black students with

Students at the Snow Hill Institute, 1902.

the means to become economically self-supporting.

Similarly other independent schools developed around the country. In a lecture room at the Christ Presbyterian Church, Lucy Laney in 1883 opened what would become the Haines Normal and Industrial In-

An early schoolroom.

Booker T. Washington

stitute in Savannah, Georgia. In 1901 Nannie Helen Burroughs founded the National Training School for Women and Girls in Washington, DC. By the end of the first year the school had enrolled thirty-one students; twenty-five years later more than 2,000 women had trained at the school. In Sedalia, North Carolina in 1901, Charlotte Hawkins Brown founded the Palmer Memorial Institute.

With only $1.50 and five students, in 1904 Mary McLeod Bethune founded Daytona Normal and Industrial Institute for Girls (now Bethune-Cookman College) in Daytona Beach, Florida. Nineteen years later, the institute merged with the Cookman Institute of Jacksonville, Florida, founded in 1872 by D.S.B. Darnell. Some 2,000 students now study at Bethune-Cookman College.

Early Black Institutions of Higher Education

One of the oldest of the historically black institutions of higher education, named for the English abolitionist William Wilberforce, Wilberforce College (now Wilberforce University) was founded in 1856 by the African Methodist Episcopal Church. The school awarded its first degree in 1857. The oldest institution in operation today, Cheyney State in Pennsylvania, was founded in 1837.

Between 1865–1871 several predominantly black institutions of higher learning were founded, including Atlanta University (now Clark-Atlanta University), Shaw University and Virginia Union University (1865); Fisk University and Lincoln Institute (now Lincoln University) (1866); Talladega College, Augusta Institute (now Morehouse Col-

First site of Atlanta University.

Students at Tuskegee Institute, 1902.

lege), Biddle University (now Johnson C. Smith University), Howard University and Scotia Seminary (now Barber-Scotia College) (1867); Tougaloo College (1869); and Alcorn College (now Alcorn State University) and Benedict College (1871). Religious organizations were instrumental in the founding and support of these early black institutions. Atlanta, Fisk, Talladega, and Tougaloo were founded by the American Missionary Association; Benedict, Shaw, and Virginia Union were founded and supported by the American Baptist Home Mission Society.

Fisk University, c.1868.

Alcorn College, founded in 1871, was the first black land grant college. This was made possible under the Morrill Act of 1862, which provided federal land grant funds for higher education. In 1890 Congress passed the second Morrill Act, also known as the Land Grant Act of 1890. The second act stipulated that no federal aid was to be provided for the creation or maintenance of any white agricultural and mechanical school unless that state also provided for a similar school for blacks. As a result a system of separate,

Arthur Schomburg, founder of the Negro Society for Historical Research, with staff.

black land grant institutions developed, and became the basis of black higher education in the South.

By 1900 there were some thirty-four black institutions in the United States for higher education and more than 2,000 blacks with earned degrees. (John Hope Franklin. 1988. *From Slavery to Freedom, A History of Negro Americans*, 6th ed., New York: McGraw-Hill. p. 243.)

Early Promoters of African-American Studies

From its beginnings, the purpose of African-American studies has been to disseminate knowledge about the social, cultural, political, and historical experiences of Africans (see Darlene Clark Hine. 1992. "The Black Studies Movement: Afrocentric-Traditionalist—Feminist Paradigms for the Next Stage," *The Black Scholar* 22-3:11-18).

One of the forerunners in the field of black studies, theologian and educator Reverend Alexander Crummell, along with a group of black intellectuals, in 1897 founded the American Negro Academy in Washington, DC. The purpose of the organization was to foster scholarship and promote literature, science, and art among African Americans. The organization's members hoped that through the academy, an educated black elite, which would shape and direct society, would be born. Crummell first conceived the idea of an American Negro Academy while a student at Cambridge University, England. The organization's founding members included Paul Laurence Dunbar, William Sanders Scarborough, and W.E.B.

DuBois, among other noted educators. Following Crummell's death in 1908, DuBois was elected president of the academy.

In September 1915 Carter G. Woodson, a Harvard Ph.D. graduate, organized the Association for the Study of Negro Life and History (now the Association for the Study of Afro-American Life and History). The association's primary purpose was to promote research, encourage the study of African-American history, and to publish material on black history. In 1916 the organization began publishing the *Journal of Negro History*, for which Woodson served as editor until his death in 1950.

Other early scholars of African-American studies include sociologist E. Franklin Frazier (1894–1963), historian George Washington Williams (1849–1991), John Edward Bruce (1856–1924) and Arthur Schomburg, founders of the Negro Society for Historical Research (1911), and Alain Locke, founder of the Associates in Negro Folk Education (1934).

The End of Segregation in Public Education

In the years that followed the United States Supreme Court's 1896 ruling in the case *Plessy v. Ferguson*, segregation in public education became general practice. Prior to the Court's decision in *Brown v. Board of Education*, black children were often subjected to inferior educational facilities. However, by the 1930s a string of school desegregation cases reached the Court.

When Lloyd Lionel Gaines, an African American, had been refused admission to the law school of the State University of Missouri, he applied to state courts for an order to compel admission on the grounds that refusal constituted a denial of his rights under the Fourteenth Amendment of the U.S. Constitution. At that time, the state of Missouri maintained a practice of providing funds for blacks to attend graduate and professional schools outside of the state, rather than provide facilities itself. The university defended its action by maintaining that Lin-

Daisy Bates with four black students, who will attend formerly all-white high schools in Little Rock, Arkansas, 1959.

coln University, a predominantly black institution, would eventually establish its own law school, which Gaines could then attend. Until then the state would allow him to exercise the option of pursuing his studies outside the state on a scholarship. Ruling in the case *Missouri ex rel. Gaines v. Canada* in 1938, the United States Supreme Court ruled that states were required to provide equal educational facilities for blacks within its borders.

Taking an even greater step, in 1950 the United States Supreme Court ruled that a separate law school for blacks provided by the state of Texas violated the equal protection clause of the Fourteenth Amendment, when Herman Marion Sweatt, was refused admission to the law school of the University of Texas on the grounds that substantially equivalent facilities were already available in another Texas school open to blacks only. Ruling in the case *Sweatt v. Painter*, the Court ruled that the petitioner be admitted to the University of Texas Law School, since "in terms of number of the faculty, variety of courses and opportunity for specialization, size of the student body, scope of the library, availability of law review and similar activities, the University of Texas Law School is superior."

In 1952, five different cases, all dealing with segregation in public schools but with different facts and from different places, reached the United States Supreme Court. Four of the cases, *Brown v. Board of Education of Topeka* (out of Kansas), *Briggs v. Elliott* (out of South Carolina), *Davis v. Prince Edward County School Board* (out

Predominantly black colleges and universities continue to account for the majority of black graduates.

Students being bused in Woodville, Mississippi

of Virginia), and *Gebhart v. Belton* (out of Delaware) were considered together; the fifth case, *Bolling v. Sharpe*, coming out of the District of Columbia, was considered separately (since the district is not a state).

After hearing initial arguments, the Court found itself unable to reach an agreement. In 1953, the Court heard reargument. Thurgood Marshall, legal consul for the NAACP Legal Defense and Education Fund, presented arguments on behalf of the black students. On May 17, 1954, the Court unanimously ruled that segregation in all public education deprived minority children of equal protection under the Fourteenth Amendment. (In the *Bolling* case, the Court determined that segregation violated provisions of the Fifth Amendment, since the Fourteenth Amendment is expressly directed to the states.)

Black Colleges in the Twentieth-Century

Predominantly black colleges and universities continue to account for the majority of black graduates. This is especially true in the areas of science, mathematics, and engineering. In 1964, over 51 percent of all blacks in college were still enrolled in the historically black colleges and universities. By 1970 the proportion was 28 percent, and by fall 1978, 16.5 percent. As recently as 1977, 38 percent of all blacks receiving baccalaureate degrees earned their degrees at black institutions. In 1980 some 190,989 African Americans were enrolled at historically black institutions. By 1988 the total black enrollment at these institutions reached 217,462.

Independent Schools in the Late-Twentieth Century

For years independent schools have been founded in order to exert greater control, ensure quality in education and to meet the needs of African-American children.

In 1932, in order to promote religious growth in the Muslim community, the Nation of Islam founded the University of Islam, an elementary and secondary school to educate black Muslim children in Detroit. Clara Muhammad, wife of Elijah Muhammad served as the school's first instructor. In 1934 a second school was opened in Chicago; by 1965 schools were operating in Atlanta and Washington, DC. The current system of black Muslim schools, named for Clara Muhammad, is an outgrowth of the earlier University of Islam. There are currently thirty-eight Sister Clara Muhammad schools in the United States (Hakim M. Rashid and Zakiyyah Muhammad. 1992 "The Sister Clara Muhammad Schools," *The Journal of Negro Education*, 61:178-185).

Gertrude Wilks and other black community leaders in East Palo Alto, California in 1966 organized the Nairobi Day School, a Saturday school. In 1969 the school became a full-time school. It closed in 1984.

Also founded as a Saturday school program in 1972, the New Concept Development Center in Chicago set out to create an educational institution which promoted self-respect, cooperation, and an awareness of African-American history and culture. In 1975 public school teacher and nurse, Marva Collins founded the Westside Preparatory School in Chicago.

Recently the educational and social needs of urban youth, particularly African-American males, have been given increased attention. Studies show that nearly forty percent of adult black males are functionally illiterate, and that the number of African-American males incarcerated far outnumbers the number of black males in college (Donald O. Leake and Brenda L. Leake. 1992. "Islands of Hope: Milwaukee's African American Immersion Schools," *The Journal of Negro Ed-*

Marva Collins with her class at the Westside Preparatory School, Chicago.

ucation. 61:24-29). Addressing these issues, large urban school systems, including Baltimore, Detroit, and Milwaukee, have attempted to create programs which focus on the needs of African-American males.

Although African-American students have shown improved performance on achievement tests, gaps between black students and white still exist. Although progress has been made in the quality of education for black children, inadequacies remain in the provision of resources for the education of blacks. In recent years, efforts at creating alternative schools designed to meet the needs of African-American children and to reflect the culture and social experiences of blacks have received increased attention. In 1991 the Institute for Independent Education, an organization providing technical assistance to independent neighborhood schools, reported an estimated 300 such schools serving children of color in the United States (Gail Foster. 1992 "New York City's Wealth of Historically Black Independent Schools," *The Journal of Negro Education* 61:186-200).

Toward African-Centered Education

by Kwame Kenyatta

The African centered thrust in education has sparked national enthusiasm, debates, and attacks. Whereas many people of African descent see this as a dream come true, others see African-centrism as an attack on American fundamentalism.

American fundamentalism can be defined as a Eurocentric world view, based on the myth of white supremacy. In other words, the fundamental principles of education in

America are rooted in the theory that whites are superior and that all people of color are inferior. This myth of white supremacy laid the foundation for manifest destiny and eminent domain, thereby giving justification for the annihilation of the Native Americans, and enslavement of Africans.

Based on the above views, I submit to you that the mis-education, marginalization, and out right neglect of children of African descent and other children of color is done by design and not by accident.

Attacks on African-Centered Education

The attacks on African-centered education in recent years has been concerted and consistent. Most evident has been the many books, national magazines and newspaper articles, charging African-centerism with the "dis-uniting" and "fraying" of American society. Arthur Schlesinger, author of *The Dis-Uniting of America*, and Diane Ravitch, author of *The Troubled Crusade*, have been the lead gladiators in the fight against African centered education. Schlesinger has charged that African centered education is un-American and promotes the teaching of inaccuracy and distorted history; Diane Ravitch has argued that African-centrism is "particularism that is spreading like wildfire through the educational system, promoted by organizations and individuals with a political and professional interest in strengthening ethic power bases." Schlesinger, Ravitch, and other defenders of the Euro-centric world view have worked to discredit African scholars such as Dr. Leonard Jeffries, Dr. Molefi Asante, Dr. Asa Hillard, and Dr. John Henrik-Clark. All of this is designed to convince both blacks and whites

Principal Dr. Clifford Watson with students of the Malcolm X Academy, Detroit, Michigan.

that African-centrism is nothing more than an Africanized curriculum.

However, one point that Schlesinger makes about African-centrism is true—the point that African-centrism in "un-American." He states that European ideas and culture formed the American republic and that the United States is an extension of European civilization. African-centrism, on the other hand, provides a world view that is contrary to European ideas and culture—a culture which has oppressed Africans and other people of color.

In an article that appeared in the *Wall Street Journal*, on April 23, 1990, Schlesinger argues that Native Americans and person of African descent must be able to assimilate in the same way that Russians, Jews, French, Germans and the Irish immigrants have. However, European immigrants have not been oppressed, exploited, and enslaved because of their color. Native Americans and Africans, on the other hand, have been and continue to be oppressed and exploited. Therefore, it is clear that assimilation of people of color never has been and never will be a reality in America.

In an African-centered environment, the classroom is transformed into a holistic learning environment, in which the student is the center.

The Foundations of African-Centered Education

African-centrism is not just historical facts and figures centered around time and space. African-centrism is based on the principle of MAAT—truth, justice, balance, and order. African-centrism presents to black students their own cultural life experiences. The classroom is transformed into a holistic learning environment, in which the student is the center. Although African-centrism benefits all students, the overall thrust of African-centered education is the recentering of children of African descent.

The education of African children is fundamental to the continual survival and liberation of African people. As a people, Africans have been trained to accept oppression. The educational system in America has been designed to promote and advance a racist and capitalistic agenda—an agenda which has made Africans dysfunctional and hostile to our very existence—an agenda which has trained Africans to be employees and consumers who work for and buy from someone else—an agenda which allows African children to graduate, not knowing how to read, write, or perform basic mathematical functions, not to mention how to think.

Many African children do not graduate, they simply drop out. They become statistics at juvenile centers, group homes, foster care, adoption agencies, prison yards, and grave yards. They are often referred to by such code names as "at risk" and "inner city youth". They are at risk because they have been targeted for failure.

As we move toward the twenty-first century we cannot continue to accept this Eurocentric definition of education. Educating children must be based on the principles of "self-determination." We will define, defend, and develop what is in our best interest. African-centered education is in our best interest. African-centered education will instill in our youth a sense of self-confidence, pride, and responsibility. It will replace the "dog-eat-dog" and the "do-your-own-thing" mentality with a sense of respect for all people.

When the Eurocentric style of teaching comes in conflict with the African child, the African child is then labeled "non-responsive" or "hyper-active." Children are often labeled "learning disabled" and placed in a special education program. However, the problem is with the Eurocentric style of teaching. The solution is an end to the use of the Eurocentric teaching style, since Eurocentrism is alien to the African child. It is virtually impossible to educate African children using the Eurocentric teaching style, due to the historical relationship of oppression and open hostility that continues to exist between Europeans and non-European people. One cannot prepare a child for a liberating life experience using an oppressive philosophy.

As we move toward an African-centered education, African children will no longer see the contributions of their people as a footnote of history, but rather as the center and origin of history—African-centrism will stand and be celebrated as one of the most progressive educational philosophies in the twenty-first century.

■ ADMINISTRATORS, EDUCATORS, AND SCHOLARS

Molefi Kete Asante (1942–)
Scholar

Asante was born Arthur Lee Smith, Jr. on August 14, 1942 in Valdosta, Georgia. His name was legally changed in 1975. He graduated cum laude with a B.A. from Oklahoma Christian College in 1964, received an M.A. from Pepperdine University in 1965 and a Ph.D. from UCLA in 1968.

Asante has taught speech and communications at many universities in the United States. He was an instructor at California State Polytechnic University at Pomona (1966–1967) and California State University at Northridge (1967). In 1968 he accepted an assistant professorship at Purdue University

Molefi Kete Asante

in Lafayette, Indiana where he remained until 1969 when he began teaching at UCLA where he advanced from assistant to associate professor of speech. While at UCLA he also served as the director of the Center for Afro-American Studies (1970–1973). In 1973 he accepted the position of professor of communications at the State University of New York. He soon became department chairman, a position he held until 1979 when he became a visiting professor at Howard University in Washington, DC (1979–1980). In 1981 and 1982 he was a Fullbright Professor at the Zimbabwe Institute of Mass Communications. Since 1980 he has been a professor at Temple University in Philadelphia in their Department of Pan African Studies.

Asante is a prolific author with over twenty-four books dealing with both communication theory and the African-American experience. He has published books under both names. Some of his most recent titles are *Afrocentricity: The Theory of Social Change* (1980), *African Culture: The Rhythms of Unity* (1985) and *The Historical and Cultural Atlas of African-Americans* (1991).

Asante is also a founding editor of the *Journal of Black Studies* and has been a member of the advisory board of the *Black Law Journal* (1971–1973) and *Race Relations Abstract* (1973–1977).

Mary McLeod Bethune (1875–1955)
Educator, Bethune-Cookman College Founder

Born on July 10, 1875 in Mayesville, South Carolina Mary McLeod received a sporadic education in local schools. She eventually received a scholarship and studied for seven years at the Scotia Seminary in Concord, North Carolina. In 1893 she went on to study at the Moody Bible Institute in Chicago in lieu of a missionary position in Africa. In 1895 she began teaching at the Haines Institute in Augusta, Georgia. Between 1900 and 1904 she taught in Sumter, Georgia and Palatka, Florida.

In 1904 she founded her own school in Daytona Beach, Florida— the Daytona Educational and Industrial School for Negro Girls. John D. Rockefeller became an early admirer and supporter of the school after hearing a performance by its choir. Bethune went on to found the Tomoka Missions and in 1911 the McLeod Hospital. In 1922 her school merged with the Cookman Institute to become Bethune-Cookman College.

Bethune's work received national attention and she served on two conferences under President Herbert Hoover. In 1936 President Franklin Roosevelt appointed her director of the Division of Negro Affairs of

Mary McLeod Bethune

the National Youth Administration. During World War II she served as special assistant to the Secretary of War, responsible for selecting Negro WAC officer candidates.

Bethune also served on the executive board of the National Urban League and was a vice-president of the NAACP. She received the Spingarn Award in 1935, the Frances A. Drexel Award in 1936 and the Thomas Jefferson Medal in 1942. Bethune was also instrumental in the founding of the National Council of Negro Women. She retired from public life in 1950 on her seventy-fifth birthday and died five years later on May 18, 1955.

Much of Bethune's philosophy had to do with ennobling labor and empowering African-Americans to achieve economic independence. Although a tireless fighter for equality, she eschewed rhetorical militancy in favor of a doctrine of universal love.

Nannie Helen Burroughs (1879–1961)
Educator

Known as a brilliant orator, Burroughs was a lifelong booster of women's education and a tireless civic organizer. In 1901 the National Training School for Women and Girls opened in Washington, DC, with Burroughs as president; by the end of the first school year the school had enrolled thirty-one students. In 1934 the name was changed to the National Trades and Professional School for Women. In 1964 the school was again renamed the Nannie Helen Burroughs School, with a new elementary school curriculum. Burroughs was active in the antilynching campaign and a life member of the Association for the Study of Negro Life and History. She helped organize the Women's Industrial Club of Louisville and was responsible for organizing Washington, DC's first black self-help program.

Fanny Coppin (1873–1913)
Educator

Fanny Coppin was born in slavery but rose to prominence in the field of education. After her aunt purchased her freedom, Coppin went on to become the second African-American woman to receive a degree from Oberlin College.

Coppin was appointed principal of the women's department of the Institute for Colored Youth, a high school established by Quakers in 1837, and later principal of the entire school. In 1894 Coppin founded the Women's Exchange and Girls' Home. She served as president of the local Women's Mite Missionary Society and the Women's Home and Foreign Missionary Society, and as a vice president of the National Association of Colored Women.

Coppin, an active member of the African Methodist Episcopal Church, served as president of the AME Home Missionary Society and accompanied her husband, Levi J. Coppin, on a missionary venture to South Africa.

Before her death Coppin began writing an autobiography, *Reminiscences of School Life, and Hints on Teaching.*

Joe Clark (1939–   )
Educator

Best known as the feisty, dedicated, baseball-bat-wielding school principal portrayed in the film *Lean on Me*, Clark has served as an exemplar of school discipline and boasts a distinguished record of achievements and laurels. A fourteen-year member of the New Jersey Board of Education and an elementary and secondary-school principal since 1979, he has been honored by the White House, the NAACP, his alma mater Seton Hall University, and various newspapers and magazines.

Born in Rochelle, Georgia, Clark served in the United States Army Reserve from 1958–1966. He received a B.A. from New Jersey's William Paterson College in 1960 and his master's degree from Seton Hall in 1974. Between the degrees he served on the Board of Education; from 1976–1979 he was a coordinator of language arts. He then began his career as school principal, and only a few years after he began the accolades came pouring in. Clark received the NAACP Community Service award and was named New Jerseyan of the Year by the Newark *Star Ledger* in 1983; the next year *New Jersey Monthly* named him an outstanding educator. In 1985 Clark appeared in Washington, DC to receive honors at a presidential conference on academic and disciplinary excellence, and also took awards from Seton Hall and Farleigh Dickinson University. The National School Safety Center gave Clark the Principal of Leadership award in 1986 and the National Black Policemen's Association bestowed their humanitarian award upon him in 1988.

Joe Clark

Johnetta Cole (1936–   )
Spelman College President

A distinguished scholar, Johnetta Cole has served on the faculties of Washington State University, University of Massachusetts, Hunter College, and Spelman College, the historically black women's institution in Atlanta where she is president. Born in Jacksonville, Florida, Cole attended Oberlin College, which awarded her a BA in 1957; she went on to earn her master's and doctorate at Northwestern.

Cole held her first teaching post at Washington State, where she taught anthropology and served as director of black studies; the university dubbed her Outstanding Faculty Member of the Year for 1969–70. She has served as a visiting professor of anthropology at several of the institutions named above. As an anthropologist, she has done field work in Liberia, Cuba, and in the African-American community. A prolific writer, she has published in many mainstream periodicals as well as scholarly journals. Since 1979 she has been a contributor and advising editor to *The Black Scholar*. She headed the Association of Black Anthropologists in 1980 and has been a fellow of the American Anthropological Association since 1970, as well as a board member of the Center for Cuban Studies since 1971.

Marva Collins (1936–   )
Educator

Schoolteacher Marva Delores Nettles Collins's dedication and ingenuity moved the producers of television's "60 Minutes" to do

Johnetta Cole

a feature on her and even inspired a made-for-TV film.

The Monroeville, Alabama native received a bachelor's degree from Clark College in 1957, after which she attended Northwestern University; her teaching career began at the Monroe County Training School in her hometown in 1958. She taught at Delano Elementary School from 1960–1975 and has been a fixture at Chicago's Westside Preparatory School ever since.

Collins served as director of the Right to Read Foundation in 1978, and has been a member of the President's Commission on White House Fellowships since 1981. A variety of organizations have honored her, including the NAACP, the Reading Reform Foundation, the Fred Hampton Foundation, and the American Institute for Public Service. Among the institutions that have given her honorary degrees are Washington University, Amherst, Dartmouth, Chicago State University, Howard University and Central State University.

Sarah Mapp Douglass (1806–1882)
Educator

The free-born Sarah Mapp Douglass was an outspoken antislavery activist and accomplished educator. She attended the Ladies Institute of the Pennsylvania Medical

University. In the 1820s she organized a school for black children in Philadelphia.

Douglass was an active member of the Philadelphia Female Anti-Slavery Society, which also provided support to Douglass's school. She also served as vice chairman of the Freedmen's Aid Society and was a member of the New York Anti-Slavery Women.

In 1853 Douglass was appointed head of the girls' department at the Institute of Colored Youth (forerunner of Cheney State College). She remained there until her retirement in 1877. Douglass died in Philadelphia on September 8, 1882.

John Hope Franklin

John Hope Franklin (1915–)
Scholar

Franklin's long and distinguished career has included the publication of numerous books of history and biography, numerous awards and honorary degrees and a position of great stature in the scholarly community.

Marva Collins

Franklin was born in Rentiesville, Oklahoma. He received his bachelor's degree from Fisk University in 1935 and then began graduate work at Harvard, which awarded him a master's in 1936 and a Ph.D. in 1941. He taught history at Fisk and St. Augustine's College while working on his doctorate, later moving on to North Carolina College at Durham, Howard University, Brooklyn College (where he chaired the history department), Cambridge University, the University of Chicago, and Duke University.

Among his many publications are such books as *From Slavery to Freedom, A History of Negro Americans, Militant South, Reconstruction After the Civil War, The Emancipation Proclamation, A Southern*

Odyssey, and *Race and History: Selected Essay*. Twice a Guggenheim Fellow, Franklin received honors from the Fellowship of Southern Writers, Encyclopedia Britannica and many other organizations, was made professor emeritus of history at Duke and earned the Publications Prize of the American Studies Association established in his name in 1986.

William H. Gray III (1941–)
United Negro College Fund President

Born to a minister and a high school teacher in Baton Rouge, Louisiana, William H. Gray III began his professional life as an assistant pastor at Union Baptist Church in New Jersey. He earned a bachelor's degree from Franklin and Marshall College in 1963, serving during his senior year as an intern for Pennsylvania congressman Robert C. Nix. He received a Master's of Divinity from Drew Theological School in 1966 and a Master of Theology degree from Princeton Theological Seminary in 1970. In between he attended the University of Pennsylvania, Temple and Oxford. He then served as pastor of Union Baptist.

In 1976 Gray moved into politics, challenging Nix for his congressional seat. He lost the first time, but returned to unseat Nix in 1979. He became a vocal and influential member of the House, challenging the administration of Ronald Reagan on such issues as social spending and U.S. support for the government of South Africa. He served on the House Budget Committee, becoming chair in 1985; he there earned the admiration and respect of even his most implacable political foes. Gray left the House of Representatives in 1991 to head the United Negro College Fund.

William Gray

Franklin G. Jenifer (1939–)
Howard University President

A distinguished scholar, Franklin Jenifer was trained as a biologist and taught in the biology departments of such institutions as Livingston College at Rutgers University, where he chaired the biology department from 1974–77. He obtained his doctorate from the University of Maryland, but it was to his alma mater, Howard University—where he received his bachelor's and master's degrees—that he would return to take up his most visible position: university president. He became Howard's president in 1990 after a series of assignments ranging from vice chancellor of the New Jersey Department of Higher Education to chancellor of the Massachusetts Board of Regents.

A native of Washington, DC, Jenifer is chairman of the AAAS National Council for Science & Technology Education and a board member of the American Council on Education and the Council for Aid to Education. He holds honorary doctorates from Babson College, Boston College, Mount Holyoke College, the University of Medicine and Dentistry of New Jersey, and Wheelock College.

Charles S. Johnson (1893–1956)
Scholar, Former Fisk University President

Charles Spurgeon Johnson was born in Bristol, Virginia. He earned a B.A. degree from Virginia Union University and in a Ph.D. from the University of Chicago.

Johnson occupied a number of diverse positions, from editor to administrator. He served as the assistant executive secretary of the Chicago Commission on Race Relations and as research director of the National Urban League, where he founded the organization's journal, *Opportunity*. In 1928 Johnson was made chairman of Fisk University's department of social sciences. While at Fisk he established the Fisk Institute of Race Relations. In 1933 he was appointed director of Swarthmore College's Institute of Race Relations. In 1946 Johnson was appointed president of Fisk University—the first black to hold the position.

Johnson wrote several books including *The Negro in American Civilization* (1930), *The Economic Status of the Negro* (1933), *The Negro College Graduate* (1936), and *Educational and Cultural Crisis* (1951).

Alain Locke (1886–1954)
Scholar

Born on September 3, 1886 in Philadelphia, Locke graduated Phi Beta Kappa with a B.A. degree from Harvard University in 1907. He was then awarded a Rhodes Scholarship for two years of study at Oxford University in England and did further graduate study at the University of Berlin (1910–1911). Upon returning to the United States, Locke took an assistant professorship in English and philosophy at Howard University in Washington, DC. He received his Ph.D. from Harvard in 1918 and the same year was made chairman of the philosophy department at Howard where he stayed until his retirement in 1953.

Alain Locke

In 1934 Locke founded the Associates in Negro Folk Education. In 1942 he was named to the Honor Role of Race Relations. A prolific author, Locke's first book was entitled *Race Contacts and Inter-Racial Relations* (1916). His best known works include, *The New Negro: An Interpretation* (1925), a book that introduced America to the Harlem Renaissance, and *The Negro in Art: A Pictorial Record of the Negro Artist and of the Negro Theme in Art* (1940). Locke died in New York City on June 9, 1954.

Benjamin Mays and others meet with President John F. Kennedy.

Benjamin E. Mays (1894–1984)
Former Morehouse College President

In addition to occupying the president's office at Morehouse, Benjamin Mays wrote, taught mathematics, worked for the Office of Education, served as chairman of the Atlanta Board of Education, preached in a Baptist church, acted as an advisor to the Southern Christian Leadership Council, and was a church historian.

Born in Epworth, South Carolina, Dr. Mays attended Bates College and later received his master's and Ph.D. from the University of Chicago. He served as a pastor at Georgia's Shiloh Baptist Church from 1921–24, and later taught at Morehouse College and South Carolina's State College at Orangeburg. After a stint at the Tampa Urban League, he worked for the YMCA as National Student Secretary and then directed a study of black churches for the Institute of Social and Religious Research. From 1934–40 he acted as dean of Howard University's School of Religion, before taking up the presidency of Morehouse from 1940–67. He served in several other distinguished posts, including the Atlanta Board of Education chairmanship and positions at HEW and the Ford Foundation. Awards earned by Dr. Mays include 43 honorary degrees, the Dorie Miller Medal of Honor, and the 1971 Outstanding Older Citizen award.

Jesse Edward Moorland (1863–1940)
Archivist, Clergyman

Moorland was born on September 10, 1863 in Coldwater, Ohio. Following the untimely death of his parents, Moorland was reared by his grandparents. His early education consisted of sporadic attendance at a small rural schoolhouse and being read to by his grandfather. Moorland eventually attended Normal University in Ada, Ohio, married and taught school in Urbana, Ohio. He went on to Howard University in Washington and graduated with a degree in theology in 1891.

Moorland was ordained a congregational minister and between 1891 and 1896 he served at churches in South Boston, Virginia, Nashville and Cleveland. In 1891 he also became active in the YMCA, an association he would maintain for much of his life.

In 1909 Moorland's well known essay "Demand and the Supply of Increased Efficiency in the Negro Ministry" was published by the American Negro Academy. In it Moorland called for a more pragmatic ministry, both in terms of the education of its members and its approach to dealing with social issues.

By 1910 Moorland had become quite active in the YMCA and was appointed secretary of the Colored Men's Department. In this position Moorland raised millions of dollars for the YMCA's construction and building fund.

Having reached the mandatory retirement age in 1923, Moorland resigned from the YMCA and began devoting his time and considerable energy to other pursuits. Moorland was active with the Association for the Study of Negro Life and History, the National Health Circle for Colored People, and the Frederick Douglass Home Association.

From 1907 on Moorland served as a trustee of Howard University. In 1914 he donated his private library of African-American history to the university. Out of this gift grew the Moorland Foundation. The collection was renamed the Moorland-Spingarn Collection and later renamed the Moorland-Spingarn Research Center. This collection of documents on black history and culture was the first African-American research collection in a major American university. Moorland died in New York on April 30, 1940.

Frederick D. Patterson (1901–1988)
United Negro College Fund Founder

Frederick Douglass Patterson was born in Washington, DC. He received a D.V.M degree, in 1923, and a M.S. degree, in 1927, from Iowa State University. In 1932 he received a Ph.D. from Cornell University.

Patterson joined the faculty of Tuskegee Institute in 1928, first as an instructor of veterinary science, later as director of the school of agriculture, and finally as president. He also chaired the R.R. Moton Memorial Institute and served as director of education for the Phelps-Stokes Fund.

In 1944 Patterson organized the United Negro College Fund, a cooperative fundraising organization to provide financial assistance to predominantly black colleges and universities.

Benjamin F. Payton (1932–)
Tuskegee University President

Born in Orangeburg, South Carolina, Benjamin Franklin Payton took a bachelor's degree with honors from South Carolina State College in 1955. Earning a Danforth Graduate Fellowship, he proceeded to distinguish himself with a B.D. from Howard University, a master's from Columbia and, in 1963, a Ph.D. from Yale. He then took a position as assistant professor at Howard University before working for the National Council of Churches as the Commission on Religion and Race's executive director of social justice, a position which he retained even as he took over the presidency of Benedict College in 1967. He left Benedict in 1972 for a position at the Ford Foundation, where he remained until he became Tuskegee's president in 1981.

Payton holds honorary degrees from Eastern Michigan University, Morris Brown, Benedict, and Morgan State. A recipient of the Napoleon Hill Foundation Gold Medal Award and the Benjamin E. Mays Award, he served as educational advisor to Vice President George Bush on Bush's seven nation tour of Africa in 1982. Payton has also served as a member of myriad organizations, including the National Association for Equal Opportunity in High Education, the Alabama Industrial Relations Council, the National Association of Independent Colleges and Universities, the Executive Board of the National Consortium for Educational Access.

Arthur A. Schomburg (1874–1938)
Archivist, American Negro Academy President

Born in Puerto Rico, Arturo Schomburg led a richly varied public life. He worked as a law clerk and was a businessman, journalist, editor, lecturer, New York Public Library curator, and teacher of Spanish.

In 1911 Schomburg co-founded the Negro Society for Historical Research. He was also a lecturer for the United Negro Improvement Association. Schomburg was a member of the New York Puerto Rico Revolutionary Party and served as secretary of the Cuban Revolutionary Party. In 1922 he headed the American Negro Academy, an organization founded by Alexander Crummell in 1879 to promote black art, literature, and science.

Schomburg collected thousands of works on black culture over his life time. In 1926 Schomburg's personal collection was purchased by the Carnegie Corporation and given to the New York Public Library. In 1973 the collection became known as the Schomburg Collection of Negro Literature and History, the name was later changed to the Schomburg Center for Research in Black Culture.

Shelby Steele (1946–)
Scholar

Steele was born January 1, 1946 in Chicago but grew up in Phoenix, Illinois, a blue collar suburb of Chicago. He attended high school in Harvey, Illinois, where he was student council president his senior year prior to graduating in 1964. Steel then attended Coe College in Cedar Rapids, Iowa where he was active in SCOPE—an organization associated with Martin Luther King's Southern Christian Leadership Council. He graduated in 1968 and in 1971 received an M.S. in socio-

Arthur Schomburg

Shelby Steele

logy from Southern Illinois University. He went on to receive a Ph.D. in English literature from the University of Utah in 1974. While at Southern Illinois University he taught African-American literature to impoverished children in East Saint Louis. Steele is currently a professor of English literature at San Jose State University.

In 1990 Steele published *The Content of Our Character: A New Vision of Race in America*, which won the National Book Critics Circle Award. In this controversial book Steele argued that African-American self-doubt and it's exploitation by the white and black liberal establishment is as great a cause of problems for African Americans as more traditional forms of racism. Steele has also written articles on this theme for such respected publications as *Harper's*, *New Republic*, *American Scholar*, and *Commentary*.

Because of his beliefs Steele has been identified as part of an emerging black neoconservative movement, but in an interview with *Time* magazine (August 12, 1991) he categorized himself as a classical liberal focusing on the freedom and sacredness of the individual.

Clifton R. Wharton, Jr. (1926–)
Former University President

Clifton R. Wharton was the first African American to head the largest university system in the United States—the State University of New York. He also helmed Michigan State University and served as chairman and CEO of the Teachers Insurance and Annuity Association and College Retirement Equities Fund.

A native Bostonian, Wharton took a bachelor's degree cum laude from Harvard in 1947. He received a master's at Johns Hopkins the following year, as the first African American admitted into the university's

Clifton Wharton

School for Advanced International Studies. In 1956 he took a second MA from the University of Chicago, which awarded him a Ph.D. in 1958. Between master's degrees he worked as a research associate for the University of Chicago. He then proceeded to the Agricultural Development Council, Inc., where he worked for twelve years. He also held a post as visiting professor at the University of Malaya and served as director and eventually vice president of the American Universities Research Program. Wharton took over the presidency of Michigan State in 1970 and stayed there for eight years; he moved on to the SUNY system from 1978–87. He then worked for the Teachers Insurance and Annuity Association and has since become the first African American to chair the Rockefeller Foundation.

Carter G. Woodson

Carter G. Woodson (1875–1950)
Scholar

Carter Godwin Woodson was born December 9, 1875, in New Canton, Virginia. He received a B.Litt. degree from Berea College in 1903, a B.A. and an M.A. in 1907 and 1908 from the University of Chicago, and a Ph.D. from Harvard University in 1912.

Known as the "Father of Modern Black History," Woodson was a passionate exponent of African-American economic self-sufficiency. In 1915 Woodson founded the Association for the Study of Negro Life and History (now the Association for the Study of Afro-American Life and History). One year later, the organization began publishing the *Journal of Negro History*. In 1920 he founded Associated Publishers, Inc. and in 1921 he founded the *Negro History Bulletin*. In 1926 Woodson launched Negro History Week (now Black History Month) to promote the study of African-American history.

An historian, author, editor, and teacher, Woodson served as dean of the Howard University School of Liberal Arts and of the West Virginia Institute, and was a Spingarn Medalist. His works include *The Education of the Negro Prior to 1861* (1915), *A Century of Negro Migration* (1918), *The Negro in Our History* (1922), and *The Miseducation of the Negro* (1933).

Ivan Van Sertima (1935–   )
Scholar

Born in British Guyana, anthropologist, linguist, and literary critic Ivan Van Sertima is currently professor of African studies at Rutgers University.

In 1977 Van Sertima published *They Came Before Columbus: The African Presence in Ancient America*. Drawing from various disciplines, Van Sertima, presents evidence of pre-Columbian contact with the New World by Africans.

In 1979 Van Sertima founded *The Journal of African Civilizations*, which presents a revisionist approach to world history. He is also the author of *Caribbean Writers*, a collection of essays.

HISTORICALLY AND PREDOMINANTLY BLACK COLLEGES AND UNIVERSITIES

Alabama A&M University
PO Box 285
Normal, AL 35762
(205)851-5245

Alabama State University
915 S. Jackson St.
Montgomery, AL 36195
(205)293-4291

Albany State College
504 College Dr.
Albany, GA 31705

Alcorn State University
PO Box 359
Lorman, MS 39096
(601)877-6147

Allen University
1530 Harden St.
Columbia, SC 29204
(803)254-9735

Arkansas Baptist College
1600 Bishop St.
Little Rock, AR 72202
(501)374-7856

Atlanta Metropolitan College
1630 Stewart Ave. SW
Atlanta, GA 30310
(404)756-4441

Barber-Scotia College
145 Cabarrud Ave.
Concord, NC 28025
(704)786-5171

Benedict College
Harden and Blanding Sts.
Columbia, SC 29204
(803)256-4220

Bennett College
900 E. Washington St.
Greensboro, NC 27401
(919)370-8624

Bethune-Cookman College
640 2nd Ave.
Daytona Beach, FL 32015
(904)255-1401

Bishop State Community College
351 N. Broad St.
Mobile, AL 36690
(205)690-6800

Bowie State College
Jericho Park Rd.
Bowie, MD 20715
(301)464-6563

Central State University
1400 Brush Row Rd.
Wilberforce, OH 45384
(513)376-6478

Charles R. Drew University of Medicine and Science
1621 E. 120th St.
Los Angeles, CA 900059
(213)563-4960

Cheyney University of Pennsylvania
Cheyney and Creek Rds.
Cheyney, PA 19319
(215)399-2275

Chicago State University
95th St. at King Dr.
Chicago, IL 60628
(312)995-2513

Chaflin College
College Ave. NE
Orangeburg, SC 29115
(803)534-2710

Clark-Atlanta University
240 James P. Brawley Dr.
Atlanta, GA 30314
(404)880-8018

Clinton Junior College
1020 Crawford Rd.
PO Box 968
Rock Hill, SO 29731
(803)327-5587

Coahoma Community College
Rt. 1, Box 616
Clarksdale, MS 38614
(601)627-2571

Concordia College
1804 Green St.
Selma, AL 36701
(205)847-5736

Coppin State College
2500 W. North Ave.
Baltimore, MD 21216
(301)333-5990

Delaware State College
1200 N. Dupont Hwy.
Dover, DE 19901
(302)736-4917

Denmark Technical College
PO Box 327
Denmark, SC 29042
(803)793-3301

Dillard University
2601 Gentilly Blvd.
New Orleans, LA 70122
(504)283-8822

Edward Waters College
1658 Kings Rd.
Jacksonville, FL 32209
(904)355-3030

Elizabeth City State University
1704 Weekszill Rd.
Elizabeth City, NC 27909
(919)355-3305

Fayetteville State University
Murchison Rd.
Fayetteville, NC 28301
(919)486-1371

Fisk University
1000 17th Ave. N
Nashville, TN 37203
(615)329-8665

Florida A&M University
Tallahassee, FL 32307
(904)599-3796

Florida Memorial College
15800 NW 42nd Ave.
Miami, FL 33054
(305)623-4145

Fort Valley State College
1005 State College Dr.
Fort Valley, GA 31030
(912)825-6307

Grambling State University
PO Box 864
Grambling, LA 71245
(318)274-2435

Hampton University
Hampton, VA 23368
(804)727-5328

Harris-Stowe State University
3026 Laclede Ave.
St. Louis, MO 63103
(314)533-3000

Howard University
2400 6th St. NW
Washington, DC 20059
(202)636-6150

Huston-Tillotson College
1820 E. 8th St.
Austin, TX 78702
(512)476-7421

Interdenominational Theological Center
671 Beckwith St. Sw
Atlanta, GA 30314
(404)527-7709

Jackson State University
1400 John R. Lynch St.
Jackson, MS 39217
(601)968-2100

Jarvis Christian College
Hwy. 80 W
Drawer G
Hawkins, TX 75765
(214)769-2174

Johnson C. Smith University
100-152 Beatties Ford Rd.
Charlotte, NC 28216
(704)378-1010

Kentucky State University
E. Main St.
Frankfort, KY 40601

Knoxville College
901 College St. NW
Knoxville, TN 36921
(615)524-6525

Lane College
545 Lane Ave.
Jackson, TN 38301
(901)424-4600

Langston University
PO Box 907
Langston, OK 73050
(405)466-2231

Lawson State Community College
3060 Wilson Rd. SW
Birmingham, AL 35221
(205)925-2515

LeMoyne-Owen College
807 Walker Ave.
Memphis, TN 38126
(901)942-7302

Lewis College of Business
17370 Meyer Rd.
Detroit, MI 48235
(313)862-6300

Lincoln University (Missouri)
820 Chestnut St.
Jefferson City, MO 65101
(314)681-5599

Lincoln University (Pennsylvania)
Lincoln University, PA 19352
(215)932-8300

Livingstone College
702 W. Monroe St.
Salisbury, NC 28144
(704)638-5502

Mary Holmes Junior College
Hwy. 50 W
PO Box 1257
West Point, MS 39773
(601)494-6820

Medgar Evers College of City University of New York
1650 Bedford Ave.
Brooklyn, NY 11225
(718)735–1948

Meharry Medical College
1005 D.B. Todd Blvd.
Nashville, TN 37208
(615)327-6223

Miles College
PO Box 3800
Birmingham, AL 35208
(205)923-2771

Mississippi Valley State University
Itta Bena, MS 38941
(601)254-9041

Morehouse College
830 Westview Dr. Sw
Atlanta, GA 30314
(404)681-2800

Morgan State University
Cold Spring Ln. and Hillen Rd.
Baltimore, MD 21239
(301)444-3430

Morris Brown College
643 Martin Luther King Dr. NW
Atlanta, GA 30311
(404)525-7831

Morris College
N. Main St.
Sumter, SC 29150
(803)775-9371

Natchez College
1010 N. Yunion St.
Natchez, MS 39120
(601)445-9702

Norfolk State University
2401 Corprew Ave.
Norfolk, VA 23504
(804)683-8391

North Carolina A&T State University
815 W. Market St.
Greensboro, NC 27411
(919)334-7946

North Carolina Central University
PO Box 19717
Durham, NC 27707
(919)560-6066

Oakwood College
Oakwood Rd. NW
Huntsville, AL 35806
(205)837-1630

Paine College
1235 15th St.
Augusta, GA 30901
(404)722-4471

Paul Quinn College
1020 Elm Ave.
Waco, TX 76704
(817)753-6415

Philander-Smith College
812 W. 13th
Little Rock, AR 72202
(501)375-9845

Prairie View A&M College
PO Box 2818
Prairie View, TX 77446
(409)857-2618

Prentiss Normal and Industrial Institute
PO Box 1107
Prentiss, MS 39474

Roxbury Community College
1234 Columbus Ave.
Roxbury Crossing, MA 02120
(617)541-5310

Rust College
1 Rust Ave.
Holly Spring, MS 38565
(601)252-4461

Saint Augustine's College
1315 Oakwood Ave.
Raleigh, NC 27610
(919)828-4451

Saint Paul's College
406 Windsor Ave.
Lawrenceville, VA 23868
(804)848-3984

Savannah State College
PO Box 2029
Savannah, GA 31404
(912)356-2181

Selma University
1501 Lapsley
Selma, AL 36701
(205)872-2533

Shaw University
118 E. South St.
Raleigh, NC 27611
(919)546-8200

Shorter College
604 Locust St.
North Little Rock, AR 72114
(501)374-6305

Simmons Bible College
1811 Dumesnil St.
Louisville, KY 40210
(502)776-1443

Sojourner-Douglass College
500 N. Caroline St.
Baltimore, MD 21205
(301)276-0306

South Carolina State College
300 College St.
Orangeburg, SC 29117
(803)536-7185

Southern University
J.S. Clark Administration Bldg.
Baton Rouge, LA 70813
(504)282-4401

Southwestern Christian College
PO Box 10
Terrell, TX 75160
(214)563-3341

Spelman College
Spelman Ln. SW
Atlanta, GA 30314

Stillman College
PO Box 1430
Tuscaloosa, AL 35403

Talladega College
637 W. Battle St.
Talladega, AL 35160
(205)362-0206

Tennessee State University
3500 John Merritt Blvd.
Nashville, TN 37203
(615)320-3420

Texas College
2404 N. Grand Ave.
Tyler, TX 75702
(214)598-8311

Texas Southern University
3100 Cleburne Ave.
Houston, TX 77004
(713)527-7070

Tougaloo College
Tougaloo, MS 39174
(601)956-4941

Tuskegee University
Tuskegee, AL 36088
(205)727-8500

University of Arkansas, Pine Bluff
University Dr.
PO Box 4038
Pine Bluff, AR 71601
(501)541-6559

University of Maryland, Eastern Shore
Princess Anne, MD 21853
(301)651-2200

University of the District of Columbia
4200 Connecticut Ave. NW
Washington, DC 20008
(202)282-8637

Virginia State University
Petersburg, VA 23803
(804)524-5900

Virginia Union University
1500 N. Lombardy St.
Richmond, VA 23220
(804)257-5885

Voorhees College
Voorhees Rd.
Denmark, SC 29042
(803)793-3351

Wilberforce University
1055 N. Bickett Rd.
Wilberforce, OH 45384
(513)376-2911

Wiley College
711 Wiley Ave.
Marshall, TX 75670
(214)938-8341

Winston-Salem State University
Martin Luther King Blvd.
Winston-Salem, NC 27110

Xavier University
7325 Palmetto St.
New Orleans, LA 70125
(504)486-7411

■ RESEARCH INSTITUTIONS

African American Studies Center
Boston University
138 Mountfort St.
Brookline, MA 02146
(617)353-2795

African American Studies Program
University of Houston
College of Humanities and Fine Arts
Agnes Arnold Hall
Houston, TX 77204-3784
(713)749-2900

African and Afro-American Studies Center
University of Texas at Austin
Jester A232A
Austin, TX 78712
(512)471-1784

African Studies Program
University of Wisconsin, Madison
1454 Van Hise Hall
1220 Linden Dr.
Madison, WI 53706
(608)262-2380

Africana Research Center
Brooklyn College of City University of New York
3105 James Hall Bldg.
Brooklyn, NY 11210
(718)780-5485

Africana Studies and Research Center
Cornell University
310 Triphammer Rd.
Ithaca, NY 14850
(607)255-5218

Africana Studies and Research Institute
Queens College of City University of New York
65-30 Kissena Blvd.
Flushing, NY 11367
(718)520-7545

Afro-American Arts Institute
Indiana University Bloomington
109 N. Jordan Ave.
Bloomington, IN 47405
(812)855-9501

Afro-American Studies and Research Program
University of Illinois at Urbana-Champaign
606 S. Gregory
Urbana, IL 61801
(217)333-7781

Afro-American Studies Center
Purdue University
326 Stone Hall
West Lafayette, IN 47907
(317)494-5680

Afro-American Studies Program
Princeton University
112 Dickinson Hall
Princeton, NJ 08544-1017
(609)258-4270

Afro-American Studies Program
Brown University
Box 1904
Providence, RI 02912
(401)863-3137

Amistad Research Center
Tulane University
6823 St. Charles Ave.
New Orleans, LA 70118
(504)865-5535

Association for the Study of Afro-American Life and History, Inc.
1407 14th St. NW
Washington, DC 20005
(202)667-2822

Black Abolitionist Papers Project
Florida State University
Department of History
Tallahassee, FL 32306
(904)644-4527

Black Americana Studies
Western Michigan University
814 Sprau Tower
Kalamazoo, MI 49008
(616)387-2661

Black Periodical Literature Project, 1827–1940
Harvard University
77 Dunster St.
Cambridge, MA 02138
(617)496-7404

Bureau of Educational Research
Howard University
School of Education
Box 311
Washington, DC 20059
(202)806-8120

Carter G. Woodson Institute for Afro-American and African Studies
University of Virginia
1512 Jefferson Park Ave.
Charlottesville, VA 22903
(804)924-3109

Center for African-American History and Culture
Temple University
Weiss Hall, Ste. B18
13th and Cecil B. Moore Ave.
Philadelphia, PA 19122
(215)787-4851

Center for Afro American Studies
University of California, Los Angeles
160 Haines Hall
405 Hilgard Ave.
Los Angeles, CA 90024-1545
(310)825-7403

Center for Afro American Studies
Ohio University
300 Lindley Hall
Athens, OH 45701
(614)593-4546

Center for Afro American Studies
Wesleyan University
Middleton, CT 06457
(203)344-7943

Center for Afroamerican and African Studies
University of Michigan
W. Engineering Bldg., Rm. 200
550 E. University
Ann Arbor, MI 48109-1092
(313)764-5513

Center for Black Music Research
Columbia College Chicago
600 S. Michigan Ave.
Chicago, IL 60605
(312)663-1600

Center for Black Studies
University of California, Santa Barbara
Santa Barbara, CA 93106-3140
(805)893-3914

Center for Black Studies
Northern Illinois University
DeKalb, IL 60115
(815)753-1709

Center for Research on Multi-Ethnic Education
University of Oklahoma
601 Elm Ave., Rm. 146
Norman, OK 73019-0315
(405)325-4529

Center for Southern History and Culture
University of Alabama
PO Box 870342
University, AL 35487-0342
(205)348-7467

Center for Studies of Ethnicity and Race in America
University of Colorado at Boulder
Ketchum 30
CB 339
Boulder, CO 80309-0339
(303)492-8852

Center for the Study and Stabilization of the Black Family
Niagara University
PO Box 367
Niagara University, NY 14109
(716)285-1212

Center for the Study of Southern Culture
University of Mississippi
Barnard Observatory
University, MS 38677
(601)232-5993

Center for the Study of Black Literature and Culture
University of Pennsylvania
3400 Walnut St., Bennett Hall
Philadelphia, PA 19104-6273
(215)898-5141

Center for the Study of the Black Experience in Higher Education
Clemson University
E-103 Martin Hall
Clemson, SC 29634-5404
(803)656-0313

Center for the Study of Civil Rights
University of Virginia
1512 Jefferson Park Ave.
Charlottesville, VA 22903
(804)924-3109

Center for the Study of Race and Ethnicity in America
Brown University
Box 1886
Providence, RI 02912
(401)863-3080

Committee on African and African-American Studies
University of Chicago
5828 S. University Ave.
Chicago, IL 60637
(312)702-8344

Frederick Douglass Institute for African and African-American Studies
University of Rochester
Rochester, NY 14627
(716)275-7235

Institute for African American Affairs
Kent State University
Department of African Studies
18 Ritchie Hall
Kent, OH 44242
(216)672-2300

Institute for African American Studies
College of Staten Island of City University of New York
130 Stuyvesant Pl.
Staten Island
New York, NY 10301
(718)390-7990

Institute for African American Studies
University of Connecticut
241 Glenbrook Rd., U-162
Storrs, CT 06269-2162
(203)486-3630

Institute for Black Leadership Development and Research
University of Kansas
1028 Dole
Lawrence, KS 66045-0048
(913)864-3990

Institute for the Preservation and Study of African-American Writing
PO Box 50172
Washington, DC 20004
(202)727-4047

Institute for Urban and Minority Education
Columbia University
ERIC Clearinghouse on Urban Education
Teachers College
Box 40
New York, NY 10027
(212)678-3433

Institute of Afro American Affairs
New York University
269 Mercer St., Ste. 601
New York, NY 10003
(212)998-2130

Institute of Jazz Studies
Rutgers University
135 Bradley Hall
Newark, NJ 07102
(201)648-5595

Joint Center for Political and Economic Studies
1301 Pennsylvania Ave. NW, Ste. 400
Washington, DC 20004
(202)626-3500

Martin Luther King, Jr. Center for Nonviolent Social Change, Inc.
449 Auburn Ave. NE
Atlanta, GA 30312
(404)524-1956

Moorland-Spingarn Research Center
Howard University
500 Howard Pl. NW
Washington, DC 20059
(202)806-7239

Morehouse Research Institute
Morehouse College
830 Westview Dr.
Atlanta, GA 30314
(404)681-2800

National Afro-American Museum and Cultural Center
Box 578
Wilberforce, OH 45384
(513)376-4944

National Black Child Development Institute
1463 Rhode Island Ave. NW
Washington, DC 20005
(202)387-1281

National Study of Black College Students
University of California, Los Angeles
Department of Sociology
405 Hilgard Ave.
Los Angeles, CA 90024-1551
(213)206-7107

New York African American Institute
State University of New York
State University Plaza
Albany, NY 12246
(518)443-5798

Program for Research on Black Americans
University of Michigan
5118 Institute for Social Research
426 Thompson St.
PO Box 1248
Ann Arbor, MI 48106-1248
(313)763-0045

Race Relations Institute
Wayne State University
College of Urban, Labor and Metropolitan Affairs
656 W. Kirby, Rm. 3208 FAB
Detroit, MI 48202
(313)577-5071

Rites and Reason
Brown University
Box 1148
Providence, RI 02912
(401)863-3558

Schomburg Center for Research in Black Culture
515 Malcolm X Blvd.
New York, NY 10037-1801
(212)491-2200

W.E.B. DuBois Institute for Afro-American Research
Harvard University
44 Brattle St.
Cambridge, MA 02138
(617)495-4192

William Monroe Trotter Institute for the Study of Black Culture
University of Massachusetts at Boston
Harbor Campus
Boston, MA 02125-3393
(617)287-5880

Women's Research and Resource Center
Spelman College
Box 115
Atlanta, GA 30314
(404)681-3643

	Total	Public		Private	
		4-year	2-year	4-year	2-year
Number of institutions, fall 1989	106	40	11	49	6
Total enrollment, fall 1980	233,557	155,085	13,132	62,924	2,416
Men, total	106,387	70,236	6,758	28,352	1,041
Men, black	81,818	53,654	2,781	24,412	971
Women, total	127,170	84,849	6,374	34,572	1,375
Women, black	109,171	70,582	4,644	32,589	1,356
Total enrollment, fall 1988	239,755	158,606	15,066	64,644	1,439
Men, total	100,561	66,097	6,772	27,219	473
Men, black	78,268	50,545	3,192	24,081	450
Women, total	139,194	92,509	8,294	37,425	966
Women, black	115,883	73,893	5,894	35,145	951

Source: *Digest of Education Statistics 1991*, November 1991, p. 215. Primary source: Department of Education, National Center for Education Statistcs.

Enrollment at historically Black Colleges and Universities, 1980 and 1988.

	Percent of 1987 secondary students in special education classes	Percent of 1980 sophomores	Disability concentration ratio
Race/ethnicity			
White	65.0	70.0	0.9
Black	24.2	12.2	2.2
Hispanic	8.1	12.6	0.6
other	2.7	5.2	0.5

Source: "Percentage of Students in Special Education Classes and Disability Concentration Ratio, by Individual and Family Characteristics at the Secondary Level: 1985-1986," *The Condition of Education 1991, Volume 1, Elementary and Secondary Education,* p.52. Primary source: U.S. Department of Education Office of Special Education and Rehabilitative Services, National Longitudinal Study, May 1989.

Note: Disability concentration ratio is the percent of all students in special education classes divided by the percent of all 1980 sophomores in a category.

Percentage of Students in Special Education Classes.

Age and Race	Number of dropouts (thousands)			Percent of population		
	1980	1985	1989	1980	1985	1989
Total dropouts*	5,212	4,456	4,109	12.0	10.6	10.7
16-17 years	709	505	395	8.8	7.0	5.9
18-21 years	2,578	2,095	2,128	15.8	14.1	15.0
22-24 years	1,798	1,724	1,516	15.2	14.1	13.7
White*	4,169	3,583	3,314	11.3	10.3	10.5
16-17 years	619	424	328	9.2	7.1	6.1
18-21 years	2,032	1,678	1,690	14.7	13.6	14.6
22-24 years	1,416	1,372	1,236	14.0	13.3	13.4
Black*	934	748	648	16.0	12.6	11.4
16-17 years	80	70	61	6.9	6.5	5.6
18-21 years	486	376	363	23.0	17.5	17.4
22-24 years	346	279	220	24.0	17.8	14.9
Hispanic*	919	820	1,168	29.5	23.3	27.9
16-17 years	92	97	80	16.6	14.6	12.5
18-21 years	470	335	538	40.3	29.3	34.9
22-24 years	323	365	524	40.6	33.9	41.1

Source: Statistical Abstract of the United States, 1991, p.156. U.S. Bureau of the Census.

*Includes person 14-15, not shown separately.

High School Dropouts by Age, Race, and Hispanic Orgin, 1980 to 1989.

	Popula-tion (1,000)	Percent of population completing--							Median school years completed
		Elementary			High School		College		
		0-4 years	5-7 years	8 years	1-3 years	4 years	1-3 years	4+ years	
White	131,092	2.0	3.9	5.3	11.1	39.5	17.2	20.9	12.7
25-29 years old	18,070	1.0	1.4	1.5	9.5	42.3	20.8	23.5	12.9
30-34 years old	18,078	1.0	1.9	1.3	7.9	41.0	21.3	25.5	12.9
35-44 years old	29,783	1.3	2.3	1.8	7.4	38.1	21.3	27.8	13.0
45-54 years old	20,448	1.7	3.2	3.7	11.4	42.3	16.0	21.6	12.7
55-64 years old	19,074	2.6	4.8	7.4	14.9	41.2	13.4	15.6	12.5
65 years and over	25,639	4.1	9.0	14.5	15.6	34.7	10.9	11.1	12.2
Black	15,929	4.8	7.7	5.5	18.6	37.1	15.0	11.3	12.4
25-29 years old	2,701	.3	.6	1.8	16.4	47.4	21.2	12.3	12.7
30-34 years old	2,571	.7	2.2	1.4	15.5	45.4	20.7	14.0	12.7
35-44 years old	3,700	1.1	2.7	2.3	16.6	42.2	19.6	15.4	12.6
45-54 years old	2,501	2.9	7.2	5.4	23.3	38.7	11.6	17.0	12.3
55-64 years old	2,074	7.3	14.8	10.6	24.0	28.0	8.3	7.0	11.0
65 years and over	2,383	20.1	24.1	14.4	18.0	15.0	3.8	4.7	8.4
Hispanic	9,940	12.2	15.7	6.9	14.2	28.3	12.6	10.0	12.0
25-29 years old	2,044	6.0	10.0	4.4	17.3	34.3	16.7	11.3	12.4
30-34 years old	1,741	6.7	14.0	4.3	14.0	30.9	17.5	12.6	12.4
35-44 years old	2,624	9.3	15.5	5.1	14.1	31.4	13.8	10.7	12.2
45-54 years old	1,488	14.1	18.3	8.9	13.8	25.9	8.5	10.4	10.7
55-64 years old	1,142	22.3	18.8	10.3	14.1	21.0	7.2	6.2	8.9
65 years and over	903	29.3	24.5	15.0	8.9	14.0	4.3	4.1	7.5

Source: U.S. Bureau of the Census, *Statistical Abstract of the United States.*

Years of School Completed by Age and Race, 1988.

	1990			1990		
	Both sexes	Male	Female	Both Sexes	Male	Female
Total, 25 years old and over	16,751	7,471	9,280	16,395	7,315	9,080
Percent	100.0	100.0	100.0	100.0	100.0	100.0
Elementary	16.1	17.1	15.3	17.3	18.6	16.3
High school	55.0	53.9	55.8	54.6	53.5	55.4
College	28.9	29.0	28.8	28.1	27.9	28.3
Percent for 4 years of high school or more	66.2	65.8	66.5	54.6	64.2	65.0

Source: *Black Population in the United States: March 1990 and 1989*, 1991, pp.31-32. Primary source: U.S. Bureau of the Census, Current Population Reports

Educational Attainment for Blacks Age 25 and Older.

In thousands

Year	White			Black		
	Total	Men	Women	Total	Men	Women
1995	11,020	4,885	6,135	1,339	568	771
1996	11,019	4,878	6,140	1,431	604	827
1997	11,259	4,967	6,292	1,376	573	802
1998	11,310	4,965	6,345	1,478	615	862
1999	11,476	5,019	6,457	1,499	622	877
2000	11,637	5,069	6,568	1,521	627	895

Source: *Black Issues in Higher Education*, Vol. 8, No. 24, January 30, 1992, p. 40. Primary source: U.S. Bureau of Census, Current Population Reports.

College Enrollment Projections, 1995–2000.

17

Religion

17

Religion

The Origins and History of Black Religious Traditions ■ Black Female Religious Leadership ■ Black Churches During Reconstruction ■ Black Churches in the Twentieth-Century ■ Black Denominations ■ Religious Leaders

by Stephen W. Angel

The first Africans who arrived on North American shores (an event traditionally dated to 1619) brought their own religious world views with them. While a minority had been Muslims or Christians prior to their kidnapping by slave traders, most adhered to their native African religions. There were hundreds of these religions, but, in general, the Africans believed that the world had been created by a high god who removed himself from direct intervention in worldly affairs after the act of creation.

■ THE ORIGINS AND HISTORY OF BLACK RELIGIOUS TRADITIONS

The Beginnings of African-American Religion

In Africa, worshipers directed their prayers to intermediary spirits, chief among whom were their ancestors, or the "living dead." If proper offering was made to an ancestor, the individual would be blessed with great prosperity, but if the ancestor was slighted, misfortune would result. In addition, the Yorubas worshiped a variety of nature spirits (or orishas). These spirits often possessed their devotees, who then became mediums of their gods. This kind of spirit-possession is a prominent feature of some modern African-American religions such as santería, which recently has spread in large urban areas, including Miami and New York. Also a part of the African world view, especially among the Bakongo, was the practice of magic, variously known in the New World as obeah, vaudou (voodoo), or conjure. This magic, designed to help friends (myalism) or to hurt enemies (obeah), at one time was widely practiced by Africans throughout the Western Hemisphere.

The type of African spirituality that took root in North America merged elements from many African cultures. Since slave masters intentionally mixed Africans from many tribal backgrounds, no "pure" African religion preserving one tradition emerged. Nevertheless, the longstanding scholarly controversy over the extent to which African traditions have been retained in African-based religions is gradually being resolved in favor of those who see extensive survivals. In addition to singing, church music, and preaching style, aspects where an African influence has generally been conceded, scholars have made persuasive arguments for African survivals in family structure, funeral practices, church organization, and many other areas.

Christian Missionary Efforts

The first sustained effort at converting African Americans to Christianity was made by the Anglican Society for the Propagation of the Gospel in Foreign Parts, which sent missionaries to North America in 1701. These missionaries had little success among the Africans; many mocked those who imitated the whites too closely, and thus resisted the missionaries. In addition, white slave masters often resented losing slaves' time to church services and feared that slaves would lay a claim to freedom through conversion. The numerous colonial laws, starting with Virginia in 1669, proclaiming that conversion failed to entitle slaves to freedom did not comfort some slave masters, who suspected that Christianity would undermine slave discipline—indeed, some remained unconvinced of the advisability of missionary efforts up until emancipation occurred. On the other hand, some slave masters believed the Christianization of Africans to be justification for enslaving them.

Subsequent efforts to convert African Americans to Christianity were more successful. In his seven missionary tours throughout North America between 1742 and 1770, the spellbinding orator George Whitefield effected the conversions of large numbers of both black and white Americans. The ministry of Methodist circuit riders, such as Francis Asbury, was also well received by African Americans at the end of the eighteenth century. Baptist and Methodist churches were the most successful in attracting black members. Since these churches did not require their ministers be well educated, doors were opened for aspiring African-American ministers, many of whom lived in states where teaching African Americans to read and write was forbidden by law. Furthermore, the Baptists and Methodists were not as hostile to the emotionalism of black preachers and congregations as were more staid denominations such as the Episcopalians. Finally, the antislavery stance of notable Methodist and Baptist leaders, such as John Wesley, Francis Asbury, and John Leland, and the greater degree of equality nurtured within many Baptist and Methodist congregations were attractive to African Americans.

Early Black Congregations

Probably the first organizing effort by African Americans to bear fruit in an independent black congregation was the Silver Bluff Baptist Church in South Carolina, which came into existence between 1773 and 1775. David George, an African American, and seven other men and women formed its organizing nucleus. George Liele, one of George's associates, often preached at the Silver Bluff Church before emigrating to Jamaica in 1782. Andrew Bryan, one of Liele's converts, founded the First African Baptist Church in Savannah, Georgia, in 1788.

Bryan's life well represented the complex predicament faced by African-American religious leaders in the antebellum South. In the early years of his ministry, Bryan was whipped and twice imprisoned by whites who feared him. But he bought his freedom, prospered, and eventually came to own much property, including eight black slaves;

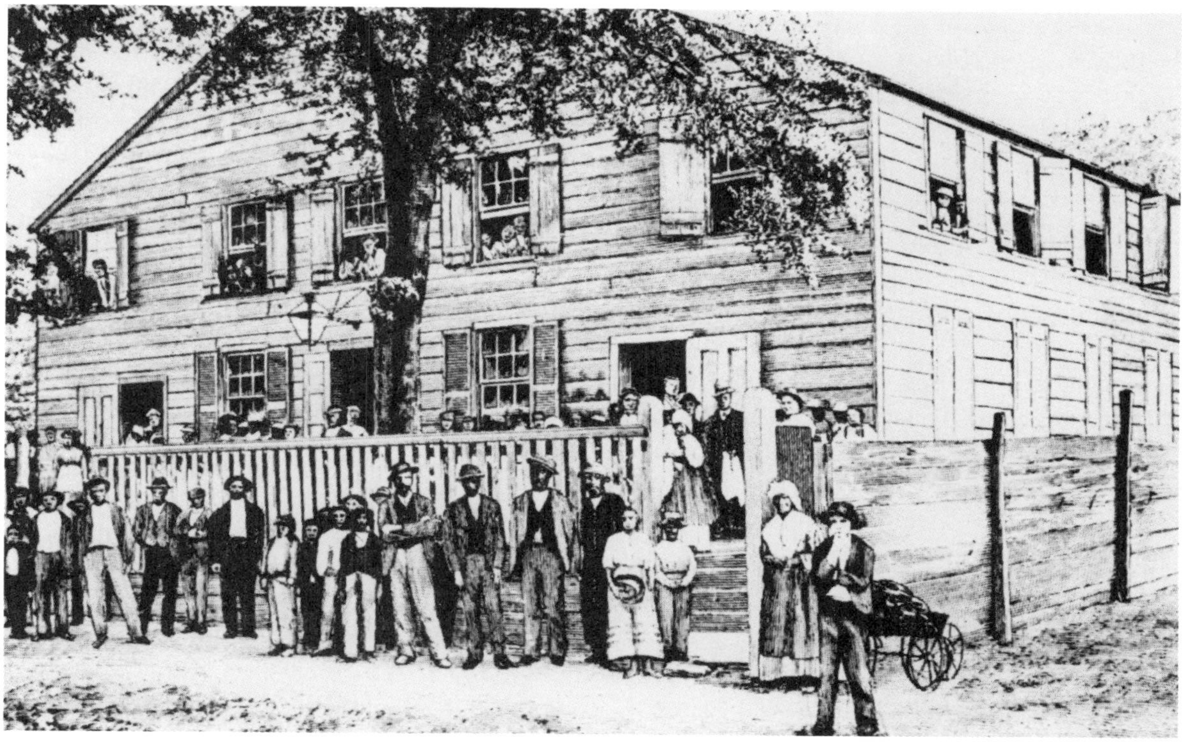

First African Baptist Church, Savannah, Georgia.

his death in 1812 was mourned by blacks and whites alike. While many black churches continued to be served by white ministers until 1865, black pastors, licensed ministers, and exhorters ministering to black Baptist and Methodist congregations were not at all unusual at this time, either in the South or the North.

Black Catholics

Before the Civil War, black Catholics were confined largely to Maryland and Louisiana. However, Catholics made greater efforts to convert African Americans after the Civil War. By the end of the nineteenth century, there were about 200,000 black Catholics in the United States. However, there were not as many black priests in the nineteenth-century Catholic churches as there were black ministers among Protestant churches.

Discrimination in White Churches

While white preachers urged black Americans to convert and many predominantly white congregations welcomed them into membership, racial prejudice was never absent from the religious scene. Although the level of discrimination varied from region to region, and congregation to congregation, some factors were relatively constant.

One such factor was the relative paucity of ordained African-American clergy. To take the Methodists as an example, some African-American ministers were ordained as deacons within the Methodist Episcopal Church prior to 1820, but none in the four decades thereafter. No African-American Methodist minister was ordained by the Methodist Episcopal Church to the higher office of elder or consecrated as a bishop prior to the Civil War, unless he was willing to emigrate to Liberia.

Other discriminatory practices also formed part of the religious landscape. The Methodists, and many other denominations, tried to reserve the administration of sacraments as the exclusive province of white clergy. Segregated seating in churches was pervasive in both the North and the South. Church discipline was often unevenly applied. Of course, racial discrimination in the churches was only a small part of the much larger political and moral controversy over slavery.

Resistance to discrimination took many forms. In the North, Peter Spencer in Wilmington, Delaware, Richard Allen in Philadelphia, and James Varick in New York, led their black followers out of white Methodist churches and set up independent black congregations. In Allen's case, his departure was preceded by a dramatic confrontation over segregated seating in Philadelphia's white Methodist church. Each of these men then used his congregation as the nucleus of a new black Methodist denomination—Spencer formed the African Union Church in 1807, Allen the African Methodist Episcopal Church(AME) in 1816, and Varick a denomination eventually called the African Methodist Episcopal Zion Church (AME Zion) in 1821.

Meanwhile, in Charleston, South Carolina, a more explosive situation was taking shape. Morris Brown, a black Methodist minister from Charleston, who had helped Richard Allen organize the African Methodist Episcopal Church, organized an independent black Methodist church in his home city. The authorities harassed Brown's church and sometimes arrested its leaders.

Reverend Richard Allen

Nevertheless, within a year, more than three-quarters of Charleston's black Methodists had united with him. The oppression of African Americans in Charleston was so severe that many members of Brown's congregation, including prominent lay leaders, joined the insurrection planned by Denmark Vesey to take over the Charleston armory and, eventually, the whole environs of Charleston. The conspirators, apprehended before they could carry out their plans, testified that Brown had not known of their scheme, and the minister was allowed to move to Philadelphia, where Richard Allen made him the second bishop of the African Methodist Episcopal Church.

A few African Americans became acquiescent as a result of Christianity. One such example was Pierre Toussaint, a black Haitian slave who fled in 1787 to New York with his white owners, the Berards, just prior to the

Haitian Revolution. In 1811, Mrs. Berard manumitted Toussaint on her death bed. Over the next forty years, Toussaint became a notable philanthropist, contributing funds to the building of St. Patrick's Cathedral. However, when the cathedral opened, Toussaint did not protest when a white usher refused to seat him for services. Some American Catholics recently revived the controversy over Toussaint, by campaigning for his canonization. Many black Catholics have strongly objected, seeing Toussaint as passive and servile and thus a poor candidate for sainthood.

The Black Church Responds to the Slavery Question

The mid-nineteenth century saw increased anti-slavery activity among many black church leaders and members. Some gave qualified support to the gradual emancipation program sponsored by the American Colonization Society, which sought to encourage free African Americans to emigrate to Africa to Westernize and Christianize the Africans. Virginia Baptist pastor Lott Cary and Maryland Methodist minister Daniel Coker were the two most prominent African-American religious leaders to emigrate to Africa in the 1820s. By the 1850s, there were enough black Methodists in Liberia for the Methodist Episcopal Church to consecrate a black bishop, Francis Burns, to serve the Liberian churches. While some black Americans were emigrating to Africa, others emigrated to the West Indies—Episcopalian Bishop James T. Holly, for example, settled in Haiti to undertake missionary work.

Because of the extreme repression in the slave states, Southern blacks were unable to express openly their views on political issues. They were, however, often able to make their views clear; for example, a white minister who dwelled too long on the Biblical text that servants should obey their masters was apt to find his African-American listeners deserting him. In addition, black Christians often held secret meetings in "brush arbors" (rude structures made of pine boughs) or in the middle of the woods. There they could sing spirituals and pray openly for the quick advent of freedom. Slave revolts provided a violent outbreak of dissent much feared by whites. The 1831 revolt of Nat Turner, a Baptist preacher, in Northampton County, Virginia, was suppressed only after tremendous bloodshed had been visited upon both blacks and whites. Frightened whites in the South intensified their surveillance of black churches in the aftermath of the Turner revolt. Even conservative black preachers such as Presbyterian John Chavis in North Carolina and the Baptist "Uncle Jack" in Virginia were prohibited from preaching.

Northern African-American leaders could afford to be more open and forthright in their political stance. Most rejected outright the views of the American Colonization Society in favor of the immediate abolition of slavery. Presbyterian minister Henry Highland Garnet was a prominent abolitionist, urging African-American slaves in 1843 to "let your motto be RESISTANCE! RESISTANCE! RESISTANCE!" African Methodist Episcopal Bishop Daniel Payne and African Methodist Episcopal Zion Bishop Christopher Rush, both emigrants from the Carolinas to the North, were outspoken abolitionists who, after the mid-1840s, became the most prominent leaders in their respective churches. Frederick Douglass was one of the few leading black abolitionists who did not pursue a ministerial career, and even he had briefly served as an African Methodist Episcopal Zion preacher in New Bedford, Massachusetts. Black clergy were extraordinarily active in recruiting black men to join

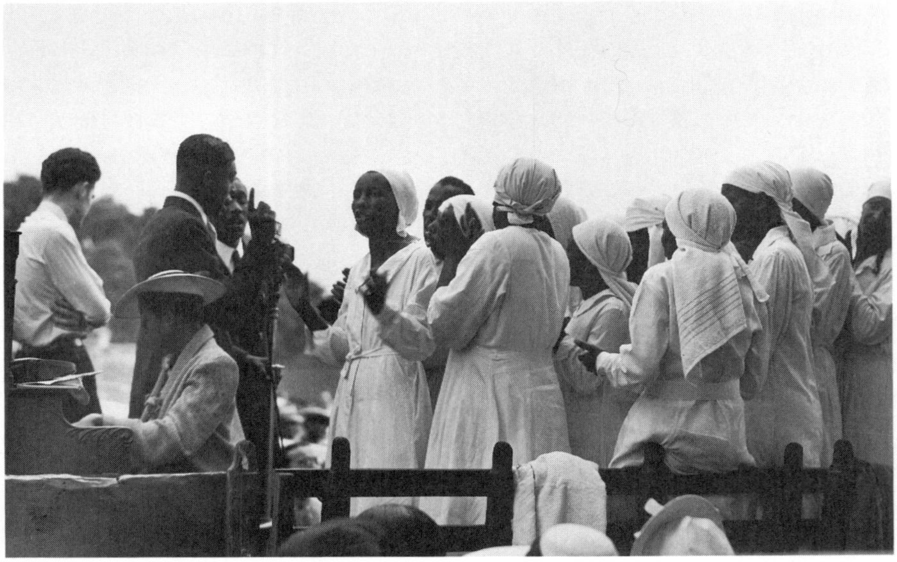

A baptism service on the Potomac River.

the Union armies during the Civil War, after the Emancipation Proclamation opened up the possibility of military service to them. During the Civil War nearly a dozen black ministers, including the African Methodist Episcopal Church's Henry McNeal Turner, served as chaplains to black army regiments.

■ BLACK FEMALE RELIGIOUS LEADERSHIP

The contributions of black women ministers were also vital. Women sometimes served as travelling evangelists, especially within the black denominations. While Sojourner Truth's oratory has become appropriately famous, Maria Stewart, Jarena Lee, Zilpha Elaw and other early nineteenth-century women also spoke eloquently and, in Lee's and Elaw's cases, travelled widely and labored diligently. None of these women were ordained, but Elizabeth (no last name known), a former slave from Maryland whose ministry began in 1796, spoke for many female preachers when she was accused of preaching without a license: "If the Lord has ordained me, I need nothing better." Rebecca Cox Jackson left the African Methodist Episcopal Church in the 1830s when she felt that men denied her the chance to exercise her ministry, and she eventually became head eldress of a predominantly black Shaker community in Philadelphia.

During the postbellum years, some black women sought and obtained formal ordination from their denominations. Sarah Ann Hughes, a successful North Carolina evangelist and pastor, was ordained by Bishop Henry McNeal Turner in 1885, but complaints from male pastors caused her ordination to be revoked two years later. Two women were ordained by African Methodist Episcopal Zion bishops not long thereafter—Mary J. Small in 1895 as a deacon and 1898 as an elder, and Julia A. J. Foote in 1894 and 1900. Many women exercised their ministry through para-ecclesiastical structures, such as women's temperance and missionary societies, while others, such as Anna Cooper and the African Methodist Episcopal Church's Frances Jackson Coppin, became renowned educators.

■ BLACK CHURCHES DURING RECONSTRUCTION

The Role of Black Churches in Reconstruction Government

Black church membership grew explosively after the Civil War, especially in the South, where the black clergy played a prominent part in the Reconstruction governments. African Methodist Episcopal minister Hiram Revels became the first African American to serve as a United States Senator, when the Mississippi legislature sent him to Washington, DC, in 1870. However, Revels, was only the ground breaker; many black ministers went on to serve in the Congress or in their state governments. African-American participation in Reconstruction politics was effective in large part because ministers in the AME and AME Zion Churches, and many black Baptist ministers, carefully and patiently educated their congregation members on every civic and political issue (although the newly established black denomination, the Colored Methodist Episcopal Church, largely stayed away from politics during Reconstruction).

Even though African Americans were largely expelled from Southern state governments after the end of political Reconstruction in the 1870s, many black ministers and laity continued to play an active political role on such issues as temperance, often campaigning on behalf of prohibition refer-

An African Methodist Episcopal congregation, 1898.

enda. The Southern white campaign of terror, lynching, and disfranchisement steadily reduced black political power and participation, however, until the onset of mid-twentieth century civil rights movements.

The Black Church's Response to Segregation

As the system of racial segregation imposed in the 1880s and 1890s took hold, black ministers coordinated a manifold response. First, they forthrightly challenged new segregation laws, engaging in civil disobedience and boycotts. For example, when the city of Nashville, Tennessee segregated its street cars in 1906, influential Baptist minister R. H. Boyd led a black boycott of the streetcars, even operating his own streetcar line for a time. No defeat was ever seen as final.

Second, black ministers helped to nurture a separate set of black institutions to serve African Americans excluded from white establishments. The Congregationalists, Baptists, and Northern Methodists established schools in the South for African Americans during Reconstruction, but the African Methodist Episcopal, African Methodist Episcopal Zion, and Christian Methodist Episcopal bishops forged ahead with establishment of their own network of schools. The black denominations also built up their publishing houses, and the books and periodicals that they published were vital to the black community. Virtually every institution with ties to African-American communities received some support from black churches.

Third, some black ministers believed that the civil rights retreats of the late nineteenth century should spur African Americans to leave the United States for a destination where their full civil rights would be respected. A "Back to Africa" movement grew to enable African Americans to find a home where they could run governments, banks, and businesses without interference from whites. Thus, Bishop Turner helped to organize a steamship line to carry black Americans back to Africa, and two shiploads of black emigrants sailed to Liberia in 1895 and 1896 as a result of his efforts. Some black church leaders, such as Christian Methodist Episcopal Bishop Lucius Holsey and AME Bishop Richard Cain, held views similar to those advocated by Turner, but many more church leaders opposed Turner's emigrationism vigorously. Simultaneously, African American missionary work continued to occupy the attention of African Americans at the end of the nineteenth century. Under the guidance of Bishops Payne and Turner, for example, the African Methodist Episcopal Church had a vigorous missionary presence in Sierra Leone, Liberia, and South Africa.

■ BLACK CHURCHES IN THE TWENTIETH CENTURY

In the past one hundred years, black religious life has become characterized by a far greater degree of diversity and pluralism. At the same time, traditional African-American concerns, including the continuing quest for freedom and justice, have been not only maintained but strengthened.

Pentecostalism, which burst on the American scene in 1906, has become a major religious force within the black community. The Church of God in Christ, a Pentecostal denomination, has become the second largest black denomination in the United States. Meanwhile, the charismatic or Neo-Pentecostal movement has revitalized many congregations within mainline black denominations. The black nationalism of Bishop Turner came to full flower in the work of such men as Marcus Garvey (and his chap-

Pentecostalism, which burst on the American scene in 1906, has become a major religious force within the black community.

lain general, George A. McGuire), Elijah Muhammad, and Malcolm X. There has been a spectacular rise of storefront churches, some of which were led by flamboyant showmen such as Father Divine and "Sweet Daddy" Grace. Each of these trends has been significantly aided by the black migrations from the South to the North, which greatly strengthened Northern black communities.

Many black ministers became advocates of a "Social Gospel." One of the most famous was Reverend Ransom of the African Methodist Episcopal Church, who came into prominence between 1901 and 1904 as pastor of an Institutional Church in Chicago. ("Institutional churches" provided a whole panoply of social services to needy members and neighbors, in addition to regular worship.) Social Gospellers highlighted the reality of collective, societal sin such as the starvation of children and the denial of human rights, and maintained that Christian repentance of these sins must be followed by concrete actions to rectify injustice and to assist the poor. The Reverend Dr. Martin Luther King, Jr., was profoundly influenced by this Social Gospel movement.

It is worth recalling that many black religious leaders in the 1960s thought that King's brand of social activism was too radical. One of King's most determined critics during the 1960s was the theologically conservative president of the National Baptist Convention of the U.S.A., Inc., Joseph H. Jackson. The attempt by King's ministerial allies to unseat Jackson as president of the Convention in 1960 and 1961 led to a schism, with King and his supporters forming a new denomination, the Progressive National

Baptist Convention. King came under further criticism when, in 1967 and 1968, he made it clear that his advocacy of pacifism extended to opposition to American military involvement in Vietnam.

The "Black Theology" movement, which grew rapidly after King's assassination, attempted to fashion a critique of the prevalent Christian theology out of the materials that King and Malcolm X provided. One such theologian, Albert Cleage, pastor of the Shrine of the Black Madonna in Detroit, argued that Jesus is a black messiah and that his congregation should follow the teachings of Jehovah, a black god. "Almost everything you have heard about Christianity is essentially a lie," he stated. Cleage was representative of black theologians in arguing that black liberation should be seen as situated at the core of the Christian gospels. In the 1980s, black women such as Jacquellyn Grant, Delores Williams, and Katie Cannon have formulated "womanist" theologies which seek to combat the triple oppression of race, class, and gender suffered by most black women.

Current Trends

African-American churches remain strong, healthy institutions in the 1990s.

Reverend Gardner Taylor, pastor of Concord Baptist Church in Brooklyn, addressing a protest rally, 1963.

Some denominations are growing substantially, and none is declining precipitously. While secularization has diminished its influence somewhat, the black church is still the central institution in the black community. Many black churches are vigorously confronting such problems as drug abuse and homelessness that are visible symptoms of the increasing desperation of the black underclass.

The largest denomination among the black churches remains the National Baptist Convention of the U.S.A., Inc. Its current president, veteran civil rights activist Theodore J. Jemison, was first elected in 1982. Under Jemison's leadership, the denomination in 1989 completed a $10,000,000 world headquarters building in Nashville, Tennessee. More recently, Jemison has come under criticism for his role in attempting to forestall Mike Tyson's 1992 trial (and eventual conviction) on rape charges. The Convention continues to extend its strong support to Jemison who, under current church rules, will not be able to succeed himself when his term expires in 1994.

Black churches continue to address a wide variety of social problems affecting the African-American community. Perhaps most urgently, many churches have strong anti-drug programs. The First AME Church of Los Angeles sponsors a "Lock In" program, which on weekends presents anti-drug messages to youth. Similarly, many congregations have undertaken vigorous action against "crack" houses. Parochial schools, feeding centers, and housing for senior citizens are also part of the black church's outreach to the black community. Many black ministers have noted, however, the growing division of the African-American community along lines of social class and have exhorted middle-class black Americans to give more generously to programs that aid the poor. James Cone, a leading black theologian, has stated that black churches need to devote less time and attention to institutional survival and more to finding ways to deal with such pressing issues as poverty, gang violence, and AIDS.

Members of the Ministers Coalition for Peace pray for an end to civil unrest in Los Angeles.

Towards this end, black churches participate in a wide variety of ecumenical projects among themselves and often additionally, in conjunction with white denominations. The Congress of National Black Churches, a consortium of six black churches, continues to sponsor a variety of projects to improve the economic and social situation of the African-American community. Partners in Ecumenism, a project of the National Council of Churches, has challenged white denominations to be more responsive to black concerns. At a grassroots level, African-American churches are successfully joining forces to combat problems that are too large for any congregation to address alone. In Marks, Mississippi, for example, the Quitman County Development Organization has sponsored a Black Church Community and Economic Development Project. This organization has assisted church leaders in developing programs on teen pregnancy and parenting.

The spirit of cooperation has inspired individual denominations to explore merging or establishing close working relationships with other denominations with similar backgrounds and traditions. Three black Methodist churches, the African Methodist Episcopal Zion, Christian Methodist Episcopal, and United American Methodist Episcopal churches have been planning a merger that they hope to consummate in the near future. In the spring of 1991, bishops of the AME, AME Zion, Christian Methodist Episcopal, and United Methodist churches requested that their denominations approve a study commission to explore an even broader reunion of churches. The Progressive National Baptists have recently entered into a formal dialogue with the Southern Baptist Alliance, an organization of more than 72,000 mostly white Baptists who recently have distanced themselves from the Southern Baptist Convention.

Black churches also have found themselves compelled to address issues related to the multi-ethnic tensions of the 1990s. Leading black pastors in Los Angeles have deplored both the violence of police revealed in the Rodney King incident and the violence of inner city rioters, while advocating urgent attention to the problems of inner-city residents. For example, James Lawson of the Holman United Methodist Church stated that those who burned build-

African-American churches remain strong, healthy institutions.

More than 1.5 million African Americans belong to the Roman Catholic Church. Pictured Reverend George Clements giving communion.

ings during the 1992 Los Angeles riots were "responding to a society of violence, not simply a society of racism," and issued "a call to repent." In Queens, New York, a black Baptist congregation in 1991 warmly welcomed the opportunity to perform an ordination service for a Korean-American minister, Chong S. Lee.

In a few recent cases, furthermore, tensions have surfaced between black pastors and predominantly white congregations. For example, after Joan Salmon Campbell resigned in 1992 as pastor of the Old Pine Presbyterian Church in Philadelphia, black ministers protested to the Philadelphia Presbyters that the differences over preaching style and theology that led to her resignation had been caused by alleged racist attitudes in her former congregation.

While many black Methodist and Baptist denominations are showing only limited membership growth, other black denominations are showing marked membership increases. Foremost among these are the Pentecostalist churches, whose lively worship and extensive social ministries are attracting members from all classes within the black community. The largest of these denominations, the Church of God in Christ, is now estimated to have over three million members. Charismatic congregations (also known as neo-Pentecostalist) within main-

Black parishioners attending mass a the Church of the Transfiguration in Los Angeles.

line black churches such as the African Methodist Episcopal Church are also thriving, and for similar reasons.

Other groups that have made substantial membership gains among African Americans include Roman Catholicism and Islam. While estimates differ, apparently more than 1.5 million African Americans now belong to the Roman Catholic Church, which has worked hard in recent years to be sensitive to their needs. In many inner cities, it has maintained churches and schools in predominantly African-American neighborhoods, although closings, mostly for financial reasons, are increasing in such dioceses as Detroit. Moreover, the Roman Catholic Church has been receptive to some liturgical variation, allowing gospel choirs and African vestments for priests in black churches. Nevertheless, Roman Catholics confront some serious problems in serving black parishioners. Fewer than 300 of the 54,000 priests in the United States are black, meaning that some black congregations must be served by white priests. In 1989, George A. Stallings, Jr., a priest in Washington, D.C., broke away from Catholicism, arguing that the Catholic Church was still racist and did not do enough for its African-American members.

Mainstream Islam, despite raising its own complexities, has also made large gains in the United States. Of the six million Muslims in this country, one million are believed to be black. Most African-American Muslims do not distinguish between people of different races and worship cordially side by side with recent Muslim immigrants from Asia and Africa. Louis Farrakhan's Nation of Islam, however, which retains Elijah Muhammad's black separatist teachings, continues to maintain a devoted following. Due to its very conservative stance on gender issues, Islam has proven to be more popular among black men than among black women.

The cause of gender equality continues to progress slowly in black churches. While two predominantly white denominations, the United Methodist and Protestant Episcopal Churches, have elevated black women to the episcopacy in the past decade, none of the largest historically black denominations have done so. Nevertheless, women in some black churches are achieving ever-more-prestigious ministerial assignments. Vashti McKenzie, a former model, disc jockey, and radio program director, has recently been appointed pastor of the Payne Memorial AME Church, an "old-line" church in Baltimore. Her innovative ministry, she says, is designed to "provide a message of hope for a hurting community." There are presently more than 600 female pastors in the African Methodist Episcopal Church.

Preaching the gospel in a faithful but relevant fashion remains the most important objective of black churches. In a recent survey, twenty-two percent of black clergy considered the most important problem of the black church to be "lack of evangelism in fulfilling its religious role." That was more than twice the figure for any other problem identified. Ministerial training and financial support is another area needing improvement in many black churches. There is no danger, however, that the black churches will lose sight of their many, vital and extremely significant functions, within both the black community and American society as a whole. It is safe to predict that the black churches will continue to sustain and develop their important and prophetic witness.

BLACK DENOMINATIONS

African Methodist Episcopal Church

The African Methodist Episcopal (AME) Church was founded in 1816 at a conference convened in Philadelphia by Richard Allen, who was elected as its first bishop. In the following years, it grew throughout the North and Midwest, and after the Civil War, it expanded quickly throughout the South and the West.

Its 1989 membership was 2.2 million, about 1 million of whom are found in churches in Africa and the Caribbean as a result of successful missionary efforts. It oversees about 5,000 churches, as well as six colleges and two seminaries. Payne Theological Seminary is located in Wilberforce, Ohio, at the site of the Church's oldest school, Wilberforce University, founded in 1856. Turner Theological Seminary is one of six schools that have joined to form the Interdenominational Theological Center in Atlanta. The African Methodist Episcopal Church's chief governing bodies are the General Conference, the Council of Bishops, and the General Board. It publishes the following periodicals: the *Christian Record*; the *Voice of Missions*; and the *AME Church Review*.

African Methodist Episcopal Zion Church

Another African Methodist Episcopal Church was founded in 1821 in New York City. James Varick was elected its first "superintendent"; the title of the presiding officer was later changed to bishop. In 1848, the word "Zion" was added to the name of this church in order to avoid confusion with that founded by Richard Allen. Thus, it became known as the African Methodist Episcopal Zion (AME Zion) Church. It only grew slightly prior to 1860, but expanded quickly in such Southern states as North Carolina and Alabama after the Civil War.

As of 1989, the African Methodist Episcopal Zion Church had 1.3 million members, 100,000 of whom lived in Africa or the Caribbean. It possesses 2,900 churches. The church supports three colleges (two of which are junior colleges) and one seminary. The four-year college and the seminary

First African Methodist Episcopal Church, Los Angeles.

are Livingstone College and Hood Theological Seminary, both located in Salisbury, North Carolina. The denomination is governed by a General Conference, a Board of Bishops, and a Correctional Council. Its publications include the weekly *Star of Zion*, the *Quarterly Review*, the monthly *Missionary Seer*, and the quarterly *Church School Herald*.

African Orthodox Church

The African Orthodox Church was founded in 1921 by Archbishop George Alexander McGuire, once a priest in the Protestant Episcopal Church. McGuire was the chaplain for Marcus Garvey's United Negro Improvement Association, but Garvey soon disavowed his chaplain's efforts to found a new denomination. This church is today an autonomous and independent body adhering to an "orthodox" confession of faith. Its nearly 6,000 members worship in some twenty-five to thirty churches.

African Union First Colored Methodist Protestant Church, Inc.

This denomination was formed in 1866 by a merger of the African Union Church and the First Colored Methodist Protestant Church. The African Union Church traced its roots to a Union Church of Africans founded in 1813 by Peter Spencer in Wilmington, Delaware. Today, this denomination has more than 309 churches and a membership of about 8,000.

Apostolic Overcoming Holy Church of God

This Pentecostal denomination, originally known as the Ethiopian Overcoming Holy Church, was incorporated in Alabama in 1919. Evangelistic in purpose, it emphasizes sanctification, holiness, and the power of divine healing. As of 1975, it claimed 350 churches and about 100,000 members.

Black Jews

Several different groups in the past century have been known by this name. Included among these are the Commandment Keepers, founded in Harlem in 1919 by a Nigerian-born man known as "Rabbi Matthew"; the Church of God and Saints in Christ, founded in 1896 in Lawrence, Kansas, by William Crowdy; and the Church of God founded in Philadelphia by Prophet F. S. Cherry. In terms of doctrine, these groups share little more than a dislike of Christianity and an affection for the Old Testament. Some black Jews claim descent from the Falasha Jews of Ethiopia, who now reside in Israel. However, few black Jews are recognized as such by orthodox rabbis. The Church of God and Saints of Christ is probably the largest of these groups, with more than 200 churches and a membership of 38,000.

Christian Methodist Episcopal Church

The Christian Methodist Episcopal (CME) Church, known until 1954 as the Colored Methodist Church, is the third largest black Methodist body in the United States. It was founded after the Civil War, when some black Methodist churches desiring to join neither the African Methodist Episcopal or African Methodist Episcopal Zion Churches successfully petitioned the Methodist Episcopal Church, South, for the right to form their own denomination. The first CME General Conference was held at Jackson, Tennessee, in 1870. There the Church's first two bishops, William H. Miles and Richard Vanderhorst, were elected.

In 1989, the Christian Methodist Episcopal Church had about 900,000 members, of

Black rabbi stands in front of his Bronx, New York synagogue.

whom 75,000 were located overseas. It possesses about 3,000 churches and maintains five church-affiliated colleges, as well as the Phillips School of Theology, a seminary which is part of the consortium known as the Interdenominational Theological Center in Atlanta. Its periodicals include the bimonthly *Christian Index* and the monthly *Missionary Messenger*.

Church of Christ (Holiness) Inc.

This denomination was organized by Bishop Charles Price Jones, a renowned and prolific gospel song and hymn writer, in 1907. Some 160 churches and 9,300 members belong to this denomination, which upholds the possibility of sanctification and Christian perfection. The Holy Ghost is seen as an indispensable gift for each believer. The church operates a college, Christ Missionary and Industrial College, in Jackson, Mississippi.

Church of God in Christ

The Church of God in Christ (COGIC) was organized in 1897 by two former Baptist preachers, Charles H. Mason and C. P. Jones. It was initially strongest in Alabama, Mississippi, and Tennessee. Mason reorganized COGIC in 1907 when he and Jones parted on the issue of speaking in tongues. At that time, Mason was appointed "General Overseer and Chief Apostle" of the Church, as well as its first bishop. It has subsequently expanded very rapidly throughout the United States, especially in black neighborhoods in the inner cities.

As of 1989, COGIC has about 3.7 million members, many of whom are located in Africa and the Caribbean, and about 10,000 churches. It possesses bible colleges and a junior college, with plans for a university (All Saints University in Memphis) some time in the future. Its Charles H. Mason Theological Seminary is part of the Interdenominational Theological Center in Atlanta. It is governed by a General Assembly, a General Council of Elders, the Board of Bishops, and the General Board composed of 12 bishops elected by the General Assembly to four-year terms.

Churches of God, Holiness

This denomination was organized by K. H. Burruss in Georgia in 1914. Membership in the group's forty-odd churches totals some 25,000.

Fire Baptized Holiness Church

This church was organized on an interracial basis as the Fire Baptized Holiness Association in Atlanta, Georgia, in 1898; its African-American members formed the Fire Baptized Holiness Church in 1908. The church subscribes to standard Pentecostalist doctrines on divine healing, speaking in tongues, and sanctification. As of 1958, it had about fifty churches and a membership of about 1,000.

Imani Temple African-American Catholic Congregation

The Imani Temple was founded in Washington, D.C., by George Augustus Stallings, Jr., a former Roman Catholic priest, in July, 1989. The schism occurred when Stallings performed a mass based on an experimental rite currently being used in Zaire, in defiance of the prohibition of his archbishop, James Hickey. This was the first schism from the Roman Catholic Church in the United States since 1904. Stallings also voiced a number of

Reverend George Stallings (right) with Reverend George Clements.

criticisms of the Roman Catholic Church at the time of the schism: "There are not enough black priests, not enough black church members, and some of the relatively few black churches that exist are being closed and consolidated. The black experience and black needs are addressed minimally in church services and life." He also asserted that "we could no longer afford to worship white gods in black houses." Thirteen black American Catholic bishops issued a statement denouncing Stallings and accused him of expressing "personal disappointment [and] individually felt frustration" under the cover of charges of racism.

Black Catholic reactions to these developments were mixed. Many expressed sympathy for Stallings's concerns but were unwilling to leave the Roman Catholic Church. Stallings assumed the title of archbishop of Imani Temple in 1991, and at the same time ordained a woman to the priesthood of the African-American Catholic Congregation. In forming his denomination, he has experienced some setbacks. Several formerly close associates split with Stallings in 1991, alleging a lack of fiscal accountability in the church and accusing him of taking his liturgical innovations too far. The denomination currently claims 3,500 members in six cities.

Nation of Islam

After the death of Elijah Muhammad in 1975, his son Warith D. Muhammad assumed leadership of the movement. Warith Muhammad shifted dramatically away from his father's teachings of black nationalism, stating that whites could become members. He

Elijah Muhammad

sought to bring his movement in accord with Orthodox Islam, and he eventually succeeded, renaming the Nation of Islam as the World Community of Al-Islam in the West and then as the American Muslim Mission before the merger was accomplished.

Not all members of the Nation of Islam followed Warith Muhammad. The largest splinter group was headed by Louis Farrakhan, who had split from Muhammad by 1978 to re-establish the Nation of Islam on the basis of Elijah Muhammad's original black separatist teachings.

National Baptist Convention of America, Unincorporated

The National Baptist Convention of America was formed in 1915 as a result of a schism with the National Baptist Convention, U.S.A., Inc., over the issue of control of the denominational publishing house. In 1989 it possessed 2.4 million members and 7,800 churches. It has missions in Jamaica, Panama, and Africa, and supports ten colleges.

National Baptist Convention of the U.S.A., Inc.

The National Baptist Convention was formed in 1895 through the union of three smaller church organizations, the oldest of which had been founded only fifteen years earlier: the Baptist Foreign Mission Convention of the U.S.A.; the American National Baptist Convention; and the National Baptist Educational Convention of the U.S.A. The Convention incorporated itself after a dispute over the publishing house led to a schism in 1915.

The National Baptist Convention, Inc., as of 1989, had 7.5 million members, 100,000 of whom were in foreign countries. It possesses more than 30,000 local churches. The convention is governed by a fifteen-member board of directors and a nine-member executive board. It is a supporter of the American Baptist Theological Seminary in Nashville, Tennessee. Its publications include the semi-monthly *National Baptist Voice.*

National Primitive Baptist Convention of America

Black and white Primitive Baptists separated after the Civil War. Although having long avowed opposition to church organization above the congregational level, it was not until 1907 that black Primitive Baptists formed the National Primitive Baptist Convention. Each congregation is independent, and a decision by officials of a local church is final. In 1975, they possessed a membership of 1,645,600 in 2,198 churches.

Progressive National Baptist Convention, Inc.

The Progressive National Baptist Convention, Inc., was formed in 1961 as a result of a schism in the National Baptist Convention of the U.S.A., Inc. The schism resulted from a dispute over leadership occasioned by differences over tactical strategies in the strug-

First Baptist Church, Washington, DC.

gle for civil rights. Those, including Martin Luther King, Jr., committed to such provocative tactics as nonviolent civil disobedience left to form the new denomination. The convention's motto is "Unity, Service, Fellowship, and Peace."

The Convention has 1.2 million members and 1,000 churches, and is governed by a sixty-member executive board. Although it has no publishing house of its own, it does publish a quarterly periodical, the *Baptist Progress*.

Rastafarians

Members of this religion regard Ethiopian Emperor Haile Selassie, who died in 1975, as God. Marcus Garvey, a Jamaican-born nationalist who advocated a back-to-Africa movement in the United States in the early 1920s, is also a central figure in the faith. Reggae musician Bob Marley, a Rastafarian, helped to increase the religion's popularity in the United States.

Today, Rastas differ on specific dogma, but they basically believe that they are descended from black Hebrews exiled in Babylon and therefore are true Israelites. They also believe that Haile Selassie (whose name before ascending the throne was Lij Ras Tafari Makonnen) is the direct descendent of Solomon and Sheba, and that God is black.

Most white men, they believe, have been worshipping a dead god and have attempted to teach the blacks to do likewise. They hold that the Bible was distorted by King James and that the black race sinned and was punished by God with slavery. They view Ethiopia as Zion, the Western world as Babylon, and believe that one day they will return to Zion. They preach love, peace, and reconciliation between races but warn that Armageddon is imminent.

Rastas don't vote, tend to be vegetarians, abhor alcohol, and wear their hair in long, uncombed plaits called dreadlocks. The hair is never cut, since it is part of the spirit, nor is it ever combed.

There are an estimated 50,000 Rastas in Britain and almost a million in the United States, approximately 80,000 of whom live in New York City, mainly in Brooklyn, where there is a high concentration of West Indians and Haitians.

■ RELIGIOUS LEADERS

Noble Drew Ali (1886–1929)
Moorish Science Temple Founder

Noble Drew Ali, whose birth name was Timothy Drew, was born in North Carolina. He is principally important for his role in establishing the first North American religious movement combining black nationalist and Muslim themes with rejection of Christianity as the religion of whites. In 1913, he established the first Moorish Science Temple in Newark, New Jersey. He taught that black Americans were "Asiatics" who had originally lived in Morocco before enslavement. Every people, including black Americans, needed land for themselves, he proclaimed, and North America, which he termed an "extension" of the African continent, was the proper home for black Americans. The holy book for the Moorish Science Temple was a "Holy Koran" which was "divinely prepared by the Noble Prophet Drew Ali." (This book should not be confused with the Q'uran of Islam). Every member of the Temple carried a card stating that "we honor all the Divine Prophets, Jesus, Mohammed, Buddha and Confucius" and that "I AM A CITIZEN OF THE U.S.A."

In the 1920s, the Moorish Science Temple expanded to Pittsburgh, Detroit, and Chicago. Noble Drew Ali also started several small businesses, which he ran together with his followers. Drew Ali was stabbed to death in his Chicago offices in apparent strife over the leadership of the Temple. The Moorish Science Temple survived Drew Ali's death, but the Nation of Islam was able to attract some of its followers.

Richard Allen (1760–1831)
African Methodist Episcopal Church Founder

Born a slave in Philadelphia, Allen converted to Christianity in 1777 and soon thereafter bought his freedom. He traveled widely through the Middle Atlantic States as an exporter. Francis Asbury, the first bishop of the Methodist Episcopal Church, asked Allen to join him as a travelling companion, stipulating that Allen would not be allowed to fraternize with slaves and would sometimes have to sleep in his carriage. Allen refused to accept such an offer, instead settling down in Philadelphia, where he helped to found the Free African Society, an African-American society for religious fellowship and mutual aid. One day in the early 1790s, Allen was worshipping in Philadelphia's St. George's Methodist Church when he was pulled off his knees during prayer by white deacons who insisted that Allen was sitting outside the area reserved for African Americans. Allen left, establishing his own church for Philadelphia's African Americans in a converted blacksmith shop in 1794. White Methodists tried to exert their control over his church in various ways, and Allen resisted successfully. In 1816, after the Pennsylvania Supreme Court settled a suit over this church in Allen's favor, Allen called for a conference of black Methodists. The African Methodist Episcopal Church was founded at this conference, and Allen was consecrated as its first bishop. Allen remained both religiously and politically active in his later years, and he was especially active in opposing schemes to colonize free African Americans in Africa.

Thea Bowman (1938–1990)
Roman Catholic Nun

Born in Canton, Mississippi, Thea Bowman, daughter of a medical doctor, joined the Roman Catholic Church at age twelve because of the Catholic education she had received. Three years later, she joined the Franciscan Sisters of Perpetual Adoration. She was extensively educated, earning a Ph.D. in literature and linguistics.

Bowman was a distinguished teacher, who taught elementary and high school as well as college. She helped to found the Institute of Black Catholic Studies at Xavier University and was a distinguished scholar known for her writings on Thomas More. But it is probably for the spiritual inspiration that she provided in numerous lectures, workshops and concerts that she will be best remembered. She said that she brought to her church "myself, my black self, all that I am, all that I have, all that I hope to become, my history, my culture, my experience, my African-American song and dance and gesture and movement and teaching and preaching and healing."

Nannie Helen Burroughs (1883–1961)
Baptist Lay Leader, Educator

Born in Orange Springs, Virginia, Nannie Helen Burroughs became one of the most significant Baptist lay leaders of the twentieth century. She addressed the National Baptist Convention in Virginia in 1900 on the subject, "How the Sisters are Hindered from Helping," and from that time until her death more than sixty years later she exercised pivotal leadership. She was elected corresponding secretary for the Woman's Convention, Auxiliary to the National Baptist Convention, U.S.A., Inc., and in 1948 she became President of the Women's Convention. She founded the National Training School for Women and Girls, emphasizing industrial arts and proficiency in African-American history, in Washington, DC. She edited such periodicals as the *Christian Banner*, and was the author of such books as the *Roll Call of Bible Women*.

James Cone (1938–)
Theologian

Born in Fordyce, Arkansas, James Cone received a B.A. from Philander Smith College, a B.D. from Garrett Evangelical Seminary, and an M.A. and Ph.D. from Northwestern University. After teaching at Philander Smith and Adrian Colleges, Cone moved to Union Theological Seminary in 1969. He is currently the Charles A. Briggs Professor of Systematic Theology. Cone is the author of numerous books, including *Black Theology and Black Power* (1969); *The Spirituals and the Blues* (1972); *For My People: Black Theology and the Black Church* (1984); and most recently, *Martin & Malcolm & America: A Dream or a Nightmare* (1991). Perhaps more than any other black theologian, Cone has provided a systematic exposition of the argument that since God, according to the Bible, is on the side of the poor and oppressed, that in the American context, God is siding with the black liberation struggle. He has made this argument using a diverse set of sources, including the writings of modern European theologians such as Karl Barth, and the writings and speeches of Malcolm X and Martin Luther King, Jr. Cone has worked painstakingly in the past two decades to build ties between black, feminist, and third world liberation theologians.

Alexander Crummell (1819–1898)
Episcopalian Minister

See Black Nationalism.

Father Divine (1877–1965)
Peach Mission Founder

Mystery shrouds the early identity and real name of Father Divine. There is reason to believe he was born George Baker in 1877 on Hutchinson's Island in Georgia. In 1907, he became a disciple of Sam Morris, a Pennsylvania black man who called himself Father Jehovia. Two years later he switched over to John Hickerson's "Lift Ever, Die Never" group before returning to Georgia where he began his own campaign to promote himself as a "divine messenger."

Threatened by local authorities (he was once booked as "John Doe, alias God"), Father Divine left Georgia in 1914 and later settled in New York City, where he worked as an "employment agent" for the few followers still loyal to him. Calling his meeting place "Heaven," he soon attracted a larger following and moved to Sayville, Long Island, in 1919. It was at this time that Father Divine began to provide shelter and food to the poor and homeless. Spiritually, Father Divine fostered what amounted to a massive cooperative agency, based on the communal spirit of the Last Supper. His movement practiced complete racial equality. Services included songs and impromptu sermons and were conducted without Scripture readings and the use of clergy.

Once he was sentenced to six months in jail as a public nuisance. Four days after his trial, the judge in his case died of a heart attack, whereupon Father Divine was

Father Divine

quoted as having said: "I hated to do it." The ensuing publicity enhanced his popularity.

The Divine movement, a non-ritualistic cult whose followers worshipped their leader as God incarnate on earth, grew rapidly in the 1930s and 1940s, with "Father" speaking out across the country and publicizing his views in the *New Day*, a weekly magazine published by his organization. He set up "Peace Mission Kingdom" throughout the United States and the world. In 1946, he married his "Sweet Angel," a twenty-one-year old Canadian stenographer known thereafter as Mother Divine.

Father Divine died peacefully at Woodmont, an estate he had acquired in the Philadelphia suburbs, and his wife pledged to continue the work of the movement.

Louis Farrakhan (1933–)
Nation of Islam National Minister, Black Nationalist

See Black Nationalism.

Elijah John Fisher (1858–1915)
Baptist Minister

Elijah Fisher exemplifies the great charismatic black preachers of the nineteenth and early twentieth centuries who, with very little formal education, built large religious institutions, counseled racial pride, and expounded the cause of blacks as a people.

Born in La Grange, Georgia, the youngest of eight boys in a family of seventeen children, Fisher's father was an unordained preacher of a Baptist congregation that met in a white church. Fisher worked in a Baptist parsonage as a boy slave, and was taught to read by a former house slave and a white missionary. In his teens, he worked in mines in Alabama and then as a butler, all the while studying theology on his own time. Though he lost a leg in an accident, Fisher in his early twenties became pastor of several small country churches, and then in 1889, of the Mount Olive Baptist Church in Atlanta. In that year, when past the age of thirty, he enrolled in the Atlanta Baptist Seminary, passed his examinations, went to preach in Nashville and then Chicago where he led the Olive Baptist Church from 1902 until his death.

Throughout his life, Fisher continued his studies, preached from coast to coast, and involved the churches in youth work, food programs for poor people, and black-run businesses. An active member of the Republican Party, Fisher strongly criticized blacks who advised their brethren to rely solely on the good will of whites and publicly criticized Booker T. Washington for not speaking out against lynching.

"Sweet Daddy" Grace (1881–1960)

United House of Prayer for all People Founder

Born in the Cape Verde Islands, "Sweet Daddy" Grace probably opened his first church in New Bedford, Massachusetts, in 1921, but his first success occurred five years later when he opened a church in Charlotte. Grace's church, the United House of Prayer for All People, had an ecstatic worship style, where speaking in tongues was encouraged. Grace claimed great powers, including the power of faith healing, and he stated that "Grace has given God a vacation, and since God is on His vacation don't worry Him . . . If you sin against God, Grace can save you, but if you sin against Grace, God cannot save you." Even the numerous products that he sold, such as "Daddy Grace" coffee, tea, soaps, and hand creams, were reputed to have healing powers. By the time of his death, the church had 375 branches and about 25,000 members nationwide.

Barbara C. Harris (1930–)

Episcopalian Bishop

Born in Philadelphia, Barbara Harris, a former public relations executive, was ordained a deacon in the Protestant Episcopal Church in 1979 and a priest one year later. She served as the priest-in-charge of an Episcopalian Church in Norristown, Pennsylvania, the interim pastor of a church in Philadelphia, and the executive director of the publishing company associated with the Episcopal Church. In February, 1989, she was consecrated as suffragan (or assistant) bishop for the diocese of Massachusetts. She thus became the first woman bishop in the history of the Episcopal Church. She received considerable support despite the concerns of some that her views were too liberal. Her supporters said that despite the lack of a college degree or seminary training, she would broaden the outreach of her church.

James Augustine Healy (1830–1900)

Roman Catholic Bishop

James Augustine Healy was the first black Catholic bishop in the United States. For twenty-five years he presided over a diocese covering the states of Maine and New Hampshire.

Barbara Harris

A native of Macon, Georgia, Healy received his education in the North, first at Franklin Park Quaker School in Burlington, New York, and later at Holy Cross in Worcester, Massachusetts. Healy graduated from the latter with first honors. Healy continued his studies abroad, and was ordained in Paris at Notre Dame Cathedral in 1854. He then returned to the United States.

Pastor of a predominantly Irish congregation which was at first reluctant to accept him, Bishop Healy performed his priestly duties with devotion and eventually won the respect and admiration of his parishioners—particularly after performing his office during a typhoid epidemic.

Thereafter, he was made an assistant to Bishop John Fitzpatrick of Boston, who appointed him chancellor and entrusted him with a wide variety of additional responsibilities. In 1875, he was named Bishop of Port-

Bishop James A. Healy

land, Maine, and in this capacity, he founded sixty parishes, as well as eighteen schools.

Healy's brother, Patrick Francis Healy, was a Jesuit priest who served as president of Georgetown University from 1873 to 1882.

Joseph H. Jackson (1904–1990)
National Baptist Convention, U.S.A., Inc. Former President

From 1953 to 1982, Joseph H. Jackson was the president of the National Baptist Convention, U.S.A., Inc., the third largest Protestant denomination in the United States and the largest of the predominantly black churches.

Born in Rudyard, Mississippi, Jackson held a B.A. from Jackson College, a M.A. from Creighton University, and a B.D. from Rochester Colgate School of Divinity. After pastoring churches in Mississippi, Jackson accepted a call to pastor the historic Olivet Baptist Church in 1941. His role in the civil rights movement was a fairly conservative one. He was supportive of the efforts of Martin Luther King, Jr. during the Montgomery bus boycott of 1955, but criticized the massive nonviolent civil disobedience campaigns of the early 1960s. Jackson's main emphasis was on the need for African Americans to build a viable economic base. His favorite slogan was "From Protest to Production." He was supportive of Baptist missions in Africa and attempted to finance them by developing farmland in Liberia.

Dr. Joseph Jackson

Leontine T.C. Kelly (1920–)
Methodist Bishop

Leontine T.C. Kelly, the first black woman bishop in any large American denomination, was born in Washington, D.C. She received a M.Div. degree from Union Theological Seminary in Richmond, Virginia, in 1969. She served as a schoolteacher, pastor of Virginia churches, and a staff member of the Virginia Conference of Churches before being elected a bishop in the United Methodist Church in 1984. She currently presides over the California-Nevada conference of that denomination. She is married to James David Kelly and has four children.

Isaac Lane (1834–1937)
Colored Methodist Episcopal Bishop

A great religious leader and educator whose life spanned more than a century, Isaac Lane was born a slave in Jackson, Tennessee. Self-educated, in 1856 he was granted a license to exhort, a category assigned to blacks who were forbidden to preach, in the Methodist Episcopal Church South.

Lane was ordained a minister in 1865 and in 1873 was made a bishop of the Colored Methodist Episcopal Church (now known as the Christian Methodist Episcopal Church) at a salary so low he had to raise cotton to supplement his income and support his family—which contained eleven children. His missionary work was instrumental in establishing the CME Church in Louisiana and Texas. In the 1880s, he established Lane College in Jackson with $9,000 he himself raised.

Jarena Lee (1783– ?)
Methodist Church Pioneer

Born in Cape May, New Jersey, she worked as a servant for a family who lived near Philadelphia. She had a conversion experience in 1804, but was unable to find a church with which to unite until she heard Richard Allen, founder of the African Methodist Episcopal Church, preach in Philadelphia. She experienced a call to preach about 1808, and sought permission twice from Richard Allen for exercise of her call. On her first attempt in 1809, Allen refused her request, but eight years later, he granted it and licensed her as a preacher. Subsequently she traveled widely throughout the North and Midwest, and many of her listeners, especially women, were moved by her eloquent preaching. After Allen's death in 1831, male African Methodist Episcopal preachers in Philadelphia attempted to deny her permission to preach from their pulpits, but she continued her ministry despite such harassment. In 1848, she attempted to form a connection of female African Methodist Episcopal preachers for mutual support, but her organization soon fell apart. Many black women, especially within the African Methodist Episcopal Church, have seen Jarena Lee as a courageous foremother and a model for church activism.

George Liele (c.1750–1820)
Baptist Minister

Born a slave in Virginia, George Liele was sold while very young into Georgia. He experienced a Christian conversion after hearing a sermon by Matthew Moore, a white preacher, in 1773. Liele began conducting worship services on nearby plantations, and, with Moore's sponsorship, he soon became the first ordained black Baptist preacher in America. Liele's slave master, Henry Sharp, granted him his freedom before Sharp was killed in the American Revolution. Liele preached at the Silver Bluff Baptist Church in Silver Bluff, South Carolina, probably the first independent black congregation formed in North America, and at a location outside Savannah. One of his notable converts was Andrew Bryan, who founded the First African Baptist Church in Savannah. Some whites attempted to re-enslave Liele, but a British officer in Savannah ensured that he would maintain his freedom. Liele emigrated to Jamaica in 1784, and he started a school and preached to a small Baptist congregation in Kingston. Liele was married to a woman he converted in Savannah, and his four American-born children accompanied him to Jamaica.

Eugene A. Marino (1934–)
First African-American Roman Catholic Archbishop

Born May 29, 1934, in Biloxi, Mississippi, Marino received his training at Epiphany Apostolic College, St. Joseph Seminary, Fordham University, and Catholic University. He was ordained to the priesthood in 1962. In 1963 he was made director of St. Joseph.

In 1971 he was made vicar general of the Josephites and was consecrated a bishop in 1974. Marino became the first black Roman Catholic archbishop in the United States in

Eugene Marino as Archbishop

1988, when he was made archbishop of the Atlanta Archdiocese. Marino retired in 1990.

Charles H. Mason (1866–1961)
Church of God in Christ, Founder

Born to former slaves on a farm outside Memphis, Tennessee, Charles Mason was converted at the age of fourteen and he joined a Missionary Baptist Church. Mason obtained a preaching license from the Missionary Baptists in 1893, and, in the same year, he claimed to have the experience of entire sanctification, thus aligning himself with the Holiness Movement. He had little formal education beyond a brief period of study at the Arkansas Bible College. In 1895, the Baptists expelled him because of his beliefs on sanctification. Mason then held holiness revivals in Mississippi with the help of Charles Price Jones, a prolific writer of hymns and gospel songs, and others. In Lexington, Mississippi, his meetings were held in an abandoned cotton gin house. Despite an armed attack, probably by hostile African Americans, he achieved much success and many new converts with his revival preaching. In 1897, Mason and Jones founded a new Holiness Church and called it the Church of God in Christ; they worked together harmoniously over the next decade.

In 1907, Mason attended the Azusa Street Revival, conducted by William Seymour in Los Angeles, and he received the gift of speaking in tongues. He believed that the ability to speak in tongues was a necessary precondition for Baptism of the Spirit. He and Jones disagreed on this point and parted company. Mason re-formed the Church of God in Christ along the lines of his new spiritual insights. Over the next four decades, Mason, as bishop, general overseer, and "chief apostle," shepherded his denomination through a period of tremendous growth. He traveled extensively, preaching at revivals throughout the United States and the world. He was imprisoned for making pacifist statements during World War I. He died in 1961.

William Henry Miles (1828–1892)
Christian Methodist Episcopal Bishop

Born a slave in Kentucky, Miles was manumitted by his owner in her will. He joined the Methodist Episcopal Church, South, and soon perceived a call to preach. In 1859, he was ordained a deacon. Uncertain about church affiliation after the war, he investigated the possibility of joining the African Methodist Episcopal Zion Church, but soon thought better of it. Thus he remained a preacher in the Methodist Episcopal Church, South, until its African American members, those who had decided not to join the African Methodist Episcopal or African Methodist Episcopal Zion Churches, were allowed to form a separate denomination, the Colored Methodist Episcopal Church. At the first General Conference of the Colored Methodist Episcopal Church in 1870, Miles was elected one of the denomination's first two bishops. He was an active advocate of black colleges, especially those affiliated with the CME Church, such as Lane College in Jackson, Tennessee, and Paine Seminary in Atlanta, Georgia.

Elijah Muhammad (1897–1975)
Nation of Islam Spiritual Leader, Black Nationalist

See Black Nationalism.

Daniel Alexander Payne (1811–1893)
African Methodist Episcopal Bishop, Educator

Payne is a towering figure in the history of African-American religion and probably the greatest educator in the history of the African Methodist Episcopal Church. Born to free parents in Charleston, South Carolina, Payne received an excellent education and opened a school for black Charlestonians in 1829. An act of the South Carolina legislature forced him to close the school six years later. Payne travelled north and studied at the Lutheran Theological Seminary in Gettysburg, Pennsylvania. He delivered forceful anti-slavery speeches, and in 1841, switched his affiliation to the African Methodist Episcopal Church. He was ordained one year later and was elected a bishop in 1852.

Payne visited President Lincoln in the White House in 1862 and was a persistent advocate for emancipation and the freed people. In 1863, Payne bought Wilberforce University from the Methodist Episcopal Church. That university was the flagship school for the African Methodist Episcopal Church, and as its president and chief booster, Payne was the dominant presence there for the next thirty years. After the Civil War, Payne plunged himself deeply into oversight of the missionary work to the southern and western states and eventually to Africa. He was one of the first African Americans to visit Charleston after its liberation by the Union Army in 1865. He initially was a strong supporter of black ministerial involvement in Reconstruction governments in the South, but Payne (widely known to have an impeccable character) changed his mind after exposures of southerners' corruption and misdeeds soured him on political participation. In 1882, he refused a conductor's order to move to a segregated smoking car, and after the conductor evicted him from the train, protest meetings were held in many American cities. In his last five years of life, he published two important books, *Recollections of Seventy Years* (1888) and his well-researched *History of the African Methodist Episcopal Church* (1891).

Harold Robert Perry (1916–)
Roman Catholic Bishop

Harold Robert Perry was consecrated a Bishop of New Orleans on January 6, 1966—and thus became the first Catholic bishop in the United States in the twentieth century.

One of six children, Perry was born the son of a rice-mill worker and a domestic cook in Lake Charles, Louisiana. He entered the Divine Word Seminary in Mississippi at the age of thirteen, was ordained a priest in 1944, and spent the next fourteen years in parish work. In 1958, he was appointed rector of the seminary.

Louisiana has the largest concentration of black Catholics in the South, some 200,000

Reverend Harold Perry

in all. As of 1989, Perry was one of thirteen African-American bishops serving Catholic parishes around the nation.

Adam Clayton Powell, Jr. (1945–1971)
Baptist Minister, United States Representative

See Politics.

Adam Clayton Powell, Sr. (1865–1953)
Baptist Minister

Adam Clayton Powell, Sr. father of the late Harlem congressman, was largely responsible for building the Abyssinian Baptist Church into one of the most celebrated black congregations in the world.

Born in the backwoods of Virginia in 1865, Powell attended school locally, and between sessions, worked in the coal mines of West Virginia. After deciding to enter the ministry, he began his studies at Wayland Academy (now Virginia Union University), working his way through as a janitor and waiter. He later attended the Yale University School of Divinity and served as pastor of the Immanuel Baptist Church in New Haven.

Powell became pastor of Abyssinian in 1908 when it had a membership of only 1,600 and indebtedness of over $100,000. By 1921, the church had not been made solvent but was able to move into a $350,000 Gothic structure at its present location on 138th Street in Harlem.

During the Depression, Powell opened soup kitchens for Harlem residents and served thousands of meals. Later he and his son campaigned vigorously to expand job

Reverend Adam Clayton Powell, Sr.

opportunities and city services in Harlem. Powell retired from Abyssinian in 1937.

Joseph Charles Price (1854–1893)
African Methodist Episcopal Zion Minister, Educator

Born in Elizabeth City, North Carolina, to a free mother, Price was educated in the school established for freed people, and later at Shaw and Lincoln Universities, graduating from the latter in 1879. At age twenty-one, he was licensed to preach in the African Methodist Episcopal Zion Church, and he received the ordination of elder six years later. Price was renowned for the eloquence of his public addresses. It was Price who was the most responsible for the African Methodist Episcopal Zion Church's success in establishing a church college—Livingstone College in North Carolina—after ministers in that denomination had failed in several previous attempts. As president of Livingstone College, he quickly gave his school a solid grounding both academically and financially. For example, he raised $10,000 for his school during a lecture tour of England. He was an active participant in politics, campaigned for civil rights and prohibition, and assumed such offices as chairman of the Citizens' Equal Rights Association of Washington, D.C. He died a tragically early death from kidney failure.

William Joseph Seymour (1870–1922)
Pentecostal Minister

Born in Centerville, Louisiana, to parents who had been slaves, Seymour taught himself to read and write. In 1900, Seymour encountered the prominent promoter of Holiness doctrine, Martin Knapp, and studied under him. He suffered a bout of smallpox which left him blind in one eye. He was ordained as an evangelist by the "Evening Light Saints," a group that eventually became known by the title Church of God (Anderson, Indiana). Moving to Houston, he sat immediately outside the door of white evangelist Charles Parham's segregated classroom, while Parham lectured on Christian doctrine and, especially, on the importance of speaking in tongues.

In 1906, Seymour moved to Los Angeles to pastor a small black Holiness church, but his congregation, opposed to Seymour's contention that speaking in tongues was a very important part of Christian experience, dismissed him after one week. Seymour continued to hold religious meetings, attracting an interracial audience. A widely publicized outburst of speaking in tongues brought him an ever-larger audience, so he moved his "Apostolic Faith Gospel Mission" to a former AME Church building on Azusa Street. The extremely successful meetings that he held before ecstatic, interracial throngs of listeners over the next three years have been universally acknowledged as the beginnings of modern Pentecostalism in the United States and around the world. Seymour was greatly saddened when the racial unity displayed in the early stages of Pentecostalism began to break apart under the pressures exerted by racial discrimination in the nation at large. He was holding services at the Azusa Street mission until his death in 1922.

Amanda Berry Smith (1837–1915)
Holiness Evangelist, Missionary

Born in Long Green, Maryland, Smith was manumitted during her childhood after her father paid for her freedom. She had a emotional conversion experience in 1856. She began attending religious meetings faithfully, and while she resisted identification with any single denomination, her religious practice was most strongly influenced by Quakers and Methodists. Attendance at the religious meetings of white evangelists Phoebe Palmer and John Inskip introduced her to Holiness doctrine, and she experienced entire sanctification in 1868. Her husband died the following year, and Smith soon became a full-time traveling evangelist. She never sought to breach the barriers against women's ordination erected by male preachers, stating that the calling she had received directly from God was justification enough for her ministry.

From 1878 to 1890, Smith worked as a missionary in England, Ireland, Scotland, India, and Liberia. A Methodist bishop who heard her preach in India stated that he "had never known any one who could draw and hold so large an audience as Mrs. Smith." On her return to the United States in 1890, she preached widely and wrote her autobiography in 1893, an extremely detailed work now regarded as a classic. Her last twenty years were devoted to the construction and management of the Amanda Smith Orphan's Home for Colored Children in Illinois.

Stephen Gill Spottswood (1897–1974)
African Methodist Episcopal Bishop

Bishop of the African Methodist Episcopal Zion Church from 1952 to 1972 and board chairman of the National Association for the Advancement of Colored People

Bishop Stephen Spottswood

from 1961 until his death in 1974, Bishop Spottswood embodied the religious faith and intellectual incisiveness that has produced so many effective black religious activists.

Spottswood was born in Boston, attended Albright College, Gordon Divinity School, and then received a Doctor of Divinity from Yale University. As a religious leader, Bishop Spottswood was president of the Ohio Council of Churches and served on the boards of numerous interfaith conferences as well as heading the African Methodist Episcopal Zion Church. His activity with the NAACP started in 1919, when he joined the organization. He was appointed to the national board in 1955. In 1971, he became the center of a political storm when he chastised the Nixon administration for its policies toward blacks and refused, under strong pressure from the administration, to retract his comments.

George Augustus Stallings, Jr. (1948–)
Imani Temple African-American Catholic Congregation Founder and Bishop

Born in New Bern, North Carolina, Stallings received his bachelor of arts degree from St. Pius X Seminary in 1970. He received his bachelor of science degree in theology from the University of St. Thomas Aquinas in 1973 and his master of arts degree in pastoral theology the following year. In 1974 Stallings was ordained and in 1976 was named pastor of St. Teresa of Avila, located in one of Washington, DC's poor black neighborhoods. In 1975 he was granted a licentiate in sacred theology by the University of St. Thomas Aquinas. While pastor at St. Teresa, Stallings stressed that the contributions of Africans and African Americans to Christianity should be recognized and that the needs of blacks must be addressed by the church. In an effort to confront what he considered the church's racial insensitivity, he made use of what is known as the Rite of Zaire, incorporated jazz and gospel music to the Mass, and added readings by celebrated African-American writers to the litgery. Stallings received much criticism and in 1988 was removed from St. Teresa and named head of evangelism for Washington, DC. In 1989 Stallings, still convinced that the church was not meeting the cultural, spiritual, and social needs of African-American Catholics, announced that he would leave the diocese to found a new congregation, the Imani Temple African-American Catholic Congregation. In 1991, Bishop Stallings ordained former Roman Catholic nun Rose Vernell a priest. The congregation's membership is currently estimated at 3,500 members.

Leon Howard Sullivan (1922–)
Baptist Minister

Born in Charleston, South Carolina, Sullivan was ordained to the ministry at age nineteen. He was educated at the Union Theological Seminary in New York, and served as pastor of the Zion Baptist Church in Philadelphia from 1950 to 1988.

Much of his efforts during his ministry were directed toward improving employment prospects of African Americans. During the 1950s, he organized a selective patronage campaign, boycotting Philadelphia-area businesses which employed too few black employees. Sullivan's campaign experienced some success, but businesses requested black workers with technical skills that few possessed. Accordingly, Sullivan founded the Opportunities Industrialization Center in 1964 in order to impart employment skills to inner city youths. By 1980, the O.I.C. operated programs in 160 cities. He was also a major force in many other economic development initiatives, such as the

Philadelphia Community Investment Cooperative. His acceptance within the American business community is well symbolized by his long-time membership on the boards of General Motors and Philadelphia's Girard Bank.

Sullivan is also renowned for his leadership in addressing international issues as they affect the African-American community, and in particular, for his intensive involvement in political and economic reform in South Africa. In the mid-1970s, he devised his "Sullivan Principles," which successfully encouraged American-owned companies to hire more black South African workers and to treat them equitably in relation to promotions and working conditions. Sullivan, however, parted company with President Reagan's "constructive engagement" policy toward South Africa, and endorsed a policy of South African divestment in 1987.

Gardner C. Taylor (1918–)

Baptist Minister

Reverend Taylor is widely regarded as the dean of the nation's black preachers. He received a B.A. degree from Leland College in 1937 and a B.D. degree from the Oberlin Graduate School of Theology in 1940.

Taylor has long been a community activist. He demonstrated for civil rights and suffered arrest for civil disobedience with Martin Luther King, Jr. in the 1960s, and introduced Nelson Mandela to a New York audience in 1990. He is a trusted counselor to New York Mayor David Dinkins. Taylor served on the New York City Board of Education. He is the past president of the New York Council of Churches and the past vice president of the Urban League in New York, City. After forty-two years as pastor of the Concord Baptist Church in Brooklyn, Taylor resigned his post in 1990.

Howard Thurman (1899–1981)

Theologian, Educator

Born in Daytona Beach, Florida, Thurman studied at Morehouse College, Rochester Theological Center, and Haverford College. Thurman, named by *Life* magazine as one of the twelve great preachers of the twentieth century, served as a pastor to a Baptist church in Ohio and, from 1944 to 1953, an interracial and interdenominational Fellowship Church he founded in San Francisco. He also served as dean of the chapel at Howard University from 1932 to 1944, and Boston University from 1953 until his retirement. Thurman was one of the leading theologians of his time, writing *The Negro Spiritual Speaks of Life and Death* and his opposition to segregation and support of the civil rights movement in *This Luminous Darkness*. Altogether, he authored nineteen books, including an autobiography published in 1979.

Henry McNeal Turner (1834–1915)

African Methodist Episcopal Bishop

See Black Nationalism.

James Varick (c.1750–1827)

African Methodist Episcopal Zion Bishop

Born near Newburgh, New York, to a slave mother, Varick was a leader in the movement among African-American Methodists in New York to set up a separate congregation. This was accomplished with the formation of the Zion Church in 1796. Varick was ordained a deacon by Bishop Francis Asbury ten years later. Varick sought to obtain full ordination (as elder) for himself and other African-American ministers, and would have preferred to have received such an ordination within the Methodist Episcopal Church, but this did not prove possible.

Reverend Howard Thurman (left) with O.D. Foster, 1952.

He did not favor joining Richard Allen's African Methodist Episcopal Church, especially since Allen had been attempting to set up a New York congregation seen by Varick as in competition with the Zion Church. Eventually, Varick participated in setting up the African Methodist Episcopal Zion Church, and he was elected the first superintendent or bishop. He was also deeply involved in issues relating to freedom and human rights, preaching against the slave trade in 1808 and subscribing to the first newspaper in the country owned by African Americans, *Freedom's Journal.*

18

Literature

18

Literature

African-American Writers Before the Harlem Renaissance ■ The Harlem Renaissance ■ African-American Writers After the Harlem Renaissance ■ The Black Aesthetic Movement ■ The Post Aesthetic Movement ■ African-American Novelists, Poets, Playwrights

Essay by Nancy Rampson

African-American literature in the United States reached an artistic pinnacle in the period between the two world wars with the Harlem Renaissance. Since then the fate of African-American writing has reached a level of high visibility; the themes have varied from highly charged and political to private and introspective. The Black Aesthetic Movement of the 1960s and 1970s brought acclaim and prominence to many African-American writers and fostered the growth of many black studies departments at universities around the country. In the 1980s and 1990s, African-American writers were working in every genre—from scriptwriting to poetry—and the names of African-American writers consistently were found on best-seller lists around the country.

■ AFRICAN-AMERICAN WRITERS BEFORE THE HARLEM RENAISSANCE

Perhaps the greatest satisfaction for black writers before the 1920s, or the Harlem Renaissance was to have the freedom to write; in fact, knowing how to read and write was a tremendous accomplishment for many post-Reconstruction African-Americans.

For Frederick Douglass, to write stirring diatribes against slavery powerful enough to shake the consciousness of a nation was more of a political than an artistic accomplishment. Likewise, when Jupiter Hammon, George Moses Horton, and Frances Harper prosaically wrote about the evils of slavery and racism, their verse seemed somewhat stilted; they followed the molds of Methodism, neoclassicism, and the Bible, traditions ill suited to their subject matter. However admirable their writing was, they never quite found a vehicle that fit their revolutionary thoughts.

As the bonds of slavery were loosened, black writers clamored to be heard, but the range of their work was limited. Since slavery and plantations were practically the only subjects in their repertoire, early African-

American works were often locked into these themes. In addition, being a black writer before 1920 was certainly a unique profession, almost an oddity. Many writers were essentially unknown during their lives. Still others, like Phillis Wheatley and Horton, gained a certain amount of acclaim. In fact, a number of blacks, including Paul Laurence Dunbar and Charles W. Chestnutt, became truly appreciated as writers.

White society, however, still controlled much of publishing in America; African-American work was often filtered and distorted through this lens. As a result, much of the post-Reconstruction era work by African-Americans was an attempt to prove that blacks could fit into middle-American society. In fact, much of the literature of this era was an attempt by blacks to appear happy with their assigned lot. Yet some writers, Dunbar and Chestnutt for example, tried to break the chains of this imposed expression. They attempted to present a view of black life as it really was, not as society wanted it to be.

Although the accomplishments of writers of this era were remarkable, existing conditions seemed to keep African-American letters from truly flourishing. What these authors most notably did was to pave the way for the Harlem Renaissance and to provoke authors to think about and develop a truly African-American culture.

Phillis Wheatley's first poem was printed in 1770 under the title "A Poem by Phillis, A Negro Girl on the Death of Reverend George Whitefield."

■ THE HARLEM RENAISSANCE

Resistant to the easy categorization of a timeline, the Harlem Renaissance began roughly around World War I and extended into the early 1930s. It began mostly as a movement of African-American artists and writers into Harlem from practically every state in the country. At the same time, another hub of artistic activity was forming in Washington, DC. In fact, Harlem artists often journeyed to Washington for a break and a new perspective.

What was on the conscious agenda of these mostly young, African-American artists was to define and celebrate black art and culture and to change the preconceived and erroneous notions most Americans had of black life.

As African-American journals such as *Crisis* and *Opportunity* began to appear, it became much easier for black writers to publish in a style that suited their tastes. Also, African-American writers were finding that some white patrons in the publishing fields were, in fact, interested in promoting their work. Bohemianism was flourishing, and many of the Harlem Renaissance artists fit this label. Being called "New Negroes," they sought to chisel out a unique, African-centered culture for blacks, and to improve race relations while maintaining a distinct cultural identity.

Important writers of this era include Langston Hughes, Countee Cullen, Claude McKay, Nella Larsen, and Zora Neale Hurston. These younger writers were encouraged by the older, established writers, critics and editors, including W.E.B. DuBois, with his journal, *Crisis* and Charles S. Johnson, editor of *Opportunity*, a sponsor of many literary contests. In fact, Langston Hughes actually believed that the Renaissance was due to the nurturing of older writers, including Jessie Fauset and Alain Locke.

The Harlem Renaissance was marked by a shift away from the moralizing work, which had been characteristic of much post-reconstruction writing that decried racism. Even though much of this writing was excellently written and eloquently executed, people like DuBois and Locke realized that it was doing very little to change the consciousness of the country. For this reason, they decided instead to challenge these new writers to produce works that came directly out of personal experience—to communicate the ills of the racist world with art rather than essay. In this way, readers were not struck so bluntly with the grim realities presented by African-American writers. These issues could be experienced through the lives of characters and in verse, and the message delivered more subtly and effectively.

Jessie Fauset, Langston Hughes, and Zora Neale Hurston.

AFRICAN-AMERICAN WRITERS AFTER THE HARLEM RENAISSANCE

As the economic Depression deepened, the Harlem Renaissance slowly faded. Richard Wright's publication in 1940 of *Native Son* marked a new era in African-American literature. The years from 1940 to 1955 served as a transition period for black letters; they bridged the wildly creative period of the Renaissance with the more intense creativity and political activity that was to define the work produced during the civil rights movement.

With the publication of his classic novel, Wright maintained that the era of the Harlem Renaissance—with its motto of 'art for art's sake'—must die and be replaced instead with works directly intended to end racism. He believed that blacks were an essential part of American society. This seeming dichotomy was one of the foundations for the ideology of the civil rights movement.

During this time, other black writers, notably poets, were taking a different road in their quest to be heard. Poets such as

Richard Wright

Gwendolyn Brooks, Melvin B. Tolson and Robert Hayden were using classical and mythical themes in their works. Indeed, Brooks was to win a Pulitzer prize in 1950 for her book *Annie Allen*. These poets used a blend of extreme eclecticism with realistic, African-American issues. The blend seemed to work, as their writing was met with acceptance in the university community and beyond.

Ralph Ellison's *Invisible Man*, arguably one of the best novels published in America during this century, and James Baldwin's *Go Tell It on the Mountain* were two other books that brought serious African-American issues to mainstream culture. In addition, many African-American works were gaining acceptance with the literary establishment and being taught in English classes around the country.

■ THE BLACK AESTHETIC MOVEMENT

The Black Aesthetic Movement, or the Black Arts Movement, has been the first major African-American artistic movement since the Harlem Renaissance. Beginning in the early 1960s and lasting through the mid-1970s, this movement was brought on not by white patrons (as the Renaissance had been in part). Rather, it was made possible by the anger of Richard Wright, Ralph Ellison, and other notable African-American writers.

This artistic movement was closely paralleled by the civil rights marches and the call for independence being experienced in the African-American community. As phrases like "Black is beautiful" were popularized, African-American writers of the Aesthetic Movement consciously set out to define what it meant to be a black writer in a white culture. While writers of the Harlem Renaissance seemed to stumble upon their identity within, writers of the Aesthetic Movement were serious about defining themselves and their era before being defined by others.

For the most part, Black Aesthetics were supportive of separatist politics and a black nationalist ideology. Rebelling against the mainstream society by being essentially anti-white, anti-American and anti-middle class, these artists moved from the Renaissance view of art for art's sake into a philosophy of art for politics' sake.

The Black Aesthetic Movement attempted to produce works of art that would be meaningful to the black masses. Towards this end, popular black music of the day, including John Coltrane's jazz and James Brown's R&B, as well as street talk, were some of the inspirational forces for their art. In fact, much of the language used in these works was vulgar and shocking—this was often a conscious attempt to show the vitality and power of black activists. These writers tended to be revolutionaries rather than diplomats—Malcolm X was more of an idol than Martin Luther King, Jr. In addition, they believed that artists had more of a responsibility than just art: artists also had to be political activists in order to achieve nationalist goals.

Leading writers in this movement include Imamu Amiri Baraka (Leroi Jones), whose poetry was as well known as his political prowess; Haki R. Madhubuti (Don L. Lee), a poet and essayist who was overwhelmingly popular—selling over 100,000 copies of his books without a national distributor. Ishmael Reed, on the other hand, an early organizer of the Black Aesthetic Movement, later dissented with some of the movement's doctrines; he became inspired more and more by the black magic and spiritual practices of the West Indies (in what he called the "HooDoo Aesthetic").

Imamu Amiri Baraka

Sonia Sanchez was another leading voice of the movement. She managed to combine feminism with her commitment to nurturing children and men in the fight for black nationalism. She joined up with the Nation of Islam from 1972–75, and through her association with the Black Aesthetic Movement, managed to instill stronger support for the role of some in that religion.

THE POST AESTHETIC MOVEMENT

Many women, however, were writing in response to the Black Aesthetic Movement—protesting the role which they felt women were placed into in the male-oriented black nationalist movement. Zora Neale Hurston's work was resurrected and used for inspiration and impetus in their work. These women were also supported by the women's liberation movement, allowing their works to reach a wider audience. In this way, the somewhat female-repressive politics of the Black Aesthetic Movement provoked women writers to express their own unique voice. Alice Walker, Gayl Jones, Toni Morrison, Terry McMillan, and Gloria Naylor are examples of successful women authors who have become prominent figures in the publishing world. In fact, during the 1980s, black women writers were at the leading edge of publishing—in quality as well as quantity of work.

Since the Black Aesthetic Movement, African-American writing has become more legitimized in America, and black studies departments have emerged in many universities around the country. Variety was the key to African-American writing after 1950, and barriers went down in various genres. For example, Octavia Butler and Samuel Delany broke into the world of science fiction. Donald Goines wrote detective fiction that rivaled his contemporaries. Novels of both folk history and the urban

Gloria Naylor

experience were equally well received, and many artists found that they could straddle more than one genre—Alice Walker and Gayl Jones being good examples—and delve into the worlds of fiction, poetry, essay and children's books.

Alex Haley's *Roots* was perhaps one of the greatest African-American writing coups of the post 1950s era. With his book, as well as the highly popular television mini-series that followed, many blacks became interested in their African ancestors. Other books explored the history of blacks in other areas, namely the American West, the South and the North.

Writers after the 1960s seem to have changed the tone a bit—no longer was there as much emphasis on the disparity between black and white in America. In the words of Toni Morrison, John Edgar Wideman and Kristin Hunter, the themes of self-reflection and healing were evident. African Americans were portrayed looking into their own inner worlds for answers, rather than letting themselves be defined by the outer world.

AFRICAN-AMERICAN NOVELISTS, POETS, PLAYWRIGHTS

Raymond Andrews (1934–)
Novelist

Born in Madison, Georgia, Raymond Andrews left his sharecropper farm home at fifteen to live, work, and attend high school at night in Atlanta. After graduation, he served in the United States Air Force (1952–1956) and attended Michigan State University before moving to New York City where he worked in a variety of jobs: airline reservations clerk, hamburger cook, photo librarian, proofreader, inventory taker, mail room clerk, messenger, air courier dispatcher, and bookkeeper. During his spare time, Andrews perfected his literary skills.

His first novel, *Appalachee Red* (1978), set in the black neighborhood of a northern Georgia town called Appalachee, was widely acclaimed. In the view of the reviewer for the *St. Louis Globe Democrat*, it marked the literary debut of a significant modern American novelist of the stature of a Richard Wright or James Baldwin. The following year Raymond Andrews was the first recipient of the annual James Baldwin Prize presented by The Dial Press at a ceremony attended by Baldwin.

Andrews' second work, *Rosiebelle Lee Wildcat Tennessee: A Novel* (1980), chronicled the 40-year reign in Appalachee, beginning in 1906, of the spiritual and temporal leader of the black community there. And like his previous novel, it was illustrated by his brother Benny.

His third novel titled *Baby Sweets* (1984), was also published by Dial Press and illustrated by his brother Benny. Baby Sweets is the name given to the brothel opened by the eccentric son of Appalachee's leading citizen to provide black prostitutes to the white population. This novel examines how the intermingling of the races affects an entire community.

Maya Angelou

Maya Angelou (1928–)
Novelist, Poet

Born Marguerite Johnson, Angelou spent her formative years shuttling between St. Louis, Missouri, a tiny, totally segregated town in Arkansas, and San Francisco where she realized her ambition of becoming that city's first black streetcar conductor.

During the 1950s, she studied dancing with Pearl Primus in New York, later appearing as a nightclub singer in New York and San Francisco. She worked as an editor for *The Arab Observer*, an English-language weekly published in Cairo; lived in Accra, Ghana, where under the black nationalist regime of Kwame Nkrumah she taught music and drama; and studied cinematography in Sweden. She became a national celebrity in 1970 with the publication of *I Know Why the Caged Bird Sings*, the first volume of her autobiography, which detailed her encounters with southern racism and a prepubescent rape by her mother's lover.

In 1971, she produced *Just Give Me a Cool Drink of Water 'fore I Die: The Poetry of Maya Angelou*; in 1975, *Oh Pray My Wings Are Gonna Fit Me Well*; in 1979, *And Still I Rise*; and in 1983, *Shaker Why Don't You Sing?*. In 1977, she was nominated for an Emmy award for her portrayal of Nyo Boto in the television adaptation of the best-selling novel *Roots*.

Three more volumes of her autobiography have been published: *Gather Together in My Name* (1974); *Singin' and Swingin' and Gettin' Merry Like Christmas* (1976); and *The Heart of a Woman* (1981). In 1986, *All God's Children Need Traveling Shoes* was published. Angelou's other works include*Mrs. Flowers: A Moment of Friendship* , and *Now Sheba Sings the Song.*

On January 20, 1993, Angelou read her poem "On the Pulse of Morning" during the inauguration of President Bill Clinton.

James Baldwin (1924–1987)
Novelist, Essayist, Playwright

Born in New York City, Baldwin turned to writing after an early career as a boy preacher in Harlem's storefront churches. He attended Frederick Douglass Junior High

School in Harlem and later graduated from DeWitt Clinton High School, where he was editor of the school magazine. Three years later, he won a Eugene Saxton Fellowship, which enabled him to write full-time. After leaving the United States, Baldwin resided in France as well as in Turkey.

Baldwin's first novel, *Go Tell It on the Mountain*, was published in 1953, and received critical acclaim. Two years later, his first collection of essays, *Notes of a Native Son*, again won favorable critical acclaim. This was followed, in 1956, by the publication of his second novel, *Giovanni's Room*. His second collection of essays, *Nobody Knows My Name*, brought him into the literary spotlight and established him as a major voice in American literature.

In 1962, *Another Country*, Baldwin's third novel, was a critical and commercial success. A year later, he wrote *The Fire Next Time*, an immediate best-seller regarded as one of the most brilliant essays written in the history of the black protest.

Since then, two of Baldwin's plays, *Blues for Mister Charlie* and *The Amen Corner*, have been produced on the New York stage, where they achieved modest success.

His novel *Tell Me How Long The Train's Been Gone* was published in 1968. Baldwin himself regards it as his first "grown-up novel," but it has generated little enthusiasm among critics.

Much to the distress of his public, Baldwin then entered an extended fallow period, and the question of whether he had stopped writing was widely debated. After a silence of several years, he published the 1974 novel *If Beale Street Could Talk*. In this work, the problems besetting a ghetto fam-

James Baldwin

ily, in which the younger generation is striving to build a life for itself, are portrayed with great sensitivity and humor. Baldwin's skill as a novelist is evident as he sets and solves the difficult problem of conveying his own sophisticated analyses through the mind of his protagonist, a young woman. To many critics, however, the novel lacks the undeniable relevance and fiery power of Baldwin's early polemical essays.

Baldwin's other works include *Going to Meet the Man* (short stories); *No Name in the Street*; *One Day When I Was Lost*, a scenario based on Alex Haley's *The Autobiography of Malcolm X*; *A Rap on Race* with Margaret Mead; and *A Dialogue* with Nikki Giovanni. He was one of the rare authors who worked well alone or in collaboration. Other books by Baldwin are *Nothing Personal* (1964) with photographs by Richard Avedon; *The Devil Finds Work* (1976), about the movies; his big sixth novel *Just Above My Head* (1979); and *Little Man, Little Man: A Story of Childhood* (1977) a book for children. He wrote 16 books and co-authored three others. There are six books about Baldwin's life and writings including a reference guide and bibliography.

Just Above My Head, published in 1979, dealt with the intertwined lives from childhood to adulthood of a gospel singer, his brother, and a young girl who is a child preacher. The next year Baldwin's publisher announced *Remember This House*, described as his "memoirs, history and biography of the civil rights movement" interwoven with the biographies of three assassinated leaders: Martin Luther King Jr. Malcolm X, and Medgar Evers. Meanwhile, in his lectures Baldwin remained pessimistic about the future of race relations.

His last three books were *The Evidence of Things Not Seen* (1985) about the killing of 28 black youths in Atlanta, Georgia in the early 1980s; *The Price of the Ticket: Collected Non-fiction 1948–1985* (1985), and *Harlem Quartet* (1987).

Baldwin spent most of the remainder of his life in France. In 1986, the French government made him a commander of the Legion of Honor, France's highest civilian award. He died at his home in France, on November 30, 1987, at the age of sixty-three.

Imamu Amiri Baraka (Leroi Jones) (1934–)

Poet, Playwright, Essayist

Baraka was born in Newark in 1934. He attended Rutgers University, in Newark, New Jersey, and Howard University, in Washington, DC. In 1958 he founded *Yugen* magazine and Totem Press. From 1961 to 1964 Baraka worked as an instructor at New York's New School for Social Research. In 1964 he founded the Black Arts Repertory Theater. He has since taught at the State University of New York at Stony Brook, University of Buffalo, Columbia University, George Washington University, and San Francisco University, and has served as director of the community theater Spirit House, in Newark.

In 1961 Baraka published his first book of poetry, *Preface to a Twenty Volume Suicide Note*. His second book, *The Dead Lecturer*, was published in 1964. However, he did not achieve fame until the publication of his play *Dutchman* in 1964, which received the Obie award for the best Off-Broadway play of the season. The shocking honesty of Baraka's treatment of racial conflict in this and later plays became the hallmark of his work.

During the late 1960s Baraka became a leading black power spokesman in Newark. He became head of the Temple of Kawaida, which Baraka describes as an "African religious institution—to increase black consciousness." The Temple and Baraka soon became a focal point of black political activism in the racially polarized city. In 1972 Baraka achieved prominence as a black leader as chairman of the National Black Political Convention

In 1966 Baraka's play *The Slave* won second prize in the drama category at the First World Festival of Dramatic Arts in Dakar, Senegal. Baraka's other published plays include: *The Toilet* (1964); *The Baptism* (1966); *The System of Dante's Hell* (1965); *Four Black Revolutionary Plays* (1969); *J-E-L-L-O* (1970); and *The Motion of History and Other Plays* (1978).

He has edited, with Larry Neal, *Black Fire: An Anthology of Afro-American Writing* (1968) and *Afrikan Congress: A Documentary of the First Modern Pan-African Congress* (1972). His works of fiction include *The System of Dante's Hell* (novel, 1965) and *Tales* (short stories, 1967). Baraka has also published *Black Music, Blues People: Negro Music in White America, Home: Social Essays, In Our Terribleness: Some Elements and Meanings in Black Style* with Billy Abernathy, *Raise Race Rays Raze: Essays Since 1965, It's Nation Time, Kawaida Studies: The New Nationalism, A Black Value System and Strategy and Tactics of a Pan Afrikan Nationalist Party.*

Arna Bontemps (1902–1973)
Poet, Novelist

Arna Bontemps was one of the most productive black writers of the twentieth century. Born in Alexandria, Louisiana and raised in California, Arna Bontemps received his B.A. degree from Pacific Union College in Angwin in 1923. The next year, his poetry first appeared in *Crisis* magazine, the NAACP periodical edited by Dr. W.E.B. DuBois. Two years later, *Golgotha Is a Mountain* won the Alexander Pushkin Award, and in 1927, *Nocturne at Bethesda*

Arna Bontemps

achieved first honors in the *Crisis* poetry contest. *Personals*, Bontemps' collected poems, was published in 1963.

In the late 1920s, Bontemps decided to try his hand at prose, and over the next decade produced such novels as *God Sends Sunday* (1931); *Black Thunder* (1936); and *Drums at Dusk* (1939).

His books for young people include *We Have Tomorrow* (1945); and *Story of the Negro* (1948). Likewise of literary merit are such children's books as *Sad-Faced Boy* (1937); and *Slappy Hooper* (1946). He edited *American Negro Poetry* and two anthologies, with Langston Hughes among others.

In 1968, he completed the editing of a volume of children's poetry. Other publications were *One Hundred Years of Negro Freedom* (1961); *Anyplace But Here* (published in 1966 in collaboration with Jack Convoy); *Black Thunder* (1968 reprint); *Great Slave Narratives* (1969); *The Harlem Renaissance Remembered: Essays* (1972, 1984); and *The Old South.* He also edited several anthologies.

Gwendolyn Brooks (1917–)
Poet

Gwendolyn Brooks is one of many blacks to win a Pulitzer Prize. Brooks received this prestigious award in 1950 for *Annie Allen*, a volume of her poetry which had been published a year earlier.

Brooks was born in Topeka, Kansas, moved to Chicago at an early age, and was educated there, graduating from Wilson Junior College in 1936.

In 1945, she completed a book of poems, *A Street in Bronzeville*, and was selected by *Mademoiselle* as one of the year's ten most outstanding American women. She was made a fellow of the American Academy of Arts and Letters in 1946, and received Guggenheim Fellowships for 1946 and 1947.

In 1949, she won the Eunice Tietjen Prize for Poetry in the annual competition sponsored by *Poetry* magazine. She was poet laureate of the state of Illinois.

Gwendolyn Brooks

Her other books include a collection of children's poems, *Bronzeville Boys and Girls* (1956); a novel, *Maud Martha* (1953); and two books of poetry, *The Bean Eaters* (1960); and *Selected Poems* (1963). She has also written *In the Mecca*; *Riot*; *The World of Gwendolyn Brooks*; *Report from Part One: The Autobiography of Gwendolyn Brooks*; *Family Pictures*; *Beckonings*; *Aloneness*; *Primer for Blacks*; and *To Disembark*.

Her poems and stories have also been published in magazines and two anthologies *Soon, One Morning*; and *Beyond the Angry Black*. She has edited *A Broadside Treasury* and *Jump Bad, A New Chicago Anthology*.

Claude Brown (1937–)
Novelist

Claude Brown's claim to literary fame rests largely on his best-selling autobiography *Manchild in the Promised Land*, which was published in 1965 when its author was 28.

The book is the story of Brown's life in Harlem and, in the process, becomes a highly realistic documentary of life in the ghetto. It tells of Brown's escapades with the Harlem Buccaneers, a "bopping gang," and of his later involvement with the Forty Thieves, an elite stealing division of this same gang.

After attending the Wiltwyck School for emotionally disturbed and deprived boys, Brown returned to New York, was later sent to Warwick Reform School three times, and eventually made his way downtown to a small loft apartment near Greenwich Village. Changing his style of life, Brown finished high school and went on to graduate from Howard University in 1965.

Brown began work on his book in 1963, submitting a manuscript of some 1,500 pages which was eventually cut and reworked into the finished product over a two-year period. Brown completed law school in the late 1960s and is now practicing in California. In 1976, he published *The Children of Ham* about a group of young blacks living as a family in a condemned Harlem tenement, begging, stealing, and doing whatever is necessary to survive.

William Wells Brown (1815–1884)
Novelist, Playwright

Williams Wells Brown was the first American black to publish a novel, the first to publish a drama, and the first to publish a travel book.

Born a slave in Lexington, Kentucky and taken to St. Louis as a young boy, Brown worked for a time in the offices of the *St. Louis Times*, and then took a job on a riverboat in service on the Mississippi. In 1834, Brown fled to Canada, taking his name from a friendly Quaker whom he met there. While working as a steward on Lake Erie ships, he educated himself and became well known as a public speaker. In 1849, he went to England and Paris to attend the Peace Congress, remaining abroad for five years.

His first published work, *The Narrative of William H. Brown*, went into three editions within eight months. A year later, a collection of his poems was published, *The Anti-Slavery Harp*, and in 1852 his travel book *Three Years in Europe* appeared in London.

Brown's *Clotel, or the President's Daughter*, a melodramatic novel about miscegenation, was first published in London in 1853. As the first novel by an American black (it subsequently went through two revisions), its historical importance transcends its aesthetic shortcomings.

Brown's other books include the first black drama *The Escape, or a Leap for Freedom* (1858); *The Black Man: His Antecedents, His Genius, and His Achievements* (1863); *The Negro in the American Rebellion: His Heroism and Fidelity* (1867); and *The Rising Son* (1874).

Ed Bullins (1935–)
Playwright, Essayist, Poet

Ed Bullins was born in Philadelphia and grew up in Los Angeles. Bullins is a writer of drama, and one of the founders of the Black Arts/West in the Fillmore District of San Francisco. He patterned this experiment after the Black Arts Repertory Theater School in Harlem, which was founded and directed by Imamu Baraka. In 1977, when *Daddy*, the sixth play in his "Twentieth-Century Cycle" opened at the New Federal Theatre in New York's Henry Street Settlement, Bullins in an interview with the *New York Times* foresaw black theatrical producers taking plays to cities with large black populations and spreading out unless something happens to kill the economy. A leader of the black theater movement and creator of more than fifty plays, he has yet to have a play produced on Broadway.

Bullins' main themes are the violence and tragedy of drug abuse and the oppressive life style of the ghetto. He presents his material in a realistic and naturalistic style. Between 1965 and 1968 he wrote *The Rally*; *How Do You Do*; *Goin' a Buffalo*; *Clara's Old Man*; *The Electronic Nigger*; and *In The Wine Time*. He has also produced *The Fabulous Miss Marie*.

He has been a creative member of Black Arts Alliance, working with Baraka in producing films on the West Coast.

Bullins has been connected with the New Lafayette Theater in Harlem where he was a

Ed Bullins

resident playwright. His books include *Five Plays; New Plays from the Black Theatre* (editor); *The Reluctant Rapist*; *The New Lafayette Theatre Presents*; *The Theme Is Blackness*; *Four Dynamite Plays*; *The Duplex*; *The Hungered One: Early Writings*; and *How Do You Do: A Nonsense Drama.*

Octavia E. Butler (1947–)
Novelist

Born in Pasadena, California, Octavia Butler is a graduate of Pasadena City College. She has attended science fiction workshops and is a member of Science Fiction Writers of America. Her writing has focused on the impact of race and gender on future society.

In 1985 Butler won three of science fiction's highest honors for her novella *Blodchild*: the Nebula Award, the Hugo Award, and the Locus Award. Her other works include: *Patternmaster*; *Mind of My Soul*; *Survivor*; *Kindred*; *Wild Seed*; *Clay's Ark*; *Dawn*; *Xenogensis*. She has also served as a contributor to such science fiction publications as *Clarion*, *Future Life*, *Isaac Asimov's Science Fiction Magazine*, and *Transmission*.

Charles Waddell Chesnutt (1858–1932)
Novelist

Born in Cleveland, Ohio, in 1858, Chesnutt moved to North Carolina with his family at the age of eight. Largely self-educated, he was admitted to the Ohio bar in 1887, the same year in which his first story, "The Gophered Grapevine," was published in the *Atlantic Monthly*. This was followed in 1899 by two collections of his stories, *The Conjure Woman* and *The Wife of His Youth.*

His first novel, *The House Behind the Cedars* (1900), dealt with a young girl's attempt to "pass" for white. A year later, *The Marrow of Tradition* examined the violence of the post-Reconstruction period. His final novel, *The Colonel's Dream*, was published in 1905 and typified Chesnutt's basically ingratiating approach to his art, one which the writers of the Harlem School were later to reject. Chesnutt also wrote a biography, *Frederick Douglass* (1899).

Alice Childress (1920–   )
Playwright, Novelist

Born in Charleston, South Carolina, Childress studied acting at the American Negro Theatre and attended Radcliffe Institute from 1966 to 1968 through a Harvard University appointment as a scholar-writer. Her plays are *Florence* (one-act play); *Gold Through the Trees*; *Just a Little Simple* (based on Langston Hughes' *Simple Speaks His Mind*); *Trouble in Mind*; *Wedding Band*; *Wine in the Wilderness*; and *When the Rattlesnake Sounds: A Play about Harriet Tubman*. Childress also edited *Black Scenes* (1971), excerpts from plays in the Zenith series for children. Her other books include *Like One of the Family: Conversations from a Domestic's Life* (1956); *A Hero Ain't Nothing but a Sandwich* (1973) (novel); and *A Short Walk* (1979), *Rainbow Jordan* (1981), and *Many Closets* (1987). Childress' play *Trouble in Mind* won the Obie Award in 1956 as the best original off-Broadway production. Her book *Rainbow Jordan* for young people was published in 1982. She wrote, in the 1980s, a play based on the life of the black woman comedian Jackie (Moms) Mabley. The play was produced in New York City.

Countee Cullen (1903–1946)
Poet

Born Countee Porter on May 30, 1903 in Baltimore, he was orphaned at an early age and adopted by Reverend Frederick Cullen, pastor of New York's Salem Methodist Church. At New York University, Cullen won Phi Beta Kappa honors and was awarded the Witter Bynner Poetry Prize. In 1925, while still a student at New York University, Cullen completed *Color*, a volume of poetry which received the Harmon Foundation's first gold medal for literature two years later.

In 1926, he earned his M.A. at Harvard and a year later finished both *The Ballad of the Brown Girl* and *Copper Sun*. This was followed in 1929 by *The Black Christ*, written during a two-year sojourn in France on a Guggenheim Fellowship. In 1927, he edited

Countee Cullen

Caroling Dusk: An Anthology of Verse by Negro Poets. The book was reprinted in 1972.

Upon his return to New York City, Cullen began a teaching career in the public school system. During this period, he also produced a novel, *One Way to Heaven* (1932); *The Medea and Other Poems* (1935); *The Lost Zoo* (1940); and *My Lives and How I Lost Them* (1942, 1971).

In 1947, a year after his death, Cullen's own selections of his best work were collected in a volume published under the title *On These I Stand.*

Samuel R. Delany (1942–)
Novelist

Born in Harlem, and a published writer at the age of nineteen, Delany has been a prolific writer of science fiction, novelettes and novels. His first book was *The Jewels of Aptor* (1962); followed by *Captives of the Flame* (1963); *The Towers of Toron* (1964); *City of a Thousand Suns* (1965); *The Ballad of Beta-2* (1965); *Babel-17* (1966); *Empire Star* (1966); *The Einstein Intersection* (1967); *Out of the Dead City* (1968); and *Nova* (1968). *Babel-17* and *The Einstein Intersection* both won Nebula Awards from the Science Fiction Writers of America, as have his short stories "Aye, and Gomorrah" and "Time Considered as a Helix of Semi-Precious Stones," which also won a Hugo Award at the World Science Fiction Convention at Heidelberg. Delany co-edited the speculative fiction quarterly *Quark, Nos. 1, 2, 3, 4* with his former wife, National Book Award winning poet Marilyn Hacker. He also wrote, directed, and edited the half-hour film *The Orchid.* In 1975, Delany was Visiting Butler Chair Professor of English at the State University of New York at Buffalo.

His other books include: *Distant Stars* (1981); *Stars in My Pocket Like Grains of Sand* (1984); *The Splendor and Misery of Bodies of Cities* (1985); *Flight from Neveryon* (1985); *Neveryona* a (1986); and *The Bridge of Lost Desire* (1988). His nonfiction works include: *The Jewel-Hinged Jaw*; *The American Shore*; *Starboard Wine*; *The Straits of Messina*; and *The Motion of Light in Water* (autobiography) (1988).

Rita Dove (1952–)
Poet, Educator

Dove was born on August 28, 1952 in Akron, Ohio. She received a B.A. from Miami University in Oxford, Ohio in 1973 and a Master of Fine Arts from the University of Iowa in 1977. Dove also attended the University of Tubingen in Germany in 1974 and 1975.

Dove began her teaching career at Arizona State University in 1981 as an assistant professor. By 1984 she was an associate professor and by 1987 a full professor. In 1989 she joined the University of Virginia's English department where she continues to teach creative writing.

Dove is a renowned poet having won the 1987 Pulitzer Prize for Poetry for a collection titled *Thomas & Beulah.* Her themes are universal, encompassing much of the human condition and occasionally commenting on racial issues. She has also published *Yellow House on the Corner* (1980), *Museum* (1983), *Grace Notes* (1989), and a collection of short stories, *Fifth Sunday* (1985).

Besides the Pulitzer Prize Dove has many honors including Presidential Scholar (1970), Fulbright Scholar (1974, 1975), a Literary Grant from the National Endowment for the Humanities (1978, 1989), Guggenheim Fellow (1983, 1984), General Electric

Foundation Award for Younger Poets (1987), Ohio Governor's Award (1988), Andrew W. Mellon Fellowship (1988, 1989), Fellow, Center For Advanced Studies, University of Virginia (1989–1992), and the Walt Whitman Award (1990). In 1993 she was named United States Poet Laureate.

Dove has also been a Writer in Residence at the Tuskegee Institute in 1982 and has served on the editorial boards of the literary journals *Callaloo*, *Gettysburg Review* and *TriQuarterly*.

Paul Laurence Dunbar (1872–1906)
Poet

The first black poet to gain a national reputation in the United States, Paul Laurence Dunbar was also the first to use black dialect within the formal structure of his work.

Born of former slaves in Dayton, Ohio, Dunbar went to work as an elevator operator after graduating from high school. His first book of poetry, *Oak and Ivy*, was privately printed in 1893 and was followed by *Majors and Minors*, which appeared two years later. Neither book was an immediate sensation, but there were enough favorable reviews in such magazines as Harper's to encourage Dunbar in the pursuit of a full-fledged literary career. In 1896, Dunbar completed *Lyrics of a Lowly Life*, the single work upon which his subsequent reputation was irrevocably established.

Before his untimely death in 1906, Dunbar had become the dominant presence in the world of American Negro poetry. His later works included *Lyrics of Sunshine and Shadow* (1905), *Li'l Gal* (1904), *Howdy, Honey, Howdy* (1905), *A Plantation Portrait* (1905), *Joggin'erlong* (1906), and *Complete Poems*, published posthumously in 1913. This last work contains not only the dialect poems which were his trademark, but many poems in conventional English as well. The book has enjoyed such enormous popularity that it has, to this day, never gone out of print. He also published four novels including *The Sport of Gods*, *The Love of Landry*, and *The Uncalled*, and four volumes of short stories.

Ralph Ellison (1914–)
Novelist, Essayist

Ralph Ellison's critical and artistic reputation rests largely on a single masterpiece, his first and only novel, *Invisible Man*. Acclaimed by virtually all who have read it, the novel was given the National Book Award for fiction in 1952. It had been years in the making, and its success heralded the emergence of a major writing talent.

Ellison was born in Oklahoma City, Oklahoma and came to New York City in the late 1930s, after having studied music at Tuskegee Institute for three years. At first interested in sculpture, he turned to writing after coming under the influence of T.S. Eliot's poetry, and as a direct consequence of his friendship with Richard Wright.

In 1955, the American Academy of Arts and Letters awarded Ellison the Prix de Rome, which enabled him to live and write in Italy for a time. Since then, he has lectured at New York University and at Bennington College, and has been writer-in-residence at Rutgers University.

His second published work was *Shadow and Act*, a book of essays which appeared in 1964. Excerpts from his second novel have been published in several literary journals. There are three books of essays on him and his novel.

He has retired as Albert Schweitzer Professor of Humanities at New York University (1970–1980), and in 1974, was awarded an

Ralph Ellison

honorary Doctor of Letters degree by Harvard University.

The thirtieth anniversary edition of *Invisible Man* with a new introduction by Ellison was published in 1982.

Elected to the National Institute of Arts and Letters and the American Academy of Arts and Letters, Ellison was the subject of a *New Yorker* magazine profile in 1976. He received the Medal of Freedom from President Richard M. Nixon in 1969, and an honorary Doctor of Letters degree from Wesleyan University in June 1980 "for his insight into the role of the artist in American culture."

His third book and second book of essays and speeches, *Going To The Territory* (1986, 1987), was hailed as highly literate essay writing although some reviewers disagreed with some of his opinions. Ellison's writings are in many literary anthologies and collections and there are chapters about his work in scores of books as well as masters theses and thirty or more doctoral dissertations on him as a writer.

Mari Evans (1923–)
Poet

Born in Toledo, Ohio, Evans studied at the University of Toledo. In 1963, her poetry was published in *Phylon*, *Negro Digest*, and *Dialog*. Two years later she was awarded a John Hay Whitney Fellowship.

One of her better known works is *The Alarm Clock*, which deals with the rude awakening of the black American to the white "establishment." It captures and summarizes the scene of the sixties in the United States.

Her books include *I Am A Black Woman*; *Where Is All the Music?*; *Black Women Writers (1950–1980): A Critical Evaluation* (1984) edited by Evans, covering fifteen black women poets, novelists, and playwrights; *Nightstar: Poems From 1973–1978* (1982); *I Look at Me; Singing Black; The Day They Made Benani;* and *Jim Flying High.*

Charles Fuller (1939–)
Playwright

Fuller became "stagestruck" in his high-school days when he went to the Old Walnut Street Theater in his native Philadelphia, and saw a Yiddish play starring Molly Picon and Menasha Skulnik. He didn't understand a word of it, "but it was live theater, and I felt myself responding to it."

In 1959, Fuller entered the Army and served in Japan and South Korea, after which he attended Villanova University and La Salle College. While Fuller was working as a housing inspector in Philadelphia, the McCarter Theater in Princeton, New Jersey

Charles Fuller

produced his first play. The theme was intermarriage, and its creator is quick now to tag it "one of the world's worst interracial plays." However, during this time he met members of The Negro Ensemble Company, and in 1974 he wrote his first play for them, *In the Deepest Part of Sleep*. For NEC's tenth anniversary Fuller wrote *The Brownsville Raid* about the black soldiers who were dishonorably discharged on President Teddy Roosevelt's orders in 1906 after a shoot-out in Brownsville, Texas. The play was a hit and Fuller followed it a few seasons later with *Zooman and the Sign*, a melodrama that won two Obie awards.

A Soldier's Play, which won a Pulitzer Prize in 1982, is his fourth play for The Negro Ensemble Company. This drama dealing with a murder set in a back water New Orleans Army camp in 1944, opened NEC's fifteenth anniversary season in 1981 with a long run and was hailed by the *New York Times* as "tough, taut and fully realized." *A Soldier's Play* became *A Soldier's Story* when it was produced as a film in 1984 by Columbia Pictures. Fuller wrote the screenplay and black actor Howard E. Rollins Jr. was the film's star.

The recipient of the Guggenheim Foundation Fellowship, the Rockefeller Foundation, and the National Endowment for the Arts and CAPS Fellowships in playwrighting, Fuller describes himself as a playwright who happens to be black, rather than a black playwright.

Ernest J. Gaines (1933–)
Novelist, Short Story Writer

Gaines was born on a plantation in Louisiana. He moved to California in 1949 where he did his undergraduate study at San Francisco State College. In 1959, he received the Wallace Stegner Fellowship in creative writing. The following year he was awarded the Joseph Henry Jackson Literary Award.

His first novel to be published was *Catherine Carmier* (1964). Other novels by Gaines are *Of Love and Dust* (1967); *Barren Summer* (completed in 1963 but never published); *The Autobiography of Miss Jane Pittman* (1971); *A Warm Day in November* (for young people); and *In My Father's House* (1978). The 1974 television production of *The Autobiography of Miss Jane Pittman* with Cicely Tyson boosted his reputation. Another work by Gaines, the novel *A Gathering of Old Men*, published in 1983, has been made into a movie.

Nikki Giovanni (1943–)
Poet

Nikki Giovanni was born in Knoxville, Tennessee. She studied at Fisk University and at the University of Pennsylvania. Her first book of poetry, *Black Feeling, Black Talk*, published in the mid-1960s, was followed by *Black Judgment* in 1968. These two were combined as *Black Feeling, Black Talk, Black Judgment* in 1970.

By 1974, her poems were to be found in many black literature anthologies and she had also become a media personality through her TV appearances where she read her poetry. Many of her poems were put to soul or gospel music accompaniment. One such recording is *Truth Is on Its Way.*

Giovanni is a prolific author. Her other books include *Recreation*; *Spin a Soft Black Song*; *Night Comes Softly: Anthology of Black Female Voices*; *My House*; *Gemini: An Extended Autobiographical Statement*; *Ego Tripping and Other Poems for Young People*; *A Dialogue* (with James Baldwin); and *A Poetic Equation: Conversations Between Nikki Giovanni and Margaret Walker*. Her other works include: *The Women and the Men: Poems* (1975); *Cotton Candy on a Rainy Day* (1978); and *Vacation Time*, a collection of poems for children (1980) which was dedicated to her son, Tommy; *Those Who Ride the Night Winds* (1984) and *Sacred Cows . . . and Other Edibles* (1988).

Alex Haley (1921–1992)
Journalist, Novelist

The author of the widely acclaimed novel *Roots* was born in Ithaca, New York and reared in Henning, Tennessee. The oldest of three sons of a college professor father and a mother who taught grade school, Haley graduated from high school at fifteen and attended college for two years before enlisting in the United States Coast Guard as a messboy in 1939.

A voracious reader, he began writing short stories while working at sea, but it took eight years before small magazines began accepting some of his stories. By 1952, the Coast Guard had created a new rating for Haley, chief journalist, and he began handling United States Coast Guard public relations. In 1959, after 20 years of military service, he retired from the Coast Guard and launched a new career as a freelance writer. He eventually became an assignment writer for *Reader's Digest* and moved on to *Playboy* where he initiated the "Playboy Interviews" feature.

One of the personalities Haley interviewed was Malcolm X—an interview that inspired Haley's first book, *The Autobiography of Malcolm X* (1965). Translated into eight languages, the book has sold over 6 million copies.

Alex Haley

Pursuing the few slender clues of oral family history told him by his maternal grandmother in Tennessee, Haley spent the next 12 years traveling three continents tracking his maternal family back to a Mandingo youth, named Kunta Kinte, who was kidnaped into slavery from the small village of Juffure, in The Gambia, West Africa. During this period, he lectured extensively in the United States and in Great Britain on his discoveries about his family in Africa, and wrote many magazine articles on his research in the 1960s and the 1970s. He received several honorary doctor of letters degrees for his work.

The book *Roots*, excerpted in *Reader's Digest* in 1974 and heralded for several years, was finally published in the fall of 1976 with very wide publicity and reviews. In January 1977, ABC-TV produced a 12-hour series based on the book, which set records for the number of viewers. With cover stories, book reviews, and interviews with Haley in scores of magazines and many newspaper articles, the book became the number one national best-seller, sold in the millions, and was published as a paperback in 1977. *Roots* became a phenomenon. It was serialized in the *New York Post* and the *Long Island Press*. Instructional packages, lesson plans based on *Roots* and other books about *Roots* for schools were published along with records and tapes by Haley.

Haley's book stimulated interest in Africa and in black genealogy. The United States Senate passed a resolution paying tribute to Haley and comparing *Roots* to *Uncle Tom's Cabin* by Harriet Beecher Stowe in the 1850s. The book received many awards, including the National Book Award for 1976 special citation of merit in history and a special Pulitzer Prize in 1976 for making an important contribution to the literature of slavery. *Roots* was not without its critics, however. A 1977 lawsuit brought by Margaret Walker charged that *Roots* plagiarized her novel *Jubilee*. Another author, Harold Courlander also filed a suit charging that *Roots* plagiarized his novel *The African*. Courlander received a settlement after several passages in *Roots* were found to be almost verbatim from *The African*. Haley claimed that researchers helping him had given him this material without citing the source.

Haley received the NAACP's Spingarn Medal in 1977. Four thousand deans and department heads of colleges and universities throughout the country in a survey conducted by *Scholastic Magazine* selected Haley as America's foremost achiever in the literature category. (Dr. Martin Luther King Jr. was selected in the religious category.) The ABC-TV network presented another series, *Roots: The Next Generation*, in February 1979 (also written by Haley). *Roots* had sold almost 5 million copies by December 1978 and had been reprinted in 23 languages.

In 1988, Haley conducted a promotional tour for a novella titled *A Different Kind of Christmas* about slave escapes in the 1850s. He also promoted a drama, *Roots: The Gift*, a 2-hour television program shown in December 1988. This story revolved around two principal characters from *Roots* who are involved in a slave break for freedom on Christmas Eve.

Haley died February 10, 1992, of a heart attack.

Jupiter Hammon (1720?–1800?)
Poet

Hammon was the first black poet to have his work published in America. *An Evening Thought, Salvation by Christ, with Penitential Cries* appeared in 1761, when Hammon was a slave belonging to a Mr. Lloyd of Long Island, New York.

Due to his fondness for preaching, the major portion of Hammon's poetry is religious in tone, and is usually dismissed by critics as being of little aesthetic value because of its pious platitudes, faulty syntax, and forced rhymes. Hammon's best-known work is a prose piece, *An Address to the Negroes of the State of New York*, delivered before the African Society of New York City on September 24, 1786. This speech was published the following year and went into three editions.

Lorraine Hansberry (1930–1965)
Playwright

Born in Chicago, Hansberry studied art at Chicago's Art Institute, the University of Wisconsin, and, finally, in Guadalajara, Mexico.

Hansberry wrote the award winning *A Raisin in the Sun* while living in New York's Greenwich Village, having conceived the play after reacting distastefully to what she called "a whole body of material about Negroes. Cardboard characters. Cute dialect bits. Or hip-swinging musicals from exotic scores." The play opened on Broadway on March 11, 1959, at a time when it was generally held that all plays dealing with blacks were "death" at the box-office. Produced, directed, and performed by blacks, it was

Lorraine Hansberry

later made into a successful movie starring Sidney Poitier. It was then adapted into *Raisin*, a musical which won a Tony Award in 1974.

Her second Broadway play, *The Sign in Sidney Brustein's Window*, dealt with "the western intellectual poised in hesitation before the flames of involvement." Shortly after its Broadway opening, Hansberry succumbed to cancer on January 12, 1965 in New York City.

Her books, in addition to the two published plays, include *To Be Young, Gifted and Black*; *The Movement: Documentary of a Struggle for Equality*; and *Les Blancs: The Collected Last Plays of Lorraine Hansberry*.

Robert E. Hayden (1913–1980)
Poet

Robert E. Hayden, a graduate of Detroit City College, now Wayne State University, who was chief researcher on African-American history and folklore for the Federal Writers Project in 1936, later went on to do advanced work in English, play production, and creative writing at the University of Michigan. While there, he won the Jule and Avery Hopwood Prize for poetry twice. Hayden also completed radio scripts and a finished version of a play about the Underground Railroad, *Go Down Moses*.

His first book of poems, *Heart-Shape in the Dust*, was published in 1940 shortly before he assumed the music and drama critic function for the *Michigan Chronicle*. He taught at Fisk University from 1946 to the early 1970s and later at the University of Michigan. His works include *The Lion and the Archer* (with Myron O'Higgins); *A Ballad of Remembrance*; *Selected Poems*; *Words in the Mourning Time*; and *The Night-Blooming Cereus*. He edited *Kaleidoscope: Poems by American Negro Poets*; and *Afro American Literature: An Introduction* (with David J. Burrows and Frederick R. Lapsides). His other books include *Figure of Time*; *Angle of Ascent: New and Selected Poems*; and *American Journal* (poems). In 1975, the Academy of American Poets elected him its Fellow of the Year, and in 1976, he was awarded the Grand Prize for Poetry at the First World Festival of Negro Arts in Dakar, Senegal. From 1976 to 1978, he served as Consultant in Poetry at the Library of Congress. He was a professor of English at the University of Michigan at the time of his death on February 25, 1980.

Chester Himes (1909–1984)
Novelist

Born in Jefferson City, Missouri, Himes was educated at Ohio State University, and later lived in France and in Spain.

In 1945, he completed his first novel *If He Hollers Let Him Go*, the story of a black working in a defense plant. His second book, *The Lonely Crusade* (1947), was set in similar surroundings.

His other books include *The Third Generation, Cotton Comes to Harlem, Pinktoes, The Quality of Hurt: The Autobiography of Chester Himes*, and *Black on Black: Baby Sister and Selected Writings.*

Following a stroke, which confined him to a wheelchair, he and his wife lived in Alicante, Spain. In 1977 they returned to New York for the publication of the concluding volume of his autobiography *My Life of Absurdity.*

Himes died in Spain in November 1984, at the age of seventy-five. A prolific author of almost twenty books, several of his popular novels are being reprinted posthumously in hard and paperback editions.

Chester Himes

George Moses Horton (1797–1883?)
Poet

George Moses Horton, was the first black professional man of letters in America and one of the first professional writers of any race in the South. Horton was the first black southerner to have a volume of poetry published.

Horton was born into slavery in North Carolina. While growing up on a farm, and between chores, Horton was able to cultivate a love of learning. With the aid of his mother and her Wesley hymnal, Horton learned to read. He did not learn to write until years later. While working as a janitor at the University of North Carolina, Horton wrote light verse for some students in exchange for spending money.

Some of his early poems were printed in the newspapers of Raleigh and Boston. When Horton published his first book of poems in 1829, he entitled it *The Hope of Liberty* in the belief that profits from its sales would be sufficient to pay for his freedom. His hopes did not materialize, however, with the result that he remained a slave until the coming of Emancipation. This book was reprinted in 1837 under the title *Poems by a Slave.*

In 1865, he published *Naked Genius*, a poem containing many bitter lines about his former condition which are in sharp contrast to the conformist verse of earlier black poets. Richard Walser's *The Black Poet* was written about Horton and published in 1967.

Langston Hughes (1902–1967)
Poet, Novelist, Playwright

Born in Joplin, Missouri, Hughes moved to Cleveland at the age of fourteen, graduated from Central High School, and spent a year in Mexico before studying at Columbia University. After roaming the world as a seaman and writing some poetry as well, Hughes returned to the United States, winning the Witter Bynner Prize for undergraduate poetry while attending Lincoln University. In 1930, he received the Harmon Award, and in 1935, with the help of a Guggenheim Fellowship, traveled to Russia and Spain.

The long and distinguished list of Hughes' prose works includes *Not Without Laughter* (1930), a novel; *The Big Sea* (1940); and *I Wonder as I Wander* (1956), his autobiography. To this must be added such collections of poetry as *The Weary Blues* (1926); *The Dream Keeper* (1932); *Shakespeare in Harlem* (1942); *Fields of Wonder* (1947); *One Way Ticket* (1947); and *Selected Poems* (1959).

Hughes was also an accomplished song lyricist, librettist, and newspaper columnist. Through his newspaper columns, he created Jesse B. Simple, a Harlem character who saw life on the musical stage in *Simply Heavenly*. There are also several volumes of the Simple columns.

Throughout the 1960s, Hughes edited several anthologies in an attempt to popularize black authors and their works. Some of these are *An African Treasury* (1960); *Poems from Black Africa* (1963); *New Negro Poets: U.S.A.* (1964); and *The Best Short Stories by Negro Writers* (1967). Published posthumously were, *The Panther and the Lash: Poems of Our Times* (1969); and *Good Morning Revolution: Uncollected Writings of Social Protest*. Hughes wrote many plays, including *Emperor of Haiti*, and *Five Plays by Langston Hughes*. *Mulatto* was produced on Broadway in the 1930s. He also wrote gospel song plays such as *Tambourines to Glory; Black Nativity;* and *Jericho—Jim Crow*.

Langston Hughes

Zora Neale Hurston (1903–1960)
Novelist, Folklorist

After traveling north as a maid with a Gilbert and Sullivan company, Hurston acquired her education at Morgan State, Howard, and Columbia. While at Howard, under Alain Locke's influence, she became a figure in the Harlem Renaissance, publishing short stories in *Opportunity* and serving with Langston Hughes and Wallace Thurman on the editorial board of the magazine *Fire*.

In 1934, *Jonah's Gourd Vine* was published after her return to Florida. Her most important novel, *Their Eyes Were Watching God*, appeared three years later. *Moses, Man of the Mountain* (1939), was followed in 1948 by *Seraph on the Suwanee*. Her other three works are two books of folklore, *Mules and Men* (1935) and *Tell My Horse* (1938); and *Dust Tracks on a Road* (1942), her autobiography which was reprinted in

Zora Neale Hurston

1985 with a new introduction and with several altered or expunged chapters restored.

Toward the end of her life, Hurston was a drama instructor at the North Carolina College for Negroes in Durham. She died in obscurity and poverty on January 28, 1960. Since then, six of her works have been reprinted with new introductions.

Georgia Douglas Johnson (1886–1966)
Poet

As one of the first modern black female poets to gain recognition, Georgia Douglas Johnson, whose collections of verse were published between 1918 and 1930, is an important link in the chain of American black female lyric poets. Johnson's life spanned most of the literary movements of this century, and her Washington, DC home was the popular gathering place of early Harlem Renaissance writers.

Johnson was born in Atlanta, Georgia, on September 10, 1886. She was educated in the public schools of the city and at Atlanta University, and she went on to attend Howard University in Washington, DC, and Oberlin Conservatory of Music in Ohio.

Initially, she was interested in musical composition, but gradually she turned toward lyric poetry. After teaching school in Alabama, she moved to Washington, DC with her husband, who had been appointed as Recorder of Deeds by President William Howard Taft. While in the nation's capital, she too engaged in government work while completing such books as *The Heart of a Woman* (1918); *Bronze* (1922); *An Autumn Love Cycle* (1928); and *Share My World*, published in 1962.

Johnson was a prolific writer; over 200 of her poems were published in her four literary works; other poems and several dramas have appeared in journals and books primarily edited by blacks.

James Weldon Johnson (1871–1938)
Poet, Lyricist, Civil Rights Leader

Like W.E.B. DuBois, black intellectual James Weldon Johnson played a vital role in the civil rights movement of the twentieth century—as poet, teacher, critic, diplomat, and NAACP official. Johnson is perhaps most often popularly remembered as the lyricist for *Lift Every Voice and Sing*, the poem which is often referred to as the black national anthem.

Born in 1871 in Jacksonville, Florida, Johnson was educated at Atlanta and Columbia Universities. His career included service as a school principal, a lawyer, and a diplomat (United States Consul at Puerto Cabello, Venezuela, and later, in Nicaragua).

From 1916 to 1930, he was a key policy maker of the NAACP, eventually serving as the organization's executive secretary.

In his early days, Johnson's fame rested largely on his lyrics for popular songs, but in 1917 he completed his first book of poetry, *Fifty Years and Other Poems*. Five years later, he followed this with *The Book of American Negro Poetry*, and in 1927, he established his literary reputation with *God's Trombones*, a collection of seven folk sermons in verse. Over the years, this work has been performed countless times on stage and television.

In 1930, Johnson finished *St. Peter Relates an Incident of the Resurrection*, and three years later, his lengthy autobiography *Along This Way*.

Johnson died in 1938 following an automobile accident in Maine.

Gayl Jones (1949–)
Novelist, Poet, Short Story Writer

Born in Lexington, Kentucky, Jones received a bachelor's degree in English from Connecticut College in 1971 and an master's degree in creative writing from Brown University in 1973. Jones' work includes two novels, *Corregidora* (1975) and *Eva's Man* (1976), short stories, and several collections of poetry, including *Song for Anninho* (1981), *The Hermit Woman* (1983), and *Xarque and Other Poems* (1985).

June Jordan (1936–)
Poet, Novelist

Born in Harlem of parents from Jamaica, in the West Indies, June Jordan attended Barnard College and the University of Chicago. She has been married and has a son. She has taught Afro-American literature, English, and writing at several colleges and universities and was co-founder and co-director of The Voice of the Children, Inc., a creative workshop. Her poems have been published in many magazines, newspapers, and anthologies. She received a Rockefeller Grant in creative writing for 1969. Her books for children and young people include: *Fannie Lou Hamer* (1972); *His Own Where* (1971), her first novel nominated for the National Book Award; *Who Look at Me* (1969); *Dry Victories* (1972); *New Room, New Life* (1974); and *The Voice of the Children: Writings by Black and Puerto Rican Young People* (1970, 1974), edited by Jordan and Terri Bush. Her books for adults include: *Soulscript* (1970), edited by Jordan; *Some Changes* (1971); *New Days: Poems of Exile and Return* (1973); *Things That I Do in the Dark: Selected Poems* (1976); and *Passion: New Poems 1977–1980* (1980).

Nella Larsen (1891–1964)
Novelist

Nella Larsen was born in Chicago, Illinois of a Danish mother and a West Indian father. She attended Fisk University, in Nashville, Tennessee, and the University of Copenhagen, in Denmark. Larsen's two novels are *Quicksand* (1928), for which she received a bronze medal from the Harmon Foundation, and *Passing* (1929).

Audre Lorde (1934–1993)
Poet

Audre Lorde was born in New York City, educated at Hunter College with a masters in library science from Columbia University; was poet-in-residence at Tougaloo College; taught at Lehman College, Bronx; and is now teaching at John Jay College, CCNY. She received a National Endowment for the Arts grant for poetry and a Cultural Council Foundation grant also for poetry.

Her books of poetry include: *Cables to Rage* (1970); *The First Cities* (1968); *From a Land Where Other People Live* (1973); *Coal* (1968); *The New York Head Shop and Museum* (1974); *Between Ourselves* (1976); *The Black Unicorn* (1978); *Chosen Poems-Old and New* (1982); *Zami: A New Spelling of My Name* (1982); *Sister/Outsider: Essays & Speeches* (1984); *Lesbian Poetry: An Anthology* (1982); and *Woman Poet—The East* (1984). Lorde's poetry has been published in many anthologies, magazines and lesbian books and periodicals.

Claude McKay (1890–1948)
Poet

Born the son of a farmer in Jamaica (then British West Indies), McKay began writing early in life. Two books of his poems, *Songs of Jamaica* and *Constab Ballads*, were published just after he turned twenty. In both, he made extensive use of Jamaican dialect.

In 1913, McKay came to America to study agriculture at Tuskegee Institute and at Kansas State University, but his interest in poetry induced him to move to New York City, where he published his work in small literary magazines.

McKay then made a trip abroad, visiting England. While there, he completed a collection of lyrics entitled *Spring in New Hampshire.* When he returned to the United States, he became associate editor of *The Liberator* under Max Eastman. In 1922, he completed *Harlem Shadows*, a landmark work of the Harlem Renaissance period.

McKay then turned to the writing of such novels as *Home to Harlem* (1928), *Banjo* (1929), and four other books including an autobiography and a study of Harlem. *The Passion of Claude McKay: Selected Prose and Poetry 1912–1948* edited by Wayne Cooper, was published in 1973. McKay traveled extensively abroad before returning to the United States, where he died. His final work, *Selected Poems*, was published posthumously in 1953.

During World War II, when Winston Churchill addressed a joint session of the United States Congress in an effort to enlist American aid in the battle against Nazism, the climax of his oration was his reading of the famous poem "If We Must Die", originally written by McKay to assail lynchings and mob violence in the South. McKay's *Trial by Lynching* (1967), edited and translated stories, and his *The Negroes in America* (1979 or 1980), edited and translated from the Russian language, have also been published. Many of his books or works have been reprinted since his death: *Home to Harlem; Banana Bottom; Banjo* (1970); *A Long Way From Home* (1970); *Harlem: Negro Metropolis* (1972), and *Selected Poems of Claude McKay* (1971). *Songs of Jamaica* and *Constab Ballads* have been bound together as *The Dialect Poems of Claude McKay.* Wayne F. Cooper's *Claude McKay: Rebel Sojourner in the Harlem Renaissance* (1987) is an important book detailing McKay's life and work.

Terry McMillan (1951–)
Novelist

McMillan was born and raised in Port Huron, Michigan. She attended Los Angeles City College, but later transferred to Berkeley and then to Columbia University to study film. She later enrolled in a writing workshop at the Harlem Writers Guild and was accepted at the MacDowell Colony in 1983.

McMillan's novels include *Mama* (1987), *Disappearing Acts* (1989), and *Waiting to Exhale* (1992). Her novel, *Waiting to Exhale* remained on the best-seller list for several months, proving that there is a demand for African-American literature. She has also edited the anthology of contemporary African-American fiction entitled *Breaking Ice* (1992).

James Alan McPherson (1943–)
Short Story Writer

James McPherson, born in Savannah, Georgia, received his B.A. degree in 1965 from Morris Brown College in Atlanta, a law degree from Harvard University in 1968, and an M.F.A. degree from the University of Iowa in 1969. He has taught writing at several universities, presently at the University of Iowa, and is a contributing editor of *Atlantic Monthly*. His short stories have appeared in several magazines. *Hue and Cry*, a collection of short stories published in 1969, was highly praised by Ralph Ellison. A Guggenheim Fellow in 1972–1973, McPherson's second book of short stories, *Elbow Room*, was published in 1977 and was given the Pulitzer Prize for fiction in 1978. He taught fiction writing for several years at the University of Virginia in Charlottesville. McPherson was one of the three black writers who in 1981, with Elma Lewis, were awarded five-year grants by the McArthur Foundation of Chicago for exceptional talent.

Loften Mitchell (1919–)
Playwright

Raised in the Harlem of 1920s, Loften Mitchell first began to write as a child, creating scripts for backyard shows he and his brother put on. After completing junior high school, he decided to enroll at New York Textile High because he had been promised a job on the school newspaper there. But Mitchell soon realized that he needed the training of an academic high school, and with the help of one of his teachers, transferred to DeWitt Clinton.

Graduating with honors, Mitchell found a job as an elevator operator and a delivery boy to support himself while he studied play writing at night at the City College of New York. However, he met a professor from Talladega College in Alabama who helped him win a scholarship to study there. He graduated with honors in 1943, having won an award for the best play written by a student.

After two years of service in the Navy, Mitchell enrolled as a graduate student at Columbia University in New York. A year later, he accepted a job with the Department of Welfare as a social investigator and continued to go to school at night. During this time, he wrote one of his first successful plays, *Blood in the Night*, and in 1957 he wrote *A Land Beyond the River*, which had a long run at an off-Broadway theater and was published as a book.

The following year Mitchell won a Guggenheim award, which enabled him to return to Columbia and write for a year. Since then, he has written a new play, *Star of the Morning*, the story of Bert Williams, famous black entertainer.

In 1967 Mitchell published a study African-American theater entitled *Black Drama*. His other books include: *Tell Pharaoh*, a play; *The Stubborn Old Lady Who Resisted Change* (1973), a novel; and *Voices of the Black Theatre* (1976). Mitchell also wrote the books for the Broadway musicals *Ballads for Bimshire* (1963); *Bubbling Brown Sugar* (1975); *Cartoons for a Lunch Hour* (1978); *A Gypsy Girl* (1982); *Miss Ethel Waters* (1983).

Toni Morrison (1931–)
Novelist, Editor

Born Chloe Anthony Wofford in Lorain, Ohio, Morrison received a B.A. degree from Howard University in 1953 and an M.A. from

Cornell in 1955. After working as an instructor in English and the humanities at Texas Southern University and Howard University, Morrison eventually became a senior editor at Random House in New York City. She has been responsible for the publication of many books by blacks at Random House: Middleton Harris' *The Black Book*, which she edited, and books by Toni Cade Bambara and others. In 1971–1972, she was also an associate professor at the State University of New York at Purchase. Formerly married, she has two sons. Her first novel, *The Bluest Eye*, was published in 1969. Her second novel, *Sula*, was published in 1974 and won a 1975 Ohioana Book Award. Morrison's third novel, *Song of Solomon* (1977), was critically acclaimed and received the 1977 National Book Critics Circle Award and the 1978 American Academy and Institute of Arts and Letters Award. Her fourth novel, *Tar Baby* (1981) also received positive reviews. She was elected to the American Institute of Arts and Letters in 1981 and gave the keynote address at the American Writers' Congress in New York City in the fall of that year. Barbara Christian's *Black Women Novelists* (1980) has a section on her first three novels; and there is an interview with Morrison in Michael S. Harper and Robert B. Stepto's *Chant of Saints: A Gathering of Afro-American Literature, Art and Scholarship* (1979). She has written the story for the musical *Storyville*, which is about jazz music originating in the brothels of New Orleans.

Toni Morrison

From 1984–1989, Morrison served as Albert Schweitzer Professor of the Humanities at the State University of New York at Albany, after twenty years as a senior editor for Random House. She wrote the lyrics or story for the musical *New Orleans*, a New York Public Theater workshop production and also a screenplay of her novel *Tar Baby*.

Morrison's fifth novel *Beloved* was published in 1987. A historical novel, it received rave reviews. In 1988, *Beloved* won both the Pulitzer Prize for fiction and the Robert F. Kennedy Award. *Beloved* was a finalist for the 1988 National Book Critics Circle Award and was one of the three contenders for the Ritz Hemingway prize in Paris, from which no winner emerged. This novel by Morrison was also a finalist for the National Book Award for 1987. Her most recent works include a collection of essays and *Jazz*, a novel.

Gloria Naylor (1950–)
Novelist

Gloria Naylor was born in New York City and still lives there. She received a B.A. in English from Brooklyn College in 1981 and a M.A. in Afro-American studies from Yale University in 1983. She has taught writing and literature at George Washington University, New York University, Brandeis University, Cornell University, and Boston University. In 1983, she won the American Book Award for first fiction for her novel *The Women of Brewster Place*, which was produced on television in 1988. Her second novel was *Linden Hills* published in 1985. Her third novel, *Mama Day* (1988), was written with the aid of a grant from the National Endowment for the Arts. In 1988, Naylor was awarded a Guggenheim Fellowship. In 1993, Naylor published a new novel, *Bailey's Cafe*.

Ann Petry (1908–)
Novelist, Short Story Writer

Ann Petry was born in Old Saybrook, Connecticut, where her father was a druggist. After graduating from the College of Pharmacy at the University of Connecticut, she went to New York where she found employment as a social worker and newspaper reporter, studying creative writing at night.

Her early short stories appeared in *Crisis* and *Pylon*. In 1946, after having received a Houghton Mifflin Fellowship, she completed and published her first novel, *The Street*. This was followed by *Country Place* (1947); *The Narrows* (1953) and *Miss Muriel and Other Stories* (1971). Her works for children and young people include: *The Drugstore Cat; Harriet Tubman; Tituba of Salem Village;* and *Legends of the Saints*. Many of her earlier novels are being reprinted.

Ann Petry

Ishmael Reed (1938–)
Novelist, Poet

Born in Chattanooga, Tennessee, Reed grew up in Buffalo, New York. His first volume of poetry published in the United States, *Conjure* (1972), was nominated for the National Book Award, as was his third novel, *Mumbo Jumbo* (1972). He has also published *Chattanooga*, a second volume of poetry, and four other novels, *The Freelance Pallbearers, Yellow Back Radio Broke Down, The Last Days of Louisiana Red,* and *Flight to Canada*.

Reed edited the breakthrough anthology *19 Necromancers from Now* and *Yardbird Lives!*. His poetry has appeared in numerous anthologies and magazines, including *The Poetry of the Negro, The New Black Poetry, The Norton Anthology, Cricket,* and *Scholastic* magazine. *His Shrovetide in Old New Orleans* (1978) is a collection of essays.

Reed published two novels in the 1980s, *The Terrible Twos* (1982), a political satire; and *Reckless Eyeballing* (1986), a farce in which the sinister Flower Phantom punishes feminists for defaming black manhood. Both

Ishmael Reed

novels were reissued in paperback in 1988 by Atheneum Publishers. Reed's two books of essays, editorials, and book reviews for this period are *God Made Alaska for the Indians: Selected Essays* (1983) and *Writin' Is Fightin': Thirty-Seven Years of Boxing on Paper* (1988). Reed's novel, *The Terrible Threes*, was published in 1989.

Sonia Sanchez (1934–)

Poet, Playwright

Sonia Sanchez was born in Birmingham, Alabama. She studied at New York University and Hunter College in New York City. She is married to Etheridge Knight, a black writer of poetry and fiction. She has taught at San Francisco State College and is now teaching in the Black Studies Department of Temple University in Philadelphia. Her plays are published in the special black drama number of *The Drama Review* (Summer 1968), and in *New Plays from the Black Theatre* (1969) edited by Ed Bullins. Her poems have been published in many magazines and anthologies. Books written or edited by her include six volumes of poetry: *Homecoming* (1969); *We a BaddDDD People* (1970), *It is a New Day* (1971); *A Blues Book for Blue Black Magical Women* (1973); *Love Poems* (1975); and *I've Been a Woman* (1978). Sanchez has edited two anthologies: *Three Hundred and Sixty Degrees of Blackness Comin at You, An Anthology of the Sonia Sanchez Writers Workshop at Countee Cullen Library in Harlem* (1971); and *We Be Word Sorcerers: Twenty-five Stories by Black Americans* (1973). She has also written *A Sound Investment* (1979), a collection of short stories; and *homegirls and handgrenades* (1984).

Ntozake Shange (1948–)

Playwright, Poet, Novelist

Born in Trenton, New Jersey, Ntozake Shange graduated from Barnard College and received her masters degree from the University of Southern California. She studied Afro-American dance and gave many poetry readings in California. Shange taught at Sonoma Mills College in California from 1972–1975. Her play *For Colored Girls Who Have Considered Suicide When the Rainbow is Enuf*, a choreopoem, was first produced in California after her dance-drama *Sassafrass* was presented in 1976. *For Colored Girls* showed real talent and was later produced in New York City where it had a long run before going on to other cities. Other works by Shange that have been produced on the stage are *Spell 7*; *A Photograph: Lovers in Motion* (1979), and *Boogie Woogie Landscapes* (1979). *For Colored Girls* has been published twice as a book and Shange's book *Three Pieces* (1981) con-

Ntozake Shange

tains *Spell 7, A Photograph: Lovers in Motion*, and *Boogie Woogie Landscapes*. Her other books include: *Sassafrass, Cypress & Indigo* (1982), *A Daughter's Geography* (1983) and *From Okra to Greens* (1984). Earlier she published *Nappy Edges* (1978), a book of poetry. Her novel *Betsey Brown* was published in 1985. *See No Evil: Prefaces & Accounts, 1976–1983* was published in 1984. A version of *Betsey Brown* for the stage, with music by the jazz trumpeter and composer Baikida Carroll, opened the American Music Theater Festival in Philadelphia March 25 1989.

Lucy Terry (1730–1821)
Poet

Lucy Terry is generally considered to be the first black poet in America. In a ballad which she called "Bars Fight," she recreated an Indian massacre which occurred in Deerfield, Massachusetts in 1746 during King George's War; "Bars Fight" has been hailed by some historians as the most authentic account of the massacre.

A semi-literate slave in the household of Ensign Ebenezer Wells, she won her freedom and was married to a freed man named Prince. The Prince house served as a center for young people who gathered to listen to their hostess's storytelling. Lucy Terry was a strong woman who argued eloquently for her family's rights in several cases.

Jean Toomer (1984–1967)
Novelist, Poet

Jean Toomer's *Cane*, published in 1923, has been called one of the three best novels ever written by an American black—the others being Richard Wright's *Native Son* and Ralph Ellison's *Invisible Man*. According to Columbia University critic Robert Bone, "Cane is by far the most impressive product of the Negro Renaissance."

A mixture of poems and sketches, *Cane* was written during that period in which most black writers were reacting against earlier "polite" forms by creating works marked by literary realism. Toomer even went beyond this realm to the threshold of symbol and myth, using a "mystical" approach which is much more akin to the contemporary mood than it was to the prevailing spirit of his own day. *Cane* sold only 500 copies on publication, and was still little known until it was reprinted recently with new introductions. A lot has been written about Toomer and *Cane* in recent years including a *Cane* casebook.

Born in Washington, DC in 1894, Toomer was educated in law at the University of Wisconsin and City College of New York before he turned to writing. The transcendental nature of his writings is said to have stemmed in part from his early study under Gurdjieff, the Russian mystic.

Toomer also published quite a bit of poetry. Darwin T. Turner edited *The Wayward and The Seeking: A Collection of Writings by Jean Toomer* (1980), a book of his poetry, short stories, dramas, and autobiography. Other books about Toomer and his writings are Therman O'Daniel (editor) *Jean Toomer: A Critical Evaluation* (1985), over 40 essays of the most thorough, up-to-date scholarship on Toomer; Robert B. Jones and Margery Toomer Latimer (editors) *The Collected Poems of Jean Toomer* (1988), 55 poems; and Nellie Y. McKay's *Jean Toomer, Artist: A Study of His Literary Life and Work, 1894–1936* (1984, 1987).

Gustavus Vassa

Gustavus Vassa (Oloudah Equiano) (c. 1745–c. 1801)
Narrative writer

Gustavus Vassa was born in 1745, in Southern Nigeria. At the age of eleven, he was kidnapped and shipped to the New World as a slave. His masters included a Virginia plantation owner, a British officer, and a Philadelphia merchant from whom he eventually purchased his freedom.

Vassa then settled in England where he worked diligently for the elimination of slavery. He even went so far as to present a petition to Parliament calling for its abolition.

His autobiography, *The Interesting Narrative of the Life of Oloudah Equiano, or Gustavus Vassa,* was published in London in 1789 and went through five editions in the next five years. It is regarded as a highly informative account of the evils of slavery as it affected both master and slave. Vassa died around 1801.

Alice Walker (1944–)
Poet, Novelist

Alice Walker was born in Eatonton, Georgia and has lived in Mississippi, New York City, and San Francisco, California. She was educated at Spelman College, Atlanta, Georgia, and at Sarah Lawrence College, Bronxville, New York.

Her short stories and poems have been published in *Freedomways*, *Essence*, and other magazines and anthologies. She has been writer-in-residence and teacher at Jackson State College and Tougaloo College in Mississippi and is a prolific writer. Her first book was poetry entitled *Once*, published in 1968. Her second book, published in 1970, was a novel, *The Third Life of Grange Copeland*. A second book of poetry, *Revolutionary Petunias and Other Poems*, was published in 1973. She also wrote *In*

Love and Trouble: Stories of Black Women (1973); *Langston Hughes, American Poet* (1974), for children; *Meridian* (1976), a novel; *Good Night, Willie Lee, I'll See You in the Morning* (1979), poetry; and *You Can't Keep A Good Woman Down* (1981), short stories.

Her book *In Love and Trouble: Stories of Black Women* (1973) won the American Academy and Institute of Arts and Letters' Rosenthal Award. *Revolutionary Petunias and Other Poems* (1973) was nominated for the National Book Award and was given the Lillian Smith Award. She has received the Merrill Fellowship for Writing, the National Endowment for the Arts Grant, the Radcliffe Institute Fellowship and other honors.

In 1983, her third novel *The Color Purple* (1982), won the American Book Award in the hardcover category and also the Pulitzer Prize. The book was reviewed negatively by black men and some women reviewers for its degrading depiction of black men. *The Color Purple* became a best seller in hardcover and paperback. It was released in 1985 as a widely acclaimed film.

Alice Walker

Walker's other books include: *In Search of Our Mothers' Gardens: Womanist Prose* (1983); *Horses Make the Landscape Look More Beautiful* (1984), a book of poems; *To Hell With Dying* (1988), a book for children; *Living By The Word: Selected Writings, 1973–1987* (1988), a book of essays; *The Temple of My Familiar* (1989), which was both panned and praised by critics, and *Possessing the Secret of Joy* (1992). Walker also edited *A Zora Neale Hurston Reader*, published in 1980.

Margaret Abigail Walker (Margaret Walker Alexander) (1915–)
Poet, Novelist

Margaret Walker was born on July 7, 1915 in Birmingham, Alabama, and received her early education in Alabama, Louisiana, and Mississippi. She earned her B.A. from Northwestern University and her M.A. from the University of Iowa (1940).

In 1942, Walker published *For My People* and two years later was awarded a Rosenwald Fellowship for creative writing. She has taught English and literature at Livingston College in North Carolina, at West Virginia State College, and at Jackson State College in Mississippi. Her novel appeared in 1965 and is entitled *Jubilee*. *For My People* was reprinted in 1969. Her other works are *Prophets for a New Day*, *How I Wrote Jubilee*, *October Journey*, and *A Poetic Equation: Conversations Between Nikki Giovanni and Margaret Walker*. June 17, 1976, was proclaimed Margaret Walker Alexander Day by the mayor of her native Birmingham.

Margaret Walker

Walker's other works include *Richard Wright: Daemonic Genius* (1988). A second edition of *A Poetic Equation: Conversations between Nikki Giovanni and Margaret Walker* was published in 1983.

Phillis Wheatley (1753–1784)
Poet

Born in Senegal, Phillis Wheatley was brought to the United States as a slave and received her name from Mrs. Susannah Wheatley, the wife of the Boston tailor who had bought Phillis.

Wheatley received her early education in the household of her master. Her interest in writing stemmed from her reading of the Bible and the classics under the guidance of the Wheatley's daughter, Mary.

In 1770, her first poem was printed under the title "A Poem by Phillis, A Negro Girl on the Death of Reverend George Whitefield." Her book *Poems on Various Subjects: Religious and Moral* was published in London in 1773. After a trip to England for health reasons she later returned to the United States, and was married. She published the poem "Liberty and Peace" in 1784, shortly before her death. Most of the old books of her poems, letters, and memories about her life were reprinted in the late 1960s and early 1970s. Two books about her are Julian D. Mason Jr.'s *The Poems of Phillis Wheatley* (1966); and William H. Robinson's *Phillis Wheatley, A Biography* (1981). Robinson also compiled and published *Phillis Wheatley: A Bio-Bibliography* (1981).

Although George Washington was among her admirers (she had once sent him a tributary poem, which he graciously acknowledged), her poetry is considered important today largely because of its historical role in the growth of American Negro literature. Wheatley's poetry reflects Anglo-Saxon models, rather than her African heritage. It is, nevertheless, a typical example of the verse manufactured in a territory—the British colonies—not yet divorced from its maternal origins.

August Wilson (1945–)
Playwright

The first of Wilson's plays, was *Ma Rainey's Black Bottom.* First produced at the Yale Repertory Theater and directed by Lloyd Richards, then brought to New York, the play was the New York Drama Critics Circle's best new play in 1985. Wilson's next play *Fences*, about the 1930s, 1940s, and 1950s, was the best new play in 1987 for the New York Drama Critics Circle, after first being produced at the Yale Repertory Theater. Wilson's third play produced in New York, *Joe Turner's Come and Gone* also started at the Yale Repertory Theater and was named the best new play in 1988 by the New York Drama Critics Circle. *Joe Turner's Come and Gone* is about 1911 and the earlier period of black migration from the South, sharecropping and being dispossessed; about a search for cultural roots and identity in a dark and distant past and the psychic burden of years of slavery.

August Wilson

In 1986, Wilson was one of ten writers to win the Whiting Writer's Awards of ten tax-free checks for $25,000 each. The awards were established in 1985 by the Whiting Foundation to reward "exceptionally promising, emerging talent." In 1988, Yale University gave Wilson an honorary degree.

Wilson's *Joe Turner* opened in Boston before coming to New York. It was produced in 1987 by the Seattle Repertory Theater. *Fences* was also produced in San Francisco in 1987, and received a Pulitzer Prize and a Tony award. In 1990, Wilson's *The Piano Lesson* was awarded a Pulitzer Prize.

Richard Wright (1908–1060)
Novelist

Born on a plantation near Natchez, Mississippi, Wright drew on his personal experience to dramatize racial injustice and its brutalizing effects. In 1938, under the auspices of the WPA Illinois Writers Project, Wright published *Uncle Tom's Children*, a collection of four novellas based on his Mississippi boyhood memories. The book won an award for the best work of fiction by a WPA writer, and Wright received a Guggenheim Fellowship.

Two years later, *Native Son*, a novel of Chicago's Negro ghetto, further enhanced Wright's reputation. A Book-of-the-Month Club choice, it was later a successful Broadway production under Orson Welles' direction and was filmed in South America with Wright himself in the role of Bigger Thomas. He published *Twelve Million Black Voices* in 1941.

In 1945, Wright's largely autobiographical *Black Boy* was selected by the Book-of-the-Month Club and went on to become a second best-seller.

Wright later moved to Paris where he continued to write fiction and nonfiction including *The Outsider* (1953); *Black Power* (1954); *Savage Holiday* (1954, 1965); *The Color Curtain* (1956); *White Man Listen* (1957); *The Long Dream* (1958); *Lawd Today* (1963); *Eight Men* (1961); and *American Hunger* (1977), a continuation of Wright's autobiographical work *Black Boy*.

Wright died of a heart attack on November 28, 1960. There are over a dozen books written about Richard Wright, two casebooks on *Native Son*, a children's book, and a critical pamphlet in a writers series.

Bibliography

Bibliography

Compiled by Donald Franklin Joyce

Included in this selected bibliography are titles which were published between 1990 and 1992, reviewed favorably in the reviewing media, and judged to be significant contributions to the study of black history and culture in the United States and in Africa. The titles are arranged under two major divisions: "Africana" and "African Americana." Within these two divisions titles are arranged alphabetically by author under categories indicative of their subject matter. A list of the names, addresses and telephone numbers of all publishers included follows the bibliography.

■ AFRICANA

Agriculture

Barnett, Tony, and Abbas Abdelkarim. *Sudan: The Gezira Scheme and Agricultural Transition.* London: Frank Cass, 1991.

Freeman, Donald B. *A City of Farmers: Informal Urban Agriculture in the Open Spaces of Nairobi, Kenya.* Montreal: McGill-Queen's University Press, 1991.

Gyllstrom, Bjorn. *State Administrative Rural Change: Agricultural Cooperatives in Rural Kenya.* New York: Routledge, 1991.

Kidane, Mengisteab. *Ethiopia: Failure of Land Reform and Agricultural Crisis.* Westport, CT: Greenwood Press, 1990.

Apartheid

Burman, Sandra, and Pamela Reynolds, eds. *Growing Up In a Divided Society.* With forewords by Archbishop Desmond Tutu and Robert Coles. Evanston, IL: Northwestern University Press, 1992.

Cohen, Robin, Yvonne G. Muthien, and Abebe Zegeye, eds. *Repression and Resistance: Inside Accounts of Apartheid.* London; New York: Hans Zell Publishers, 1990.

Davis, R. Hunt, ed. *Apartheid Unravels.* Gainesville, FL: University of Florida Presses, 1991.

Dumor, E.K. *Ghana, OAU and Southern Africa: An African Response to Apartheid.* Accra: Ghana University Press, 1991.

Ellis, Stephen. *Comrades Against Apartheid: The ANC and the South African Communist Party in Exile.* London: James Currey/Indiana University Press, 1992.

Ellman, Stephen. *In a Time of Trouble: Law and Liberty in South Africa's State of Emergency.* New York: Oxford University Press, 1992.

Giliomee, Herman, and Laurence Schlemmer. *From Apartheid to Nation-Building.* Capetown, S.A.: Oxford University Press, 1990.

Grundy, Kenneth. *South Africa: Domestic Crisis and Global Challenge.* Boulder, CO: Westview Press, 1991.

Heard, Anthony Hazlett. *The Cape of Storms: A Personal History of the Crisis in South Africa.* Fayetteville: University of Arkansas Press, 1990.

Holland, Heidi. *The Struggle: A History of the African National Congress.* New York: Braziller, 1990.

Hull, Richard W. *American Enterprise in South Africa: Historical Dimensions of Engagement and Disengagement.* New York: New York University Press, 1990.

Human Rights Watch. *The Killings of South Africa: The Role of the Security Forces and the Response of the State.* New York: Human Rights Watch, 1991.

Johns, Sheridan, and R. Hunt Davis, eds. *Mandela, Tambo and the African National Congress: The Struggle Against Apartheid, 1948-1990: A Documentary Survey.* New York: Oxford University Press, 1991.

Kalley, Jacqueline A. *South Africa's Road to Change, 1987–1990.* Westport, CT: Greenwood Press, 1991.

Lemon, Anthony, ed. *Homes Apart: South Africa's Segregated Cities.* Bloomington: Indiana University Press, 1991.

Maasdorp, Gavin, and Alan Whiteside, eds. *Towards a Post-Apartheid Future: Political and Economic Relations in South Africa.* New York: St. Martin's Press, 1992.

Mallaby, Sebastian. *After Apartheid: The Future of South Africa.* New York: Times Books, 1992.

Moss, Rose. *Shouting at the Crocodile: Popo Molefe, Patrick Lekota, and the Freeing of South Africa.* Boston: Beacon Press, 1990. (Dist. by Farrar, Strauss, Giroux)

Price, Robert M. *The Apartheid State in Crisis: Political Transformation in South Africa, 1975–1990.* New York: Oxford University Press, 1991.

Shepherd, George W., ed. *Effective Sanctions on South Africa: The Cutting Edge of Economic Intervention.* Westport, CT: Greenwood Press, 1991.

Sparks, Allister. *The Mind of South Africa.* New York: Knopf, 1990.

Spink, Kathryn. *Black Sash: The Beginning of a Bridge in South Africa.* With a foreword by Archbishop Desmond Tutu. London: Methuen, 1991.

Art

Courtney-Clarke, Margaret. *African Canvas: The Art of West African Women.* New York: Rizzoli, 1990.

Okediji, Mayo, ed. *Principles of "Traditional" African Art.* Ile Ife: Bard Book, 1992 (Dist. by Avon).

Smithsonian Institution. Libraries. National Museum of African Art Branch. *Catalog of the Library of the National Museum of African Art Branch of the Smithsonian Library.* Boston: G.K. Hall, 1991.

Vogel, Susan. *Africa Explores: Twentieth Century African Art.* New York: The Center for African Art, 1991.

Williams College Museum of Art. *Assuming the Guise: African Masks Considered and Reconsidered.* Williamstown, MA: Williams College Museum of Art, 1991.

Williamson, Sue. *Resistance Art in South Africa.* New York: St. Martin's Press, 1990.

Autobiography and Biography

Appiah, Joseph. *Joe Appiah: The Autobiography of an African Patriot.* New York: Praeger, 1990.

Bunche, Ralph Johnson. *An African American in South Africa: The Travel Notes of Ralph J. Bunche, 28 September 1937–1 January 1938.* Edited by Roger R. Edgar. Athens: Ohio University Press, 1992.

Gastrow, Shelagh, ed., *Who's Who in South African Politics.* 3rd ed., London: Hans Zell Publishers, 1990.

Glickman, Harvey, ed., *Political Leaders of Contemporary Africa South of the Sahara: A Biographical Dictionary.* Westport, CT: Greenwood Press, 1992.

Harris, Eddy L. *Native Stranger: A Black American's Journey into the Heart of Africa.* New York: Simon & Schuster, 1992.

Isert, Paul Erdmann. *Letters on West Africa: Paul Erdmann Isert's Journey to Guinea and the Caribbean Islands in Columbia (1788).* Translated by Selena Axelrod Winsnes. New York: Oxford University Press, 1992.

Lockot, Hans Wilhelm. *The Mission: The Life, Reign and Character of Haile Selassie I.* New York: St. Martin's Press, 1990.

Mashinini, Emma. *Strikes Have Followed Me All My Life: A South African Autobiography.* New York: Routledge, 1991.

Meer, Fatima. *Higher Than Hope: The Authorized Biography of Nelson Mandela.* New York: Harper & Row, 1990.

Mendelsohn, Richard. *Sammy Marks: the Uncrowned King of the Transvaal.* Athens: Ohio University Press, 1991.

Modisan, Blake. *Blame Me on History.* New York: Simon & Schuster, 1990.

Nkrumah, Kwame. *Kwame Nkrumah: The Conakry Years: His Life and Letters.* Compiled by June Milne. New York: Zed Books, 1991. (Dist. by Humanities Press)

Rake, Alan. *Who's Who in Africa: Leaders for the 1990s.* Metuchen, NJ: Scarecrow, 1992.

Rodney, Walter. *Walter Rodney Speaks: The Making of an African Intellectual.* With introduction by Robert Hill. Foreword by Howard Dodson. Trenton, NJ: Africa World Press, 1990.

Vaillant, Janet G. *Black, French and African: A Life of Leopold Sedar Senghor.* Cambridge: Harvard University Press, 1990.

Vigne, Randolph, ed. *A Gesture of Belonging: Letters from Bessie Head, 1965–1979.* Portsmouth, NH: Heinemann, 1991.

Wiseman, John A. *Political Leaders in Black Africa: A Biographical Dictionary of the Major Politicians Since Independence.* Brookfield, VT: Gower Publishing Co., 1991.

Economics

Blumenfield, Jesmond. *Economic Interdependence in Southern Africa: From Conflict to Cooperation.* New York: Printer/St. Martin's Press, 1991.

Chole, Eschetu, ed. *Food Crisis in Africa: Policy and Management Issues.* New Delhi: Vikas Publishing House, 1990. (Dist. by Advent House)

Claessen, Henri J.M., and Pieter van de Velde, eds. *Early State Economies.* New Brunswick, NJ: Transaction Publishers, 1991.

Cock, Jacklyn, ed. *Going Green: People, Politics and the Environment in South Africa.* New York: Oxford University Press, 1991.

Crockcroft, Laurence. *Africa's Way: A Journey from the Past.* UK: Tauris, 1990. (Dist. by St. Martin's Press)

Crush, Jonathan, Alan Jeeves, and Donald Yudelman *Africa's Labor Empire: A History of Black Migrancy to the Gold Mines.* Boulder, CO: Westview Press/D. Philip, 1991.

Edington, J.A.S. *Rubber in West Africa.* Anaheim, CA: Collings, 1991.

Henige, David, and T.C. McCaskie, eds. *West African Economic and Social History: Studies in Memory of Marion Johnson.* Madison: African Studies Program, University of Wisconsin, 1990.

Hodd, Michael. *The Economies of Africa: Geography, Population, History, Stability, Performance, Forecasts.* Boston: G. K. Hall, 1991.

Mahjoub, Azzam, ed. *Adjustment or Delinking? The African Experience.* London: Zed Press, 1990. (Dist. by Humanities Press)

Martin, Matthew. *The Crumbling Facade of African Debt Negotiations: No Winners.* New York: St. Martin's Press, 1991.

Mingst, Karen A. *Politics and the African Development Bank.* Lexington: University of Kentucky Press, 1990.

Nyango'oro, Julius, and Timothy Shaw, eds. *Beyond Structural Adjustment in Africa: The Political Economy of Sustainable and Democratic Development.* New York: Praeger, 1992.

Okolo, Julius Emeka, and Stephen Wright, eds. *West African Regional Cooperation and Development.* Boulder, CO: Westview Press, 1990.

Peckett, James, and Hans Singer, eds. *Towards Economic Recovery in Sub-Saharan Africa: Essays in Honor of Robert Gardner.* New York: Routledge, 1991.

Pradervand, Pierre. *Listening to Africa: Developing Africa from the Grassroots.* New York: Praeger, 1990.

Pryor, Frederic L. *The Political Economy of Poverty, Equity and Growth: Malawi and Madagascar.* New York: Oxford University for the World Bank, 1990.

Rau, Bill. *From Feast to Famine: Official Cures and Grassroots Remedies to Africa's Food Crisis.* New York: Zed Books, 1991 (Dist. by Humanities Press).

Riddell, Roger C. *Manufacturing Africa: Performance and Prospects of Seven Countries in Sub-Saharan Africa.* Portsmouth, NH: Heinemann, 1990.

Sarhof, Joseph A. *Hydropower Development in West Africa: A Study in Resource Development.* New York: P. Lang, 1990.

Siddle, David, and Ken Swindell. *Rural Change in Tropical Africa: From Colonies to Nation-States.* Cambridge, MA: Basil Blackwell, 1990.

Stewart, Frances, ed. *Alternative Development Strategies in Sub-Saharan Africa.* New York: St. Martin's Press, 1992.

Education

King, Kenneth, ed., *Botswana: Education, Culture and Politics.* Edinburgh: University of Edinburgh Press, 1990.

Mungazi, Dickson A. *Colonial Education for Africana: George Starks in Zimbabwe.* Westport, CT: Praeger, 1991.

Njobe, M.W. *Education for Liberation.* Johannesburg: Skotaville, 1990.

Okeem, E.O., ed. *Education in Africa: Search for Realistic Alternatives.* London: Institute for African Alternatives, 1990.

Okunor, Shiame. *Politics, Misunderstandings, Misconceptions: The History of Colonial Universities.* New York: P. Lang, 1991.

Folklore and Folk Culture

Berry, Jack, comp. and trans. *West African Folktales.* Edited with introduction by Richard Spears. Evanston, IL: Northwestern University Press, 1991.

Gunner, Liz, and Mafika Gwala, eds. and trans., *Musho!: Zulu Popular Praises.* East Lansing: Michigan State University Press, 1991.

McDermott, Gerald. *Zomo the Rabbit: A Trickster Tale from West Africa.* San Diego: Harcourt Brace Jovanovich, 1992.

Mohindra, Kamlesh. *Folk Tales of West Africa.* New Delhi: Sterling Pubs., 1991. (Dist. by APT Books)

Njoku, John E. Eberegbulaum. *The Igbos of Nigeria: Ancient Rites, Changes and Survival.* Lewiston, NY: Edwin Mellen Press, 1990.

Schipper, Mineke. *Source of All Evil: African Proverbs and Sayings on Women.* Chicago: Ivan R. Dee, 1991.

Smith, Alexander McCall. *Children of Wax: African Folk Tales.* New York: Interlink Books, 1991.

Ugorji, Okechukwu K. *The Adventures of Torti: Tales from West Africa.* Trenton, NJ: Africa World Press, 1991.

General Reference

Asante, Molafi Keto *The Book of African Names.* Trenton, NJ: Africa World Press, 1991.

Blackhurst, Hector, comp. *Africa Bibliography 1989.* Manchester, UK: Manchester University Press, 1991. (Dist. by St. Martin's Press, Inc.)

Fredland, Richard. *A Guide to African International Organizations.* New York: Hans Sell Publishers, 1991.

Morrison, Donald George, Robert Cameron Mitchell, and John Naber Paden. *Black Africa: A Comparative Handbook.* 2nd ed., New York: Paragon House/Irvington, 1990.

Moss, Joyce, and George Wilson. *Peoples of the World: Africans South of the Sahara.* Detroit: Gale Research Inc., 1991.

Sarfoh, Joseph A. *Energy in the Development of West Africa: A Selected Annotated Bibliography.* New York: Greenwood Press, 1991.

Thurston, Anne. *Guide to Archives and Manuscripts Relating to Kenya and East Africa in the United Kingdom.* New York: Hans Zell Publishers, 1991.

Zell, Hans M. *The African Studies Companion: A Resources Guide and Directory.* Providence, NJ: Hans Zell Publishers, 1990.

Government and Politics

Bowman, Larry W. *Mauritius: Democracy and Development in the Indian Ocean.* Boulder, CO: Westview Press, 1991.

Charlick, Robert B. *Niger: Personal Rule and Survival in the Sahel.* Boulder, CO: Westview Press, 1991.

Clingman, Stephen, ed. *Regions and Repertoires: Topics in South African Politics and Culture.* Johannesburg: Raven Press, 1991. (Dist. by Ohio University Press.)

Clough, Marshall S. *Fighting Two Sides: Kenyan Chiefs and Politicians, 1918–1940.* Niwot, CO: University Press of Colorado, 1990.

Cowell, Alan. *Killing the Wizards: Wars of Power and Freedom from Zaire to South Africa.* New York: Simon & Schuster, 1992.

Deng, Frances M., and I. William Zartman, eds. *Conflict Resolution in Africa.* Washington: Brookings Institution, 1991.

Forrest, Joshua B. *Guinea-Bissau: Power, Conflict and Renewal in a West African Nation.* Boulder, CO: Westview Press, 1992.

Gambari, I.A. *Political and Comparative Dimensions of Regional Integration: The Case of ECOWAS.* New York: The Humanities Press, 1991.

Hanlon, Joseph. *Mozambique: Who Calls the Shots.* Bloomington: Indiana University Press, 1991.

Hansen, Holger Bernt, ed. *Changing Uganda: The Dilemmas of Structural Adjustment and Revolutionary Change.* Athens: Ohio University Press, 1991.

Henze, Paul B. *The Horn of Africa: From War to Peace.* New York: St. Martin's Press, 1991.

Herbst, Jeffrey. *State Politics in Zimbabwe.* Berkeley: University of California, 1990.

Hughes, Arnold, ed. *The Gambia: Studies in Society and Politics.* Birmingham, UK: University of Birmingham, Centre for African Studies, 1991.

Ingham, Kenneth. *Politics in Modern Africa: The Uneven Tribal Dimension.* New York: Routledge, 1990.

Johnson, Willard R. *West African Governments and Volunteer Development Organizations: Priorities for Partnerships.* Lanham, MD: University Press of America, 1990.

Khalid, Mansour. *The Government They Deserve: The Role of the Elite in Sudan's Political Evolution.* New York: Kegan Paul International, 1990.

Kriger, Norma J. *Zimbabwe's Guerrilla War: Peasant Voices.* New York: Cambridge University Press, 1991.

Machobane, L.B.B.J. *Government and Change in Lesotho, 1800–1966: A Study of Political Institutions.* New York: Macmillan, 1990.

Moss, Glenn, and Ingrid Obery, eds. and comps. *South Africa Contemporary Analysis.* London: Hans Zell Publishers, 1990.

Nyang'oro, Julius E., and Timothy M. Shaw, eds. *Beyond Structural Adjustment in Africa: The Political Economy of Sustainable and Democratic Development.* New York: Praeger, 1992.

O'Brien, Donal B. Cruise, John Dunn, and Richard Rathbone, eds. *Contemporary West African States.* New York: Cambridge University Press, 1990.

Ogunsanwo, Alaba. *The Transformation of Nigeria: Scenarios and Metaphors.* Lagos: University of Lagos Press, 1991.

Reyna, Stephen P. *Wars Without End: The Political Economy of a Precolonial African State.* Hanover, NH: University Press of New England, 1990.

Riley, Eileen. *Major Political Events in South Africa, 1948–1990.* New York: Facts on File, 1991.

Schlosser, Dirk Berg, and Rainer Siegler. *Political Stability and Development: A Comparative Analysis of Kenya, Tanzania and Uganda.* Boulder, CO: Lynne Rienner, 1990.

Sklar, Richard L., and C. S. Whitaker. *African Politics and Problems in Development.* Boulder, CO: Lynne Rienner, 1991.

Tareke, Gebru. *Ethiopia, Power and Protest: Peasant Revolts in the Twentieth Century.* New York: Cambridge University Press, 1991.

Vines, Alex. *Renamo: Terrorism in Mozambique.* Bloomington: Indiana University Press, 1991.

Wunsch, James S., and Dele Olowu, eds. *The Failure of the Centralized State: Institutions and Self-Governance in Africa.* Boulder, CO: Westview Press, 1990.

Wylie, Diana. *A Little God: The Twilight of Patriarchy in a Southern Africa Chiefdom.* Hanover, NH: University Press of New England, 1990.

Health

Baron, Vida C. *African Power: Secrets of the Ancient Ibo Tribe.* San Diego, Barez Publishing Co., 1992.

Falala, Toyin, ed. *The Political Economy of Health in Africa.* Athens: Ohio University for International Studies/Ohio University Press, 1992.

King, Richard D. *African Origin of Biological Psychiatry.* Germantown, TN: Seymour-Smith, Inc., 1990.

Turner, Edith L.B., et al. *Experiencing Ritual: A New Interpretation of African Healing.* Philadelphia: University of Pennsylvania Press, 1992.

Williams, A. Olufemi. *AIDS: An African Perspective.* Boca Rotan, FL: CRC Press, 1992.

Wolff, James, et. al. *Beyond Clinic Walls, Case Studies in Community-Based Distribution.* West Hartford, CT: Kumarian Press, 1990.

History

Ayittey, George B.N. *Indigenous African Institutions.* Ardsley-on-Hudson, NY: Transnational Publishers, 1991.

Banbera, Tayiru. *A State of Intrigue: The Epic of Bamana Segu According to Tayiru Banbera.* Edited by David Conrad; transcribed and translated with the assistance of Soumaila Diakit'e. Oxford, UK: Oxford University Press, 1990.

Cammack, Diana. *The Rand at War, 1899–1902: The Witwatersrand and the Anglo-Boer War.* Berkeley: University of California Press, 1990.

Collelo, Thomas. *Angola: A Country Study* 3rd ed., Washington, DC: Government Printing Office, 1991.

Collins, Robert O. *Western African History.* New York: W. Wiener, 1990.

Crais, Clifton C. *White Supremacy and Black Resistance in Pre-Industrial South Africa: The Making of the Colonial Order in the Eastern Cape, 1770–1865.* Cambridge, UK: Cambridge University Press, 1992.

Digre, Brian. *Imperialism's New Clothes: The Repartition of Tropical Africa, 1914–1919.* New York: P. Lang, 1990.

Diop, Cheikh Anta. *Civilization or Barbarism: An Authentic Anthropology.* Translated by Yaa-Lengi Meema Ngemi; edited by Harold J. Salemson and Marjolijn de Jager. Brooklyn: Lawrence Hill Books, 1991.

Echenberg, Myron J. *Colonial Conscripts: The Tirailleurs S'en'egalais in French West Africa, 1857–1960.* Portsmouth, NH: Heinemann, 1991.

Friedman, Kajsa Ekholm. *Catastrophe and Creation: The Transformation of an African Culture.* Philadelphia: Hardwood Academic Publishers, 1991.

Gann, L.H., and Pete Duignan. *Hope for Africa.* Stanford, CA: Stanford University Press, 1991.

Gordon, April, ed. *Understanding Contemporary Africa.* Boulder, CO: Lynne Reinner Publishers, 1992.

Hair, P.E.H. *Black Africa in Time Perspective: Four Talks on Wide Historical Themes.* Liverpool, UK: Liverpool University Press, 1990. (Dist. by University of Pennsylvania Press).

Hair, P.E.H. *English Seamen and Traders in Guinea, 1553–1565: The New Evidence of their Wills.* Lewiston, NY: E. Mellen Press, 1992.

Hansen, Emmanuel. *Ghana Under Rawlings: Early Years.* Lagos: Malthouse Press, 1991.

Hassen, Mohammed. *The Oromo of Ethiopia: A History.* New York: Cambridge University Press, 1990.

Hudson, Peter. *Two Rivers: In the Footsteps of Mungo Park.* London: Chapmans Publishers, 1991.

Human Rights Watch. *Evil Days: Thirty Years of War and Famine in Ethiopia.* New York: Human Rights Watch, 1990.

Ki-Zerbo, J., ed.*UNESCO General History of Africa, Vol. 1: Methodology and African Prehistory.* Berkeley: University of California Press, 1990.

Lamphear, John. *The Scattering Time: Turkans Responses to Colonial Time.* New York: Oxford University Press, 1992.

Law, Robin. *The Slave Coast of West Africa, 1550–1750: The Impact of the Atlantic Slave Trade on African Society.* New York: Oxford University Press, 1991.

Manning, Patrick. *Slavery and African Life: Occidental, Oriental and African Slave Trades.* New York: Cambridge University Press, 1990.

Metaferia, Getchew. *The Ethiopian Revolution of 1974 and the Exodus of Ethiopia's Trained Human Resources.* Lewiston, NY: Edwin Mellen Press, 1991.

Mokhtar, G., ed. *UNESCO General History of Africa, Vol. II: Ancient History of Africa.* Berkeley: University of California Press, 1990.

Mooncraft, Paul L. *African Nemesis: War and Revolution in Southern Africa (1945–2010).* Riverside, NJ: Pergamon Press, 1990.

Morton, Fred. *Children of Ham: Freed Slaves and Fugitive Slaves on the Kenya Coast, 1873–1907.* Boulder, CO: Westview, 1990.

Mostert, Noel. *Frontiers: The Epic of South Africa's Creation and the Tragedy of the Xhosa People.* New York: Knopf, 1992.

Munford, Clarence J. *The Black Ordeal of Slavery and Slave Trading in the French West Indies, 1625–1715.* Lewiston, NY: Edwin Mellen Press, 1991.

Nasson, Bill. *Abraham Esau's War: A Black South African War in the Cape, 1899–1902.* New York: Cambridge University Press, 1991.

Obasanjo, Olusegun, and Hans d'Orville, eds. *The Impact of Europe in 1992 on West Africa.* New York: C. Russak, 1990.

Ochieng, William, ed. *Themes in Kenyan History.* Nairobi: Heinmann Kenya, 1990.

Ogot, B.A., ed. *Africa from the Sixteenth to the Eighteenth Century.* Berkeley: University of California Press, 1992.

Remmer, Douglas, ed. *Africa Thirty Years Ago.* Portsmouth, NH: Heinemann, 1991.

Shillington, Kevin. *History of Africa.* New York: St. Martin's Press, 1990.

Solow, Barbara L., ed. *Slavery and the Rise of the Atlantic System.* Cambridge, UK; New York: Cambridge University Press, 1991.

Stauton, Irene, comp. and ed. *Mothers of the Revolution: The War Experiences of Thirty Zimbabwean Women.* Bloomington: Indiana University Press, 1991.

Stedman, Stephen John. *Peacemaking in the Civil War: International Mediation in Zimbabwe, 1974–1980.* Boulder, CO: Lynne Rienner, 1991.

Temperley, Howard. *White Dreams, Black Africa: The Anti-Slavery Expedition to the River Niger, 1841–42.* New Haven: Yale University Press, 1991.

Thompson, Leonard. *A History of South Africa.* New Haven: Yale University Press, 1990.

Wyse, Akintola J.G., and H.C. Bankhole-Bight. *Politics in Colonial Sierra Leone, 1919–1958.* New York:Cambridge University Press, 1991.

Yarak, Larry W. *Asante and the Dutch, 1744–1873.* New York: Oxford University Press, 1990.

Young, John. *They Fell Like Stones: Battles and Casualties of the Zulu War, 1879.* Novato, CA: Presidio Press, 1991.

International Relations

Kent, John. *The Internationalization of Colonialism: Britain, France and Black Africa.* New York: Oxford University Press, 1992.

Russell, Sharon Stanton, Karen Jacobsen, and William Deane Stanley. *International Migration and Development in Sub-Sahara Africa.* Washington, DC: The World Bank, 1991.

Thompson, Joseph E. *American Policy and African Famine: The Nigeria-Biafra War, 1966–1970.* New York: Greenwood Press, 1970.

Winros, Gareth M. *The Foreign Policy of GDR in Africa.* Cambridge, UK: Cambridge University Press, 1991.

Language and Literature

Abraham, Cecils ed. *The Tragic Life: Bessie Head and Literature in South Africa.* Trenton, NJ: Africa World Press, 1990.

Achebe, Chinua. *Hopes and Impediments: Selected Essays.* New York: Doubleday, 1990.

Bjornson, Richard. *The African Quest for Freedom and Identity: Cameroonian Writing and the National Experience.* Bloomington: Indiana University Press, 1991.

Dram'e, Kandioura. *The Novel as Transformation Myth: A Study of the Novels of Mongo Beti and Ngugi wa Thiongo.* Syracuse, NY: Syracuse University, 1990.

Dunton, Chris. *Make Man Talk True: Nigerian Drama in English Since 1970.* New York: Hans Zell Publishers, 1992.

Elimimian, Isaac Iraber. *Theme and Style in African Poetry.* Lewiston, NY: E. Mellen, 1991.

February, V.A. *Mind Your Colour: The Coloured Stereotype in South African Literature.* London and New York: Kegan Paul International, 1991. (Dist. by Routledge, Chapman & Hall, Inc.).

Gikandi, Simon. *Reading Chinua Achebe: Language and Ideology in Fiction.* Portsmouth, NH: Heinemann, 1991.

Gunner, Liz, ed., and trans. *Musho!: Zulu Popular Praises.* East Lansing: Michigan State University Press, 1991.

Hale, Thomas A. *Scribe, Griot and Novelist: Narrative Interpreters of the Songhay Empire Followed by the Epic of Askia Mohammed Recounted,* Gainesville, FL: University of Florida Press/Center for African Studies, 1990.

Harrow, Kenneth, ed., *Faces of Islam in African Literature.* Portsmouth, NH: Heinemann, 1991.

Harrow, Kenneth, Jonathan Ngate, and Clarissa Zimra, eds. *Crisscrossing Boundaries in African Literatures, 1986.* Washington, DC: Three Continents Press/African Literature Association, 1991.

Ikonne, Chidi, Emelia Oko, and Peter Onwudinjo, eds. *African Literature and African Historical Experience.* New York: Heinemann, 1991.

Innes, Catherine Lynette. *Chinua Achebe.* New York: Cambridge University Press, 1990.

Innes, Catherine Lynette. *The Devil's Own Mirror: The Irishman and the African Modern Literature.* Washington, DC: Three Continents Press, 1990.

James, Adeola, ed., *In Their Own Voices: African Women Writers Talk.* Portsmouth, NH: Heinemann, 1990.

Jones, Eldred Durosimi, ed. *The Question of Language in African Literature Today: Borrowing and Carrying: A Review.* Trenton, NJ: Africa World Press, 1991.

Julien, Eileen. *African Novels and the Question of Orality.* Bloomington: Indiana University Press, 1992.

Lazarus, Neil. *Resistance in Postcolonial African Fiction.* New Haven, CT: Yale University Press, 1991.

Lindfors, Bernth. *Popular Literature in Africa.* Trenton, NJ: Africa World Press, 1991.

Liyong, Taban Lo. *Another Last Word.* New York: Heinemann, 1990.

Miller, Christopher L. *Theories of Africans: Franco-Phone Literature and Anthropology in Africa.* Chicago: University of Chicago Press, 1990.

Mortimer, Mildred. *Journey Through the French African Novel.* Portsmouth, NH: Heinemann, 1990.

Nethersole, Reingard, ed. *Emerging Literature.* New York: P. Lang, 1990.

Ngara, Emmanuel. *Ideology and Form in African Poetry: Implications for Communication.* Portsmouth, NH: Heinemann, 1990.

Obiechina, Emmanuel N. *Language and Theme: Essays on African Literature.* Washington, DC: Howard University Press, 1990.

Orisawayi, Dele, et. al., eds. *Literature and Black Aesthetics.* New York: Heinemann, 1990.

Owomoyela, Onjekan. *Visions and Revisions: Essays on African Literatures and Criticisms.* New York: P. Lang, 1991.

Research in African Literatures: Critical Theory and African Literature. Bloomington: Indiana University Press, 1990.

Research in African Literature: Dictatorship and Oppression. Bloomington: Indiana University Press, 1990.

Roscoe, Adrian A., and Hangson Msika. *The Quiet Chameleon: Modern Poetry from Central Africa.* New York: Hans Zell Publishers, 1992.

Scheub, Harold. *The African Storyteller: Stories from African Oral Traditions.* Dubuque, IA: Kendell/Hunt, 1991.

Schipper, Mineke. *Beyond the Boundaries: Text and Context in African Literature.* Chicago: Ivan R. Dee, 1990.

Sicherman, Carol. *Ngugi wa Thiong: A Source Book on Kenyan Literature and Resistance.* New York: Hans Zell Publishers, 1990.

Soyinka, Wole. *Myth, Literature, and the African World.* New York: Cambridge University Press, 1990.

Trump, Martin, ed. *Rendering Things Visible: Essays on South African Literary Culture.* Athens: Ohio University Press, 1991.

Wilentz, Gay Alden. *Binding Cultures: Black Women Writers in Africa and the Diaspora.* Bloomington: Indiana University Press, 1992.

Wylie, Hal, Dennis Brutus, and Juris Silenieks, eds. *African Literature, 1988: New Masks.* Washington, DC: Three Continents Press/The African Literature Association, 1990.

Law, Law Enforcement, Civil and Human Rights

Ahire, Philip Terdo. *Imperial Policing: The Emergence and Role of the Police in Nigeria, 1860–1960.* Philadelphia: Open University Press, 1991.

Bazille, Susan, ed. *Putting Women on the Agenda.* Johannesburg, S.A.: Raven Press, 1991. (Dist. by Ohio University Press).

Braham, Peter, ed. *Racism and Antiracism: Inequalities in Opportunities and Policies.* Philadelphia: Sage/Open University Press, 1992.

Hansson, Desiree, and Dirk van Zyl Smit, eds. *Toward Justice? Crime and State Control in South Africa.* New York: Oxford University Press, 1990.

Mann, Kristin, ed. *Law in Colonial Africa.* Portsmouth, NH: Heinemann, 1991.

Shepherd, George W., and Mark O.G. Anikpo, eds. *Emerging Human Rights: The African Political Economy Concept.* Westport, CT: Greenwood Press, 1990.

Media

Faringer, Gunilla L. *Press Freedom in Africa.* Westport, CT: Praeger, 1991.

Harden, Blaine. *Africa: Dispatches from a Fragile Continent.* London: Harper Collins, 1990.

Hawk, Beverly G., ed. *Africa's Media Image.* New York: Praeger, 1992.

Sturges, Paul, and Richard Neill. *The Quiet Struggle: Libraries and Information for Africa.* New York: Mansell, 1990.

Music

Arom, Simha. *African Polyphony and Polyrhythm: Musical Structure and Methodology.* Translated by Martin Thom and Barbara Tucker. New York: Cambridge University Press, 1991.

Bender, Wolfgang. *Sweet Mother: Modern African Music.* Translated by Wolfgang Freis. Chicago: University of Chicago Press, 1991.

Collins, John. *West African Pop Roots.* Philadelphia: Temple University Press, 1992.

Gray, John. *African Music: A Bibliographic Guide to the Traditional Popular Art and Liturgical Music of Sub-Saharan Africa.* Westport, CT: Greenwood Press, 1991.

Lems-Dworkin, Carol. *African Music: A Pan-African Annotated Bibliography.* New York: Hans Zell Publishers, 1991.

Stewart, Gary. *Breakout: Profiles in African Rhythm.* Chicago: University of Chicago Press, 1992.

Waterman, Christopher Alan. *Juju: A Social History and Ethnography of an African Popular Music.* Chicago: University of Chicago Press, 1990.

Pan-Africanism

Agyeman, Opoku. *Nkrumah's Ghana and East Africa: Pan-Africanism and African Interstate Relations.* Cranbury, NJ: Fairleigh Dickinson University Press, 1992.

Clarke, John H. *Africans at the Crossroads: Notes for an African World Revolution.* Trenton, NJ: Africa World Press, 1992.

Staniland, Martin. *American Intellectuals and African Nationalists, 1950–1970.* New Haven: Yale University Press, 1991.

Performing Arts

Diawara, Manthia. *African Cinema: Politics and Culture.* Bloomington: Indiana University Press, 1992.

Erlman, Veit. *African Stars: Studies in Black South African Performance.* Chicago: University of Chicago Press, 1991.

Lee, Jacques K. *Sega: The Mauritius Folk Dance.* London: Nautilus Publishing Co., 1990.

Orkin, Martin. *Drama and the South African State.* Manchester, UK: Manchester University Press, 1991. (Dist. by St. Martin's Press)

Religion and Philosophy

Dankwa, Nano O., III. *Christianity and African Traditional Beliefs.* Edited by John W. Branch. New York: Power of the World Publishing Co., 1990.

Felder, Cain Hope, ed. *Stony the Road We Trod: African American Biblical Interpretation.* Minneapolis: Fortress Press, 1991.

Gbadegesin, Segun. *African Philosophy: Traditional Yoruba Philosophy and Contemporary African Realities.* New York: Lang, 1991.

Gifford, Paul. *The New Crusaders: Christianity and the New Right in Southern Africa.* London: Pluto, 1991.

Gray, Richard. *Black Christians and White Missionaries.* New Haven: Yale University Press, 1991.

Oldfield, J.R. *Alexander Crummell (1819–1898) and the Creation of an African-American Church in Africa.* Lewiston, NY: Edwin Mellin Press, 1990.

Olupona, Jacob K. *African Traditional Religions in Contemporary Society.* New York: Paragon, 1991.

Oruka, H. O. *Trends in Contemporary African Philosophy.* Nairobi, Kenya: Shirikon Publishers, 1990.

Peek, Philip M., ed. *African Divination Systems: Ways of Knowing.* Bloomington: Indiana University Press, 1991.

Prozesky, Martin, ed. *Christianity Amidst Apartheid.* New York: London, Macmillan, 1990.

Soyinka, Wole. *The Credo of Being and Nothingness.* Ibadan: Spectrum Books, 1990.

Vanderaa, Larry A. *A Survey of Christian Reformed World Missions and Churches in West Africa.* Grand Rapids, MI: Christian Reformed World Missions, 1991.

Sociology and Psychology

Barnes, James Franklin. *Gabon: Beyond the Colonial Legacy.* Boulder, CO: Westview Press, 1992.

Bell, Leland V. *Mental and Social Disorder in Sub-Saharan Africa: The Case of Sierra Leone, 1787–1990.* Westport, CT: Greenwood Press, 1991.

Carr-Hill, Roy A. *Social Conditions in Sub-Saharan Africa.* London; New York: Macmillan, 1991.

Cleaver, Tessa, and Marion Wallace. *Namibia: Women in War.* Foreword by Glenys Kinnock. Atlantic Highlands, NJ: Zed Books, 1990.

Cobley, Alan Gregord. *Class and Consciousness: The Black Petty Bourgeoisie in South Africa, 1924–1950.* Westport, CT: Greenwood Press, 1990.

Coles, Catherine, and Beverly Mack, eds. *Hausa Women in the Twentieth Century.* Madison: University of Wisconsin Press, 1991.

Gordon, Robert J. *The Bushman Myth: The Making of a Namibian Underclass.* Boulder, CO: Westview Press, 1992.

Hill, Martin J.D., ed. *The Harambee Movement in Kenya: Self-Help Development and Education Among the Kamba of Chat District.* Atlantic Highlands, NJ: Athlone Press, 1991.

Kilbride, Philip Leroy. *Changing Family Life in East Africa: Women and Children at Risk*, Philadelphia: Pennsylvania State University Press, 1990.

Mohammad, Duri, ed., *Social Development in Africa: Strategies, Policies and Programmes After the Lagos Plan.* Providence, NJ: H. Zell Publishers, 1991.

Moran, Mary. *Civilized Women: Gender and Prestige in Southeastern Liberia.* Ithaca, NY: Cornell University Press, 1991.

Nsamenang, A. Bame. *Human Development in Cultural Conflict.* Foreword by Michael Lamb. Newbury Park, CA: Sage Publications, 1992.

Ominde, S. H., ed. *Kenya' s Population Growth and Development to the Year 2000.* Columbus: Ohio University Press, 1990.

Reynolds, Pamela. *Dance Cat: Child Labour in the Zambezi Valley.* London: Hans Zell Books, 1991.

Riseman, Paul. *First Find Your Child A Good Mother: The Construction of Self in Two African Communities.* New Brunswick, NJ: Rutgers University Press, 1992.

Robertson, Struan. *The Cold Choice: Pictures of a South African Reality.* Grand Rapids, MI: Wm. B. Erdmans Publishing Co., 1992.

■ AFRICAN AMERICANA

Art, Architecture, and Photography

Bearden, Romare. *Memory and Metaphor: The Art of Romare Bearden, 1940–1987.* New York: Studio Museum of Harlem/Oxford University Press, 1991.

Durham, Michael S. *Powerful Days: The Civil Rights Photography of Charles Moore.* Introduction by Andrew Young. New York: Stewart, Tabori & Chang, 1991.

Easter, Eric, D. Michael Cheers, and Dudley M. Brooks, eds. *Songs of My People: African Americans: A Self-Portrait.* Introduction by Gordon Parks. Essays by Sylvester Monroe. Boston: Little, Brown, 1992.

McElroy, Guy C. *Facing History: The Black Image in American Art, 1710–1940.* Edited by Christopher C. French. Washington, DC: Bedford Arts/Corcoran Gallery, 1990.

Powell, Richard J. *Homecoming: The Art and Life of William H. Johnson.* New York: National Museum of American Art/Rizzoli, 1991.

Rozelle, Robert V., et. al. eds. *Black Art: Ancestral Legacy: The African-American Impulse in African-American Art.* New York: Abrams, 1990.

Thomison, Dennis, comp. *The Black Artist in America: An Index to Reproductions.* Metuchen, NJ: Scarecrow Press, 1991.

Travis, Jack, ed. *African-American Architects in Current Practice.* New York: Princeton Architecture Press, 1991.

Autobiography and Biography

Baker, Donald P. *Wilder: Hold Fast to Dreams: A Biography of L. Douglas Wilder.* Cabin John, MD: Seven Locks, 1990.

Baldwin, Lewis V. *There Is a Balm in Gilead: The Cultural Roots of Martin Luther King, Jr.* Minneapolis: Fortress Press, 1991.

Bigelow, Barbara Carlisle, ed. *Contemporary Black Biography.* Detroit: Gale Research Inc., 1992.

Bjarkman, Peter C. *Ernie Banks.* Introduction by Jim Murray. New York: Chelsea House, 1992.

Brown, Drew T., III. *You Gotta Believe!: Education + Hard Work − Drugs = The American Dream.* New York: Morrow, 1991.

Brown, James, and Bruce Tucker. *James Brown: The Godfather of Soul.* New York: Thunder's Mouth Press, 1990.

Buchmann-Moller, Frank. *You Just Fight for Your Life: The Story of Lester Young.* New York: Praeger, 1990.

Campbell, James. *Talking at the Gate: A Life of James Baldwin.* New York: Viking, 1991.

Carson, Clayborne. *Malcolm X; The FBI File.* Introduction by Spike Lee. Edited by David Gallen. New York: Carroll & Graf Publishers, Inc., 1991.

Carson, Clayborne, ed. *The Papers of Martin Luther King, Jr.* Berkeley: University of California Press, 1991.

Chilton, John. *The Song of the Hawk: The Life and Recordings of Coleman Hawkins.* New York: St. Martin's Press, 1990.

Davis, Benjamin O., Jr. *Benjamin O. Davis, Jr., American: An Autobiography.* Washington, DC: Smithsonian Institution, 1991.

Davis, Miles, and Quincy Troupe. *Miles, The Autobiography.* New York: Simon & Schuster, 1990.

Deane, Bill. *Bob Gibson.* Introduction by Jim Murray. New York: Chelsea House, 1992.

Dees, Morris. *A Season for Justice: The Life and Times of Civil Rights Lawyer Morris Dees.* New York: Scribner, 1991.

Faser, Jane. *Walter White.* New York: Chelsea House, 1991.

Goldman, Roger, and David Gallen. *Thurgood Marshall: Justice for All.* New York: Carroll & Graf, 1992.

Hamilton, Charles V. *Adam Clayton Powell, Jr.: The Political Biography of an American Dilemma.* New York: Atheneum, 1991.

Hawkins, Walter L. *African American Biographies: Profiles of 558 Current Men and Women.* Jefferson, NC: McFarland & Co., 1992.

Hayes, Bob. *Run, Bullet, Run.* New York: Harper Collins, 1990.

Kranz, Rachel C. *The Biographical Dictionary of Black Americans.* New York: Facts on File, 1992.

Kremer, Gary R. *James Milton Turner and the Promise of America: The Public Life of a Post-Civil War Black Leader.* Columbia: University of Missouri Press, 1991.

Levi, Darrell E. *Michael Manley: The Making of a Leader.* Athens: University of Georgia Press, 1990.

McFeely, William S. *Frederick Douglass.* New York: Norton, 1990.

Mosby, Dewey F., and Darrel Sewell. *Henry Ossawa Tanner.* New York: Rizzoli, 1991.

Naughton, Jim. *Taking to the Air: The Rise of Michael Jordan.* New York: Warner Books, 1992.

Pallister, Janis L. *Aime Cesaire.* New York: Twayne, 1991.

Perry, Bruce. *Malcolm: The Life of a Man Who Changed Black America.* Barrytown, NY: Station Hill, 1991.

Pfieffer, Paula F. *A. Philip Randolph, Pioneer of the Civil Rights Movement.* Baton Rouge: Louisiana State University Press, 1990.

Phelps, J. Alfred. *Chappie: America's First Black Four-Star General.* Novato, CA: Presidio Press, 1991.

Phelps, Shirelle, ed. *Who's Who Among Black Americans, 1993–94.* 7th ed., William C. Matney, Jr., Consulting Editor. Detroit: Gale Research Inc., 1993.

Pickens, William. *Bursting Bonds: Enlarged edition (of) The Heir of Slaves: The Autobiography of a "New Negro".* Edited by William L. Andrews. Bloomington: Indiana University Press, 1991.

Rattenbury, Ken. *Duke Ellington, Jazz Composer.* New Haven: Yale University Press, 1991.

Rivlin, Benjamin, ed. *Ralph Bunche, The Man and His Times.* Foreword by Donald F. Henry. New York: Holmes & Meier, 1990.

Rose, Cynthia. *Living in America: The Soul Saga of James Brown.* London: Serpent Tale, 1990 (Dist. by Consortium Book Sales Distribution.)

Rout, Kathleen. *Eldridge Cleaver.* Boston: Twayne/G.K. Hall, 1991.

Schwartzman, Myron. *Romare Bearden: His Life and Art.* New York: Abrams, 1990.

Shapiro, Leonard. *Big Man on Campus: John Thompson and the Georgetown Hoyas.* New York: Holt, 1991.

Shapiro, Miles. *Bill Russell.* Introductory essay by Coretta Scott King. New York: Chelsea House, 1991.

Sifford, Charlie. *Just Let Me Play: The Story of Charlie Sifford: The First Black PGA Golfer.* Latham, NY: British American Publishers, 1992.

Smith, Eric Ledell. *Bert Williams: A Biography of the Pioneer Black Comedian.* Jefferson, NC: McFarland, 1992.

Stewart, James Brewer. *William Lloyd Garrison and the Challenge of Emancipation.* Arlington Heights, IL: Harlan Davidson, 1992.

Strode, Woody, and Sam Young. *Goal Dust: An Autobiography.* Lantham, MD: Madison Books, 1990.

Tucker, Ken. *Ellington: The Early Years.* Champaign: University of Illinois Press, 1991.

Urban, Wayne J. *Black Scholar: Horace Mann Bond, 1904–1972.* Athens: University of Georgia Press, 1992.

Vache, Warren W. *Crazy Fingers: Claude Hopkins' Life in Jazz.* Washington, DC: Smithsonian Institution Press, 1992.

Watts, Jill. *God, Harlem U.S.A.: The Father Divine Story.* Berkeley: University of California Press, 1992.

Weland, Gerald. *Of Vision and Valor: General O. O. Howard, A Biography.* Canton, OH: Daring Publishing Group, 1991.

Wells, Dicky. *The Night People: The Jazz Life of Dicky Wells.* As told to Stanley Dance. rev. ed., Washington, DC: Smithsonian Institution Press, 1991.

Wills, Maury, and Mike Celizic. *On the Run: The Never Dull and Often Shocking Life of Maury Wills.* New York: Carroll & Graf, 1991.

Black Nationalism and Pan-Africanism in the United States

Crosby, Edward W., and Linus A. Hoskins, eds. *Africa for the Africans: Selected Speeches of Marcus Mosiah Garvey; Malcolm X; and Nelson Kolihlahla Mandela.* Kent, OH: The Institute for African American Affairs, Department of Pan-African Studies, Kent State University, 1991.

Crummell, Alexander. *Destiny and Race: Selected Writings, 1840–1898.* Edited with introduction by Wilson J. Moses. Amherst: University of Massachusetts Press, 1992.

Drake, St. Clair. *Black Folks Here and There: An Essay in History and Anthropology.* 2 vols. Los Angeles: University of California, Los Angeles, Center for Afro-American Studies, 1991.

Harris, Robert, et. al. *Carlos Cooks: And Black Nationalism from Garvey to Malcolm.* Dover, MA: Majority Press, 1992.

Jacques, Geoffrey. *The African-American Movement Today.* New York: Watts, 1992.

Lemelle, Sid. *Pan-Africanism for Beginners.* New York: Writers and Readers Publishing, Inc., 1992.

Lewis, Rupert, ed. *Garvey: His Work and Impact.* Trenton, NJ: Africa World Press, 1991.

Martin, Tony, comp. and ed. *African Fundamentalism: A Literary and Cultural Anthropology of Garvey's Harlem Renaissance.* Dover, MA: Majority Press, 1991.

Moses, Wilson J. *Alexander Crummell: A Study of Civilization and Discontent.* Amherst: University of Massachusetts Press, 1992.

Civil Rights, Law, and Civil Protests

Administrative History of the Civil Rights Division of the Department of Justice During the Johnson Administration. 2 vols., New York: Garland Publishing Co., 1991.

Aguirre, Adalberto, Jr., and David V. Baker. *Race, Racism and the Death Penalty in the United States.* Barrien Springs, MI: Vande Vere Publishers, 1992.

Belknap, Michal. *Racial Violence and Law Enforcement in the South.* New York: Garland Publishing Co., 1991.

Belknap, Michal. *Securing the Enactment of Civil Rights Legislation, 1965–1968.* New York: Garland Publishing Co., 1991.

Belknap, Michal. *Urban Race Riots.* New York: Garland Publishing Co., 1991.

Belknap, Michal. *Voting Rights.* New York: Garland Publishing Co., 1991.

Belz, Herman. *Equality Transformed: A Quarter-Century of Affirmative Action.* New Brunswick, NJ: Transaction, 1991.

Blumberg, Rhoda L. *Civil Rights, the Freedom Struggle.* rev. ed., Boston: Twayne G.K. Hall, 1991.

Bolick, Clint. *Unfinished Business: A Civil Rights Strategy for America's Third Century.* San Francisco: Research Institute of Public Policy, 1990.

Cagin, Seth, and Philip Dray. *We Are Not Afraid: The Story of Goodman, Schwerner and Chaney and the Civil Rights Campaign for Mississippi.* New York: Bantam Books, 1991.

Capeci, Dominic, and Martha Wilkerson. *Layered Violence: the Detroit Rioters of 1943.* Jackson: University Press of Mississippi, 1991.

Carson, Clayborne, et. al. eds. *"The Eyes on the Prize" Civil Rights Reader: Documents, Speeches, and Firsthand Accounts from the Black Freedom Struggle, 1954–1990.* New York: Viking, 1991.

Cashman, Sean Dennis. *African-Americans and the Quest for Civil Rights, 1900–1990.* New York: New York University Press, 1991.

Cashmore, Ellis, and Eugene McLaughlin, eds. *Out of Order?: Policing Black People.* New York: Routledge, 1991.

Cone, James H. *Martin and Malcolm and America: A Dream or a Nightmare.* New York: Orbis Books, 1991.

Cook, Anthony. *Law, Race and Social Theory.* Boston: New England School of Law, 1991.

Detefsen, Robert R. *Civil Rights Under Reagan.* San Francisco: ICS Press, 1991.

Encyclopedia of African American Civil Rights: From Emancipation to the Present. Westport, CT: Greenwood Press, 1992.

Epstein, Richard Allen. *Forbidden Grounds: The Case Against Employment Discrimination Laws.* Cambridge: Harvard University Press, 1992.

Ezorsky, Gertrude. *Racism and Justice: The Case for Affirmative Action.* Ithaca, NY: Cornell University Press, 1991.

Fendrich, James Max. *Ideal Citizens: The Legacy of the Civil Rights Movement.* Albany: State University of New York Press, 1993.

Finkelman, Paul, ed. *African Americans and the Law.* New York: Garland Publishing Co., 1991 (*Race, Law and American History, 1700–1900. The African American Experience.*)

Finkelman, Paul, ed. *African-Americans and the Legal Profession in Historical Perspective.* New York: Garland Publishing Co., 1991 (*Race, Law, and American History, 1700–1990. The African American Experience*, vol. 10).

Finkelman, Paul, ed. *African-Americans and the Right to Vote.* Edited by Paul Finkelman. New York: Garland Publishing Co., 1992. (*Race, Law, and American History, 1700–1900. The African-American Experience*, vol. 6).

Finkelman, Paul, ed. *Lynching, Racial Violence, and Law.* New York: Garland Publishing Co., 1992. (*Race, Law, and American History, 1700–1990. The African-American Experience*, vol. 9.)

Finkelman, Paul, ed. *Race and Criminal Justice.* New York: Garland Publishing Co., 1992. (*Race, Law, and American History, 1700–1900. The American Experience*, vol. 8.)

Finkelman, Paul, ed. *Race and Law Before Emancipation.* New York: Garland Publishing Co., 1992. (*Race, Law and American History, 1700–1990. The African American Experience*, vol. 2.)

Finkelman, Paul, ed. *The Era of Integration and Civil Rights, 1930–1990.* New York: Garland Publishing Co., 1992. (*Race, Law, and American History, 1700–1990. The African American Experience*, vol. 5).

Fiscus, Ronald Jerry. *The Constitutional Logic of Affirmative Action.* Edited by Stephen Wasby. Durham, NC: Duke University Press, 1992.

Fisher, Sethard. *From Margin to Mainstream: The Social Progress of Black Americans.* 2nd ed., Savage, MD: Rowman & Littlefield, 1992.

Goings, Kenneth W. *The NAACP Comes of Age: The Defeat of Judge Parker.* Bloomington: Indiana University Press, 1990.

Goldwin, Robert A. *Why Blacks, Women and Jews Are Not Mentioned in the Constitution, and Other Unorthodox Views.* Washington, DC: American Enterprise Institute, 1990.

Graetz, Robert S. *Montgomery, A White Preachers Memoir.* Minneapolis: Fortress Press, 1991.

Grafman, Bernard, ed. *Controversies in Minority Voting: The Voting Rights Act in Perspective.* Washington, DC: Brookings Institute, 1992.

Graham, Hugh Davis. *The Civil Rights Era: Race, Gender and National Policy, 1960–1972.* New York: Oxford University Press, 1990.

Hampton, Henry, and Steve Fayer, comps. *Voices of Freedom: An Oral History of the Civil Rights Movement from the 1950s Through the 1980s.* New York: Bantam Books, 1990.

Harding, Vincent. *Hope and History: Why We Must Share the Story of the Movement.* Maryknoll, NY: Orbis Books, 1990.

Harris, Jacqueline. *A History of the NAACP.* New York: Watts, 1992.

Jackson, James E. *The Bold Bad '60s: Pushing the Point for Equality Down South and Out Yonder.* New York: International Publishers, 1992.

James, Hunter. *They Didn't Put That on the Huntley-Brinkley Report!: A Vagabound Reporter Encounters the New South.* Athens: University of Georgia, 1993.

Justice Department Briefs in Crucial Civil Rights Cases. 2 vols., New York: Garland, 1991.

Kapur, Sudarshan. *Raising Up a Prophet: The African-American Encounter with Gandhi.* Boston: Beacon, 1992.

King, Richard. *Civil Rights and the Idea of Freedom.* New York: Oxford University Press, 1992.

Kull, Andrew. *The Color-Blind Constitution.* Cambridge: Harvard University Press, 1992.

Levy, Peter B., ed. *Dictionary History of the Modern Civil Rights Movement.* New York: Greenwood Press, 1992.

Levy, Peter B., ed. *Let Freedom Ring: A Documentary History of the Modern Civil Rights Movement.* New York: Praeger, 1992.

Lyon, Danny. *Memories of the Civil Rights Movement.* Text and photographs by Danny Lyon; foreword by Julian Bond. Chapel Hill: University of North Carolina Press, 1992.

Meier, August, et. al. eds. *Black Protest in the Sixties.* New York: M. Wiener, 1991.

Meier, August. *A White Scholar and the Black Community, 1945–1965: Essays and Reflections.* Afterword by John H. Bracey, Jr. Amherst: University of Massachusetts Press, 1992.

Mills, Nicolaus. *Like a Holy Crusade: Mississippi, 1964—The Turning of the Civil Rights Movement in America.* Chicago: I.R. Dee, 1992.

Nieli, Russell, ed. *Racial Preference and Racial Justice: The New Affirmative Action Controversy.* Washington, DC: Ethics and Public Policy Center, 1991 (Dist. by National Book Network.)

Nieman, Donald G. *Promises to Keep: African Americans and the Constitutional Order, 1776 to the Present.* New York: Oxford University Press, 1991.

O'Reilly, Kenneth. *Racial Matters: The FBI's Secret File on Black America, 1960–1972.* New York: Free Press, 1991.

Powledge, Fred. *Free At Last?: The Civil Rights Movement and the People Who Made It.* Boston: Little, Brown, 1990.

Reed, Merl E. *Seedtime for the Modern Civil Rights Movement: The President's Committee on Fair Employment Practice, 1941–1946.* Baton Rouge: Louisiana State University Press, 1991.

Robinson, Amelia Boynton. *Bridge Across Jordan.* rev. ed., Washington, DC: Schiller Institute, 1991.

Robinson, Armistead L., and Patricia Sullivan, eds. *New Directions in Civil Rights Studies.*

Charlottesville: University Press of Virginia, 1991.

Sigelman, Lee, and Susan Welch. *Black Americans' Views of Racial Inequality: The Dream Deferred.* New York: Cambridge University Press, 1991.

Sikora, Frank. *Until Justice Rolls Down: The Birmingham Church Bombing Case.* Tuscaloosa: University of Alabama Press, 1991.

Stern, Mark. *Calculating Visions: Kennedy, Johnson and Civil Rights.* New Brunswick, NJ: Rutgers University Press, 1992.

Swift, Jeanne, ed. *Dream and Reality: The Modern Black Struggle for Freedom and Equality.* New York: Greenwood Press, 1991.

Thomas, Clarence. *Clarence Thomas: Confronting the Future: Selections from the Senate Confirmation Hearing and Prior Speeches.* Washington, DC: Regnery Gateway, 1992.

Urofsky, Melvin I. *A Conflict of Rights: The Supreme Court and Affirmative Action.* New York: Scribners, 1991.

Watson, Denton L. *Lion in the Lobby: Clarence Mitchell, Jr.'s Struggle for the Passage of Civil Rights Laws.* New York: Morrow, 1990.

Wright, Roberta Hughes. *The Birth of the Montgomery Bus Boycott.* Southfield, MI: Charro Book Co., 1991.

Economics, Entrepreneurship, and Labor

Broadnax, Derek. *The Black Entrepreneurs Guide to Million Dollar Business Opportunities.* Austin, TX: Black Entrepreneurs Press, 1990.

Broadnax, Derek. *The Black Entrepreneurs Guide to Money Sources: How to Get Your Share.* Austin, TX: Black Entrepreneurs Press, 1990.

Butler, John Sibley. *Entrepreneurship and Self-Help Among Black Americans: A Reconsideration of Race and Economics.* Albany: State University of New York Press, 1991.

Dewart, Janet, ed. *The State of Black America, 1991.* New York: National Urban League, 1991.

Duncan, Mike. *Reach Your Goals In Spite of the Old Boy Network: A Guide for African American Employees.* Edgewood, MD: M.E. Duncan and Co., 1990.

Grant, Nancy L. *TVA and Black Americans: Planning for the Status Quo.* Philadelphia: Temple University Press, 1990.

Green, Shelley, and Paul Pryde. *Black Entrepreneurship in America.* Brunswick, NJ: Transactions Publishers, 1990.

Greenberg, Jonathan D. *Staking a Claim: Jake Simmons and the Making of an African-American Oil Dynasty.* New York: Atheneum, 1991.

Reed, Wornie, ed. *Social, Political and Economic Issues in Black America.* Amherst: University of Massachusetts, William Monroe Trotter Institute, 1990.

Rosen, George H. *Black Money.* Chelsea, MI: Scarborough House, 1990.

Education

Allen, Walter R., Edgar Epps, and Nesha Z. Haniff, eds. *College in Black and White: African American Students in Predominately White and Historically Black Public Universities.* Albany: State University of New York Press, 1991.

Altbach, Philip G., and Kofi Lomotey, eds. *The Racial Crisis in American Higher Education.* Albany: State University of New York Press, 1991.

Bowman, J. Wilson. *America's Black Colleges.* South Pasadena, CA: Sandcastle Publishing Co., 1992.

Fife, Brian L. *Desegregation in American Schools: Comparative Intervention Strategies.* New York: Praeger, 1992.

Finkelman, Paul, ed. *The Struggle for Equal Education.* New York: Garland Publishing Co., 1992. (*Race, Law, and American History, 1700–1990. African-American Experience,* vol. 7.)

Formisano, Ronald P. *Boston Against Busing: Race, Class, and Ethnicity in the 1960s and 1970s.* Chapel Hill: University of North Carolina Press, 1991.

Harmon, Marylen E. *The Infusion of African and African American Studies into the Curriculum.* Roanoke, VA: Absolute Writings Ltd., 1991.

Irvine, Jacqueline Jordan. *Black Students and School Failure: Policies, Practices, and Prescriptions.* Westport, CT: Greenwood Press, 1990.

Lomotey, Kofi, ed. *Going to School: The African-American Experience.* Albany: State University of New York Press, 1990.

Lusane, Clarence. *The Struggle for Equal Education.* New York: F. Watts, 1992.

Margo, Robert A. *Race and Schooling in the South, 1880–1950.* Chicago: University of Chicago Press, 1991.

National Afro-American Museum and Cultural Center. *From Victory to Freedom: The African American Experience: Curriculum Guide, Secondary School Course of Study.* Wilberforce, OH: National Afro-American Museum and Cultural Center, 1991.

Neufeldt, Harvey G., and Leo McGee, eds. *Education of the African American Adult: An Historical Overview.* Westport, CT: Greenwood, 1990.

Pratt, Robert A. *The Color of Their Skin: Education and Race in Richmond, Virginia, 1954–89.* Charlottesville: University of Virginia Press, 1992.

Sachar, Emily. *Shut Up and Let the Lady Teach: A Teacher's Year in a Public School.* New York: Poseidon Press, 1991.

Thompkins, Susie Powers. *Cotton-Patch Schoolhouse.* Tuscaloosa: University of Alabama Press, 1992.

Willie, Charles V., Antoine M. Garibaldi, and Wornie L. Reed, eds. *The Education of African Americans.* Westport, CT: Auburn House/Greenwood Publishing Group, 1991.

Folklore and Folk Culture

Abrahams, Roger D. *Singing the Master: The Emergence of African American Culture in the Plantation South.* New York: Pantheon Books, 1992.

Hall, Gwendolyn Midlo. *Africans in Colonial Louisiana: The Development of Afro-Creole Culture.* Baton Rouge: Louisiana State University Press, 1992.

Hazzard-Gordon, Katrina. *Jookin': The Rise of Social Dance Formation in African-American Culture.* Philadelphia: Temple University Press, 1990.

Hill, James L., ed. *Studies in African and African American Culture.* New York: P. Lang, 1990.

Holloway, Joseph E., ed. *Africanisms in American Culture.* Bloomington: Indiana University Press, 1990.

Njeri, Itabari. *Every Good-Bye Ain't Gone: Family Portraits and Personal Escapades.* New York: Times Books, 1990.

Roberts, John W. *From Trickster to Badman: The Black Folk Hero in Slavery and Freedom.* Philadelphia: University of Pennsylvania Press, 1990.

Spalding, Henry D., comp. and ed. *Encyclopedia of Black Folklore and Humor.* Introduction by J. Mason Brewer. Middle Village, NY: Jonathan David Publishers, 1990.

Sundquist, Eric J. *The Hammers of Creation: Folk Culture in Modern African-American Culture.* Athens: University of Georgia Press, 1992.

Twining, Mary A., and Keith E. Baird, eds. *Sea Island Roots: African Presence in Carolina and Georgia.* Trenton, NJ: Africa World Press, 1991.

General Reference

Asante, Molefi K. *The Historical and Cultural Atlas of African Americans.* New York: Macmillan, 1991.

The Black Resource Guide, 1990–1991 Edition. Washington, DC: Black Resource Guide, Inc., 1991.

Bogle, Donald, ed. *Black Arts Annual, 1988/89.* New York: Garland, 1990.

Donovan, Richard X. *Black Scientists of America.* Portland, OR: National Book Co., 1990.

Fitzpatrick, Sandra, and Maria Godwin. *The Guide to Black Washington: Places and Events of Historical and Cultural Significance in the Nation's Capital.* New York: Hippocrene, 1990.

Furtaw, Julia C., ed. *Black American Information Directory.* 2nd ed., Detroit: Gale Research Inc., 1992.

Hancock, Sybil. *Famous Firsts of Black Americans.* Gretna, LA: Pelican Publishing Co., 1991.

Horton, Carrell Peterson, and Jessie Carney Smith, comps. and eds. *Statistical Record of Black America.* 2nd ed., Detroit: Gale Research Inc., 1991.

Smithsonian Institution. *African and African American Resources at the Smithsonian.* Washington, DC: Smithsonian Institution, 1991.

Southern, Eileen, and Josephine Wright, comps. *African American Traditions in Song, Sermon, Tale, and Dance, 1600s–1920: An Annotated Bibliography of Literature, Collections, and Artworks.* Westport, CT: Greenwood Press, 1990.

Thum, Marcella. *Hippocrene U.S.A. Guide to Black America: A Directory of Historic and Cultural Sites Relating to Black America.* New York: Hippocrene Books, 1992.

Health

Bailey, A. Peter. *The Harlem Hospital Story: 100 Years of Struggle Against Illness.* Richmond, VA: Native Sun Publishers, 1991.

Bailey, Eric J. *Urban African American Health Care.* Lantham, MD: University Press of America, 1991.

The Black Women's Health Book: Speaking for Ourselves. Seattle: Seal Press, 1990.

Duh, Samuel V. *Blacks and AIDS: Genetic or Environmental Causes.* Newbury Park, CA: Sage Publications, 1991.

Health of Black Americans from Post Reconstruction to Integration, 1871–1960: An Annotated Bibliography of Contemporary Sources. Westport, CT: Greenwood Press, 1990.

McBride, David. *From TB to AIDS: Epidemics Among Urban Blacks Since 1900.* Albany: State University of New York Press, 1991.

National Black Health Leadership Directory, 1990–91. Washington, DC: NRW Associates, 1991.

History

The African American Experience: A History. Sharon Harley, Stephen Middleton, and Charlotte Stokes, Consultants. Englewood Cliffs, NJ: Prentice-Hall, 1992.

America, Richard, ed. *The Wealth of Races: The Present Value of Benefits from Past Injustices.* Westport, CT: Greenwood Press, 1991.

Anderson, Eric, and Alfred Moss, Jr., eds. *The Facts of Reconstruction: Essays in Honor of John Hope Franklin.* Baton Rouge: Louisiana State University Press, 1991.

Andrews, George Reid. *Blacks and Whites in Sao Paulo Brazil, 1888–1988.* Madison: University of Wisconsin Press, 1992.

Aptheker, Herbert. *Anti-Racism in U.S. History: The First Hundred Years.* New York: Greenwood Press, 1992.

Aptheker, Herbert. *To Be Free: Pioneering Studies in Afro-American History.* Introduction by John Hope Franklin. New York: Citadel Press, 1991.

Bailey, Richard. *Neither Carpetbaggers Nor Scalawags: Black Officeholders During the Re-*

construction in Alabama. Montgomery, AL: R. Bailey Publishers, 1991.

Beeth, Howard, and Cary E. Wintz, eds. *Black Dixie: Afro-Texan History and Culture in Houston.* College Station, TX: Texas A&M University Press, 1992.

Berlin, Irs, and Philip D. Morgan, eds. *The Slaves' Economy: Independent Production by Slaves in the Americas.* London: F. Cass, 1991.

Berlin, Irs, et. al., eds. *Slaves No More: Three Essays on Emancipation and the Civil War.* New York: Cambridge University Press, 1992.

The Black Abolitionist Papers, Vol. 3: The United States, 1830–1846. Chapel Hill: University of North Carolina Press, 1991.

Boney, F.N., Richard L. Hume, and Rafia Zafar. *God Made Man, Man Made the Slave.* Macon, GA: Mercer University Press, 1990.

Bryan, Patrick. *The Jamaican People, 1880–1902: Race and Social Control.* New York: Macmillan, 1991.

Bush, Barbara. *Slave Women in Caribbean Society, 1650–1838.* Bloomington: University of Indiana Press, 1990.

Campbell, Randolph B. *An Empire for Slavery: The Peculiar Institution in Texas, 1821–1865.* Baton Rouge: Louisiana State University Press, 1991.

Cantor, George. *Historic Landmarks of Black America.* Detroit: Gale Research Inc., 1991.

Cohen, William. *At Freedom Edge: Black Mobility at the Southern Quest for Racial Control, 1861–1915.* Baton Rouge: Louisiana State University Press, 1991.

Cornelius, Janet Duitsman. *"When I Can Read My Title Clear": Literacy, Slavery, and Religion in the Antebellum South.* Columbia: University of South Carolina Press, 1991.

Counter, S. Allen. *North Pole Legacy: Black, White and Eskimo.* Amherst: University of Massachusetts Press, 1991.

Crouch, Berry A. *The Freedmen's Bureau and Black Texans.* Austin: University of Texas Press, 1992.

Davis, Lenwood G. *A Travel Guide to Black Historical Sites and Landmarks in North Carolina.* Winston-Salem, NC: Bandit Books, 1991.

Deromantizing Black History: Critical Essays and Reappraisals. Knoxville: University of Tennessee Press, 1991.

Dillon, Merton L. *Slavery Attacked: Southern Slaves and Their Allies, 1619–1865.* Baton Rouge: Louisiana State University Press, 1990.

Downey, Dennis B., and Raymond M. Hyser. *No Crooked Death: Coatsville, Pennsylvania, and the Lynching of Zachariah Walker.* Champaign: University of Illinois Press, 1991.

Drago, Edmund L., ed. *Broke by the War: Letters of a Slave Trader.* Columbia: University of South Carolina Press, 1991.

Dykstra, Robert. *Bright Radical Star: Black Freedom and White Supremacy on the Hawkeye Frontier.* Cambridge: Harvard University Press, 1993.

Fede, Andrew. *People Without Rights: An Interpretation of the Fundamentals of the Law of Slavery in the U.S. South.* New York: Garland Publishing Co., 1992.

Ferguson, Leland G. *Uncommon Ground: Archaeology and Early African America, 1650–1800.* Washington, DC: Smithsonian Institution Press, 1992.

Finkelman, Paul, ed. *The Age of Jim Crow: Segregation from the End of Reconstruction to the Great Depression.* New York: Garland Publishing Co., 1992. (*Race, Law, and American History, 1760–1990. The African American Experience,* vol. 4.)

Finkelman, Paul, ed. *Emancipation and Reconstruction.* New York: Garland Publishing Co., 1992. (*Race, Law and American History, 1700–1990. The African American Experience,* vol. 3.)

Franklin, Vincent P. *Black Self-Determinism: A Cultural History of African-American Resistance.* 2nd ed., Brooklyn, NY: Lawrence Hill Books, 1992.

Frey, Sylvia. *Water from the Rock: Black Resistance in a Revolutionary Age.* Princeton, NJ: Princeton University Press, 1992.

Gatewood, Willard B. *Aristocrats of Color: The Black Elite, 1880–1920.* Bloomington: Indiana University Press, 1990.

Genovese, Eugene D. *The Slaveholders' Dilemma: Freedom and Progress in Southern Conservative Thought, 1820–1860.* Columbia: University of South Carolina Press, 1992.

Greenberg, Cheryl Lynn. *"Or Does It Explode?": Black Harlem in the Great Depression.* New York: Oxford University Press, 1991.

Hamilton, Kenneth Marvin. *Black Towns and Profit, Promotion and Development in the Trans-Appalachian West, 1877–1915.* Champaign: University of Illinois Press, 1991.

Harley, Sharon. *The African American Experience: A History.* Englewood Cliffs, NJ: Globe, 1992.

Harris, Richard S. *Politics & Prejudice: A History of Chester, Pennsylvania Negroes.* Apache Junction, AZ: Relmo Pubs., 1991.

Harrison, Alfredteen, ed. *Black Exodus: The Great Migration from the American South.* Oxford: University Press of Mississippi, 1991.

Henry, Paget, and Paul Buhle, eds. *C.L.R. James' Caribbean.* Durham, NC: Duke University Press, 1992.

Hornsby, Jr., Alton. *Chronology of African-American History: Significant Events and People from 1619 to the Present.* Detroit: Gale Research Inc., 1991.

Horton, James Oliver. *Free People of Color: Inside the African American Community.* Washington, DC: Smithsonian Institution, 1993.

Inikoroi, Joseph E., and Stanley L. Engerman, eds. *The Atlantic Slave Trade: Effects on Economic Societies, and Peoples in Africa, the Americas and Europe.* Durham, NC: Duke University Press, 1992.

Jackson, Terrance. *Putting It All Together: World Conquest, Global Genocide and African Liberation.* Bronx, NY: AKASA, 1991.

Jones, Howard. *The Red Diary: A Chronological History of Black Americans in Houston and Some Neighboring Harris County Communities-122 Years Later.* Austin, TX: Nortex Press, 1992.

Jones, Norrece T. *Born a Child of Freedom, Yet A Slave: Mechanisms of Control and Strategies of Resistance in Antebellum South Carolina.* Middletown, CT: Wesleyan University Press, 1990.

Jordan, Winthrop. *Tumult and Silence at Second Creek: An Inquiry into a Civil War Slave Conspiracy.* Baton Rouge: Louisiana State University Press, 1993.

Katz, William Loren. *Breaking the Chains: African American Slave Resistance.* New York: Atheneum, 1990.

Lane, Roger. *William Dorsey's Philadelphia and Ours: On the Origins and Future Prospects of Urban Black America.* New York: Oxford University Press, 1991.

Lesko, Kathleen M., ed. *Black Georgetown Remembered: A History of Its Black Community from the Founding of "The Town of George" in 1751 to the Present Day.* Washington, DC: Georgetown University Press, 1991.

Malone, Ann Patton. *Sweet Chariot: Slave Family and Household Structure in Nineteenth Century Louisiana.* Chapel Hill: University of North Carolina Press, 1992.

McLaurin, Melton A. *Celia, a Slave.* Athens: University of Georgia Press, 1991.

McMillen, Sally Gregory. *Southern Women: Black and White in the Old South.* Arlington Heights, IL: Harlan Davidson, 1992.

Meillassaux, Claude. *The Anthropology of Slavery: The Womb of Iron and Gold.* Translated by

Alide Dasnois. Chicago: University of Chicago Press, 1991.

Meyer, Mary K. *Free Blacks in Hartford, Somerset, and Talbort Counties, Maryland.* Mt. Airy, MD: Pipe Creek Publications, 1991.

Middleton, Stephen. *The Black Laws in the Old Northwest: A Documentary History.* New York: Greenwood Press, 1992.

Munford, Clarence J. *The Black Ordeal of Slavery and Slave Trading in the French West Indies, 1625–1715.* Lewiston, ME: Edwin Mellen, 1991.

Nash, Gary B. *Freedom by Degrees: Emancipation in Pennsylvania and Its Aftermath.* New York: Oxford University Press, 1991.

Nash, Gary B. *Race and Revolution.* Madison, WI: Madison House, 1990.

Oakes, James. *Slavery and Freedom: An Interpretation of the Old South.* New York: Knopf, 1990.

Pearson, Edward. *Slave Work and Culture in Town and Country.* Williamsburg, VA: Institute of Early American History and Culture, 1991.

Perdue, Charles L., ed. *Weevils in the Wheat: Interviews with Virginia Ex-Slaves.* Charlottesville: University Press of Virginia, 1992.

Reidy, Joseph. *From Slavery to Agrarian Capitalism in the Cotton Plantation South: Central Georgia, 1800–1880.* Chapel Hill: University of North Carolina Press, 1992.

Richardson, Bonham C. *The Caribbean in the Wide World, 1492–1922.* New York: Cambridge University Press, 1992.

Richter, William L. *Overreached on All Sides: The Freedmen's Bureau Administrators in Texas, 1865–1868.* College Station: Texas A&M University Press, 1991.

Schwartz, Stuart B. *Slaves, Peasants, and Rebels: Reconsidering Brazilian Slavery.* Champaign: University of Illinois Press, 1992.

Schweninger, Loren. *Black Property Owners in the South, 1790–1915.* Champaign: University of Illinois Press, 1990.

Slaughter, Thomas P. *Bloody Dawn: The Christiania Riot and Racial Violence in Antebellum North.* New York: Oxford University Press, 1991.

Solow, Barbara L., ed. *Slavery and the Rise of the Atlantic System.* New York: Cambridge University Press/W.E.B. DuBois Institute for Afro-American Research, 1991.

Stanisland, Martin. *American Intellectuals and African Nationalists; 1955–1970.* New Haven, CT: Yale University Press, 1991.

Stevenson, Lisbeth Gant. *African-American History: Heroes in Hardship.* Cambridge, MA: Cambridgeport Press, 1992.

Stone, Albert E. *The Return of Nat Turner: History, Literature, and Cultural Politics in Sixties America.* Athens: University of Georgia, 1992.

Stone, Frank Andrews. *African American Connecticut: African Origins, New England Roots.* Storrs, CT: Isaac N. Thut World Education Center, 1991.

Terry, Ted. *American Black History: Reference Manual.* Tulsa, OK: Myles Publishing Co., 1991.

Thomas, Richard W. *Life for Us: Building Black Community in Detroit, 1915–1945.* Bloomington: Indiana University Press, 1992.

Thornton, John. *Africa and Africans in the Making of the Atlantic World, 1400–1680.* New York: Cambridge University Press, 1992.

White, Shane. *Somewhat More Independent: The End of Slavery in New York City 1770–1870.* Athens: University of Georgia Press, 1991.

Williams, Jacob C. *Lillie: Black Life in Martins Ferry, Ohio During the 1920s and 1930s.* Ann Arbor, MI: Braun-Brumfield, 1991.

Williams, Lee E. *Post-War Riots in America, 1919 and 1946: How the Pressures of War Exacerbated American Urban Tensions to the Breaking Points.* Lewiston, NY: E. Mellen, 1991.

Language, Literature, and Drama

Babb, Valerie Melissa. *Ernest Gaines.* Boston: Twayne/G.K. Hall, 1991.

Bailey, Guy, Natalie Maynor, and Patricia Cukor-Avila, eds. *The Emergence of Black English: Text and Commentary.* Philadelphia: J. Benjamins Publishing Co., 1991.

Baker, Houston A., and Patricia Redmond, eds. *Afro-American Literary Study in the 1990s.* Chicago: University of Chicago Press, 1990.

Baraka, Imamu Amiri. *The Leroi Jones/Amiri Baraka Reader.* Edited William J. Harris. New York: Thunder's Mouth Press, 1991.

Barksdale, Richard K. *Praisesong of Survival: Lectures and Essays, 1957–1989.* Introduction by R. Baxter Miller. Urbana: University of Illinois, 1992.

Bassett, John E. *Harlem in Review: Critical Reactions to Black American Writers, 1917–1939.* Selinsgrove, PA: Susquehanna University Press, 1992.

Benitoz-Rojo, Antonio. *The Repeating Island: The Caribbean and the Postmodern Perspective.* Durham, NC: Duke University Press, 1992.

Blackshire-Belay, Carol Aisha, ed. *Language and Literature in the African American Imagination.* Westport, CT: Greenwood Press, 1992.

Bloom, Harold, ed. *Bigger Thomas.* New York: Chelsea House, 1990.

Brown, Stewart, ed. *The Art of Derek Walcott.* UK: Seren Books, 1992. (Dist. by Dufour Editions, Inc.)

Busby, Mark. *Ralph Ellison.* Boston: Twayne/G.K. Hall, 1991.

Butler, Robert. *Native Son: The Emergence of a New Black Hero.* Boston: Twayne/G.K. Hall, 1991.

Cartey, Wilfred. *Whispers from the Caribbean: I Going Away, I Going Home.* Los Angeles: University of California, Los Angeles, Center for Afro-American Studies, 1991.

DeJongh, James. *Vicious Modernism: Black Harlem and the Literary Imagination.* New York: Cambridge University Press, 1990.

Dieke, Ikenna. *The Primordial Image: African, Afro-American, and Caribbean Mythopoetic Text.* New York: P. Lang, 1991.

Draper, James P., ed. *Black Literature Criticism: Excerpts from Criticism of the Most Significant Works of Black Authors over the Past 200 Years.* 3 vols., Detroit: Gale Research Inc., 1992.

Edwards, Walter F., and Donald Winford, eds. *Verb Phrase Patterns in Black English and Creole.* Detroit: Wayne State University Press, 1991.

Fabre, Michel. *Richard Wright: Books and Writers.* Oxford: University Press of Mississippi, 1990.

Gates, Henry Louis, Jr. *Loose Canons: Notes on the Culture Wars.* New York: Oxford University Press, 1992.

Hamalian, Leo, and James V. Hatch, eds. *The Roots of African American Drama: An Anthology of Early Plays, 1858–1938.* Detroit: Wayne State University Press, 1991.

Hord, Fred L. *Reconstructing Memory: Black Literary Criticism.* Chicago: Third World Press, 1991.

Johnson, Dianne. *Telling Tales: The Pedagogy and Power of African American Literature for Youth.* New York: Greenwood Press, 1990.

Jones, Gayl. *Liberating Voices: Oral Tradition in African American Literature.* Cambridge, MA: Harvard University Press, 1991.

Joseph, Margaret Paul. *Caliban in Exile: The Outsider in Caribbean Fiction.* New York: Greenwood Press, 1992.

Kinnamon, Kenneth, ed. *New Essays on Native Son.* New York: Cambridge University Press, 1990.

Metzger, Linda, Hal May, Deborah A. Straub, and Susan M. Trosky, eds. *Black Writers.* Detroit: Gale Research Inc., 1989.

Mikolyzk, Thomas A. comp. *Langston Hughes: A Bio-Bibliography.* Westport, CT: Greenwood Press, 1990.

Miller, R. Baxter. *The Art and Imagination of Langston Hughes.* Lexington: University of Kentucky Press, 1990.

Morrison, Toni. *Playing in the Dark: Whiteness and the Literary Imagination.* Cambridge, MA: Harvard University Press, 1992.

Newby, James Edwards. *Black Authors: A Selected Annotated Bibliography.* New York: Garland, 1990.

Ntire, Daphne Williams, ed., and comp. *Roots and Blossoms; African American Plays for Today.* Troy, MI: Bedford Publishers, 1991.

Peterson, Bernard L. *Early Black American Playwrights and Dramatic Writers: A Biographical Dictionary and Catalog of Plays, Films and Broadcasting Scripts.* Westport, CT: Greenwood Press, 1990.

Rajiv, Sudhi. *Forms of Black Consciousness.* New York: Advent Books, 1992.

Rollock, Barbara. *Black Authors and Illustrators of Children's Books: A Biographical Dictionary.* 2nd ed., New York: Garland, 1992.

Smith, Valerie. *Self-Discovery and Authority in Afro-American Narrative.* Cambridge, MA; Harvard University Press, 1991.

Stepto, Robert B. *From Behind the Veil: A Study of Afro-American Narrative.* 2nd ed., Urbana: University of Illinois Press, 1991.

Thurman, Wallace. *Infants of the Spring.* With foreword by Amritjit Singh. Boston: Northeastern University Press, 1992.

Toomer, Jean. *Essentials.* Edited by Rudolph P. Bird. Athens: University of Georgia Press, 1991.

Washington, Mary Helen, ed. *Memory of Kin: Stories About Family by Black Writers.* New York: Doubleday, 1991.

Wilson, August. *Two Trains Running.* New York: Dutton, 1992.

Media, Publishing, and Book Collecting

Chester, Thomas Morris. *Thomas Morris Chester, Black Civil War Correspondent: His Dispatches from the Virginia Front.* With Biographical Essay and Notes by R.J.M. Blackett. New York: DeCapo Press, 1991.

Dates, Jannette L., and William Barlow. *Split Image: African Americans in the Mass Media.* Washington, DC: Howard University Press, 1990.

Hill, George. *Black Women in Television: An Illustrated History and Bibliography.* New York: Garland Publishing Co., 1990.

Joyce, Donald Franklin. *Black Book Publishers in the United States: A Historical Dictionary of the Press, 1817–1990.* Westport, CT: Greenwood Press, 1991.

Schuyler, George S. *Black Empire: George S. Schuyler Writing As Samuel I. Brooks.* Edited by Robert A. Hill and R. Kent Rasmussen. Boston: Northeastern University, 1991.

Silk, Catherine, and John Silk. *Racism and Anti-Racism in American Popular Culture: Portrayals of African-Americans in Fiction and Film.* Manchester, UK: Manchester University Press, 1990. (Dist. by St. Martin's Press)

Sinnette, Elinor Des Verney, W. Paul Coates, and Thomas C. Battle, eds. *Black Bibliophiles and Collectors: Preservers of Black History.* Washington, DC: Howard University Press, 1990.

Military Participation

Collum, Danny Duncan, ed. *African Americans in the Spanish Civil War: "This Ain't Ethiopia, but It'll Do".* New York: G.K. Hall, 1992.

Cox, Clinton. *Undying Glory: The Story of the Massachusetts 54th Regiment.* New York: Scholastic, Inc., 1991.

Donaldson, Gary. *The History of African-Americans in the Military: Double V.* Malabar, FL: Krieger Publishing Co., 1991.

Gooding, James Henry. *On the Altar of Freedom: A Black Soldier's Civil War Letters from the Front.* Edited by Virginia Matzke Adams. Amherst: University of Massachusetts Press, 1991.

Johnson, Charles. *African American Soldiers in the National Guard: Recruitment and Deploy-*

ment During Peacetime and War. New York: Greenwood Press, 1992.

Redkey, Edwin S., ed. *A Grand Army of Black Men: Letters from African-American Soldiers in the Union Army.* New York: Cambridge University Press, 1992.

Music

Allen, Ray. *Singing in the Spirit: African-American Sacred Quartets in New York City.* Philadelphia: University of Pennsylvania Press, 1991.

Boggs, Vernon W. *Salsiology: Afro-Cuban Music and the Evolution of Salsa in New York City.* Westport, CT: Greenwood Press, 1992.

Booth, Stanley. *Rhythm Oil: A Journey Through the Music of the American South.* New York: Pantheon, 1991.

Cantor, Louis. *Wheelin' on Beale.* Foreword by B.B. King. New York: Pharos, 1992.

Costello, Mark, and David Foster Wallace. *Signifying Rappers: Rap and Race in the Urban Present.* New York: Ecco Press, 1990.

Donovan, Richard X. *Black Musicians of America.* Portland, OR: National Book Co., 1991.

Finn, Julio. *The Bluesman: The Musical Heritage of Black Men and Women in the Americas.* New York: Interlink Books, 1991.

Floyd, Samuel A., ed. *Black Music in the Harlem Renaissance: A Collection of Essays.* Westport, CT: Greenwood Press, 1990.

Friedwall, Will. *Jazz Singing: America's Great Voices from Bessie Smith to Bebop and Beyond.* New York: Scribner's, 1990.

Harris, Michael W. *The Rise of Gospel Blues: The Music of Thomas Andrew Dorsey in the Urban Church.* New York: Oxford University Press, 1992.

Horne, Aaron, comp. *Keyboard Music of Black Composers: A Bibliography.* Westport, CT: Greenwood Press, 1992.

Horne, Aaron, comp. *String Music of Black Composers: A Bibliography.* Westport, CT: Greenwood Press, 1991.

Horne, Aaron. comp. *Woodwind Music of Black Composers* Westport, CT: Greenwood Press, 1990.

Jackson, John A. *Big Beat Heat: Alan Freed and the Early Years of Rock & Roll.* New York: Schirmer/Macmillan, 1991.

Merrill, Hugh. *The Blues Route.* New York: Morrow, 1990.

Morgan, Thomas L. *From Cakewalk to Concert Hall: An Illustrated History of African American Popular Music from 1895 to 1930.* Washington, DC: Elliott & Clark Publishers, 1992.

Morton, David C. and Charles K. Wolfe. *DeFord Bailey: A Black Star in Early Country Music.* Knoxville: University of Tennessee Press, 1991.

Peretti, Burton W. *The Creation of Jazz: Music, Race and Culture in Urban America.* Urbana: University of Illinois Press, 1992.

Perry, Frank. *Afro-American Vocal Music: A Select Guide to Fifteen Composers.* Berrien Springs, MD: Vande Verde Publishers, 1991.

Porter, Lewis, ed. *A Lester Young Reader.* Washington, DC: Smithsonian Institution Press, 1991.

Price, Sammy. *What Do They Want: A Jazz Autobiography.* Edited by Caroline Richmond. Chronological discography compiled by Bob Weir. Urbana: University of Illinois Press, 1990.

Roach, Hildred. *Black American Music Past and Present: Pan-African Composers.* 2nd ed., Malabar, FL: Kruger, 1992.

Rosenthal, David H. *Hard Bop: Jazz and Black Music, 1955–1965.* New York: Oxford University Press, 1992.

Scott, Frank. *The Down Home Guide to the Blues.* Pennington, NJ: A Capella Books, 1990.

Spencer, Jon Michael, ed. *The Emergency Black and the Emergence of Rap.* Durham: Duke University Press, 1991.

Spencer, Jon Michael, ed. *Sacred Music of the Secular City: From Blues to Rap*. Durham: Duke University Press, 1992.

Story, Rosalyn. *And So I Sing: African American Divas of Opera and Concert*. New York: Warner Books, 1990.

Tate, Greg. *Flyboy in the Buttermilk: Essays on Contemporary America*. New York: Simon and Schuster, 1992.

Turner, Patricia. *Dictionary of Afro-American Performers: 78 RPM and Cylinder Recordings of Opera, Choral Music and Song, ca. 1900–1949*. New York: Garland, 1990.

Walker-Hill, Helen. *Piano-Music by Black Women Composers: A Catalogue of Solo and Ensemble Works*. New York: Greenwood Press, 1992.

Wright, Josephine, and Samuel A. Floyd, Jr., eds. *New Perspectives on Music: Essays in Honor of Eileen Southern*. Warren, MI: Harmonie Park Press, 1992.

Performing Arts

Adamczke, Alice J. *Black Dance: An Annotated Bibliography*. New York: Garland Publishing Co., 1990.

Ely, Melvin Patrick. *The Adventures of Amos 'n' Andy: A Social History of an American Phenomenon*. New York: Free Press, 1991.

Gray, John, comp. *Black Theatre and Performance: A PanAfrican Bibliography*. Westport, CT: Greenwood Press, 1990.

Gray, John, comp. *Blacks in Film and Television: A Pan-African Bibliography of Films, Filmmakers, and Performers*. Westport, CT: Greenwood Press, 1990.

Hansberry, Lorraine. *A Raisin in the Sun: The Unfilmed Original Screenplay*. Edited by Robert Nemiroff. Foreword by Jewell Gres. Afterword by Spike Lee. New York: Dutton, 1992.

Hughes, Langston, and Zora Neale Hurston. *Mule Bone: A Comedy of Negro Life*. Edited by George H. Bass and Henry L. Gates. New York: Harper Collins, 1991.

Jhally, Sut, and Justin Lewis. *Enlightened Racism: The Cosby Show, Audiences, and the Myth of the American Dream*. Boulder, CO: Westview Press, 1992.

Jones, G. William. *Black Cinema Treasurey: Lost and Found*. Denton, TX: University of North Texas Press, 1991.

Klotman, Phyllis Rauch, ed. *Screenplays of the African American Experience*. Bloomington: Indiana University Press, 1991.

Mapp, Edward. *Directory of Blacks in the Performing Arts*. 2nd ed., Metuchen, NJ: Scarecrow Press, 1990.

Politics

Barker, Lucius J., ed. *Ethnic Politics and Civil Liberties*. New Brunswick, NJ: Transaction Books, 1992.

Clavel, Pierre, and Wim Wiewel, eds. *Harold Washington and the Neighborhoods: Progressive City Government in Chicago, 1983–1987*. New Brunswick, NJ: Rutgers University Press, 1991.

Gomes, Ralph C., and Linda Faye Williams eds. *From Exclusion to Inclusion: The Long Struggle for African American Political Power*. Westport, CT: Greenwood Press, 1992.

Henry, Charles P. *Culture and African American Politics*. Bloomington: Indiana University Press, 1990.

Henry, Charles P. *Jesse Jackson: The Search for Common Ground*. Oakland, CA: Black Scholar Press, 1990.

Jennings, James. *The Politics of Black Empowerment: The Transformation of Black Activism in Urban America*. Detroit: Wayne State University Press, 1992.

Joint Center for Political and Economic Studies. *Black Elected Officials: A National Roster*. Washington, DC: Joint Center for Political and Economic Studies Press, 19–.

Kimball, Penn. *Keep Hope Alive: Super Tuesday and Jesse Jackson's 1988 Campaign for the Presidency.* Washington, DC: Joint Center for Political and Economic Studies, 1992.

Lawson, Steven. *Running for Freedom: Civil Rights and Black Politics in America Since 1941.* Philadelphia: Temple University Press, 1990.

Marable, Manning. *The Crisis of Color and Democracy: Essays on Race, Class and Power.* Monroe, ME: Common Courage Press, 1992.

McCartney, John T. *Black Power Ideologies: An Essay in African American Political Thought.* Philadelphia: Temple University Press, 1992.

Natanson, Nicholas. *The Black Image in the New Deal: The Politics of FSA.* Knoxville: University of Tennessee Press, 1992.

Orfield, Gar, and Carole Ashkinaze. *The Closing Door: Conservative Policy and Black Opportunity.* Chicago: University of Chicago Press, 1991.

Parker, Frank R. *Black Votes Count: Political Empowerment in Mississippi After 1965.* Chapel Hill: University of North Carolina Press, 1990.

Rees, Matthew. *From the Deck to the Sea: Blacks and the Republican Party.* Wakefield, NH: Longwood Press, 1991.

Rivlin, Gar. *Fire on the Prairie: Chicago's Harold Washington and the Politics of Race.* New York: Holt, 1992.

Van DeBurg, William L. *New Day in Babylon: The Black Power Movement and American Culture.* Chicago: University of Chicago Press, 1992.

Race Relations

Brady, Paul L. *A Certain Blindness: A Black Family's Quest for the Promise of America.* Atlanta: ALP Publishers, 1990.

Brooks, Roy L. *Rethinking the American Race Problem.* Berkeley: University of California, 1991.

Collier, Peter, ed. *Second Thoughts About Race in America.* Lanham, MD: Madison Books, 1991.

Crouch, Stanley. *Notes of a Hanging Judge: Essays and Reviews.* New York: Oxford University Press, 1990.

Davis, F. James. *Who Is Black: One Nation's Definition.* University Park: Pennsylvania State University Press, 1991.

DeSantis, John. *For the Color of His Skin: The Murder of Yusuf Hawkins and the Trial of Bensonhurst.* Introduction by Alan M. Dershowitz. New York: Pharos Books, 1991.

Essed, Philomena. *Understanding Racism: An Interdisciplinary Theory.* Newbury Park, CA: Sage, 1991.

Hacker, Andrew. *Two Nations: Black and White, Separate, Hostile, Unequal.* New York: Scribner's, 1992.

Horowitz, Irving Louis. *Daydreams and Nightmares: Reflections on a Harlem Childhood.* Jackson: University Press of Mississippi, 1990.

Hynes, Charles J., and Bob Drury. *Incident at Howard Beach: The Case for Murder.* New York: Putnam, 1990.

Leiman, Melvin M. *Racism in the U.S.A.: History and Political Economy.* Concord, MA: Paul & Co., 1992.

Lewis, Earl. *In Their own Interests: Race, Class, and Power in Twentieth-Century Nolf, Virginia.* Berkeley: University of California Press, 1991.

McFadden, Robert, et. al. *Outrage: The Story Behind the Tawana Brawley Hoax.* New York: Bantam, 1990.

Pemberton, Gayle. *The Hottest Water in Chicago: One Family, Race, Time and American Culture.* Winchester, MA: Faber & Faber, 1992.

Perlmutter, Philip. *Divided We Fall: A History of Ethnic, Religious, and Racial Prejudice in America.* Ames: Iowa State University Press, 1992.

Rasberry, William. *Looking Backward at Us.* Jackson: University Press of Mississippi, 1991.

Salzman, Jack, ed. *Bridges and Boundaries: African Americans and American Jews.* New York: Braziller, 1992.

Steele, Shelby. *The Contest of Our Character: A New Vision of Race in America.* New York: St. Martin's Press, 1990.

Stepan, Nancy Leys. *The Hour of Eugenics: Race, Gender, and Nation.* Ithaca, NY: Cornell University Press, 1991.

Terkel, Studs. *Race: How Blacks and Whites Think and Feel About the American Obsession.* New York: New Press/Norton, 1992.

Welch, Susan, and Lee Sigelman. *Black America's Views of Racial Equality: The Dream Deferred.* New York: Cambridge University Press, 1991.

Zegeye, Abebe, ed. *Exploitation and Exclusion: Race and Class in Contemporary U.S. Society.* London: Hans Zell Publishers, 1991.

Zweigenhaft, Richard L., and G. William Domhoff. *Blacks in the White Establishment: A Study of Race and Class in America.* New Haven, CT: Yale University Press, 1991.

Religion and Philosophy

Baer, Hans, and Merrill Singer. *African-American Religion in the Twentieth Century: Varieties of Protest and Accommodation.* Knoxville: University of Tennessee, 1992.

Davis, Lenwood G. *Daddy Grace: An Annotated Bibliography.* New York: Greenwood Press, 1992.

Dvorak, Katherine L. *An African-American Exodus: the Segregation of Southern Churches.* With preface by Jerald C. Brauer. Brooklyn, NY: Carlson Publishing Co., 1991.

Harris, Leonard, ed. *The Philosophy of Alain Locke.* Philadelphia: Temple University Press, 1990.

Haynes, Lemuel. *Black Preacher to White America: the Collected Writings of Lemuel Haynes, 1774–1833.* Edited by Richard Newman. New York: Carlson Publishing Co., 1990.

Hopkins, Dwight N., and George C.L. Cummings, eds. *Cut Loose Your Stammering Tongue: Black Theology in the Slave Narratives.* Maryknoll, NY: Orbis Books, 1991.

Howard, Victor B. *Conscience and Slavery: the Evangelistic Calvinistic Domestic Missions, 1837–1861.* Kent, OH: Kent State University Press, 1990.

Irvin, Dona L. *The Unsung Heart of Black America: A Middle-Class Church at Midcentury.* Columbia: University of Missouri Press, 1992.

Jacobs, Claude F., and Andrew J. Kaslow. *The Spiritual Churches of New Orleans: Origins, Beliefs and Rituals of an African-American Religion.* Knoxville: University of Tennessee Press, 1991.

Johnson, John L. *Black Biblical Heritage.* Nashville: Winston-Derek Publishers, 1990.

Lincoln, C. Eric, and Lawrence H. Mamiya. *The Black Church in the American Experience.* Durham, NC: Duke University Press, 1990.

Martin, Sandy D. *Black Baptists and African Missions: the Origins of a Movement, 1880–1915.* Macon, GA: Mercer University Press, 1990.

Ochs, Stephen J. *Desegregating the Altar: The Josephites and the Struggle for Black Priests, 1871–1960.* Baton Rouge: Louisiana State University Press, 1990.

Payne, Wardell J., ed. *Directory of African American Religious Bodies: A Compendium by the Howard University School of Divinity.* Prepared under the auspices of the Research Center on Black Religious Bodies, Howard University School of Divinity. Washington, DC: Howard University Press, 1991.

Seymour, Robert E. *Whites Only: A Pastor's Retrospective on Signs of a New South.* Valley Forge, PA: Judson Press, 1991.

Spencer, Jon Michael. *Black Hymnody: A Hymnological History of the African-American Church.* Knoxville: University of Tennessee Press, 1992.

Spencer, Jon Michael. *Protest and Praise: Sacred Music of Black Religion.* Minneapolis: Augsburg Fortress Publishers, 1990.

Walker, Theodore, Jr. *Empower the People: Social Ethics for the African-American Church.* Maryknoll, NY: Orbis Books, 1991.

Walker, Wyatt Tee. *Spirits That Dwell in Deep Woods III: The Prayer and Praise Hymns of the Black Religious Experience.* New York: Martin Luther King Press, 1991.

Wood, Forrest G. *The Arrogance of Faith: Christianity and Race in America from the Colonial Era to the Twentieth Century.* New York: Knopf, 1990.

Sociology and Psychology

Andersen, Margaret L. *Race, Class and Gender: An Anthology.* Belmont, CA: Wadsworth Publishing Co., 1992.

Anderson, Elijah. *Streetwise: Race, Class and Social Change in an Urban Community.* Chicago: University of Chicago Press, 1990.

Baer, Hans, and Yvonne Jones, eds. *African Americans in the South: Issues of Race, Class and Gender.* Athens: University of Georgia Press, 1992.

Benjamin, Lois. *The Black Elite: Facing the Color Line in the Twentieth Century.* Chicago: Nelson-Hall, 1991.

Billingsley, Andrew. *Climbing Jacob's Ladder: The Future of the African-American Family.* New York: Simon and Schuster, 1991.

Blackwell, James Edward. *The Black Community: Diversity and Unity.* 3rd ed., New York: Harper Collins, 1991.

Bowser, Benjamin, ed. *Black Male Adolescents: Parenting and Education in Community Context.* Latham, MD: University Press of America, 1991.

Consortium for Research on Black Adolescence Staff and Patricia Bell-Scott. *Black Adolescence: Current Issues and Annotated Bibliography.* Boston: G.K. Hall, 1990.

Edelman, Marian Wright. *The Measure of Our Success: A Letter to My Children and Yours.* Boston: Beacon Press, 1992.

Hay, Fred J. *African-American Community Studies from North America. A Classified, Annotated Bibliography.* New York: Garland, 1991.

Hopson, Darlene, and Derek Hopson. *Different and Wonderful: Raising Black Children in a Race Conscious Society.* New York: Simon and Schuster, 1992.

Jones, Howard, and Wanda Jones. *Heritage and Hope: The Legacy and Future of the Black Family in America.* Wheaton, IL: Victor Books, 1992.

Kunjufu, Jawanza. *Countering the Conspiracy to Destroy Black Boys.* Chicago: African American Images, 1990.

Leigh, Wilhelmina A., ed. *The Housing Status of Black Americans.* New Brunswick, NJ: Transaction Books, 1992.

Lemann, Nicholas. *The Promised Land: The Great Black Migration and How It Changed America.* New York: Knopf, 1991.

Platat, Anthony M. *E. Franklin Frazier Reconsidered.* New Brunswick, NJ: Rutgers University Press, 1991.

Trotter, Joe William, ed. *The Great Migration in Historical Perspective: New Dimensions of Race, Class and Gender.* Bloomington: Indiana University Press, 1991.

Sports

Cooper, Michael L. *Playing America's Game: The Story of Negro League Baseball.* New York: Lodestar Books, 1993.

Page, James A. *Black Olympian Medalists.* Englewood, CO: Libraries Unlimited, 1991.

Women

Alexander, Adele Logan. *Free Women of Color in Rural Georgia, 1789–1879.* Fayetteville: University of Arkansas Press, 1991.

Baker, Houston A. *Working of the Spirit: The Poetics of Afro-American Women's Writings.* Chicago: University of Chicago Press, 1991.

The Black Women Oral History Project. *Guide to the Transcripts.* Edited by Ruth E. Hill. Westport, CT: Meckler, 1991.

Braxton, Joanne M. *Black Women Writing Autobiography: A Tradition Within a Tradition.* Philadelphia: Temple University Press, 1990.

Braxton, Joanne M., and Andree Nicola McLaughlin, eds. *Wild Women in the Whirlwind: Afro-American Culture and the Contemporary Literary Renaissance.* New Brunswick, NJ: Rutgers University Press, 1990.

Brown, Karen McCarthy. *Mama Lola: A Voodoo Priestess in Brooklyn.* Berkeley, University of California Press, 1991.

Brown-Guillory, Elizabeth, ed., and comp. *Wines in the Wilderness: Plays by African American Women from the Harlem Renaissance to the Present.* Westport, CT: Greenwood Press, 1990.

Bundles, A'Lelia Perry. *Madam C. J. Walker.* New York: Chelsea House, 1991.

Busby, Margaret, ed. *Daughters of Africa: An International Anthology of Words and Writings by Women of African Descent; From the Ancient World to Present.* New York: Pantheon, 1992.

Butler-Evans, Elliott. *Race, Gender, and Desire: Narrative Strategies in the Fiction of Toni Cade Bambara, Toni Morrison, and Alice Walker.* Philadelphia: Temple University Press, 1990.

Caraway, Nancie. *Segregated Sisterhood: Racism and the Politics of American Feminism.* Knoxville: University of Tennessee Press, 1991.

Celsi, Teresa N. *Rosa Parks and the Montgomery Bus Boycott.* Brookfield, CT: Millbrook Press, 1991.

Crawford, Vicki L., Jacqueline Anne Reese, and Barbara Woods, eds. *Women in the Civil Rights Movement: Trailblazers and Torchbears, 1941–1965.* Brooklyn, NY: Carlson Publishing Co., 1990. (*Black Women in United States History,* vol. 16.)

Davis, Michael D. *Black American Women in Olympic Track and Field: A Complete Illustrated Reference.* Jefferson, NC: McFarland, 1992.

Gates, Henry Louis, Jr. *Reading Black, Reading Feminist.* New York: Meridan, 1991.

Glassman, Steve, and Kathryn Lee Seidel, eds. *Zora in Florida.* Gainesville: University Presses of Florida, 1991.

Guy-Sheftall, Beverly. *Daughters of Sorrow: Attitudes Toward Black Women.* New York: Carlson Publishing Co., 1990. (*Black Women in United States History,* vol. 11.)

Harris, Trudier. *Fiction and Folklore: The Novels of Toni Morrison.* Knoxville: University of Tennessee Press, 1991.

Hine, Darlene Clark, ed. *Black Women in American History, From Colonial Times Through the Nineteenth Century.* Brooklyn, NY: Carlson Publishing Co., 1990.

Hooks, Bell. *Black Looks: Race and Representation.* Boston: South End Press, 1992.

Ihle, Elizabeth L., ed. *Black Women in Higher Education: An Anthology of Essays, Studies and Documents.* New York: Garland Publishing Co., 1992.

Jackson, Carlton. *Hattie: The Life of Hattie McDaniel.* Lantham, MD: Madison Books, 1990.

Jones, Adrienne Lash. *Jane Edna Hunter: A Case Study of Black Leadership.* Brooklyn, NY: Carlson Publishing Co., 1990. (*Black Women in United States History,* vol. 12)

Jones, Beverly Washington. *Quest for Equality: The Life and Writing of Mary Eliza Church Terrell, 1863–1954.* Brooklyn, NY: Carlson Publishing Co., 1990. (*Black Women in United States History,* vol. 13.)

Kent, George E. *A Life of Gwendolyn Brooks.* Lexington: University of Kentucky Press, 1990.

King, Joyce Elaine, and Carolyn Ann Mitchell. *Black Mothers to Sons: Juxtaposing African American Literature and the Social Practice.* New York: Peter Lang, 1990.

Kubitschek, Missy Dehn. *Claiming the Heritage: African-American Women Novelists and History.* Oxford: University Press of Mississippi, 1991.

Mabalia, Dorethea Drummond, *Toni Morrison's Developing Class Consciousness.* Cranbury, NJ: Susquehanna University Press/Associated University Presses, 1991.

Morton, Patricia. *Disfigured Images: The Historical Assault on Afro-American Women.* Westport, CT: Greenwood Press, 1991.

Nathiri, N.Y., ed. *Zora! Zora Neale Hurston: A Woman and Her Community.* Orlando, FL: Sentinel Books, 1991.

Neverdon-Morton, Cynthia. *Afro-American Women of the South and the Advancement of the Race, 1895–1925.* Knoxville: University of Tennessee Press, 1990.

Otfinoski, Steven. *Marian Wright Edelman—Defender of Children's Rights.* New York: Rosen Publishing Group, 1991.

Reckley, Ralph. *Twentieth Century Black Women in Print: Essays.* Acton, MA: Copley Publishers, 1991.

Roses, Lorraine Elena, and Ruth Elizabeth Randolph. *Harlem Renaissance and Beyond: Literary Biographies of 100 Black Women Writers, 1900–1945.* Boston: G.K. Hall, 1990.

Salem, Dorothy. *To Better Our World: Black Women in Organized Reform.* Brooklyn, NY: Carlson Publishing Co., 1990. (*Black Women in United States History*, vol. 14.)

Samuels, Wilfred D., and Clenora Hudson-Weems. *Toni Morrison.* Boston: G.K. Hall, 1990.

Scott, Kesho Yvonne. *The Habit of Surviving: Black Women's Strategies for Life.* New Brunswick, NJ: Rutgers University Press, 1991.

Smith, Jesse Carney, ed. *Notable Black American Women.* Detroit: Gale Research Inc., 1991.

Smith, Rita Webb, and Tony Chapelle. *The Woman Who Took Back Her Streets: One Woman Fights the Drug Wars and Rebuilds Her Community.* Far Hill, NJ: New Horizon, 1991.

Thompson, Mildred I. *Ida B. Wells-Barnett: An Exploratory Study of An American Black Woman, 1893–1930.* Brooklyn, NY: Carlson Publishing Co., 1990. (*Black Women in United States History*, vol. 15)

Walker, Melissa. *Down From the Mountaintop: Black Women's Novels in the Wake of the Civil Rights Movement, 1966–1989.* New Haven, CT: Yale University Press, 1991.

Walker, Robbie Jean, ed. *The Rhetoric of Struggle: Public Addresses by African American Women.* New York: Garland Publishing Co., 1992.

Werner, Craig. *Black American Women Novelists: An Annotated Bibliography.* Englewood Cliffs, NJ: Salem Press, 1990.

Williams, Constance Willard. *Black Teenage Mothers: Pregnancy and Child Rearing from Their Perspective.* Lexington, MA: Lexington Books, 1991.

Woody, Bette. *Black Women in the Workplace: Impacts of Structural Change in the Economy.* Westport, CT: Greenwood Press, 1992.

Yee, Shirley J. *Black Women Abolitionists: A Study in Activism, 1828–1860.* Knoxville: University of Tennessee Press, 1992.

NAMES AND ADDRESSES OF PUBLISHERS OF BOOKS WHICH APPEAR IN THIS BIBLIOGRAPHY

A

A cappella Books, PO Box 380, Pennington, NJ 08534, Tel.: (609)737-6525.

ABC-Clio, Inc., PO Box 1911, Santa Barbara, CA 93116-1911, Tel.: (800)422-2546.

Harry N. Abrams, Inc., 100 5th Ave., New York, NY 10011, Tel.: (800)345-1359.

AKASA Press, 2440-10 Hunter Ave., Ste. lOG, Bronx, NY 10475, Tel.: (212)671-9639.

Advent Books, Inc., 141 E. 44th St., Ste. 511, New York, NY 10017, Tel.: (212)697-0887.

Africa World Press, PO Box 1892, Trenton, NJ 08607, Tel.: (609)771-1666.

African Studies Association, Emory University, Credit Union Bldg., Atlanta, GA 30322, Tel.: (404)329-6410.

Algonquin Books, PO Box 2225, Chapel Hill, NC 27515, Tel.: (919)933-0108.

American Enterprise Institute for Public Policy Research, 1150 17th St. NW, Washington, DC 20036, Tel.: (202)862-5800.

Apt Books, Inc., 141 E. 44th St., Ste. 511, New York, NY 10017, Tel.: (212)697-0887.

Associated University Presses, 440 Forsgate Dr., Cranbury, NJ 08512, Tel.: (609)655-4770.

Atheneum, c/o MacMillan Publishing Co., 866 3rd Ave., New York, NY 10022, Tel.: (800)257-5755.

B

Backwards & Backwards Press, 7561 Pearl Rd., Cleveland, OH 44130, Tel.: (216)243-5335.

Richard Bailey, Box 1264, Montgomery, AL 36102, Tel.: (205)271-6565.

Bandit Books, Inc., PO Box 11721, Winston-Salem, NC 27106, Tel.: (919)785-7414.

Bantam Books, 666 5th Ave., New York, NY 10103, Tel.: (212)765-6500.

Barez Publishing Co., 8690 Aero Dr., Ste. M-332, San Diego, CA 92123-1734, Tel.: (800)247-5900.

Beacon Press, 25 Beacon St., Boston, MA 02108, Tel.: (617)742-2110.

Bedford Arts/Corcoran Gallery of Art, 301 Brannon St., Ste. 410, San Francisco, CA 94107, Tel.: (415)882-7870.

Bedford Publishers, Inc., 779 Kirts, Troy, MI 48084, Tel.: (313)362-0369.

John Benjamins North America, Inc., 821 Bethlehem Pike, Philadelphia, PA 19118, Tel.: (215)836-1200.

Black Entrepreneurs Press, 4502 S. Congress Ave., Ste. 254, Austin, TX 78744, Tel.: (512)444-9962.

The Black Resources Guide, Inc., 501 Oneida Pl. NW, Washington, DC 20011, Tel.: (202)291-4373.

George Braziller, Inc., 60 Madison Ave., Ste. 1001, New York, NY 10010, Tel.: (212)889-0909.

British American Publishing Ltd., 19 British American Blvd., Latham, NY 12148, Tel.: (518)786-6000.

C

Calyx Books, PO Box B, Corvalis, OR 97339, Tel.: (503)753-9384.

Cambridge University Press, 40 W. 20th St., New York, NY 10011, Tel.: (212)924-3900.

Cambridgeport Press, 15 Chalk St., Cambridge, MA 02139, Tel.: (617)497-4437.

Carlson Publishing Co., 52 Remsen St., Brooklyn, NY 11201, Tel.: (718)875-7460.

Carol Publishing Group, 600 Madison Ave., New York, NY 10022, Tel.: (212)486-2200.

Carroll & Graf Publishers, Inc., 260 5th Ave., New York, NY 10001, Tel.: (212)889-8772.

The Center for African-Art, 560 Broadway, Ste. 206, New York, NY 10012-3945, Tel.: (212)966-1313.

Charro Books Co., Inc., 29777 Telegraph Rd., No. 2500, Southfield, MI 48034, Tel.: (313)356-0950.

Chelsea House Publishers, 95 Madison Ave., New York, NY 10011, Tel.: (212)683-4400.

Christian Reformed World Missions, 2850 Kalamazoo SE, Grand Rapids, MI 49560.

Citadel Press, c/o Carol Publishing Group, 600 Madison Ave., New York, NY 10022, Tel.: (212)486-2220.

Adam Randolph Collings, Inc., PO Box 8658, Anaheim, CA 92812, Tel.: (714)534-7976.

Common Courage Press, Box 702, Jackson Rd. and Rte. 19, Monroe, ME 04951, Tel.: (207)525-0900.

Consortium Book Sales & Distribution, 287 E. 6th St., Ste. 365, St. Paul, MN 55101, Tel.: (612)221-9035.

Copley Publishing Group, 138 Great Rd., Acton, MA 01720, Tel.: (508)263-9090.

Cornell University Press, 124 Roberts Pl., PO Box 250, Ithaca, NY 14851, Tel.: (607)257-7000.

CRC Press, Inc., 2000 Corporate Blvd. NW, Boca Raton, FL 33431, Tel.: (407)994-0555.

D

Daring Publishing Group, 913 Tuscarawas St. W., Canton, OH 44702, Tel.: (216)454-7519.

Ivan R. Dee, Inc., 1332 N. Halsted St., Chicago, IL 60622, Tel.: (312)787-6262.

Doubleday, 666 5th Ave., New York, NY 10103, Tel.: (800)223-6834.

Dufour Editions, Inc., PO Box 449, Chester Springs, PA 19425-0449, Tel.: (215)458-5005.

Duke University Press, PO Box 6697, College Sta., Durham, NC 27108, Tel.: (919)684-2173.

E

ECA Associates, PO Box 15004, Great Bridge Sta., Chesapeake, VA 23320, Tel.: (804)547-5542.

William B. Eerdmans Publishing Co., 255 Jefferson Ave. SE, Grand Rapids, MI 49503, Tel.: (800)253-7521.

F

Faber & Faber, Inc., 50 Cross St., Winchester, MA 01890, Tel.: (617)721-1427.

Facts on File, Inc., 460 Park Ave. S., New York, NY 10016, Tel.: (212)683-2214.

Fairleigh Dickinson University Press, 440 Forsgate Dr., Cranbury, NJ 08512, Tel.: (609)655-4770.

Farrar, Straus & Giroux, Inc., 19 Union Sq. W., New York, NY 10003, Tel.: (800)631-8571.

Augsburg Fortress, Publishers, 426 S. 5th St., PO Box 1209, Minneapolis, MN 55440, Tel.: (800)848-2738.

Free Press, 866 3rd Ave., New York, NY 10022, Tel.: (212)702-3130.

G

Gale Research Inc., 835 Penobscot Bldg., Detroit, MI 48226-4094, Tel.: (800)877-4253.

Garland Publishing, Inc., 717 5th Ave., New York, NY 10016, Tel.: (212)751-7447.

Georgetown University Press, Intercultural Center, Rm. 111, Washington, DC 20057, Tel.: (202)687-6063.

Gower Publishing Co., Old Post Rd., Brookfield, VT 05036, Tel.: (802)276-3162.

Greenwood Publishing Group, Inc., 88 Post Rd. W., PO Box 5007, Westport, CT 06881, Tel.: (203)226-3571.

Grove Weidenfeld, 841 Broadway, 4th Fl., New York, NY 10003-4793, Tel.: (212)614-7850.

Guilford Publications, Inc., 72 Spring St., New York, NY 10012, Tel.: (212)431-9800.

H

G.K. Hall & Co., Inc., 70 Lincoln St.1, Boston, MA 02111, Tel.: (617)423-3990.

Harlan Davidson, Inc., 110 N. Arlington Heights Rd., Arlington Heights, IL 60004, Tel.: (708)253-9720.

Harmonie Park Press, 23630 Pinewood, Warren, MI 48091, Tel.: (313)755-3080.

Harmony Books, c/o Crown Publishers, Inc., 201 E. 50th St., New York, NY 10022, Tel.: (212)572-6120.

HarperCollins Inc., 10 E. 53rd St., New York, NY 10022, Tel.: (800)331-3761.

Harvard University Press, 79 Garden St., Cambridge, MA 02138, Tel.: (617)495-2600.

Heinemann Educational Books, Inc., 361 Hanover St., Portsmouth, NH 03801-3912, Tel.: (603)431-7894.

Hemisphere Publishing Corp., 1900 Frost Rd., Ste. 101, Bristol, PA 19007, Tel.: (215)785-5000.

Hippocrene Books, Inc., 171 Madison Ave., New York, NY 10016, Tel.: (212)685-4371.

Holmes & Meier Publishers, Inc., 30 Irving Pl., New York, NY 10003, Tel.: (212)254-4100.

Holt, Rinehart & Winston, Inc., 6277 Sea Harbor Dr., Orlando, FL 32887, Tel.: (407)345-2500.

Hoover Institute Press, Stanford University, Stanford, CA 94305-6010, Tel.: (415)723-3373.

Howard University Press, 2900 Van Ness St. NW, Washington, DC 20008, Tel.: (202)806-8450.

Human Rights Watch, 485 5th Ave., New York, NY 10017-6104, Tel.: (212)972-8400.

Humanities Press International, Inc., 165 1st Ave., Atlantic Highlands, NJ 07716-1289, Tel.: (908)872-1441.

I

ICS Press, 243 Kearny St., San Francisco, CA 94108, Tel.: (415)981-5353.

Independent Publishers Group, 814 N. Franklin St., Chicago, Il 60610, Tel.: (312)337-0747.

Indiana University Press, 601 N. Morton St., Bloomington, IN 47404-3797, Tel.; (812)855-4203.

Institute of Early American History and Culture, PO Box 220, Williamsburg, VA 23187, Tel.: (804)221-1110.

Interlink Publishing Group, Inc., 99 7th Ave., Brooklyn, NY 11215, Tel.: (718)797-4292.

International Publishers Co., Inc., 239 W. 23rd St., New York, NY 10011, Tel.: (212)366-9816.

International Specialized Book Services, 5602 NE Hassalo St., Portland, OR 97213-3640, Tel.: (503)287-3093.

Ivy Books, 201 E. 50th St., New York, NY 10022, Tel.: (212)572-2573.

J

Joint Center for Political and Economic Studies, Inc., 1301 Pennsylvania Ave. NW, Ste. 400, Washington, DC 20041-1797, Tel.: (202)626-3500.

Jonathan David Publishers, Inc., 68-22 Eleat Ave., Middle Village, NY 11379, Tel.: (718)456-8611.

Judson Press, PO Box 851, Valley Forge, PA 19482-0851, Tel.: (800)331-1053.

Just Us Books, Inc., 301 Main St., Ste. 22-24, Orange, NJ 07050, Tel.: (800)762-7701.

K

Kendell/Hunt Publishing Co., 2460 Kerper Blvd., Dubuque, IA 52001, Tel.: (319)588-1451.

Kent State University Press, 101 Franklin Hall, Kent, OH 44242, Tel.: (800)666-2211.

Kluwer Academic Publishers, 101 Philip Dr., Assinippi Park, Norwell, MA 02061, Tel.: (617)871-6600.

Alfred A. Knopf, Inc., 201 E. 50th St., New York, NY 10022, Tel.: (212)572-2103.

Krieger Publishing Co., Inc., PO Box 9542, Melborne, FL 32902, Tel.: (407)724-9542.

Kumarian Press, Inc., 630 Oakwood Ave., Ste. 119, West Hartford, CT 06110-1505, Tel.: (203)953-0214.

L

Lexington Books, 125 Spring St., Lexington, MA 02173, Tel.: (617)862-6650.

Little, Brown & Co., Inc., 34 Beacon St., Boston, MA 02108, Tel.: (800)343-9204.

Louisiana State University Press, Highland Rd., Baton Rouge, LA 70893, Tel.: (504)388-6294.

Lynne Rienner Publishers, Inc., 1800 30th St., Ste. 314, Boulder, CO 80301, Tel.: (303)444-6684.

M

McFarland & Co., Inc., Publishers, Box 611, Jefferson, NC 28640, Tel.: (919)246-4460.

MacMillan Publishing Co., 866 3rd Ave., New York, NY 10022, Tel.: (800)257-6509.

Madison Books, 4720 Boston Way, Lantham, MD 20706, Tel.: (800)462-6420.

Madison House Publishers, Inc., PO Box 3100, Madison, WI 53704, Tel.: (608)244-6210.

Majority Press, PO Box 538, Dover, MA 02030, Tel.: (617)828-8450.

Martin Luther King Press, 132 W. 116th St., New York, NY 10026, Tel.: (212)866-0301.

Meckler Corp., 11 Ferry Ln. W., Westport, CT 06880, Tel.: (203)226-6967.

Edwin Mellen Press, PO Box 450, Lewiston, NY 14092, Tel.: (716)754-2266.

Mercer University Press, 1400 Coleman Ave., Macon, GA 31207, Tel.: (912)752-2880.

Michigan State University Press, 1405 S. Harrison Rd., East Lansing, MI 48824, Tel.: (517)355-9543.

Millbrook Press, Inc., Old New Milford Rd., Brookfield, CT 06804, Tel.: (203)740-2220.

Myles Publishing Co., 436 E. Ute St., Tulsa, OK 74106, Tel.: (918)663-7701.

N

NRW Associates Directory, 1315 Hamlin St. NE, Washington, DC 20017, Tel.: (202)635-4808.

National Academy Press, 2101 Constitution Ave. NW, Washington, DC 20418, Tel.: (800)624-6242.

National Afro-American Museum and Cultural Center, PO Box 578, Wilberforce, OH 45384, Tel.: (513)376-4944.

National Book Co., PO Box 8795, Portland, OR 97207-8795, Tel.: (503)228-6345.

National Book Network, 4720 Boston Way, Lanham, MD 20706-4310, Tel.: (301)459-8696.

National Urban League, Inc., 500 E. 62nd St., New York, NY 10021, Tel.: (212)310-9000.

Native Sun Publishers, Inc., PO Box 13394, Richmond, VA 23225, Tel.: (804)233-8249.

New York University Press, 70 Washington Sq. S., New York, NY 10012, Tel.: (212)998-2575.

Northeastern University Press, 360 Huntington Ave., 272 Huntington Plaza, Boston, MA 02115, Tel.: (617)437-5480.

Northwestern University Press, 625 Colfax St., Evanston, IL 60201, Tel.: (708)491-5315.

W.W. Norton & Co., Inc., 500 5th Ave., New York, NY 10110, Tel.: (212)354-5500.

O

Ohio University Press, 220 Scott Quadrangle, Athens, OH 45701, Tel.: (614)593-1155.

Open University Press, c/o Taylor & Francis, Inc., 79 Madison Ave., Ste. 1106, New York, NY 10016, Tel.: (212)725-1999.

Orbis Books, Fathers & Brothers of Maryknoll, Walsh Bldg., Maryknoll, NY 10545, Tel.: (800)258-5838.

Oxford University Press, Inc., 200 Madison Ave., New York, NY 10016, Tel.: (800)334-4349.

P

Pacific Research Institute for Public Policy, 177 Post St., Ste. 500, San Francisco, CA 94108, Tel.: (415)989-0833.

Pantheon Books, Inc., 201 E. 50th St., New York, NY 10022, Tel.: (212)872-8238.

Paragon House Publishers, 90 5th Ave., New York, NY 10011, Tel.: (212)620-2820.

Pathfinder Press, 410 West St., New York, NY 10014, Tel.: (212)741-0690.

Paul & Co. Publishers, Consortium, Inc., PO Box 442, Concord, MA 01742, Tel.: (508)369-3049.

Pelican Publishing Co., Inc., 1101 Monroe St., Gretna, LA 70053, Tel.: (800)843-4558.

Pennsylvania State University Press, 820 N. University Dr., Ste. C, University Park, PA 16802, Tel.: (814)865-1327.

Pergamon Press, Inc., Front & Braun Sts., Riverside, NJ 08075-1197, Tel.: (609)461-6500.

Peter Lang Publishing, Inc., 62 W. 45th St., New York, NY 10036, Tel.: (212)302-6740.

Pharos Books, 200 Park Ave., New York, NY 10166, Tel.: (212)692-3830.

Power of the Word Publishing Co., 176-03 Jamaica Ave., Jamaica, NY 11432, Tel.: (718)949-1987.

Praeger Publishers, c/o Greenwood Press Publishing Group, Inc., 88 Post Rd., W., Box 5007, Westport, CT 06881, Tel.: (203)226-3571.

Presidio Press, 31 Pamaron Way, Novato, CA 94949, Tel.: (415)883-1373.

Princeton Architectural Press, 37 E. 7th Ave., New York, NY 10003, Tel.: (800)458-1131.

Princeton University Press, 41 William St., Princeton, NJ 08540, Tel.: (800)777-4726.

Putnam Publishing Group, 200 Madison Ave., New York, NY 10016, Tel.: (800)631-8571.

R

Raintree Steck-Vaughn Publications, 11 Prospect St., Madison, NJ 07940, Tel.: (800)531-5015.

Regnery Gateway, Inc., 1130 17th Ave. NW, Ste. 600, Washington, DC 20036, Tel.: (202)457-0978.

Rizzoli International Publications, Inc., 300 Park Ave. S., New York, NY 10010, Tel.: (800)462-2387.

Rosen Publishing Group, Inc., 29 E. 21st St., New York, NY 10010, Tel.: (212)777-3017.

Routledge, Chapman & Hall, Inc., 29 W. 35th St., New York, NY 10001-2291, Tel.: (212)244-3336.

Rowman & Littlefield, Publishers, Inc., 4720 Boston Way, Lanham, MD 20706, Tel.: (301)459-3366.

Russell Sage Foundation, 112 E. 64th St., New York, NY 10021, Tel.: (415)931-6000.

Rutgers University Press, 109 Church St., New Brunswick, NJ 08901, Tel.: (201)932-7764.

S

Sage Publications, Inc., 2455 Teller Rd., Newbury Park, CA 91320, Tel.: (805)499-0721.

St. Martin's Press, Inc., 175 5th Ave., New York, NY 10010, Tel.: (800)325-5525.

Salem Press, Inc., PO Box 1097, Englewood Cliffs, NJ 07632, Tel.: (201)871-3700

Sandcastle Publishing Co., PO Box 3070, South Pasadena, CA 91031-6070, Tel.: (213)255-3616.

K.G. Saur, 121 Chanlon Rd., New Providence, NJ 07974, Tel.: (908)665-2828.

Scarborough House, PO Box 459, Chelsea, MI 48118, Tel.: (313)475-1210.

Scarecrow Press, Inc., 52 Liberty St., Box 4167, Metuchen, NY 08840, Tel.: (800)537-7107.

Schiller Institute, Inc., PO Box 66082, Washington, DC 20005, Tel.: (202)628-0272.

Scholastic, Inc., 730 Broadway, New York, NY 10003, Tel.: (212)505-3000.

Charles Scribner's Sons, c/o MacMillan Publishing Co., 866 3rd Ave., New York, NY 10022, Tel.: (212)702-2000.

Seal Press-Feminist, 3131 Western Ave., No. 410, Seattle, WA 98121-1028, Tel.: (206)283-7844.

Seven Locks Press, PO Box 27, Cabin John, MD 20818, Tel.: (800)537-9359.

Seymour-Smith, Inc., PO Box 381063, Germantown, TN 38138-1063, Tel.: (901)754-4418.

Simon & Schuster, Inc., 1230 Avenue of Americas, New York, NY 10020, Tel.: (212)698-7000.

Smithsonian Institution Press, 470 L'Enfant Plaza, Ste. 7100, Washington, DC 20560, Tel.: (202)287-3748.

South Asia Books, PO Box 502, Columbia, MO 75205, Tel.: (314)474-0116.

South End Press, 116 St. Botolph St., Boston, MA 02115, Tel.: (617)266-0629.

State University of New York Press, State University Plaza, Albany, NY 12246-0001, Tel.: (800)666-2211.

Station Hill Press, Station Hill Rd., Barrytown, NY 12507, Tel.: (914)758-5840.

Steward, Tabori & Chang Publishers, 575 Broadway, New York, NY 10012, Tel.: (212)941-2929.

Summit Books, 1230 Avenue of the Americas, New York, NY 10020, Tel.: (212)698-7501.

Syracuse University Foreign & Comparative Studies Program, 321 Sims Hall, Syracuse, NY 13244, Tel.: (315)443-4667.

T

Temple University Press, 1601 N. Broad St., University Services Bldg., Rm. 305, Philadelphia, PA 19122, Tel.: (800)447-1656.

Texas A&M University Press, Drawer C, College Stat., TX 77843, Tel.: (800)826-8911.

Third World Press, 7524 S. Cottage Grove Ave., PO Box 730, Chicago, IL 60619, Tel.: (312)651-0700.

Three Continents Press, 1901 Pennsylvania Ave. NW, Ste. 407, Washington, DC 20006, Tel.: (202)223-2554.

Thunder's Mouth Press, 54 Greene St., Ste. 45, New York, NY 10013, Tel.: (212)226-0277.

I.N. Thut World Education Center, University of Connecticut, School of Education, Box U-93, Storrs, CT 06269-2093, Tel.: (203)486-4812.

Times Books, c/o Random House, Inc., 201 E. 50th St., New York, NY 10022, Tel.: (800)726-0600.

Times Change Press, PO Box 1380, Ojai, CA 93023, Tel.: (800)488-8595.

Transaction Publishers, Rutgers University, New Brunswick, NJ 08903, Tel.: (201)932-2280.

Transnational Publishers, Inc., PO Box 7282, Ardsley-on-Hudson, NY 10503, Tel.: (914)693-0089.

Turman Publishing Co., 1319 Dexter Ave. N., Ste. 30, Seattle, WA 98119, Tel.: (206)282-6900.

Twayne, c/o G.K. Hall, 70 Lincoln St., Boston, MA 02111, Tel.: (617)423-3990.

Tycooly Publishing USA, PO Box 2178, Riverton, NJ 08077, Tel.: (509)486-1755.

U

University of Alabama Press, PO Box 870380, Tuscaloosa, AL 35487-0380, Tel.: (205)348-5180.

University of Arkansas Press, 201 Ozark St., Fayetteville, AR 72701, Tel.: (509)575-5647.

University of California, Los Angeles, Center for Afro-American Studies, 160 Haines Hall, 405 Hilgard Ave., Los Angeles, CA 90024-1545, Tel.: (213)825-3528.

University of California Press, 2120 Berkeley Way, Berkeley, CA 94720, Tel.: (415)642-4247.

University of Chicago Press, 5801 S. Ellis Ave., Chicago, IL 60637, Tel.: (800)621-2736.

University of Illinois Press, 54 E. Gregory Dr., Champaign, IL 61820, Tel.: (217)333-0950.

University of Massachusetts, William Monroe Trotter Institute for the Study of Black Culture, Harbor Campus, Boston, MA 02125, Tel.: (617)287-5880.

University of North Carolina Press, PO Box 2288, Chapel Hill, NC 27515-2288, Tel.: (800)848-6224.

University of North Texas Press, PO Box 13856, Denton, TX 76203, Tel.: (817)565-2142.

University of Pennsylvania Press, 418 Service Dr., Philadelphia, PA 19104-6097, Tel.: (215)898-6261.

University of South Carolina Press, 1716 College St., Columbia, SC 29208, Tel.: (803)777-5243.

University of Tennessee Press, 293 Communications Bldg., Knoxville, TN 37996-0325, Tel.; (615)974-3321.

University Press of America, Inc., 4720 Boston Way, Lanham, MD 20706, Tel.: (301)459-3366.

University Press of Kentucky, 663 S. Limestone St., Lexington, KY 40508-4008, Tel.: (606)257-2951.

University Press of Mississippi, 3825 Ridgewood Rd., Jackson, MS 39211, Tel.: (601)982-6205.

University Press of New England, 17 1/2 Lebanon St., Hanover, NH 03755, Tel.: (603)646-3340.

University Press of Virginia, PO Box 3608, University Sta., Charlottesville, VA 22903, Tel.: (804)924-3468.

University Presses of Florida, 15 NW 15th St., Gainesville, FL 32611, Tel.: (904)392-1351.

University Publications of America, 4520 E. West Hwy., Ste. 600, Bethesda, MD 20814-3319, Tel.: (301)657-3200.

Urban Research Press, Inc., 840 E. 87th St., Chicago, IL 60619, Tel.: (312)994-7200.

V

Vande Vere Publishing, Ltd., 8744 College Ave., Berrien Springs, MI 49103, Tel.: (616)473-1510.

Vantage Press, Inc., 516 W. 34th St., New York, NY 10001, Tel.: (212)736-1767.

Victor Books, 1825 Wheaton Ave., Wheaton, IL 60187, Tel.: (800)323-9409.

Virago Press, c/o Trafalgar Square, PO Box 257, North Comfort, VT 05053, Tel.: (800)423-4525.

W

Wadsworth Publishing Co., 10 Davis Dr., Belmont, CA 94002, Tel.: (415)595-2350.

Warner Books, Inc., 666 5th Ave., New York, NY 10103, Tel.: (800)733-3000.

Franklin Watts, Inc., 387 Park Ave., New York, NY 10016, Tel.: (212)686-7070.

Wayne State University Press, 5959 Woodward Ave., Detroit, MI 48202, Tel.: (313)577-4601.

Wesleyan University Press, c/o University Press of New England, 17 1/2 Lebanon St., Hanover, NH 03755, Tel.: (603)646-3340.

Westview Press, 5500 Central Ave., Boulder, CO 80301-2847, Tel.: (303)444-3541.

Wiener, Moshe, 854 Newburg Ave., N., Woodmere, NY 11581.

Winston-Derek Publishers, Inc., PO Box 90883, Nashville, TN 37209, Tel.: (800)826-1888.

Y

Yale University Press, 92A Yale Sta., New Haven, CT 06520, Tel.: (203)432-0825.

Z

Hans Zell (UK), c/o K.G. Saur, 121 Chanlon Rd., New Providence, NJ 07974, Tel.: (908)665-2828.

Picture and Text Credits

Picture and Text Credits

Pictures

Cover: Colin Powell: AP/Wide World Photos; Three men: S.B. Burns M.D. and the Burns Archive; Firefighter: UPI/Bettmann.

Chronology: p. 4: The Bettmann Archive; p. 5: Library of Congress; p. 6: Library of Congress; p. 7: Library of Congress; p. 8: Library of Congress; p. 9: New York Public Library; p. 11: Library of Congress; p. 12: Archive Photos; p. 17: Library of Congress; p. 18: Library of Congress; p. 19: Library of Congress; p. 20: Library of Congress; p. 22: The Bettmann Archive; p. 23: Library of Congress; p. 24: Library of Congress; p. 25: National Archives; p. 26: Library of Congress; p. 28: Library of Congress; p. 30: National Archives; p. 32: AP/Wide World Photos; p. 33: UPI/Bettmann; p. 34: Library of Congress; p. 35: UPI/Bettmann; p. 37: Library of Congress; p. 38: Library of Congress; p. 40: AP/Wide World Photos; p. 41: Library of Congress; p. 42: UPI/Bettmann; p. 43: AP/Wide World Photos; p. 45: UPI/Bettmann; p. 46: UPI/Bettmann; p. 46: Library of Congress; p. 47: National Archives; p. 48: UPI/Bettmann; p. 49: UPI/Bettmann; p. 50: UPI/Bettmann; p. 51: UPI/Bettmann; p. 54: UPI/Bettmann; p. 55: AP/Wide World Photos; p. 57: AP/Wide World Photos; p. 58: AP/Wide World Photos; p. 59: UPI/Bettmann; p. 63: AP/Wide World Photos; p. 67: AP/Wide World Photos; p. 70: AP/Wide World Photos; p. 73: AP/Wide World Photos; p. 74: UPI/Bettmann; p. 77: UPI/Bettmann; p. 77: AP/Wide World Photos; p. 78: AP/Wide World Photos; p. 82: AP/Wide World Photos; p. 90: AP/Wide World Photos; p. 93: AP/Wide World Photos; p. 96: UPI/Bettmann; p. 97: UPI/Bettmann; p. 98: UPI/Bettmann; p. 99: AP/Wide World Photos; p. 100: AP/Wide World Photos.

African-American Firsts: p. 106: Library of Congress; p. 110: United States Army; p. 111: AP/Wide World Photos; p. 112: AP/Wide World Photos; p. 114: AP/Wide World Photos; p. 116: AP/Wide World Photos; p. 117: National Association for the Advancement of Colored People; p. 118: AP/Wide World Photos; p. 119: AP/Wide World Photos; p. 120: UPI/Bettmann; p. 120: AP/Wide World Photos; p. 121: AP/Wide World Photos.

Significant Documents in African-American History: p. 131: Library of Congress; p. 134: Library of Congress; p. 137: Library of Congress; p. 141: Library of Congress; p. 145: Library of Congress; p. 147: The Bettmann Archive; p. 148: AP/Wide World Photos; p. 155: Library of Congress; p. 165: AP/Wide World Photos; p. 171: AP/Wide World Photos; p. 177: Consulate General of Jamaica; p. 182: Library of Congress; p. 187: AP/Wide World Photos; p. 188: Eisenhower Library; p. 193: National Broadcasting Corporation; p. 197: UPI/Bettmann; p. 203: Tex Harris, *Amsterdam News*; p. 207: UPI/Bettmann.

African-American Landmarks: p. 215: AP/Wide World Photos; p. 216: AP/Wide World Photos; p. 220: AP/Wide World Photos; p. 221: National Park Service; p. 225: UPI/Bettmann; p. 232: AP/Wide World Photos; p. 231: Burton Historical Collection, Detroit Public Library; p. 239: AP/Wide World Photos; p. 242: AP/Wide World Photos; p. 244: AP/Wide World Photos; p. 253: Denver Public Library; p. 254: Schomburg Center for Research in Black Culture, New York Public Library; p. 258: UPI/Bettmann; p. 259: AP/Wide World Photos.

Africa and the Western Hemisphere: p. 263: United Nations; p. 265: National Museum of African Art; p. 270: United Nations; p. 270: National Museum of African Art; p. 271: National Museum of African Art; p. 274: United Nations; p. 276: United Nations; p. 278: United Nations; p. 280: United Nations; p. 281: United Nations; p. 282: United Nations; p. 283: United Nations; p. 287: United Nations; p. 289: National Museum of African Art; p. 290: National Museum of African Art; p. 292: United Nations; p. 294: United Nations; p. 295: National Museum of African Art; p. 296: National Museum of African Art; p. 300: United Nations; p. 301: United Nations; p. 302: United Nations; p. 304: United Nations; p. 306: United Nations; p. 307: National Museum of African Art; p. 308: National Museum of African Art; p. 310: National Museum of African Art; p. 313: Bahama News Bureau; p. 317: United Nations; p. 319: United Nations; p. 320: Judy Gurovitz, The Clement-Petrolik Co.; p. 321: United Nations; p. 322: Jamaica Tourist Board; p. 323: United Nations; p. 324: United Nations.

Africans in America: 1600–1900: p. 334: New York Public Library; p. 335 Library of Congress; p. 336 Library of Congress; p. 337: Library of Congress; p. 338: Library of Congress; p. 341: Library of Congress; p. 342: Library of Congress; p. 343: New York Historical Society; p. 343: Library of Congress; p. 346: Library of Congress; p. 347: National Portrait Gallery; p. 348: Library of Congress; p. 350: Library of Congress; p. 353: The Bettmann Archive; p. 354: Library of Congress; p. 355: Library of Congress; p. 356: Library of Congress; p. 357: New York Public Library; p. 358: AP/Wide World Photos; p. 360: New York Public Library; p. 362: Archive Photos; p. 362: Library of Congress.

Civil Rights: p. 370: Library of Congress; p. 371: Schomburg Center for Research in Black Culture, New York Public Library; p. 371: UPI/Bettmann; p. 372: AP/Wide World Photos; p. 373: AP/Wide World Photos; p. 374: AP/Wide World Photos; p. 374: Library of Congress; p. 376: UPI/Bettmann; p. 377: AP/Wide World Photos; p. 379: AP/Wide World Photos; p. 380: AP/Wide World Photos; p. 381: UPI/Bettmann; p. 383: AP/Wide World Photos; p. 384: AP/Wide World Photos; p. 387: AP/Wide World Photos; p. 388: UPI/Bettmann; p. 389: AP/Wide World Photos;p. 390: Library of Congress; p. 391: *Amsterdam News*; p. 392: UPI/Bettmann; p. 394: AP/Wide World Photos; p. 396: Library of Congress.

Black Nationalism: p. 406: Library of Congress; p. 408: The Bettmann Archive; p. 409: Archive Photos; p. 411: Library of Congress; p. 412: Library of Congress;p. 414: AP/Wide World Photos; p. 417: UPI/Bettmann; p. 418: Archive Photos; p. 418: Library of Congress.

National Organizations: p. 424: The Bettmann Archive; p. 425: National Association for the Advancement of Colored People; p. 426: Library of Congress; p. 427: AP/Wide World Photos; p. 428: Library of Congress; p. 429: Ace Creative Photos; p. 430: AP/Wide World Photos; p. 431: AP/Wide World Photos; p. 432: AP/Wide World Photos; p. 433: UPI/Bettmann; p. 434: AP/Wide World Photos; p. 435: AP/Wide World Photos; p. 437: Library of Congress; p. 438: UPI/Bettmann; p. 438: AP/Wide World Photos; p. 440: AP/Wide World Photos; p. 441: AP/Wide World Photos; p. 442: AP/Wide World Photos; p. 443: UPI/Bettmann; p. 444: A. Philip Randolph Institute; p. 445: AP/Wide World Photos; p. 446: UPI/Bettmann; p. 447: Bill Sparow, *Encore*; p. 448: National Urban League.

Law: p. 502: New York Public Library; p. 507: UPI/Bettmann; p. 508: AP/Wide World Photos; p. 509: AP/Wide World Photos; p. 515: Library of Congress; p. 516: Library of Congress; p. 517: AP/Wide World Photos; p. 517: UPI/Bettmann; p. 522: National Association for the Advancement of Colored People; p. 523: UPI/Bettmann; p. 525: UPI/Bettmann; p. 533: UPI/Bettmann; p. 524: Library of Congress; p. 536: AP/Wide World Photos; p. 537: AP/Wide World Photos;

p. 539: AP/Wide World Photos; p. 544: UPI/Bettmann; p. 549: AP/Wide World Photos; p. 550: UPI/Bettmann; p. 551: AP/Wide World Photos; p. 552: AP/Wide World Photos; p. 553: AP/Wide World Photos; p. 554: AP/Wide World Photos; p. 555: AP/Wide World Photos; p. 556: UPI/Bettmann; p. 557: UPI/Bettmann; p. 559: AP/Wide World Photos.

Politics: p. 563: UPI/Bettmann; p. 567: UPI/Bettmann; p. 568: UPI/Bettmann; p. 569: AP/Wide World Photos; p. 570: AP/Wide World Photos; p. 571: UPI/Bettmann; p. 573: AP/Wide World Photos; p. 574: UPI/Bettmann; p. 575: United States Senate Historical Office; p. 577: AP/Wide World Photos; p. 578: AP/Wide World Photos; p. 579: AP/Wide World Photos; p. 580: AP/Wide World Photos; p. 581: AP/Wide World Photos; p. 582: AP/Wide World Photos; p. 583: AP/Wide World Photos; p. 584: Archive Photos; p. 585: AP/Wide World Photos; p. 586: UPI/Bettmann; p. 587: AP/Wide World Photos; p. 588: AP/Wide World Photos; p. 590: AP/Wide World Photos; p. 592: AP/Wide World Photos; p. 593: AP/Wide World Photos; p. 594: UPI/Bettmann; p. 597: AP/Wide World Photos; p. 598: AP/Wide World Photos; p. 601: United States Senate Historical Office; p. 602: United Nations; p. 603: AP/Wide World Photos; p. 604: Library of Congress; p. 605: AP/Wide World Photos; p. 606: AP/Wide World Photos; p. 607: AP/Wide World Photos; p. 609: AP/Wide World Photos; p. 610: AP/Wide World Photos.

Population: p. 618: Kenneth Estell; p. 619: Kenneth Estell; p. 620: S.B. Burns and the Burns Archive; p. 621: Library of Congress; p. 621: National Archives; p. 626: Kenneth Estell; p. 627: Kenneth Estell.

Employment and Income: p. 644: UPI/Bettmann; p. 647: Sue Steller; p. 649: Kenneth Estell; p. 653: UPI/Bettmann; p. 654: National Aeronautics and Space Administration; p. 655: Sue Steller; p. 656: Kenneth Estell.

Entrepreneurship: p. 668: Library of Congress; p. 670: Walker Collection of A'Lelia Perry Bundles; p. 672: Andy Roy; p. 674: AP/Wide World Photos; p. 675: Kenneth Estell; p. 676: AP/Wide World Photos; p. 677: Superb Manufacturing, Inc.; p. 678: AP/Wide World Photos; p. 679: AP/Wide World Photos; p. 680: UPI/Bettmann; p. 681: AP/Wide World Photos; p. 683: Fisk University Library.

The Family: p. 694: Faustine Jones-Wilson; p. 694: Library of Congress; p. 695: Brain V. Jones; p. 696: Brain V. Jones; p. 700: Brain V. Jones; p. 702: Kenneth Estell; p. 703: Kenneth Estell; p. 709: Kenneth Estell; p. 710: Edwin L. Wilson, Sr.

Education: p. 724: Library of Congress; p. 725: Schomburg Center for Research in Black Culture, New York Public Library; p. 726: Library of Congress; p. 726: South Carolina Historical Society; p. 727: Library of Congress; p. 443: Library of Congress; p. 727: The Bettmann Archive; p. 728: The Bettmann Archive; p. 729: Library of Congress; p. 730: AP/Wide World Photos; p. 729: AP/Wide World Photos; p. 731: UPI/Bettmann; p. 733: UPI/Bettmann; p. 735: AP/Wide World Photos; p. 736: Bruce Griffin; p. 737: Beverly Hardy; p. 730: Molefi Kete Asante; p. 739: Surlock Photographers; p. 741: AP/Wide World Photos; p. 742: AP/Wide World Photos; p. 743: AP/Wide World Photos; p. 744: AP/Wide World Photos; p. 746: John F. Kennedy Library; p. 748: AP/Wide World Photos; p. 749: AP/Wide World Photos; p. 750: AP/Wide World Photos.

Religion: p. 774: New York Public Library; p. 776: Archive Photos; p. 777: SB. Burns and the Burns Archive; p. 779: Archive Photos; p. 780: AP/Wide World Photos; p. 782: AP/Wide World Photos; p. 783: AP/Wide World Photos; p. 784: AP/Wide World Photos; p. 786: AP/Wide World Photos; p. 787: *New York Daily News*; p789]791: AP/Wide World Photos; p. 790: UPI/Bettmann; p. 791: AP/Wide World Photos; p. 795: AP/Wide World Photos; p. 797: AP/Wide World Photos; p. 797: New York Public Library; p. 798: UPI/Bettmann; p. 800: UPI/Bettmann; p. 802: AP/Wide World Photos; p. 802: The Bettmann Archive; p. 804: AP/Wide World Photos; p. 807: AP/Wide World Photos.

Literature: p. 813: Schomburg Center for Research in Black Culture, New York Public Library; p. 814: AP/Wide World Photos; p. 816: AP/Wide World Photos; p. 817: AP/Wide World Photos; p. 818: AP/Wide World Photos; p. 821: UPI/Bettmann; p. 823: AP/Wide World Photos; p. 828: AP/Wide World Photos; p. 830: UPI/Bettmann; p. 833: AP/Wide World Photos; p. 834: Springer/Bettmann Film Archive; p. 835: AP/Wide World Photos; p. 839: AP/Wide World Photos; p. 840: AP/Wide World Photos; p. 841: AP/Wide World Photos; p. 842: AP/Wide World Photos; p. 843: New York Historical Society; p. 844: AP/Wide World Photos; p. 845: AP/Wide World Photos; p. 846: AP/Wide World Photos.

The Media: p. 856: AP/Wide World Photos; p. 858: AP/Wide World Photos; p. 859: AP/Wide World Photos; p. 861: American Broadcasting Company; p. 862: AP/Wide World Photos; p. 864: AP/Wide World Photos; p. 865: Tony Brown Productions, Inc.; p. 866: Black Entertainment Television; p. 867: AP/Wide World Photos; p. 869: AP/Wide World Photos; p. 870: Turner Broadcasting System Management; p. 871: Black Enterprise Magazine; p. 872: AP/Wide World Photos; p. 874: UPI/Bettmann; p. 875: Associated Publishers; p. 876: AP/Wide World Photos; p. 877: Washington Post; p. 878: AP/Wide World Photos; p. 880: AP/Wide World Photos; p. 881: AP/Wide World Photos; p. 882: AP/Wide World Photos; p. 883: AP/Wide World Photos.

Performing Arts: p. 941: Library of Congress; p. 944: AP/Wide World Photos; p. 946: AP/Wide World Photos; p. 947: AP/Wide World Photos; p. 948: Ron Scherl; p. 950: AP/Wide World Photos; p. 951: WABC-TV, New York; p. 952: AP/Wide World Photos; p. 953: New York City Ballet; p. 954: UPI/Bettmann; p. 955: AP/Wide World Photos; p. 957: AP/Wide World Photos; p. 958: AP/Wide World Photos; p. 959: AP/Wide World Photos; p. 962: AP/Wide World Photos; p. 963: AP/Wide World Photos; p. 965: AP/Wide World Photos; p. 966: AP/Wide World Photos; p. 967: AP/Wide World Photos; p. 969: AP/Wide World Photos; p. 971: AP/Wide World Photos; p. 972: AP/Wide World Photos; p. 973: AP/Wide World Photos; p. 974: AP/Wide World Photos; p. 975: AP/Wide World Photos; p. 976: Tri-Star Pictures; p. 979: Matha Swope Associates; p. 980: UPI/Bettmann; p. 980: AP/Wide World Photos; p. 981: AP/Wide World Photos; p. 982: AP/Wide World Photos; p. 982: Archive Photos; p. 983: Island Pictures; p. 984: UPI/Bettmann; p. 985: Archive Photos; p. 990: AP/Wide World Photos; p. 991: AP/Wide World Photos; p. 993: Archive Photos; p. 994: AP/Wide World Photos; p. 995: AP/Wide World Photos; p. 997: AP/Wide World Photos; p. 998: Archive Photos; p. 999: AP/Wide World Photos; p. 1000: UPI/Bettmann; p. 1000: AP/Wide World Photos; p. 1001: AP/Wide World Photos; p. 1003: Darlene Hammond/Archive Photos.

Classical Music: p. 1008: Schomburg Center for Research in Black Culture, New York Public Library; p. 1009: Schomburg Center for Research in Black Culture, New York Public Library; p. 1010: AP/Wide World Photos; p. 1011: AP/Wide World Photos; p. 1012: AP/Wide World Photos; p. 1014: AP/Wide World Photos; p. 1015: Hurok Attractions; p. 1017: AP/Wide World Photos; p. 1020: The Bettmann Archive; p. 1022: AP/Wide World Photos; p. 1027: AP/Wide World Photos; p. 1033: The Bettmann Archive; p. 1034: Archive Photos; p. 1036: UPI/Bettmann; p. 1038: AP/Wide World Photos; p. 1041: AP/Wide World Photos; p. 1043: AP/Wide World Photos; p. 1044: AP/Wide World Photos; p. 1045: Archive Photos; p. 1046: AP/Wide World Photos.

Jazz Music: p. 1055: AP/Wide World Photos; p. 1055: The Bettmann Archive; p. 1057: UPI/Bettmann; p. 1059: AP/Wide World Photos; p. 1060: *Downbeat*; p. 1061: AP/Wide World Photos; p. 1063: AP/Wide World Photos; p. 1068: Shaw Artists Corporation; p. 1070: William Morris; p. 1073: National Archives; p. 1073: AP/Wide World Photos; p. 1075: AP/Wide World Photos; p. 1076: AP/Wide World Photos; p. 1076: S.B. Burns and The Burns Archive; p. 1077: AP/Wide World Photos; p. 1078: Springer/Bettmann Film Archive; p. 1080: The Bettmann Archive; p. 1082: Columbia Records; p. 1085: Ron Rogers; p. 1088: AP/Wide World Photos; p. 1089: UPI/Bettmann; p. 1090: AP/Wide World Photos; p. 1091: The Bettmann Archive; p. 1093: AP/Wide World Photos; p. 1094: AP/Wide World Photos; p. 1096: AP/Wide World Photos; p. 1101: UPI/Bettmann.

Popular Music: p. 1108: AP/Wide World Photos; p. 1109: Archive Photos; p. 1112: AP/Wide World Photos; p. 1113: AP/Wide World Photos; p. 1114: AP/Wide World Photos; p. 1116: AP/Wide World Photos; p. 1119: AP/Wide World

Photos; p. 1121: Archive Photos; p. 1122: AP/Wide World Photos; p. 1123: AP/Wide World Photos; p. 1124: AP/Wide World Photos; p. 1126: AP/Wide World Photos; p. 1127: AP/Wide World Photos; p. 1130: AP/Wide World Photos; p. .1133: AP/Wide World Photos; p. 1134: AP/Wide World Photos; p. 1135: Archive Photos; p. 1137: AP/Wide World Photos; p. 1138: AP/Wide World Photos; p. 1141: AP/Wide World Photos; p. 1142: AP/Wide World Photos; p. 1144: UPI/Bettmann; p. 1146: AP/Wide World Photos; p. 1147: AP/Wide World Photos; p. 1149: AP/Wide World Photos; p. 1151: AP/Wide World Photos.

Fine and Applied Arts: p. 1157: National Museum of American Art/Art Resource; p. 1161: Galbreath Photo Service; p. 1162: Whitney Museum of American Art; p. 1165: Whitney Museum of American Art; p. 1167: Fairchild Publications; p. 1169: AP/Wide World Photos; p. 1171: Art Resource; p. 1173: AP/Wide World Photos; p. 1174: AP/Wide World Photos; p. 1177 AP/Wide World Photos; p. 1183: National Museum of American Art/Art Resource; p. 1185: Whitney Museum of American Art; p. 1186: UPI/Bettmann; p. 1189: UPI/Bettmann; p. 1190: UPI/Bettmann; p. 1191: AP/Wide World Photos; p. 1195: National Museum of American Art/Art Resource; p. 1197: UPI/Bettmann; p. 1198: National Museum of American Art/Art Resource; p. 1199: AP/Wide World Photos; p. 1201: General Motors, Public Relations; p. 1202: AP/Wide World Photos; p. 1205: United Nations.

Science and Medicine: p. 1224: The Bettmann Archive; p. 1224: AP/Wide World Photos; p. 1225: AP/Wide World Photos; p. 1227: The Bettmann Archive; p. 1229: AP/Wide World Photos; p. 1230: Library of Congress; p. 1233: The Granger Collection, New York; p. 1235: UPI/Bettmann; p. 1236: AP/Wide World Photos; p. 1236: AP/Wide World Photos; p. 1237: Library of Congress; p. 1239: AP/Wide World Photos; p. 1240: AP/Wide World Photos; p. 1241: AP/Wide World Photos; p. 1242: The Bettmann Archive.

Sports: p. 1254: UPI/Bettmann; p. 1255: UPI/Bettmann; p. 1257: AP/Wide World Photos; p. 1258: AP/Wide World Photos; p. 1259: AP/Wide World Photos; p. 1260: AP/Wide World Photos; p. 1261: AP/Wide World Photos; p. 1262: AP/Wide World Photos; p. 1263: AP/Wide World Photos; p. 1265: Carl Nesfield; p. 1266: AP/Wide World Photos; p. 1266: Archive Photos; p. 1268: AP/Wide World Photos; p. 1269: AP/Wide World Photos; p. 1270: AP/Wide World Photos; p. 1273: UPI/Bettmann; p. 1274: AP/Wide World Photos; p. 1275: AP/Wide World Photos; p. 1276: National Broadcasting Co.; p. 1276: UPI/Bettmann; p. 1277: AP/Wide World Photos; p. 1278: AP/Wide World Photos; p. 1279: AP/Wide World Photos; p. 1280: AP/Wide World Photos; p. 1281: UPI/Bettmann; p. 1284: AP/Wide World Photos; p. 1286: AP/Wide World Photos; p. 1288: AP/Wide World Photos; p. 1289: AP/Wide World Photos; p. 1290: AP/Wide World Photos; p. 1291: AP/Wide World Photos; p. 1299: AP/Wide World Photos; p. 1300: AP/Wide World Photos.

Military: p. 1304: AP/Wide World Photos; p. 1304: Library of Congress; p. 1305: Library of Congress; p. 1306: AP/Wide World Photos; p. 1307: National Archives; p. 1308: Library of Congress; p. 1310: National Archives; p. 1312: National Archives; p. 1314: United States Army; p. 1316: United States Air Force; p. 1319: United States Army; p. 1323: United States Army; p. 1324: United States Marine Corps; p. 1325: AP/Wide World Photos; p. 1325: United States Marine Corps; p. 1326: United States Navy; p. 1328: United States Air Force: p. 1328: United States Army; p. 1329: National Archives; p. 1331: AP/Wide World Photos; p. 1332: AP/Wide World Photos; p. 1332: United States Navy; p. 1333: UPI/Bettmann; p. 1334: AP/Wide World Photos.

Text

Significant Documents in African-American History: "Lift Every Voice and Sing," p. 176: Used by permission of Edward B. Marks Music Company. "I Have a Dream," pp. 192–95: Reprinted by arrangement with The Heirs to the Estate of Martin Luther King, Jr., c/o Joan Daves Agency as agent for the proprietor; copyright 1963 by Martin Luther King, Jr., copyright renewed 1991 by Coretta Scott King.

Law: "African-American Federal Judges," p. 510–11: courtesy of NAACP Legal Defense and Educational Fund, Inc.

Entrepreneurship: "Largest Black Companies," pp. 684–89: The Earl G. Graves Publishing co., Inc., 130 Fifth Ave., New York, NY 10011.

Index

Index

B

C

D

F

G

H

J

K

L

N

O

P

Q

R

S

T

U

V

W

X

Y

Z